D1068943

DEMOCRACY
and the
CHURCHES

James Hastings Nichols

BR
115
.P7
N52
1969

DISCARDED

GREENWOOD PRESS, PUBLISHERS
NEW YORK

Copyright © 1951 by W. L. Jenkins

Reprinted by permission
of Westminster Press

First Greenwood Reprinting 1969

SBN 8371-2695-9

PRINTED IN UNITED STATES OF AMERICA

To
ROBERT HASTINGS NICHOLS
My Father and Teacher

FOREWORD

At the close of World War II, a small group of Church leaders met under the chairmanship of Dr. John R. Mott to discuss certain matters which were troubling many regarding the relationship of the Churches to political and social freedom. It was decided to attempt an investigation and study of the situation. Among other things it was determined to seek a competent historian to prepare a book on the attitudes of the various communions toward democracy. It was our aim to discover if possible which of the communions had effectively fostered liberty and brotherhood, and which had been antagonistic. This historical background seemed essential in order to assess the position of the same communions at present. We wished an objective statement in these matters, an investigation of changes on the part of Churches, and an outlook on their positions today.

Dr. James H. Nichols, of Chicago University, was our first choice to undertake this task. We arranged to procure for him sufficient leisure from teaching to do a thorough piece of scholarly work. This book is the result. We hope that thoughtful American citizens, both within and outside the Churches, will find it informing.

The churchmen who were interested in the preparation of this volume were, in the course of time, organized as the Committee on Religious Tolerance, later related to the Federal Council of the Churches of Christ in America. The views expressed in this book, of course, are those of the author, and are not necessarily to be construed as the positions of the Federal Council, its committees, or of any one of its constituent Churches.

Henry Sloane Coffin

AUTHOR'S PREFACE

THIS is a study in the relations between religion and politics. More precisely, it is concerned with the contributions and the resistances, both direct and indirect, offered to the several types of modern democracy by the chief Christian Churches.

An analysis so defined must be intellectually complicated and will carry a high emotional voltage. While the author desires to be challenged and corrected for any deviations from accuracy and fairness, he doubts the value of a neutral objectivity in such matters. Without a considerable degree of personal engagement in the movements treated, a scholar would be unlikely to choose such a topic of inquiry, or, having chosen, to muster the requisite sympathy for historical understanding. Objectivity in these matters must be paired with empathy, and requires, over and above continual emotional self-discipline, the conscious articulation of one's starting point and convictions so that those of other persuasions will be warned where to be on guard.

This inquiry, then, has been undertaken by one who is a liberal democrat and a Christian. What liberal democracy means, as against other types of democracy, will appear in the course of the discussion. As to the Christianity, a certain misconception which might be caused by the formulation of the problem should be here anticipated. The author is a Christian, not simply because, or in as far as, Christianity seems to him to contribute to liberal democracy, but because he believes that the Christian gospel is true. It does seem to him, on the other hand, that Christianity as understood in the Puritan tradition in which he stands has democratic implications that it is very difficult to evade.

The " Puritan tradition " refers to one of the classifications of the Christian Churches that is used in this analysis. Of the several Christian Churches, only a few are treated in detail. The political impetus and ethic of Orthodox Catholicism, as in Russia and the Balkans, has been autocratic. Continental Lutheranism and High-Church Anglicanism, with some limited exceptions, have, like Orthodox Catholicism, played no role in the development of liberal democracy, but have rather opposed it. Roman Catholicism, on the other hand, has exhibited diverse tendencies. One wing of Roman Catholicism has stood in the camp of autocratic government with Lutheranism and Orthodox Catholicism. Another wing, however, has been more closely related to the type of Protestantism that has contributed most to democracy — what we shall call Puritan Protestantism. It is with liberal or democratic Roman Catholicism, and with Puritan Protestantism, consequently, that we shall have most to do.

"Puritan Protestantism" perhaps requires definition. It refers here to the common ethos of that family of Anglo-American denominations whose best-known representatives are the Congregationalists, Baptists, Presbyterians, Methodists, Unitarians, Quakers, Disciples, Salvation Army, and the evangelical party within the Anglican communion. These groups are often more preoccupied with their differences than with their common inheritance from the Puritan Revolution in seventeenth century England, but from a historical and sociological perspective they constitute a collective unity of religious and ethical attitude. Historically they represent a fusion of Calvinism, Spiritualism, and the Baptist sect movement, and may be called "neo-Calvinism" in contrast to the aristocratic and authoritarian Calvinism of the sixteenth century. Ethically and sociologically they share the orientation that Troeltsch indicated by the terms "ascetic Protestantism," and "individualistic activistic Protestantism." To quote Troeltsch, to whom this study is indebted also at many points where his name is not mentioned, "the Christian social philosophy of Puritan Calvinism, of Pietism and the sects, and to some extent, that of the mystical groups, is a great unity. . . . It is supported mainly by the Anglo-Saxon nations, but it is not confined to them, but is present in all Calvinist countries. It has also had a very great influence upon the religious and ethical thought and practise of contemporary Lutheranism [and, we might add, of contemporary High Anglicanism]. From the point of view of historical influence this 'ascetic Protestantism' is today the chief force in Protestantism. . . . Along with medieval Catholicism it constitutes the second great main type of Christian social doctrine."[1] It is to this historical tradition that reference is made with "Puritan Protestantism," which seems preferable to "ascetic Protestantism" as a designation. "Puritanism" has, to be sure, often had other meanings. Cartoonists and popular writers have used it extensively as an epithet, often associating it with things with which historical Puritanism had no connection whatever, such as teetotalism or the ban on music, dancing, and imaginative literature. Historians have also used it with more precision to refer to this or that specific type of theology or polity, separatist, presbyterian, pre-destinarian. Such efforts, however, tend to cancel each other out and do less justice to the original uses of the word than the usage here proposed.

The core of this analysis can be described in the categories of Troeltsch's great work. So stated, it consists of a comparison of the attitudes toward modern democracy of the two most massive and systematic Christian attempts to penetrate and shape civilization, that of Roman Catholicism, as originally structured in the thirteenth century, and that of Puritan Protestantism, as originally structured in the seventeenth century.

The events and movements discussed belong for the most part to a later period than the classic ages of Roman Catholicism and of Puritan Protestantism. A case can be made, to be sure, for beginning the history of modern liberal democracy with the Puritan Revolution three hundred years ago. It *has* been made conclusively indeed, as in A. D. Lindsay's profound study, *The Modern Democratic State*. But on any large scale liberal democracy is only half so old, and dates from the American and French Revolutions at the end of the eighteenth century. Up to that time, of all Christians, only certain members of the Puritan churches had admitted any positive relation to liberal democracy. Roman Catholicism, Anglicanism, Lutheranism had consistently opposed it, and the Greek Orthodox had never heard of it. Even the liberal democratic affiliations of the Puritan churches were by no means unqualified or unanimous. They were, nevertheless, significant. For this first half of the history of modern democracy, extending from the settling of New England and the Puritan Revolution in England to the French Revolution, a brief summary in one or two chapters must suffice.

The body of our investigation will deal with the nineteenth century and the first half of the twentieth. In this period the earlier relatively simple relationship to democracy of the various churches became complicated. The Industrial Revolution, and the new social structures caused by it, posed new decisions for Christians and democrats. Puritan Protestantism discovered certain inhibitions in dealing with these problems, while Anglicanism and Roman Catholicism acquired a new social and political relevance. These several traditions have worked out a variety of relations to liberal democracy in the last four generations, and the delineation of the patterns of these relations and tendencies constitutes our central theme.

Any analysis of this type is necessarily entangled in the treacherous jungle of historical " causes." How is one to discover and exhibit which of all the diverse factors in any historical development was the most efficacious, or even one of the more efficacious? We can, to be sure, examine the statements of participants as to their motives, making what allowance seems best for their intelligence, sincerity, economic interests, or supposed subconscious urges. Such imaginative re-enactment of past thoughts and decisions must remain the primary method of the historian. A certain degree of " control," in the sense of a scientific experiment, can also be sometimes achieved by means of the comparative method. In so far as one can compare two historical situations, in which the chief social and economic forces are alike but the religious convictions in play differ, one may make some rough estimate of the role played by the latter. On this method, crude as it always is in history, we must rely for estimates, both of the relative impact of the several Christian traditions, and of such religious factors in general as against other historical forces, economic, social, military. Religious movements are continually influenced by other realms of culture and politics, and at the same time their own inner impetus and character influence them. Within a religious group the intensity and sincerity of religious concern will vary widely from one individual to another, as it also will for the same individual from one time to another. In any given case, whether of an individual or of a group, religious considerations or impulses may be obscured by political, economic, or other motives. Even the Marxian proponents of economic determinism observe analogous deviations from pure class interest on the part of historical figures. It remains possible, however, for us as for the Marxian, to calculate the prevailing pressure of a given historical factor, in our case of certain religious systems of attitude and action, over the long run and over the group as a whole.

Numerous friends and colleagues cheerfully gave the time to criticize sections of this study dealing with problems better understood by them than by the author: Professors Sidney Mead and James Luther Adams, Drs. Merrill Hutchins and Robert Handy. Some of the material here summarized was discussed in historical seminars at the University of Chicago and at the University of Frankfurt and a debt of gratitude to the students in these seminars must be acknowledged. The most searching and detailed criticism, from the most comprehensive grasp of the historical material concerned, was freely contributed by my father, Dr. Robert Hastings Nichols. Those who find the style of presentation barbarous can imagine what it must have been before my wife currycombed it. A much better book would be needed for an adequate justification of all these kindnesses.

CONTENTS

❖ ❖ ❖

DEMOCRACY
and the
CHURCHES

I

THE RELIGIOUS ORIGINS OF
LIBERAL DEMOCRACY

❖ ❖ ❖

OVER fifteen centuries of Christian history give the lie to those American preachers who are accustomed to identify Christianity and democracy. For most of its history the Christian Church never dreamed that political democracy was a natural or even possible consequence of its faith and ethic. And even in the last few generations only a minority of Christians, only one tradition within the Church, has been consistently affiliated with political democracy. Most Christians still are not democrats. We should not speak, consequently, of the "Christian" basis for democracy, *tout court*. We cannot even speak of the "Protestant" basis for democracy. We must inquire with some care into the several types or branches of modern Christianity to discover which of them has been able to provide a religious basis for democracy, and what that basis is.

Another large group of Americans is inclined to fall into the error opposite to that of the clergy we have mentioned, and to suppose that democracy is independent of any religious basis. After all, it is of the essence of American democracy that government is sharply dissevered from churches. And there are large numbers of folk who support political democracy vigorously and are aware of no interest in, or debts to, Christianity. Hitherto only history could show that large debts of such a character did in fact exist, and most Americans have known little history. Only the practical confrontation with contrasting cultural traditions in the experiences of the war and occupation revealed to many Americans the fact that there are deeper springs of democratic life. "Democracy," when transplanted by military government to Shintoist, or Roman Catholic, or German Lutheran societies, appeared a threadbare formalism. There was missing the religious and moral attitude and dynamic that alone gives a political system real vitality. Most Americans had been quite unaware of the fact that the moral dynamic of their democracy was the creation of one very specific Protestant ethical tradition, and that, with a few minor exceptions, it was the peculiar product of that single tradition. And without such roots the cut flowers of democratic parliaments, ballots, constitutions, and the rest did not seem destined to bloom long in Germany or Japan or such lands as Latin America.

1. LIMITED GOVERNMENT AND CALVINISM

To clarify these divergences of political ethics within the various nations of the West it is necessary to review some history. In the life of the Western Church the Reformation constitutes the great watershed where the origins of most of the deeper contemporary political differences among Christians are to be sought. For one will find sharply contradictory judgments about the political effects of the Reformation. On the one hand it is often observed that the Reformation marked the greatest forward step in the consolidation of modern absolutist states, and that it was a forcing time of antidemocratic ideas. In the history of Germany, England, France, and Spain, the Reformation, and the religious wars that it occasioned, greatly accelerated the tendency to centralized and absolute power. Both in theory and in fact the medieval subjection of government to law disappeared before the advance of the notion of political " sovereignty." Roman Catholics, Anglicans, Lutherans, alike taught generally the " divine right of kings," with the correlative denial of the right of resistance by subjects. The characteristic political expression of both Reformation and Counter Reformation was absolute monarchy.

But this is not yet the whole picture. " The Reformation," wrote the political theorist Laski, " was the real starting point of democratic ideas." Or, in the language of another historian, " that department of modern political thought which may broadly be called democratic takes its rise in the sixteenth century." [1] For amid the great sweep toward absolutism, which dominated Roman Catholic and Lutheran societies up to the nineteenth century, a contrary current toward constitutional limitations on monarchy or toward outright republicanism was also to be observed. This tradition shaped the life of Switzerland, Holland, Scotland, England, and the English colonies in America. All these countries were profoundly influenced by that type of Protestantism called Calvinistic or Reformed or Presbyterian. The constitutionalist or republican movement in European politics had this one specific religious affiliation in the first four generations after Luther posted his Ninety-five Theses. The only enduring and successful constitutionalist revolutions of this period were carried out by Calvinists. [2] The theoretical justification of these revolutions, which was to become the basis of later democratic thought, was worked out in Switzerland, Scotland, France, and the Netherlands by Calvinists. The ideas of natural rights, the mutual obligations of ruler and people, the duty of responsible representatives to resist tyranny, these and allied conceptions were here given a form that could be practically effective in the political conditions of the day.

There can be no doubt, either, that the most essential motive in this struggle was the religious one. " The *primum mobile* of all this struggle was religious. Civil rights are secondary, a means to an end, never successfully preserved either among Protestants or Catholics except where dangers to religious belief sharpen the determination to resist by a higher than utilitarian motive. . . . The triumph of autocracy, which as a fact was very general, must have been universal but for the claim of religious bodies to limit absolutism by their own existence or even their supremacy. . . . Political liberty is the residuary legatee of ecclesiastical animosities." [3]

But while the pattern of these political affiliations of Calvinism, Anglicanism, Lutheranism, Roman Catholicism, is strikingly consistent, on the whole, certain qualifications must be noticed. It must be reiterated, first of all, that the intolerant and conservative aristocracy of the first four or five generations of the Reformed tradition was a very different thing from modern democracy. The word " democracy " was not then common, and signified about what we would mean by " mobocracy." It is not hard to assemble an album of hard sayings about democracy from leading Calvinists. The significant point is rather the Reformed contribution to limitations on absolutism, to constitutionalism.

A second consideration is that these striking correlations of constitutionalism with Calvinism, and of Romanism, Anglicanism, and Lutheranism with absolutism, are to be explained, not solely in terms of intrinsic religious or ethical bent, but also in terms of the accident of the minority status of the Reformed Church and the prevailingly established status of the Roman Church and of the Anglican and Lutheran Churches. Minorities are naturally inclined to demand toleration or liberty, and, likely enough, representative or decentralized government which would give them some local autonomy or other political organ. Political expediency obviously played an important role in the formulation of the political ethics of both communions.

" All of the great monarchs, who were overlords of Spain and Italy, of France and Germany, of Scotland and the Netherlands, and to a certain extent even the English kings, became close allies of reinvigorated Catholicism. Complete victory of the absolute monarchy would have meant extinction of the Reformation movement everywhere. The starting points for the new religion, on the other hand, were individual local circles — estates, cities, provinces (like The Netherlands), or sections of the civic element and the nobility. A natural alliance was to link the Reformation with the political opponents of centralizing absolutism. The political struggle of the cities and estates for the defense of their liberty gained a new background, a higher motive, in the defense of religion." [4]

Such a minority situation was rarely the lot of Anglican or Lutheran. In both cases the religious cause was championed by the territorial prince. Churchmen found it expedient to support monarchical authority. In Germany, to be sure, there was conflict between the emperor and the local evangelical princes, and even Luther, despite his political conservatism, claimed the "natural right of resistance of the lower ranks of government" against the emperor's injustice.[5] The manifesto issued at Magdeburg in 1550 asserted this right even more strongly. But among Lutherans the Magdeburg *Bekenntnis* was soon forgotten and religious sanctions served simply to shore up the absolutism of the Lutheran rulers. In the eighteenth century the autocrat of Russia was to find in Lutheran Germany the most attractive model for his caesaropapist reorganization of Eastern Orthodoxy.

Among Roman Catholics, however, as well as among the Reformed, the changing fortunes of the religious wars produced situations where the interests of religion argued for limitations on sovereignty. In France and England, in particular, Roman Catholics upon occasion opposed Protestant monarchs with all the weapons at their command. The Roman contribution to antimonarchical thought was thus second only in importance to that of the Reformed, and far more significant than that of Lutheranism or Anglicanism.

"The two religious bodies which have done the most to secure 'the rights of man' are those two which really cared least about individual liberty, and made the largest inroads upon private life wherever they obtained the supremacy — the Roman Catholic Church and the Presbyterian." [6]

The literary tradition to which Calvinist and antimonarchical papist appealed in these situations was the same tradition. Many or most of the Reformed leaders were humanistically trained in Greek and Roman political theory, if not also law, and could draw also on the medieval followers of liberal Greco-Roman thought, such as John of Salisbury, Aquinas, and Marsiglio. There was here a common body of ideas of natural law, popular sovereignty, governmental contract, the right to resistance and even tyrannicide. Buchanan, Knox, Calvin, Ponet, and the later Reformed thinkers moved in the same general circle of ideas as Suárez and Vasquez in political theory, even though, as we shall see, they used these materials in significantly different ways. And it must be remembered that the constitutionalist movement, which was central with the Reformed, was but a minority or occasional phenomenon among the Roman Catholics.

A brief survey of half a dozen of the chief political controversies in the century after the Reformation may illustrate in what way the cause of limited government was served by the various religious traditions.

The first important group of political theorists to oppose absolutism were the British refugees from the persecution of Bloody Mary in the 1550's. John Knox, Bishop Ponet, and Goodman, in particular, fled to the Continent and from there urged resistance and deposition. They justified Wyatt's Rebellion against Mary on both Biblical and constitutional grounds, appealing to the compact between ruler and people in natural law. The Geneva Bible, with its annotations, was to disseminate these ideas widely in Elizabethan England. Calvin himself rather guardedly followed the current, trying to moderate the more turbulent. He did not himself enter on such questions as popular sovereignty or the governmental compact. Goodman reported that Calvin had censured his *How Superior Powers Ought to Be Obeyed* as " somewhat harsh " to rulers, but nevertheless essentially true. And in the year in which Knox left to take part in the revolution in Scotland, Calvin brought out the last edition of the *Institutes* with the famous paragraph inculcating the duty of resistance on the part of " minor magistrates " such as members of Estates-General. The decade closed with declarations of constitutional rights against tyrants by the Scots Assembly and a group of the French Reformed.

Two decades later a new body of political thought was provoked by the events attendant on the murder of at least twenty thousand French Protestants on St. Bartholomew's Day of 1572. Unlike the British refugees, the Huguenots did not appeal to popular insurrection. Having suffered themselves from lynch law at the hands of a hostile majority, they had only a qualified interest in popular sovereignty. They claimed rather the historical and constitutional liberties of estates, magistrates, provinces, and cities, and professed loyalty to the crown to the limit of endurance.

The role of political expediency became apparent at this point in French developments, when from 1584 the succession suddenly favored the Huguenot cause. A radical Romanist party supporting the Guises, the *Ligue,* now exchanged briefs with the Huguenots and repeated all the Protestant arguments for resistance to the monarch with even greater violence. The *Vindiciae contra tyrannos* of the Reformed leader Duplessis-Mornay became a source book of Romanist agitators. Boucher, Louis d'Orléans, and Rossaeus now asserted the sovereignty of the people, and noting that a heretic king was by definition a tyrant, suggested that someone put Henry IV out of the way. The divine right of kings, on the other hand, found its firmest champions now among the Huguenots, when Henry granted them the royal protection of the Edict of Nantes. French Protestants were henceforth to constitute the most conspicuous exception to the main constitutionalist thrust of Reformed politics.

A similar exchange of roles had been effected in England when Queen Mary was succeeded by Elizabeth. The daughter of Anne Boleyn was a bastard in Romanist canon law and must be antipapal, even before " Saint " Pius connived at her assassination. The English Puritans, such as Cartwright and Travers, consequently treated her gently indeed in comparison to the earlier tone of John Knox. The heirs of Knox's incendiarism were now the Roman Catholics such as Allen and Doleman, calling for insurrection against an illegitimate tyrant. Under Elizabeth and James, Roman Catholics were the most strenuous opponents of royal absolutism. Puritan and Roman Catholic alike, in fact, opposed the pretensions of James I to reign by divine right, and in part on the same grounds. Further consideration of this Puritan antiabsolutist movement, however, must be deferred to a later section.

With the Dutch revolution the prevailing patterns were again in evidence. Whether or not the *Vindiciae contra tyrannos* (1579) was written primarily with an eye to The Netherlands, it was more read there than in France. The Declaration of 1581 deposed Philip of Spain on grounds of a broken contract in natural law. The Calvinist federalism of the consequent Dutch Republic was the working model of free institutions to seventeenth century Europe, as Dr. Figgis says,[7] the pioneer of liberty in modern as distinct from medieval Europe, in the age of the Roman and Anglican absolutists, Richelieu, Bossuet, Laud. Althusius was the representative political theorist and built a rounded political system uniting popular sovereignty with the liberal (and medieval) principles of the inherent and inalienable natural rights of communities within the State. Grotius, meanwhile, was the greatest Reformed contributor to the related discipline of international law.

Are we simply to conclude from this sketch of controversies that papists and Presbyterians drew on a common stock of medieval and ancient political theory to rationalize resistance to authority when they were in a minority, and that the Reformed did it more consistently because they were more consistently in the minority? Some historians have done so, but the conclusion is too easy and superficial. The fact that the papist antiabsolutist tradition was brought into political practice only in specific controversies where it served immediate ends, and died away with no effect whatever in any of the situations where the Roman Catholics held the throne, argues that it was held only of expediency. Nothing more was heard of the Jesuit antimonarchists after 1660. The fact that the comparable Reformed tradition was responsibly commended, and actually put into effect where the Reformed were in power, argues that there were here enduring religious and ethical grounds for doing so. These suppositions are borne out by a closer scrutiny of the two sets of arguments for limitations on sovereignty. We shall find on examination that the tradition of limited government is intrinsically more compatible with the theology and churchmanship of the Calvinists than with that of any of the other major religious bodies of the period.

A comparative analysis of the political influence of the two communions in question may be divided into three major parts: first, the conception and practice of corporate life in the Church itself; second, characteristic tendencies in the civil State; and lastly, the relations desired between the Church and the State.

The contrast between Romanist and Reformed as to the structure of the Church itself needs to be seen in the long perspective. For Calvin and his associates were not the inventors of their system, as Dr. McNeill reminds us. " The fundamental ideas at the basis of their bold experimentation in representative church government came to them, consciously or unconsciously, from the conciliar thinkers of the late Middle Ages." [8] Nor should we narrow our vision too sharply to Calvinists. The Reformed Church simply exhibits the most consistent working out of a principle of government normal for Protestantism in general. " Amid a variety of forms, this is indeed the underlying characteristic of the Protestant church polities." [9] The very Protest of Spires of 1529, from which the name " Protestantism " stems, was an appeal to the principle of government of the Church by representative councils.

" In the Middle Ages two opposing principles of government were contending within the Church. These we may designate as the monarchical and the conciliar principles. In the history of government at large the approximate equivalents are absolutism and constitutionalism. In the former, authority rests with a ruler who is not responsible to the ruled. In the latter it is the ruled who also rule, though ordinarily through delegated and responsible bodies. . . . Protestantism continued the tradition of conciliar, as opposed to monarchical, Catholicism. . . . While on the one side it was maintained that the mediation of the divine was through the pope, on the other it was affirmed that authority flowed from the divine Spirit diffused throughout the body of the Christian people, and accordingly that the fundamental organ of authority was a council of the Christian people or their delegated representatives. . . . While the hope of the ecumenical completion of the conciliar system, bodying forth the visible Catholic Church, has remained an unrealized project of Protestantism, the expression of conciliarism in detail has, nevertheless, been more adequate and successful in the Reformed Churches than in medieval Christianity at any period." [10]

The clearest embodiments of these two agelong rival systems of church government were to be found respectively in the modern Roman and in the Reformed communions. Anglicanism and Lutheranism were both largely affected in their development by the interference of the civil power. The former also retained a considerable element of the monarchical principle in the character of its episcopate. Lutheranism, as it developed in Germany under the control of the " godly prince " and his consistory, was a caricature of what Luther himself had desired. In Church life and organization Calvinism has been more faithful to Luther than has Lutheranism. Where freed from State control, indeed, as in the United States, Lutheranism turns naturally to a synodical type of conciliar polity. If this could have happened in sixteenth century Germany, there is some reason to think that Lutheranism would have played a much more important role in this story of the relation of the Churches to democracy than is in fact the case. As Forsyth put it, " Germany has never got over the Reformers' dragonnade of the Anabaptists any more than France has got over the Bartholomew." [11] In fact we must deal with the Reformed as the consistent Protestants on this point.

Perhaps the sharpest contrast of the two systems is to be found at the point of " infallibility." The pope-king was the archetype of modern " sovereignty." His word made law and he was subject to no man's criticism. The administrative organs of the papal Church were infallible. But in the Reformed Church no one was infallible. No one was sovereign. Christ was sole head of the Church, and Christ as presented in Scripture was the law to which all Church officers and government must yield obedience.

The considerations which produced these divergent patterns of Church life, being theologically grounded, made themselves felt, in the second place, in the civil community. The Catholic monarchs of Spain and France and the Holy Roman Empire were effectively assimilated to the ecclesiastical hierarchy through their coronation and enjoyed a sacral sanction for their absolutism. In Strasbourg and Geneva, on the

other hand, Butzer and Calvin agreed in condemning any such unlimited power in a mortal sinner as an offense against the sovereignty
of God and tending to idolatry. In the State, as in the Church, they
opposed the absolutizing of the fallible. And in the State, as in the
Church, they believed in the general capacity for participation in rule.
In the Church, the Holy Spirit might speak through a humble layman;
in the State, all men had access to the natural law engraven in their
consciences by God. And while theoretically any of the classic forms of
government — monarchy, aristocracy, democracy — could be shaped
according to the love and justice of the higher law, Calvin found that
empirically monarchy seemed the form least likely to respect law and
equity. "It is safer and more tolerable that government should be in
the hands of a number." Rulers should be elected rather than inherit
rule, and should be accountable, so that the sovereignty of the law
should be always effective. "It is much more endurable to have rulers
who are chosen and elected — and who acknowledge themselves subject to the laws — than to have a prince who gives utterance without
reason." [12] Thus in discussing the theocracy of the Old Testament, Calvin taught:

"The condition of the people most to be desired is that in which they
create their shepherds by general vote. For when anyone by force usurps the
supreme power, that is tyranny. Also where men are born to kingship, this
does not seem to be in accordance with liberty. Hence the prophet [Micah]
says: we shall set up princes for ourselves; that is, the Lord will not only give
to the Church freedom to breathe, but also institute a definite and well-
ordered government, and establish this upon the common suffrages of all." [13]

The tendency of Reformed politics was thus toward a mixture of
aristocracy and democracy. Calvin, like Luther, steadily opposed any
suggestion of resistance to authority by private citizens, who were called
under all provocations only to suffer, pray, and obey. But he joined Butzer in making resistance to unjust princes not merely permissible but an
absolute obligation for constituted representatives of the people and local authorities. Municipal authorities and, more generally, estates-
general and parliaments, were thus exhorted to call rulers to account as
a part of their high vocation before God.

This bold specification of the political responsibilities of "minor magistrates" was of the greatest significance. By its means the medieval
tradition of the higher law as the rule of government was effectively
related to the one institution which in the circumstances was in a position to make it good, the estates-general and parliaments of the European kingdoms. Sixteenth century Calvinism viewed *all* European states

as by rights constitutional. Parliamentarism was thus penetrated and disciplined by a Reformed doctrine of vocation in Holland and England, while in Roman Catholic Spain and France the Cortes and Estates-General withered away and natural law became a merely academic speculation. When in later centuries the scope of political responsibility was to widen in countries influenced by the Reformed tradition, this high responsibility of the " lesser magistrates " was to permeate the whole political community in a fashion unknown in Roman Catholic and Lutheran societies.

In Roman political ethics the tradition of divine-right monarchy was dominant, as we have seen, but not the sole school of thought. What of the *Ligue* and the antiabsolutists such as Bellarmine and Suárez? The Roman opponents of absolutism were generally more radical and violent than the Reformed. They were not constructively interested in responsible constitutional government. It was not accidental that nothing came of this Thomist " liberalism " but a series of political murders. The papists of this school utilized the concepts of popular sovereignty more than did the Reformed, but they had less to say about the governmental contract. They wanted to prove that kings held their power originally from the people and not directly by divine right. But they did not, like the Reformed, make this argument in the interests of showing the necessity of consent and review on the part of the representatives of the people. On the contrary, the Romanist antiabsolutists had no interest in parliaments or constitutional government. Bellarmine and Suárez believed monarchy to be the best form of government. They wished only to deny its *divine* right so as to remove in advance any theological defenses against deposition by the pope. The only restriction they opposed to growing monarchical absolutism was the right of clerical intervention, the very system whose failure was the original condition of the development of the national monarchies. If, as is sometimes alleged at Communion breakfasts, the American founders drew their political ideas from this Jesuit school, or from Thomas Aquinas, they should have confined their constructive actions to dispatching an Irishman to dirk George III.

The pattern of monarchical Church government was still regnant even in these Jesuit opponents of divine right. Their mental image of the State was not the constitutionalism of the Reformed, but an absolutism like that of the Jesuit order. Such an order rests ultimately on popular sovereignty, on the deliberate compact of individuals hitherto " free and equal." Once having entered into the compact, however, the individual has alienated all rights of consent and review. He is to be *quasi cadaver,* with the duty of blind obedience to the rules of the order.

The rulers of the order, again, are elected, but, once elected, admit no restrictions on their absolute authority. This may not be divine-right monarchy, but still less is it constitutional or limited monarchy. This Jesuit and Thomist political thought has less relation to liberal democracy than it has to the theories of the classical antidemocrat, Thomas Hobbes. "A Leviathan like that of Hobbes, formed by the deliberate choice of its members, with absolutely sovereign rights, and no power of renunciation of obedience, was more nearly paralleled in a monastic order than in any national state. . . . The Whig and Reformed State," in Father Figgis' epigram, "is in fact a limited, the Jesuit and Jacobin State is an unlimited, liability company." [14]

A significant index to the political spirit of these several traditions as related to popular participation in government is to be found in their attitude to general education. Roman Catholic and Anglican education was frankly aristocratic and designed to maintain social and political inequality. The notion of universal education and the common school has been inherited by modern democracy from the Reformation. The history of early public education knows no rival to the schools of Geneva, Scotland, and New England. The Reformed did not merely believe in the capacities of all men; they took pains to develop them.

Third and last, we must compare the effects of the respective views of the proper relation between Church and State held by papist and Presbyterian. Formally one may distinguish three types of Church-State relations: clericalism, in which Church officials direct the civil State; caesaropapism, or "Erastianism," in which civil officials control the Church; and a system of co-ordinate jurisdiction. Anglicanism and Lutheranism represented the Erastian pattern, in which the Church was too closely bound to the State to take an independent line. The Roman Church, on the other hand, was in principle clerical. The seventeenth century Jesuits, to be sure, modified the simple Counter Reformation program of an international papal-controlled and priest-ridden theocracy. After all they were mostly Spaniards and saw reasons to assign a degree of autonomy to such national monarchies as Spain. In contrast to the medieval theory of Church and State as one society in two aspects, the Jesuits agreed with the Reformed in distinguishing two overlapping societies, with different ends, personnel, officers. The State was thus in part independent of the Church. Bellarmine said that he was put on the Index for arguing that the pope's power of deposing rulers was only indirect rather than direct. But in practice there was little difference. On the moral aspects of politics, the Christian magistrate had no claim to an independent conscience. He was to take orders from an infallible clerical corporation. No genuinely self-governing

State could be built on such bases.

With the Reformed the delicate balance of co-ordinate jurisdiction was most nearly achieved. At times, in Switzerland and Holland especially, the Reformed Church lapsed into State control. At times a virtual clericalism seemed to be in power. But the central and normal pattern of Reformed Church-State relations was co-ordinate jurisdiction. The Reformed State was directly responsible to God — not, as in Romanist thought, to the clergy. The Christian magistrate had a vocation in as real a sense as the minister of religion. In practice, of course, the clergy would undertake to instruct the magistrate as to God's will for him. But the Reformed knew well that the clergy were not infallible. After all, the magistrates ran Calvin out of Geneva. Church and State were to be independent but co-operating bodies, distinct centers of power, in the tensions between which was to lie the greatest possibility of liberty.

In conclusion, we must set a very different estimate on the contributions of the Roman and Reformed communions to the growth of limitations on absolutism. The Roman communion contributed only where it was in a religious minority, and there only to the extent of demanding a distinct sphere for its own clerical absolutism. Where it was in power, it lent its religious sanctions to political despotism. The Reformed communion, by contrast, urged and helped in achieving the development of constitutional limitations on sovereignty as a religious duty. It was among the Reformed, with Calvin, Knox, Ponet, Goodman, Cartwright, Hotman, Beza, Duplessis-Mornay, Marnix Saint Aldegonde, William of Orange, Althusius, Grotius, that there were found the most influential sixteenth and early seventeenth century champions of popular sovereignty, government by consent, natural rights, the duty to resist tyranny. Here were the exponents and demonstrators of the virtues of local self-government, federalism, and the rights and duties of representative assemblies. And with regard to the relationship between Church and State, it was the Reformed communion that, with some variations, now effectively maintained the early medieval tradition of co-ordinate jurisdiction as against papalist clericalism on the one hand, or Lutheran or Anglican caesaropapism on the other. With respect to State, Church, and the relation between Church and State, the Reformed Churches represented the one constitutional Christian tradition.

The Reformed Church was not democratic in the first century of the Reformation. Real democracy appeared first as a further development of Reformed ethics on the crest of the revolutionary triumph in England, when the presbyterian and parliamentary party had succeeded in breaking the power of Anglican absolute monarchy. We must next analyze that modification of classical Calvinism which made liberal democracy possible.

2. THE PURITAN COVENANT AND NATURAL DEMOCRATIC RIGHTS

With the Puritan Revolution of the middle generation of the seventeenth century we reach the critical epoch of modern Anglo-American civilization. Here was forged that new pattern of forces and orientations within which the developments of the last three hundred years have been relatively superficial readjustments. The comparable break in Roman Catholic and Lutheran societies came a century and a half later, with the French Revolution and its repercussions. Today the analysis of the deeper problems of Catholic cultures forces one back to the French Revolution. While American historians, for understandable reasons, have been prone to treat the era of the American Revolution and Constitution as a comparable creative age, it palpably was neither creative nor revolutionary in fundamentals. Analysis of the deeper issues of Anglo-American culture forces one all the way back to the 1640's and 1650's, and to a perspective that sees the interplay and unity of Britain and its American colonies.

Not least among the new creations of this Puritan generation was liberal democracy. Distinguished Anglicans such as William Temple and R. H. Tawney, as well as Roman Catholics like Lord Acton and Christopher Dawson, have accounted Puritanism to be the most potent force in the shaping of modern Anglo-American democracy. In Mr. Tawney's language, " the foundation of democracy is the sense of spiritual independence, which nerves the individual to stand alone against the powers of this world, and in England, where squire and parson, lifting arrogant eyebrows at the insolence of the lower orders, combined to crush popular agitation, as a menace at once to society and to the Church, it is probable that democracy owes more to Nonconformity than to any other single movement." [15] Dawson's account is also worth quoting here:

" In England the pure Calvinist tradition was united with that of the Anabaptist and independent sects to produce a new movement which was political as well as religious and which marks the first appearance of genuine democracy in the modern world. And in this revolutionary attempt . . . the Calvinist conception of the democratic aristocracy of the saints provided the inspiration and the driving force.

" This translation of the conception of the Holy Community from an ecclesiastical ideal to a principle of revolutionary political action was not confined to the sectarian extremists such as the Baptists and Fifth Monarchy men: it was accepted by the leading Independent divines such as the two Goodwins, by intellectuals like Vane and Milton, and by the leaders of the Army itself, Cromwell and Ireton . . . and in fact it does mark the beginning of a new world, for, as Troeltsch points out, the great experiment of the Cromwellian Commonwealth, short-lived though it was, by the momentum of its religious impulse opened the way for a new type of civilization based on the freedom of the person and of conscience as rights conferred absolutely by God and Nature. The connection is seen most clearly in America where the Congregationalist Calvinism of New England, which was a parallel development to the independent Puritanism of Old England, developing from the same roots in a different environment, leads on directly to the assertion of the Rights of Man in the Constitution of the North American states and to the rise of political democracy. But it also inspired the rise of the bourgeois liberal culture in England.

" The modern Western beliefs in progress, in the rights of man, and the duty of conforming political action to moral ideals, whatever they may owe to other influences, derive ultimately from the moral ideals of Puritanism and its faith in the possibility of the realization of the Holy Community on earth by the efforts of the elect." [16]

The crucial point of interest for us is the question as to precisely what was contributed to the " pure Calvinist tradition " by the " Anabaptist and independent sects." The first stages of the Puritan Revolution followed the familiar pattern of Calvinist constitutionalist rebellions against autocracy. Charles I, ostentatiously supported by the Anglican episcopate, had ruled " personally " and collected taxes without Parliament for eleven years. His attempts to impose " Laud's Liturgy " on the Scots led to rebellion north of the Tweed, and in military embarrassment the king had to appeal to Parliament for help. The Puritans of the Parliament at last were able to attack the arbitrary and unconstitutional exercise of royal prerogative, the special courts of High Commission and Star Chamber, the irregular taxation. They provided for regular sessions of parliament, impeached the king's more notorious ministers, including Archbishop Laud, and deposed an episcopate that had come to represent royal absolutism. At length, when they levied troops without the king's will, civil war actually broke out. " Cavaliers " were defeated by " Roundheads " at Marston Moor and Naseby, and in 1646 the king at last surrendered to the parliamentary forces. The Presbyterian program was achieved and constitutional monarchy seemed within grasp. Appropriately enough, a plan for a British Reformed Church was drawn up at Westminster to bring the English and Irish Churches into conformity with the Scots Presbyterians. Politically and ecclesiastically the " pure Calvinist tradition " seemed·to have won another victory.

But the Presbyterians of Parliament no longer held control. In 1645 and 1646 the growth of the popular sects, many of them holding democratic heresies, had been extraordinary. Most important, perhaps, was the propaganda carried on within the Army by John Lilburne, even from his cell in Newgate. Fearing this Army radicalism, the Parliament sought to disband the troops. One may say that modern democracy was born in June, 1647, when at Newmarket and Triploe Heath the Army covenanted not to disband until its rights and liberties were assured. Democratic left-wing Puritanism had challenged theocratic right-wing Calvinism. A year later Colonel Pride " purged " the Parliament of Presbyterians and the Army democracy prepared to organize a new State and a new Church system for England.

Before proceeding to the analysis of the differences between right- and left-wing Puritans, we may note that the same tensions were to be observed in the English colonies. The chief New England colony, Massachusetts Bay, represented essentially the same theocratic position as did the English Presbyterians. The Congregationalists desired a somewhat looser form of ecclesiastical government, coercing schismatic or heretical individuals or churches through the civil authority rather than directly by Church courts. In both cases the elders and ministers constituted virtually a self-perpetuating corporation within the congregations. The congregationalism of the Cambridge Platform and the Presbyterian Puritanism of the Westminster Assembly alike represented the intolerant conservative republicanism of classical Reformed churchmanship.

Even before the time of the English Civil War, however, there had been symptoms of a left-wing rebellion against Congregationalist theocracy in Massachusetts Bay. The first written constitution of the English-speaking world was the " Fundamental Orders of Connecticut " of 1639. Drawn up by seceders from Massachusetts, these Orders set neither religious nor property qualifications on the franchise. Other refugees from the Bay Colony, led by Roger Williams, founded Rhode Island. Rhode Island had a strictly civil " covenant," which explicitly used the word " democraticall " and provided for majority rule, government by consent, and " due process " of law. Roger Williams was the American counterpart of John Lilburne, and the left-wing Puritans of Rhode Island * the analogue of the democratic Puritans of Cromwell's army.

* Maryland is sometimes cited as a democratic pioneer. This is due to a confusion between democracy and toleration. Maryland was the first and " most regal " of the proprietary colonies, at the very opposite extreme from the republican governments of Rhode Island and Connecticut. While the

Puritan commonwealths based their governments on popular consent and discussion, Lord Baltimore ruled Maryland as absolute feudal owner and master. He was, on the other hand, a genuinely tolerant Catholic layman, concerned to find a refuge for English Catholics. From the Protestant crown he was granted a charter permitting such toleration.

What were the chief points of distinction between these right- and left-wing Puritans of old and New England? We may instance three, beginning with the principle of the church as "gathered" by a "covenant." This was the "Anabaptist" feature which the Puritan Independents had taken over, perhaps from the Brownists, and superimposed upon their Calvinist churchmanship. A gathered church was to be distinguished from the parish system, in which the whole community of those baptized and seeking religious nurture was included. To the gathered church could belong only those mature believers who were able to make a public statement of their religious experience and were willing to undertake exacting religious requirements in a "covenant." The level of general interest and participation was consequently much higher in a Puritan gathered church than in an Anglican or Presbyterian parish. Church life was, in fact, democratic.

"The inspirers of democracy in seventeenth-century England were the Anabaptists and the Independents, and finally, the Quakers. This, not simply because they had taken more literally and centrally than others the doctrine of the priesthood of all believers, but because they had insisted on the self-governing congregation. That meant that they had practical and indeed daily experience of a fellowship united in a common purpose beyond themselves, to which purpose each and every member was found to have something to contribute. Democracy was, therefore, for them a mystical institution from the practical experience in which it realized itself." [17]

The congregational covenant of the gathered church meant an individualizing of the Reformed covenant between God and his people. The latter had its political equivalent in the "governmental compact" of the political theorists, in the name of which rulers could be called to account by the people. The gathered church was an association constituted by the voluntary adherence of each of its individual members to the specific constitution instituted by Jesus Christ. The political equivalent of the gathered church, consequently, was the "social contract," according to which the political community itself was conceived as constituted by an explicit or tacit "owning of the covenant" by each citizen. In these matters John Locke, the classic theorist of Anglo-American democracy, showed himself a true son of the Puritan Independents.

From the historical point of view what had happened was that the sixteenth century Calvinist vocation of the " lesser magistrates " to enforce the moral law had been extended to all private men as citizens. A tremendous revolution had taken place. " The consciences of common men were a new phenomenon in politics, and one that has never since disappeared." [18] Dicey refers to individual responsibility as one of the principles of the British constitution which has curbed the arbitrariness of the crown.

" The first of these . . . is that every wrongdoer is individually responsible for every unlawful or wrongful act in which he takes part, and, what is really the same thing looked at from another point of view, cannot, if the act be unlawful, plead in his defense that he did it under the orders of a master or superior. . . . This doctrine of individual responsibility is the real foundation of the legal dogma that the orders of the king himself are no justification for the commission of a wrongful or illegal act. The ordinary rule, therefore, that every wrongdoer is individually liable for the wrong he has committed, is the foundation on which rests the great constitutional doctrine of ministerial responsibility." [19]

The contrast of parish with this gathered church system was most clearly illustrated by the British Anglicans and Presbyterians on the one hand, and on the other the Baptists and other sects of the Army. In New England right and left wing were not so obviously divided on this point, because it was the very genius of the " nonseparatist congregationalists " of Massachusetts Bay to straddle this dividing line. They repudiated sectarianism and separatism and conceived themselves as part of the visible Catholic Church. They accepted responsibility for the moral and religious character of their political community, and were ready, when necessary, to use the secular power to constrain heretics and schismatics. For these reasons we have already classified them as belonging in essentials to the Presbyterian right wing of Puritanism. But in the upsurge of popular religious enthusiasm, and because of the self-selecting process of emigration, these Massachusetts Bay Puritans were also able for a time to maintain virtually the whole community at a pitch of conviction adequate for a " gathered church." The second generation, however, could no longer be both Presbyterian and Baptist in churchmanship. If they were to insist on the standards of a gathered church, they would cease to be the community church. By lowering the conditions of membership to the " halfway covenant," New England Congregationalism chose the " presbyterian way " and ceased to be in any real sense a " gathered church." As a politically established, loosely organized Presbyterianism, the Church of the standing order represented right-wing Puritanism in America, while the left-wing Puritan witness was born henceforth by the growing movement of the Baptists in New England.

A second distinction between traditional Calvinism and left-wing Puritanism must be noted. If the individualization of the idea of the covenant is to be interpreted as an Anabaptist infiltration into the Reformed tradition, a second new element might rather be described as "Spiritualist." This was a new emphasis on the continuing role of the Holy Spirit in illuminating the mind of the Church. Now Calvin had clearly shown that the Scriptures were not self-explanatory, and the gift of full understanding of them was the work of the Holy Spirit in the Church. In the intervening century, however, little had been made of the continuing work of revelation, as the Reformed retired upon a legalistic defensive formulation in reaction against polemic and persecution. The Puritan movement, however, now developed Calvin's argument extensively, and lived in a very vivid apprehension of the presence and guidance of the Spirit. Or at least the generality of Puritans, and in particular the Independents, did so, even if the legalistic Presbyterian minority resisted.

And if we are to find in the social contract and government by consent the political and secular analogy of the Independent doctrine of the covenant, the corresponding analogy to the doctrine of the Holy Spirit in the fellowship is the democratic principle of government by discussion. Principal Lindsay has delineated the rise of these democratic principles with brilliance in his little *Essentials of Democracy*. As he there emphasizes, liberal democracy does not merely mean counting noses, or establishing the strongest pressure group, even with due protection for minorities. Democracy means entering into discussion, the submission of diverse views to mutual criticism, with the intention of discovering something new. The more legalistic variety of Calvinist Presbyterian could not enter into the democratic process, any more than can the present-day Catholic clerical, because he would not admit the possibility of continuing revelation and new truth through the group. The most dramatic illustrations of this aspect of democratic practice among the Puritans are to be found in such cases as the silent waiting of Cromwell's army on the leading of the Spirit, or the general practice of the Quaker meeting. The conviction was, in John Robinson's oft-quoted words, that "the Lord has more truth yet to break forth out of His holy Word."

We may here anticipate events and point out that the political organ of this democratic discussion was to be the Anglo-American system of political parties. This system was only to be fully developed in the eighteenth century. To this day it remains the only even partially effective way, in the conditions of a modern national State, to provide for any genuine popular discussion of policy. Just as in the sixteenth century the Reformed emphasis on the vocation of the estates-general strengthened and disciplined in a unique way the only available instrument for limiting absolutism, so in the eighteenth and nineteenth and twentieth centuries the Free Church Calvinist emphasis on the duty of genuinely participating in discussion has been the unique religious support for the system of the " loyal opposition." Neither Lutheran, Roman Catholic, nor Eastern Orthodox societies have been able to produce the common dedication and the faith in discussion which is the presupposition of the loyal opposition. European parliamentarism, with its splinter parties incapable of real discussion, displays the weakness of democratic mechanics detached from its spiritual roots and presuppositions.

But before these two new emphases of Free Church Calvinism, the covenanted congregation and the continued guidance by the Holy Spirit in the fellowship, could contribute freely to the production of the parallel political structures we have mentioned, another modification of classical Reformed patterns had to be made. This was such a separation of Church and State as would break through the theocratic control of the Presbyterian Parliament, with its Westminster Assembly, or of Massachusetts Bay Congregationalism and its Cambridge Platform. So long as the Christian magistrate was duty bound to actualize the " holy community " according to the pattern of Scripture, an aristocracy of the saints (not the elect) would be inevitable. Massachusetts Bay and New Haven Colony thus confined the franchise to church members, and expected the State to enforce Church discipline.

The " Levelers," on the other hand, and Roger Williams in America, sought to free the civil authority from all theocratic and ecclesiastical intervention. The State should be guided in its action only by those moral laws accessible to the reason and conscience of even unregenerate men. To this degree, and in this sense only, they were " Rationalists," which was the name they preferred. In making this argument they were pushing to a new extreme the Reformed theories of natural law and of the co-ordinate autonomous jurisdictions of Church and State. Most conservative Puritans considered, like Roman Catholicism to this day, that the obligation in natural law to serve and worship God meant to worship him in the true Church he had called out to that end. Thus even the law of " reason and nature " argues for the Reformed or Roman Church, as the case may be! And again, most conservative Puritans, like Aquinas, felt that in any specific case the moral insight of men might be so darkened by sin as to be unable to discern the law of nature. The unregenerate must be guided, even in Milton's judgment, by a standard not fully clear to them but restored in its primal radiance in the freed minds of the regenerate. The " Rationalists " or " Levelers " contested these or any other restrictions which were proposed against the political freedom of all men under the higher law. They postulated a civil State subordinate only to the ethical norms known to all rational men. They wanted no ecclesiastical or Biblical authorities smuggled into the domain of this law of nature.

This scrupulous separation of the Church from the State, of the realm of revelation from that of reason,[20] must be clearly distinguished from latitudinarianism. Latitudinarianism proceeds by the weakening of doctrine, the undermining of the authority of revelation, by what the popes call " indifferentism." The system of Lilburne and Williams, however, maintained strict Calvinist orthodoxy *in the Church*. It was largely out of concern for such orthodoxy that they excluded the magistrate and his political expediencies from the Church and made churchmen in politics relinquish all claims to privilege or special moral insight. State Churches — Anglican, Lutheran, Roman Catholic — can come to terms with modern democracy only by latitudinarianism. In both Britain and America, as well as on the Continent, a tendency to a deist latitudinarianism was to contribute something to the rise of democracy. However, the left-wing Puritan pattern of separation was to provide the distinctive force in Anglo-American culture which promoted a democratic movement generations earlier than elsewhere, and with more lasting vigor. Only transitorily or locally successful in the mid-seventeenth century, this system of separation developed to become a general presupposition, even of formerly " right-wing" groups, such as Presbyterians and American Congregationalists in the eighteenth and nineteenth centuries. It is the key to the characteristic American system of a State in practice deist, determined by natural law and utility, yet associated with evangelical Protestantism as the dominant religious tradition.

The immediate political consequences of left-wing Puritan churchmanship were exhibited most fully in the manifesto, the " Agreement of the People," which the Army sent to the scandalized Commons. In it the " Levelers " demanded biennial parliaments, with a redistribution of seats, equality before the law, and, as to theocracy, complete freedom of religion. As good Puritans, they were proposing for the State a voluntary covenant stating a fundamental law of nature, which reserved certain inalienable rights to the individual, some of which were to be exercised by universal suffrage. Implied, moreover, in the whole procedure of the " agreements " and the general council of the Army was the belief in the progressive discovery of truth through free discussion.

The council was a genuine democratic assembly, as well as, upon occasion, a prayer meeting. The structural pattern throughout was the procedure of the Puritan congregation, constituted by a covenant in obedience to divine institution, and seeking the further guidance of the Holy Spirit in free discussion. Once the theocratic urge to control the State was relinquished, the full exercise of this pattern was available for democratic civil government.

In both Church and State, the primary motive of Puritan democracy was less to claim equal rights, or to fulfill one's personality as such — which was simply sin — than to fulfill certain specific and inalienable religious duties. And from the beginning there was a jealousy to preserve for these a sphere inviolable by government. The first Agreement specified native rights which Parliament must recognize, and in 1653 the Levelers proposed that all juries should be empowered to throw out parliamentary legislation that was not in conformity with the moral law. It must be remembered that the Independents — and most Levelers were Independents — were the most Biblicistic, the most fiercely divine-right type of Puritan. And when they ceased to refer to Scripture as the pattern for civil affairs, they transferred this intensity of devotion to the divinely given pattern of the higher law as the norm and sanction of all government. In the State as in the Church mere tradition and prerogative, to say nothing of expediency, could not stand against morality and the law of God. Thus was nourished that constant reference of political policy to moral norms which is more essential to liberal democracy than to any other modern form of government.

One other general observation about this Puritan democracy should be made to distinguish it from another type of democracy we must come to later. Both in Church and State, Puritan democracy was liberal rather than equalitarian. To be sure, there was a small section of the millenarian group that was primarily concerned for equality. The so-called " Diggers," led by Winstanley, were theocratic communists, who anticipated Marx by interpreting the " Fall of man " as the introduction of private property and acquisitiveness, and looked forward to the establishment of communism as the millennium. The Levelers and the Independents generally, however, found their deepest motive in the classic Reformed doctrine of the inalienable religious vocation of the Christian in politics, a vocation that required a sphere of liberty for its responsible exercise.

Having surveyed the three major Puritan contributions to liberal democracy — the understanding of the community as constituted by the consent of its members under the higher law, to which their consciences are bound; the practice of corporate inquiry and discussion;

and the separation of the spheres of nature and grace, State and Church — we need not follow in detail the varied course of their fortunes. They suffered a temporary eclipse in the Stuart and High Anglican restoration, but won a limited foothold after the Glorious Revolution of 1689. England had apparently decided for a sovereign parliament, rejecting the Levelers' demand for constitutional limitations enforced by an independent judiciary. But in practice the crown in parliament was limited by natural and common law rights. So far as the churches were concerned, Anglicanism still attempted to exert a theocratic influence in a very attenuated latitudinarian fashion. Puritanism, now largely domesticated as " Nonconformity," maintained a steady pressure for the principle of separation. In the attempts at a Stuart restoration in 1715 and 1745, many High Anglicans were sorely tempted, and the firmness of the Nonconformists may have been a major force in saving constitutionalism and the Protestant succession in England. In the first half of the eighteenth century, as might be expected, the Puritan Free Churchmen were the strongest supporters of the Hanoverians and the great Whig families. But the alliance weakened after George II, especially as the efforts to remove legal disabilities on Free Churchmen proved unavailing. By the time of the American War, New England was more their home than old England.

The " three old denominations " of British dissent championed the cause of their American cousins, with whom their ties were close. " The dissenters in general adopted the cause of the Americans and repudiated the measures of the ministry as impolitic and unjust." [21] All through the '70's and '80's, Price and Priestley led the campaigns for the " secularization " of politics, for political equality and freedom of conscience as " natural rights." " Modern nonconformity," wrote Robert Robinson, " naturally leads us to study government: Sidney, Locke, Montesquieu, Beccaria, teach the notions which we hold of government. All think the people the origin of power, the administrative responsible trustees and the enjoyment of life, liberty, and property, the right of all mankind." [22]

Puritan democracy had a freer hand in these years in the American colonies. The Quaker foundations — Pennsylvania, Delaware, New Jersey — extended the influence of left-wing Puritan separation, while the Anglican and especially the Congregationalist colonies attempted to strengthen theocratic barriers to democracy. Within these latter areas, as in England, the principle of separation was urged by " nonconformists," especially Baptists. The " Great Awakening " of the mid-eighteenth century markedly strengthened the proponents of the democratic solution of the Church and State question.

In the commercial and administrative controversies of the colonists with the British crown, meanwhile, the ideas of the Glorious Revolution were revived. In calculating the intellectual preparations for the American Revolution, it should be remembered that the clergy were normally the best educated men in the community, at least in New England, and that the pulpit was still the strongest influence in public opinion. In the Election and Fast Day Sermons of Massachusetts, Connecticut, Vermont, and New Hampshire, in the second half of the century, the most frequently cited guides to Christian politics were Milton, Locke, and Sidney. Hollis had carefully supplied the Harvard library with new editions of the Puritan political theorists. From Mayhew's famous attack on the High Anglican cult of King Charles " the Martyr " in 1750, the doctrine of political Calvinists such as Chauncey, the most widely read apologist for the American cause in Europe, or Cooper, the pastor of Samuel Adams and John Hancock, or Samuel Davies, under whom Patrick Henry learned oratory and political ethics, or President Witherspoon, who directed Madison's graduate studies in ethics, had an influence on the American mind that is now often underrated. In the largest churches in the colonies — Congregationalists, Presbyterians, Baptists, and Anglicans (the bulk of the last being Puritan Anglicans) — the political ethic prevailing was that of Locke's *Second Treatise on Government.* Hence came at length the ideas of the *Declaration of Independence,* which Jefferson himself referred to Locke and Sidney.

At the time of the Revolution the colonies were as solidly Protestant as is Scandinavia today. Over 99 per cent of the population was non-Catholic. The tiny Catholic minority (twenty-five thousand, half of them communicants, with perhaps thirty clergy), like the Lutherans, and the Anglicans (Methodist or otherwise) all had the choice between political expediency and the rejection of their Churches' traditional teachings on the duty of passive obedience to authority. Puritanism alone, and especially Congregationalism, Presbyterianism, and the Baptists, supplied the colonists with a consistent and unembarrassed democratic political ethic, effectively taught by a native and, in the first case at least, well-trained ministry. In contrast to such farfetched apologetic concoctions as the Jefferson-Bellarmine legend,[23] which attempts to trace democratic theory to Jesuit sources, it is not necessary, as Ralph Barton Perry writes, " that the later historian should build a bridge from Puritanism to democracy. The puritans themselves built such a bridge, and many of them crossed it." [24]

The two theological strands in this revolutionary movement are not usually sufficiently distinguished. The more articulate spokesmen — Chauncey, Mayhew, Price, Priestley, Jefferson, Franklin — were all theologically latitudinarian (deist, unitarian) whether their nominal ecclesiastical loyalties were Anglican, Presbyterian, or Congregationalist. Half or two thirds of the signers of the " Declaration " were nominally Anglican laymen from the Middle and Southern colonies, again predominantly latitudinarian. The shapers of the new United States — Madison, Jefferson, Washington — were deists. The contribution of religious latitudinarianism, consequently, is normally overrated in American histories. It is forgotten that the substantial popular support of the movement, and the bulk of the Army, so far as religious at all,[25] was orthodox Puritan, whether Presbyterian, Baptist, Congregationalist, or Low Anglican. And in the orthodox supporters of separation of Church and State were to be found the distinctive champions of what was to be the peculiar American outcome. Those who emphasize the role of the rationalistic statesmen should study more carefully the ideas of the French rationalists which will occupy us in the next chapter. It will be seen that the eye of reason alone discovers very different things to be " natural " in a Roman Catholic monarchist society·from what appears such in a society shaped by Puritanism. To this day the moral presuppositions of liberal democracy have never seemed " natural " to the self-consciously enlightened minds of Europeans shaped by Roman Catholic or Lutheran cultures. One may even suspect that the cultured rationalist generally restates in abstract terms the fundamental motifs he has heard from the despised and uncultured spokesmen for positive religious affirmations. There is more of creative originality in the latter.

Lord Bryce noticed the contrast between the ideas of the American and the French Revolutions:

" Someone has said that the American Government and Constitution are based on the theology of Calvin and the philosophy of Hobbes. This at least is true, that there is a hearty Puritanism in the view of human nature which pervades the instrument of 1787. . . . It is the work of men who believed in original sin, and were resolved to leave open for transgressors no door which they could possibly shut. Compare this spirit with the enthusiastic optimism of the Frenchmen of 1789. It is not merely a difference of race temperaments; it is a difference of fundamental ideas." [26]

Before leaving Puritanism, we may record the Puritan reaction to the French Revolution. English dissent welcomed ecstatically the first murmurs of what they took to be civil and religious liberty in France. Half a dozen or so distinguished ministers were members of the London Revolution Society which drew up in November, 1788, the famous three principles, that: (1) all civil and political authority derive from the people; (2) abuse of power justifies resistance; (3) the right of private judgment, liberty of conscience, trial by jury, freedom of press and election, ought ever to be held sacred and inviolable.[27] Price's sermon based on these three principles provoked Burke's *Reflections on the French Revolution, and on the proceedings in certain societies in London relative to that event.* And among the replies to Burke, that of the Dissenting lawyer Nash expressed the apocalyptic mood: " As I am a believer in Revelation, I, of course, live in the hope of better things; a millennium (not a fifth monarchy, Sir, of enthusiasts and fanatics, but a new heaven and a new earth) in which dwelleth righteousness; or, to drop the Eastern figure and use a more philosophic language, a state of equal liberty and equal justice for all men." [28] For the height of vision of this generation of Puritan politics we should have to turn to its poet Blake, who performed here the role played by Milton in the Commonwealth, or by Spenser for the Elizabethan Puritans.

The English Dissenters saw the Revolution from afar, and were in no position to discern the fundamental differences between French and Puritan democracy which we must analyze. From 1792 the excesses of the terror and the national interests of England militated against sympathy with the French Revolution. By 1800, Puritan Protestantism in both England and America had generally reacted with hostility against French " infidelity," and in the first decade or so of the nineteenth century the native democratic movement was conspicuously retarded and weakened in both countries.

When Anglo-American Protestantism took again a leading role in political reform in the 1820's and 1830's, the predominant vocabulary was no longer that of natural rights, but Evangelical philanthropy and utilitarianism. Even the utilitarians who laughed at natural rights, however, unwittingly availed themselves of the principle in covert ways. Natural rights remained presuppositions of most Puritan Protestant social thought in more or less rarefied form. And the whole society was saturated with the fundamental Calvinist and Puritan fear of all absolutism and the sense of the sacred obligation of political man to direct the State by the moral law. The notions of the primacy of persons and government by consent had been widely disseminated by the Puritan church covenant, while the Puritan faith in the continued guidance of the Holy Spirit taught the habit of determining policy by discussion.

For a century and a half, thus, from 1640 to 1790, only one Christian tradition, that of Anglo-American Puritanism and Nonconformity, had nurtured a mature democratic political ethic. This orientation stood out in sharp contrast to the traditionalist authoritarianism of High Church Anglicanism and early Methodism, the conservative patriarchalism of German Lutheranism, and the divine-right absolutism of Roman Catholicism. Only with the French Revolution in the 1790's did democracy of sorts appear in force on the Continent. To that Continental history we must now turn.

II

THE RECEPTION OF DEMOCRACY IN THE ROMAN CATHOLIC WORLD

✢ ✢ ✢

1. ROMAN CATHOLICISM AND THE FRENCH REVOLUTION

DEMOCRACY in the nation states of the modern Continent, Roman Catholic, Lutheran, Orthodox Catholic, dates from the French Revolution in the last decade of the eighteenth century. It was thus a full century and a half after the rise of Puritan democracy that a Roman Catholic country first broke the hold of absolutism. And while the contagion of the French Revolution spread rapidly over much of Western Europe, the Roman Church bitterly fought its democratic program. It was not until 1848, two centuries after the Puritans of Cromwell's army framed their case, that the Roman Church really gave any qualified countenance to liberalism and democracy.

Not only was Roman Catholic society much less receptive to democracy than Puritan culture; there were also striking differences in the types of democracy produced in these two environments. The French did their best to copy the Anglo-Americans. Montesquieu thought he had captured the secret of English liberty in a mechanical equilibrium of political forces. The Revolutionary leaders attempted to emulate the written constitutions, and the declarations of the rights of persons found in the American state constitutions, like that of Virginia. But the religious motives and the social forces were very different in the two cultures, and the results were in some ways opposites. As we have seen, the primary motive of Puritan democracy was liberty for the fulfillment of religious responsibility, liberty both in the State and against the State. Equality was a corollary, since every man had such duties to fulfill. In France, by contrast, the primary motive was equality, equality based on the one hand on abstract rational considerations, and on the other, on envy of the privileged. Liberty was invoked as a corollary, a participation in privileges earlier denied. But of liberty against the State, of liberty to serve a higher law, the French Revolution had no conception. To the French, the English (and even American) constitution seemed still very imperfectly egalitarian. To the Anglo-Americans the shocking realization gradually came home that the French really had no idea of what liberty was.

The contrast might be stated variously. American democracy is a government " under law," a law partially defined by constitution beyond the reach of legislative majorities, and enforceable against legislative majorities by an independent judiciary. The Levelers themselves had urged all these points. French democracy, by contrast, defined law as the general will expressed in a legislative majority and provided for no appeal from such positive law save the barricades. Just so in the Roman Church there was no appeal from the concrete institution and its canon law.

Again, Puritan democracy assumes the distinction of State and society, the latter being more comprehensive and including besides the State a variety of other forms of association, such as Churches, which may be regulated by, but are not created by or intrinsically subject to the State. French democracy, on the other hand, attempted to treat all corporations as creations of the State, and to assimilate Churches to State organs. This difference meant to the individual citizen in Puritan culture that he possessed certain spheres of activity inviolable by the State, certain claims against the State. In Latin democracy, while individual interests were recognized, the notion of real rights against the State found no basis of conviction.

Or again, Puritan democracy, functioning by free discussion, values and protects minorities and " the opposition." The French middle class, by contrast, captivated by the abolition of feudal and clerical privilege, and the prospect of government by a legislative majority which they could control, had no comprehension of the protection of minority opinion and conducted their discussions chiefly with the guillotine. Roman Catholics had no experience in settling issues by discussion. The minority was not a " recognized opposition," but was treated as minorities are treated in the Roman Church, as expressions of pride and obstinacy, to be liquidated. Continental democracy from the beginning resembled the Church which nursed its infancy; it was in principle totalitarian, intolerant, impatient of constitutional limitation and the rule of law. French democrats did not want to limit the absolute powers of the monarchy; they wanted to seize them.

Of these two traditions of democracy — libertarian pluralistic democracy under law, and despotic unitary equalitarian democracy — we still have manifestations in American and Russian divergencies over the term. The egalitarian type has been frequently willing to resort to dictatorship to gain equality, as witness the two Napoleons, or Lenin. Neither Britain, Canada, Australia, New Zealand, nor the United States, by contrast, has lapsed to dictatorship. In these countries, however, privilege, especially economic monopoly, has often been able to maintain outrageous inequalities under the protection of the appeal to liberty.

We have been suggesting that it was no accident that democracy should have run half its course in modern history before it invaded a Roman Catholic country, and that then the impetus did not come from the religious community, as with the Puritans, but was opposed by the religious community. We have also suggested that French democracy betrayed the character of the Church which had trained its exponents even in their reaction from that Church. The contrast between Anglo-American and Continental democracy, as we have outlined it, is substantially the contrast in principles between Calvinist and Jesuit. From Roman Catholic political theory to Rousseau and the Continental democracy which derives from him is only a degree more of a leap than from Reformed politics to Anglo-American democracy.

The reason why the French democrats of 1789 did not comprehend the great political contribution of Puritanism, " the consciences of private men," was directly related to the catastrophe that had fallen upon French Puritans in the seventeenth century. The general lack in French society and culture of a sense for responsible liberty was the legacy of Louis XIV, and that whole policy of enforced uniformity symbolized by the revocation of the Edict of Nantes. The elimination of religious dissent in France destroyed the most important nursery of spontaneity and independence in the culture. All critics of the Roman Church were henceforth forced to oppose Christianity as such, and the character of the Revolution of the 1790's was predetermined. " A real philosophy of freedom could have developed only if the political and philosophical Revolution of 1789 had been accompanied by a religious upheaval, by the revolt not of minds and bodies only, but of consciences, by a new Reformation." [1]

As we have already seen, those Roman Catholic principles that were appealed to against absolute Protestant monarchy, as in the case of James I of England, had no effect whatever in limiting absolute Roman Catholic monarchies. In the mid-seventeenth century, when the Puritan Revolution in England was presenting the first democratic movement in modern Europe, and some of the English colonies in America were being organized on such principles, the Catholic world was steadily moving in the opposite direction, toward the expansion of royal prerogative. Spain and Italy were congealed in decadent despotism, policed by the Spanish Inquisition as an ecclesiastical instrument of political uniformity. Cultural and political leadership of the Catholic world rested in France, and France was the private property of Czar Louis XIV.

The Jesuit " liberalism " of Suárez and Molina and the " liberal " potentialities, if any, of Thomism, had been relegated to libraries and the innocent speculations of academics. The most representative exponent of Roman Catholic political theory for the generations between the Wars of Religion and the French Revolution was Bossuet, tutor to the Dauphin at the court of Louis XIV. Bossuet undertook to shape the Roman Catholic case against the liberal democratic trend of Holland and England. He identified the English Civil War and Glorious Revolution correctly as the political consequences of the Reformation, noting that the Reformed Church made rebellion against authorities a matter of principle, in contrast to the " Catholic " doctrine of patient submission even to tyrants and pagan emperors. With horror he condemned the impious notion of Grotius and Jurieu that there are higher laws constituting rights prior to positive law. One of the fundamental axioms of seventeenth century French political theory was this absence of any idea of individual rights against the State. Bossuet ridiculed popular sovereignty, contract, and responsible government. Roman Catholicism could contrive no political actualization for the Christian doctrine of the responsible person. " It is far less inconvenient to suffer princes, however bad, than to give the least power to the people."

Bossuet shared most of his political conceptions with Hobbes and Filmer, the two chief English defenders of absolutism against whom Locke wrote. As with Filmer, kings were heirs to the paternal rule of Adam and found their archetype in the glories of David and Solomon. Bossuet sought thus to undercut Protestant exegesis and to demonstrate that the Bible teaches unlimited obedience (*Politics Extracted from Holy Scripture*). But Bossuet also argued, like Hobbes, for the necessity of sovereign power as the only cure for anarchy. Peace and order are only to be had by the irrevocable transfer of all rights and powers to the prince. These included property, personal liberty, and conscience. Bossuet cheerfully supported the great persecution of the Protestants, although he did have the hypocritical decency to deny blandly that any violence was taking place. Slavery, and taxation without representation, as well as persecution, followed from this theory of the monarch's rights. And while a fleeting reference conceded the necessity of resisting a monarch who should contravene the law of God, Bossuet effectively deprived the Church of any means of signalizing such an occasion. It will be recalled that in even more famous writings he denied to the pope even the indirect right of deposition or of invalidating laws. The French and Spanish kings had no more intention of being overruled by the Church than had Henry VIII. On the contrary, Louis XIV ruled the pope, even on doctrinal matters, making the holy father his minister of religion.

Even those who broke with the Church still bore the stamp of authoritarian uniformity in their thinking, and their very antagonism to the ruling order was based on the same assumptions. In this sense the French enlightenment was a " Catholic by-product "; its ideal was simply a more enlightened spiritual and social despotism, but still a despotism. The *philosophes* all assumed the centralization of power in the State, and the dependence on it of all individuals and associations. Most of them were educated by Jesuits or Benedictines, and continued to look for truth of the highest kind, not from the cultivation of personal insight and conscience in fellowship, but from an authoritarian political institution. Even the demand for religious freedom came not from any realization of the rights of conscience and truth against tradition and authority, but from Voltairian skepticism and from the sense of the practical futility of terrorist Catholicism.

One may run down the list of encyclopedists, physiocrats, *philosophes,* and the other varieties of French intellectuals, hunting in vain for democratic liberty. D'Holbach drafted the code of enlightened despotism, and found his model society, as did the physiocrats, in China or ancient Egypt. Voltaire disparaged parliaments and estates-general; his heroes were Louis XIV, Catherine of Russia, and Frederick of Prussia. He was neither a liberal nor a democrat, but " expected everything from the State and worked only for the State." [2] Turgot was opposed to the calling of the estates, general or provincial; he expected everything from the royal authority — as exercised by himself. They were all what is now called " totalitarian liberals," which is to say, not liberals at all. It is no wonder that 1789 found none with real conviction as to those rights of citizens against the State which they parroted from the Americans. " The indivisibility of the State, the supremacy of its rights, the dependence on it of any individual or association, all this is axiomatic; it is not a field for discussion at all." [3]

Perhaps some exception should be made for Montesquieu, who did make a cautious effort in defense of personal liberty as an interest to be preserved in the State. Impressed by the Whig oligarchy of eighteenth century England, Montesquieu supposed the basis of its liberal aspects lay in its equilibrium of forces, the mechanics of " checks and balances." He quite missed the dynamic that sustained these counterforces. But at least his influence tended toward constitutionalism, and the monarchy as reformed in 1789/90 in some measure corresponded to his aspirations. The conservative " Liberals " of the nineteenth century, such as Guizot, were to continue this tradition.

Of all the prophets of the Revolution, however, Rousseau was the most important and widely read. In his tradition came Robespierre and the tyranny of the Revolutionary Convention, and nineteenth century Jacobin nationalism. Rousseau was the master theorist of Continental democracy, as was Locke of Anglo-American democracy. Both were devout deists. Both elaborated theories of social compact and popular sovereignty; the one, however, produced a liberal and limited government under law; the other, an absolute and unlimited despotism of the majority. From Calvinist Geneva, Rousseau carried over only such elements as could be combined with the politics of pagan Greece, or of the Jesuits. Rousseau's social compact, like the vows of a Jesuit, alienates forever all rights and grounds of appeal from the community. " The social compact gives the body politic absolute power over all its members." There is no " higher law "; the general will is the source of all laws. The general will is the criterion of morals, of what is just and unjust. The voice of the people is in fact the voice of God, just as for the Jesuit the voice of the general or the pope was the voice of God, or for the Marxian the party is the voice of God. Liberty is participation in the ruling party of a one-party State. And just as the Inquisitor coerced the suspected heretic, so Rousseau's citizens would be " forced to be free." Rousseau urged the death penalty for heresy from his civic religion. The Jacobins were thus " inverted Catholics," and from the Revolution on the two dogmatic systems were to struggle without mercy. Neither was ever to understand the first principles of liberal democracy, how a responsible person faces a moral decision on principles rather than by authority, and how truth is discovered by discussion.

" Given a country in which the sole religion is based on authority, and denies freedom, is it possible for any real sense of freedom to develop, even among those who at some time or another have broken with the Church? Do not even atheists and Protestants bear the stamp of authority in their thinking, so that their very antagonism to the official system will be but a transferred philosophy of authority, just as the sovereignty of the people is after all but sovereignty theoretically transferred? Can any real philosophy of Liberalism appear in a country in which the denial of freedom of opinion and toleration have been acquiesced in by the mass of public opinion, or in which truth of the highest kind is founded not on the appeal to individual conviction but on the authority of an infallible Church, using, if needs be, the coercive powers of the State? " [4]

While Pius VI had apparently not taken the trouble to notice the American Declaration of Independence, his allocution on the French Declaration of the Rights of Man condemned also the principles of American democracy. This allocution of March 29, 1790, is the first of the long series of authoritative Roman Catholic repudiations of liberal democracy. The pope expressed scandal, not only at the legalization of freedom of thought and expression, even in religion, but also at the declaration that " no man can be bound by laws save those to which he has consented." Moreover, " all non-Catholics have been declared eligible to hold any type of municipal, civil, or military office." He yearns to call back the nation " seduced by an empty phantom of liberty " to the Christian doctrine of obedience to kings, who are God's ministers.[5] The next year he cites Augustine on divine right: "' Human society is nothing but a general compact to obey kings,' and it is not so much from the social contract as from God himself, author of all good and all justice, that the power of kings derives its force." [6] And he finds no basis of compromise with the new theories. " This equality, this liberty, so exalted by the National Assembly, thus reach their goal only in upturning the Catholic religion, and that is why it has refused to declare her ' dominant ' in the kingdom, although this title always was accorded to her." [7] He cannot acknowledge " the seventeen articles *On the Rights of Man* . . . so contrary to religion and society." [8] Thus was Rome arrayed officially against this manifesto of Continental Liberalism, and by implication against the series of Reformed charters of liberties from Holland, England, and America on which it was based. Later, Pius fixed upon Calvinism the ultimate responsibility for the execution of the king.[9]

These expressions were explicit declarations of the general principles of political ethics taken in the abstract. It was certainly true that the pope had other grievances against the men who brought the issues of principle to his attention. The Assembly had deprived the French Church of its tithes, its lands, its feudal privileges, its status as a corporation in the State. It had even gone beyond these externals to attempt revision of the very structure of the Church. Presbyterian-style election of clergy and bishops might be the ancient tradition of the Church, and the present desire of the bulk of the lower clergy, but Rome wanted none of it, much less a revived metropolitan system reducing papal jurisdiction to a minimum. It was over the oath to this new Church constitution, devised by the Assembly, that civil war finally broke out.

And on the more specifically political issues the pope had strong reasons for feeling his solidarity of interest with the old regime. The upper clergy of France were bound by all sorts of ties of friendship and blood to the aristocracy and royal family. And at Avignon and Venaissin the pope himself held French lands. When his subjects rose in the name of " popular sovereignty " and adhered to the new National Assembly and its Rights of Man, the pope was in a position to feel a lively sympathy for Louis XVI. He wrote to all the legitimate sovereigns of Europe to protest against this enormous injustice and to warn them of the possible consequences to them of such revolutionary precedents of national self-determination. He made evident to them that the Roman Church was the surest support of the authority of kings. He became, in fact, a chief agent in promoting war against the new French government. Writing to the emperor, Leopold II, for example (March 3, 1792), Pius said, " You can thus be the promoter and head of a coalition so necessary for the defense of the cause of God." [10] It was this diplomatic role of the pope in engineering an invading coalition against France, together with the rising of the " Royal and Catholic Armies " of La Vendée in the rear, that brought the Convention to its savage attack on the Church. Then followed the Terror, which dug " the bloody ditch which never can be filled in " between democracy and Roman Catholicism in France. Roman Catholic countries in general have been most deeply divided to this day by the continuing opposition of political Catholicism and anti-clerical liberal or socialist parties in the tradition of the Revolution.

The " disdainful toleration " of the revolutionary State toward the French Churches in the latter half of the nineties produced a situation of separation in some ways comparable to the pattern then existing in most of the United States. Clerical salaries, which had been paid through the Terror, were canceled, and on the other hand freedom of religion was legally proclaimed. For six years or so the system worked passably and religion experienced a revival. An obvious factor in this relative success was the multiplicity of religious groups. The Catholics were split into three groups: the schismatic Church, which had accepted the Civil Constitution; the papalist monarchists, working for the return of Louis XVIII; and the papalists willing to accept the existing government of the Directory. In addition there were the Reformed, the Lutherans, the Jews, the " theophilanthropists," and the organized free-thinkers. It seemed to be a demonstration of Voltaire's thesis that religious peace was only to be had by so multiplying sects that their mutual jealousy would prevent the dominance of any.

But in fact, Voltaire's theory, while accurate for this system of the Directory, was a superficial and external explanation of the English situation which he had in mind. As with Montesquieu's analysis of the English constitution in terms of checks and balances, he grasped the formal mechanics without the soul which animated them. The French situation was an unstable equilibrium because the Roman Church would never accept it. The Roman Church is never " free " except when it is in a position to control the State and penalize its rivals. Voltaire had wholly missed the religious and theological pressure, which, by contrast, had contributed to the ecclesiastical neutralization of the State in Puritan cultures and which would seek to maintain an equilibrium of disestab-lished Churches even when in a majority. And he had wholly missed the Puritan conception of continuing revelation, which prevented any such rigid public protection of dogma as was essential to the Roman Catholic and Lutheran and Orthodox Catholic societies. To a Puritan like Milton or Cromwell, toleration could lead to increased truth. To a Romanist, toleration could not. It could be defended only on grounds of temporary expediency, and its proponents were always under suspicion of culpable "indifferentism" to truth. Wherever the opposition is too weak to defend itself, the Roman Church will coerce it, for hypocrites are supposed to be less dangerous to neighbors and children than are open heretics. The toleration involved in democracy could come only by breaking the hold of dogma and the hierarchy in Roman Catholic countries, and could be maintained, as Voltaire indicated, only by balancing the power of that hierarchy with other powers. And so Napoleon was able to supplant the unstable system of separation and reestablish the Roman Church by that Concordat which was the basis of Church and State relations in France into the twentieth century.

2. Catholic Liberalism in the Restoration Epoch

When Napoleon himself fell, it seemed at first as if the wish of Pius VI for a restoration of the absolutist old regime everywhere in the Catholic world would be fulfilled. Such was certainly the purpose of Prince Metternich, the chief of state of the leading Catholic power, Austria, who was to be the presiding genius of the system of restored monarchies from the Congress of Vienna of 1815 to the Revolution of 1848. Metternich's diplomacy was directed to the consolidation of monarchist interests everywhere in a league against all liberal and democratic ideas, even to the point of international intervention whenever such a source of infection might appear. And the major support of this system of legitimate kings was to be a restored Roman Church. The league of "Throne and Altar" was the formula of the Restoration system, for what more consistent ally was there in the struggle to make Europe safe from democracy?

There were difficulties, however, in realizing the program. It was not merely the refusal of England to co-operate effectively in stamping out all the liberal risings in Greece, in Latin America, in Switzerland, in Belgium. Even in Catholic countries, the princes were inclined to retain some revolutionary institutions and incorporate them in their administration. Rome did not succeed in the endeavor to form a really theocratic State save in feudal Spain, Piedmont, and the papal states. She was unable in France to recover all the former Church lands; she was unable to bring about the abolition of the State school system, although she went far in controlling it. The restoration of the old juridical status of the Church as a corporate body of the State did not seem wholly practicable, nor did the legal privileges expected by the clergy.

The continuing influence of constitutional ideas also raised problems, especially in France and in Belgium. In 1814 when Pius VII heard of the proposed establishment of Louis XVIII in France, he sent him his congratulations. But he could not forbear mentioning his dismay at the constitution proposed for the new regime, which proclaimed the sovereignty of the people, civil equality, liberty of worship and of the press. The Roman Church, by consequence, " not only was not declared the only Church having the right to the support of the laws and the authority of the government in all France, but was entirely omitted even in the act of re-establishment of the monarchy! . . . In establishing the liberty of worship without distinctions, truth is confounded with error and one puts on the level of heretical sects, and even of Jewish perfidy, the holy and immaculate Bride of Christ, the Church without which there is no salvation." His astonishment was increased by the twenty-third article of the constitution, guaranteeing the freedom of the press, that menace to faith and morals. He was afflicted by the prohibition of inquiry into votes and opinions (Art. 25). He urged the bishops of France to get these laws abolished.[11] In 1821 he condemned the *Carbonari,* the secret societies of liberals and nationalists, as holding impious principles of arousing rebellions against kings as tyrants.[12]

Similar troubles arose in the Low Countries. The Congress of Vienna had sought to create a buffer state against future French aggression by giving William of Holland Luxembourg and the principalities of Liége in addition to the United Provinces. Thus Roman Catholic Belgium was joined to Reformed Holland. The powers drafted a treaty guaranteeing political and religious liberty and equality with this union and compelled William to add it to his constitution, which was otherwise highly autocratic, lacking a responsible ministry, trial by jury, and freedom of the press. But when William submitted this constitution to an assembly of notables, the Belgian episcopate, led by Bishop de Broglie of Ghent, protested violently. The bishop simply forbade the notables of his diocese to vote for a constitution injuring the inalienable privileges of the Roman Church. Most of the Belgian notables voted against it. King William juggled the figures and announced that the constitution was accepted. The hierarchy then forbade Catholics to take the oath to the constitution. A compromise was finally achieved by which Catholics could take the oath to maintain the rights of non-Catholics but only in their civil reference. In both France and Belgium, thus, the early nineteenth century found the Roman Church still opposed to democracy on the grounds taken by right-wing Calvinists in the English seventeenth century. There can be no democracy where a dominant Church claims theocratic rights over the State.

In every Catholic country the alliance of throne and altar was rationalized on the same general lines. Metternich's secretary Gentz might be taken for the Hapsburg Empire; Adam Müller, for German Catholicism. Most famous of all was the school of French Catholic "traditionalists," who interpreted the restored monarchy of the Catholic Bourbons. De Maistre and Lamennais might be mentioned in particular. De Maistre supplied in his person a link to the system of Bossuet and Louis XIV. He came from the minor provincial nobility, virtually untouched by the disintegrating ideas of the fashionable *philosophes*. After suffering personally through the Revolution and Napoleonic Wars, he came to France at the Restoration, at the age of sixty-three, to serve as advocate of the uncorrupted *ancien régime* of the seventeenth century in the nineteenth. His most famous work, *Du Pape* (1819), can be considered together with that *Essai sur l'indifférence* (1817) which had just made Lamennais the most popular priest in France.

The traditionalists took a new line in apologetics. They did not seek to prove, like classical apologetics, that Catholicism was *true*. They avoided such arguments, and were in the last analysis skeptical as to reason, science, metaphysics, conscience. They tried to prove that Catholicism was *useful,* indeed, indispensable, for the maintenance of social order. Since dogma provides symbols of social cohesion, it must be maintained for social reasons. Reason is incapable of discovering truth; no agreement can come of free discussion; anarchy can be prevented only by the imposition of authority, and such authority, to be effective, must be absolute and infallible. Hence the pope and Catholic monarchy. The horrors of the Revolution, on the other hand, were to be attributed to the Reformation, which had called up the " bloody doctrine of the sovereignty of the people," the " absurd, fatal, degrading" notions of contract and government by consent, " liberty in belief," and " equality in authority," which must always lead to " political servitude and religious anarchy."

These were representative of the ideas of the clerical party under the restored Bourbons. The " White Terror " now took its revenge for 1793, especially on the Protestants. The ranks of the episcopate were filled up with thirty new legitimist bishops. The public-school system was violently and scurrilously attacked and put under clerical control. A sacrilege law was passed, which, in its original form, revived the medieval barbarities of mutilation as punishment. Even so, it was " heretical and atheistic " to Lamennais because it protected other faiths in addition to the true one. In 1824 a solidly reactionary Chamber decided to consoli-

date its position, and voted itself in for seven years. The same year Lamennais made a pilgrimage to Leo XII, who was doing his best to put
into effect Lamennais' ideas about the Inquisition. He had the Jews of
the papal states confined to the ghetto, maintained a widespread system
of informers, and encouraged the Roman Ku-Klux Klan, the *Sanfedisti.*
It was said that Leo offered Lamennais a cardinal's hat and an apart-
ment in the Vatican. On his return Lamennais got into trouble with the
Government over his next book (*De la religion,* 1826), in which he argued not merely that Catholicism and democracy were mutually exclusive but, on the grounds of the crudest form of papal infallibility,
contended for the right of the pope to depose princes and dispense subjects from obeying laws. This was too much even for most of the French
bishops, who still held to Bossuet's position with regard to the independence of the king from the pope in temporal matters.

Significantly enough, however, it was with Lamennais, the most extreme partisan of papal absolutism, that the suggestion of a new set of
tactics for Roman Catholics in constitutional states now made its revolutionary appearance. And also significantly, it was in three countries
where Catholics were in a minority that these tactics of " Catholic liberalism " or " ultramontane democracy " were now first tried. In Poland the effort was to fail, but Ireland and Belgium, subject to Protestant England and Protestant Holland respectively, were the pioneers
in demonstrating the feasibility of the new program of Lamennais, at
least in part. Ireland and Belgium still in the twentieth century were to
be the only Catholic countries where a good measure of religious liberty and other liberal practices were honored. And Lamennais' tactics,
rejected in his own day, became the cornerstone of policy for the twentieth century papacy.

It is an interesting question how far Lamennais' thinking was affected by Irish and Belgian experience. His writing, in turn, had great
influence on the Belgian developments. In any case we may begin with
the course of events in these two countries and then notice Lamennais'
theoretical analysis. In Ireland, it will be recalled, Pitt's original scheme
of combining the Irish with the British legislature had included also the
political emancipation of the Roman Catholics. When the king ruled
out the latter, the Irish felt cheated. Nevertheless, it was the Irish who
delayed Catholic emancipation in Britain so long. It could have been
had a decade or two earlier on terms acceptable to the pope and to the
Catholics of England. For our purposes, however, the interesting developments were the devices used by O'Connell's Association in the 1820's
to force emancipation. For the first time in generations Roman Catholic demagoguery and agitation were used as a weapon against estab-

lished authority. The Irish priests were the most effective organizers of the Association and freely used ecclesiastical penalties for political ends. The tenants were released from the intimidation of their Protestant landlords by the only power that could so nerve them to rebel. The clergy supervised their voting and their political contributions and showed itself magnificently adapted to become a political machine within the procedures of parliamentarism. In fear of civil war, Peel and Wellington pushed through Roman Catholic emancipation in 1829. The clerically organized masses had mobilized pressure adequate to co-erce the British Parliament. Here was a phenomenon to cause reflection among both Catholics and liberal democrats.

In Belgium, meanwhile, an analogous movement was taking place. The autocratic Dutch king had antagonized both the Catholic Belgians and the liberal heirs of the Revolution. Against the common foe an un-precedented alliance who struck by these two. In 1828, Belgian liberals and Belgian Catholics formed a parliamentary coalition to struggle for civil and religious liberty, liberty of worship, education, and the press. When in 1830 the Brussels uprising succeeded and Belgium came in sight of independence, it was apparent that the continuance of this Catholic-liberal *mésalliance* was the only condition on which Belgium could hope to survive independently. Thus, as in Ireland, national inter-ests brought Catholics to accept and use a measure of Protestant or lib-eral democratic procedures. In both cases the hierarchy cautiously fol-lowed the lead of laymen and priests.

With the Polish national and Catholic movement against the Ortho-dox Russian overlord we need not further concern ourselves, save to no-tice how keenly it engaged the sympathies of Lamennais, whose vision-ary eye discerned the significance of the whole series of movements. The first real manifesto of Catholic liberalism as a general strategy for the Roman Church was Lamennais' *Des progrès de la révolution* of 1828. From 1827, Lamennais' support of the monarchy was highly qualified. Even earlier, of course, he had been a monarchist because a papist, and now he began to feel that the papal cause needed to be disengaged from the cause of monarchy. The French monarchy, in particular, seemed to him to be destined to share the fate of the restored Stuarts in seven-teenth century England. He had become aware of the spiritual falsity of the Restoration; these Governments did not really believe in the Church, they only wanted to use it. The Church would do better to cast off the golden chains of the Concordat and accept its status as a move-ment within a State and culture that were no longer genuinely Catholic. Lamennais became the leader of an order looking toward such a re-alignment.

The July Revolution (1830) fulfilled Lamennais' prophesies for the Bourbons and became the French counterpart to the Glorious Revolution of 1689. The clerical absolutists were driven out and a constitutionalist monarchy installed as a compromise between the Revolution and the *ancien régime*. The new constitution granted equal freedom and protection to all religions and no longer recognized Romanism as the religion of the State, but only as the " religion of the majority." The law of sacrilege was abolished. As to the franchise, it was still much more restricted than that of the English Reform Bill of 1832. Up to 1848 there were only two hundred thousand voters in France.

But while the hierarchy and the public at large seemed to agree that the July Revolution was a repudiation of Catholic politics for those of liberalism, Lamennais suddenly entered the political arena with the first Roman Catholic daily, *L'Avenir*, bearing as its motto two hitherto irreconcilable symbols, " *Dieu et liberté*." For the first time in a Catholic country, separation of Church and State was urged by Catholics. Lamennais was ready, he said, to relinquish all State salaries for the clergy, and to stand simply on the constitutional liberties of the *Charte*. He claimed liberty of education, of the press, of assembly. He would extend the franchise, decentralize administration. And he took up the cause of the Belgians, the Poles, the Irish, for national and religious self-determination. There was the beginning of international liberal Catholic correspondence around *L'Avenir*. In it the right of revolution was justified, for divine right is " in the people." The old radicalism of the Catholic *Ligue* [13] had risen from the grave, and, indeed, in the same tones of insolence, violence, and vituperation. It was demagogy and agitation more than democracy, and liberalism only in the interests of papal absolutism. For joined to his liberal program, Lamennais revived the claim to the pope's right to dispense citizens from the duty of loyalty to governments and obedience to laws. And he expected that these democratic liberties would make it possible for the Catholic masses to hold legislatures and judiciary under clerical control.

As the *philosophes* and physiocrats had earlier illustrated, it was difficult enough even for Frenchmen who were opposed to clericalism to grasp the dynamics of genuine government by discussion. In the '20's French liberals were endeavoring to appropriate the English mechanics of political parties, ministerial responsibility, and the cabinet. But

" to understand the positive value of political parties, the example of England is not enough; there is also required a religious experience which a Catholic people does not possess, the experience of religious sects [more exactly, of religious " denominations "]. If Constant came nearer than any of his contemporaries to understanding the party system, it was perhaps because he came of a Protestant family. . . . Now parties are·nothing but religious sects, upon which only religious experience can bestow that aspect of universality, that attachment to the common welfare, which compensates and counteracts their original particularism. A party is a particular way of looking at the whole, an individual conception of the common government: precisely as a religious sect is a special way of worshiping the one God. Now in Catholic countries there may be isolated and emancipated individuals capable of understanding this principle; but the mass of the population will never be able fully to grasp it." [14]

Certainly the type of political action proposed by Lamennais would not mend this inexperience; its whole tendency was to a one-party clerical State.

Lamennais the seer had foreseen the next century of Catholic politics, but he was not to be justified in his own day. It was to be expected that the Government would dislike his propaganda and that two of the first five issues of *L'Avenir* would be confiscated. The bishops, likewise, were not to be expected to repudiate a lifetime of preaching divine-right monarchy. Archbishop Quélen of Paris, who had already condemned Lamennais' *Progrès de la révolution,* revealed the hierarchy of his own values in the following recommendation of Jesus: " Not only was Jesus Christ the Son of God, but he was very well connected, and there is good reason to see in him the legitimate heir to the Jewish throne." [15] The bishops mobilized a boycott by Catholics and within a few months *L'Avenir* was on the verge of strangulation. In a gesture of defiance of the French episcopate, Lamennais, Lacordaire, and Montalembert, his fellow editors, set off to Rome to appeal to the pope, in whose interests they were making such extensive claims. They were preceded to Rome by diplomatic communications from Metternich, the czar, the king of Prussia, as well as the French Government, all requesting the pope's· condemnation of *L'Avenir* and its antimonarchical propaganda.

The decrepit Gregory XVI was no man to take the bold line opened up to him. The revolutionary fever of 1830 had spread also into Italy and his own domains. He had been forced to avail himself of Metternich's aid, and at the moment when the pilgrims of *L'Avenir* arrived, he was assiduously cultivating the French Government. Furthermore, he was too old to repudiate his own views of traditionalism, divine right, the duty of subjects to passive obedience. He cut the ground out from under the Polish rebels by giving them the advice of Bossuet: they owed obedience to their legitimate sovereign even though he was a schismatic. In condemnation of those who had raised their heads against the legitimate power of sovereigns he reminded the Polish hierarchy that " obedience, owed by all men to the powers established by God, is an absolute principle which admits of no exception, unless one should be given orders contrary to the laws of God and the Church." [16] On this point Gregory contrasted Roman with Protestant influence a few years later. Denouncing Bible societies and the work of the *Alliance chrétien* in 1844, he summoned princes to aid in the work of suppression, since " religious indifference, propagated by the sectarians in the name of religious liberty, is the surest way to withdraw peoples from the loyalty and obedience they owe to princes." The *Alliance chrétien,* indeed, " in spreading what they call full liberty of conscience among the Italians, boast that they are also giving political liberty to Italy." [17] In contrast to such Protestant political principles, and in reply to French and Belgian Catholics who wished to accept and work within constitutional liberties, Gregory laid down the authoritative Catholic principles in *Mirari vos* (1832).

The instructions of *Mirari vos,* which went to every bishop of the Catholic Church, among the Gentiles of America and Britain, as well as in France, Belgium, Austria, and Spain, were not merely the personal opinions of Gregory XVI. *Mirari vos* contained, in the words of its successor, *Singulari nos,* " the sole doctrine which may be followed on each of the points treated." [18] These were thus the only political principles permitted for teaching or practice even in constitutional countries like America or Belgium. In the course of his encyclical, the pope came to his pronouncements on civil and political liberty from a consideration of " indifferentism," the notion that salvation is to be found in various religions, provided one's morals are sound. He proceeded as follows:

" From this tainted spring of indifferentism flows that absurd and erroneous opinion, or better, that product of delirium, that it is necessary to extend and guarantee *liberty of conscience* to whomever have you. The path to this most pestilent error is being prepared by the full and unlimited freedom of opinions which is being widely diffused, to the misfortune of religion and civil society, while some keep saying with extreme impudence that religion will derive some advantage from it. . . . Experience has proved from earliest times that states distinguished for wealth, for power, for glory, have perished from this single evil, unrestrained freedom of thought, freedom of speech, and the love of novelties.

" To this is related that deadly freedom, never adequately to be execrated and detested, the liberty of the press. . . . It is evident enough how false, rash, insulting to the Holy See, and fertile in misfortune for Christian peoples is the position of those who not only reject book censorship as too heavy a yoke, but have come to the point of malignity where they maintain that it is repugnant to right and justice and where they dare deny to the Church the right of directing and exercising it.

" Since we have learned that writings circulating publicly teach certain doctrines which unsettle the loyalty and submission owed to sovereigns, and which kindle everywhere the torches of sedition, we must take care lest the people thus deceived should deviate from the path of duty. . . . These splendid examples of unremitting submission to rulers [the early Christians] . . . condemn the detestable insolence and the wickedness of those who, inflamed with unregulated desire for an insolent liberty, endeavor with all their energies to overturn and knock down all the rights of authority, while at bottom they are only bringing slavery to the peoples under the guise of liberty. . . .

" Nor can we read the omens more happily for religion and for the governments from the course of those who desire that the Church should be separated from the State. . . .

" May our very dear sons in Jesus Christ, the sovereigns, favor by their cooperation and their authority, these prayers which we make for the safety of religion and the State. May they remember . . . that everything which aids the Church contributes also to their peace and maintenance of their authority."

Gregory XVI had Cardinal Pacca send a personal letter to Lamennais, making explicit the applications to L'Avenir, which, out of regard for his past services, the pope had not done in the encyclical itself. The pope had been afflicted to have L'Avenir venture to discuss in public such questions as separation, on which no Catholics but the hierarchy should venture.

" The Holy Father also disapproves of and indeed condemns the theories relative to *civil* and political liberty which, no doubt contrary to your intentions, tend by their nature to stir up and spread everywhere the spirit of sedition and of revolt by subjects against their sovereigns. Now this spirit is in open opposition with the principles of the Gospel and of our Holy Church, which, as you know well, uniformly preaches obedience to the peoples and justice to sovereigns.

" The doctrines of L'Avenir on the *liberty of worship* and *liberty of the press,* which were treated with so much exaggeration and pushed so far by the editors, are equally reprehensible in the extreme, and in opposition to the teaching, the maxims, and the practice of the Church. They have astonished and dismayed the Holy Father very much, for if in certain circumstances prudence compels their toleration as a lesser evil, such doctrines can never be presented by a Catholic as good or desirable." [19]

The impact of Gregory's condemnation of Catholic liberalism was greater in Belgium than in France. The Belgians had just adopted the most liberal constitution on the Continent. While less democratic than liberal in the aristocratic French sense, it did provide for a measure of representative government and for the range of liberties the pope had severally condemned. What were Belgian Catholics to do? Could they take the oath to such a constitution? If they did, would they be trusted by their liberal allies? And if they didn't, how could Belgium survive as an independent country? Some Catholic leaders retired from politics altogether. Other Catholics took the oath, clinging to that last straw at which liberal Catholics have always clutched, that obedience to the pope in faith and morals does not necessarily imply following his lead in politics. The Vatican's answer to this plea has always been in substance what Cardinal Manning declared, " Politics is a branch of morals." The Belgian hierarchy was practical enough, however, to wink at this dodge for the time being, and most Catholics supported the constitution, at least for public purposes. The liberals, however, did break away and formed a separate party.

In Great Britain and the United States, the Roman Catholics were such an insignificant minority that their Church's political doctrines made no difference anyway. The whole development of American culture and the State system, including the political emancipation of Roman Catholics, had proceeded on Protestant presuppositions. If one were to think away all Catholics in the history of the United States up to the 1830's, it is difficult to see how the main course of development would have been in any way changed. And Catholics in Britain and America had adopted protective coloration. They supported the Government and issued frequent and indignant denials that they believed in the infallibility or the deposing or dispensing power of the pope. Tocqueville discovered to his surprise that the American Catholics honestly were republicans and democrats. His account of how Roman Catholicism could flourish in such a situation was to be very influential on the thinking of Continental Catholics in the '30's and '40's. Here was a demonstration of the practicability of *L'Avenir*'s program, and by the '40's, as we shall see, even the hierarchy was beginning to take it seriously. And from 1830, on the other hand, began that mass migration of Irish Catholics into Great Britain and the United States, which in two or three generations was to make the clerical aspects of Roman Catholic democracy a serious challenge to the liberal democracy of the Puritan tradition.

III

EVANGELICAL AND UTILITARIAN DEMOCRACY
IN BRITAIN AND AMERICA

❖ ❖ ❖

IN THE second half of the eighteenth century Anglo-American Protestantism entered upon a new phase, which may be collectively
described as "Evangelicalism." A new emphasis gradually but unmistakably transformed from within all the major groups, especially Anglicanism and the "three old denominations" of Anglo-American nonconformity, the Congregationalists, Presbyterians, and Baptists. The
political effect of this new Evangelical Protestantism will occupy us in
this chapter.

To appreciate the significance of Evangelicalism we should recall the
political orientations of Anglicanism and Dissent in the eighteenth century. These orientations were equally important with, but very different
from, those of the Roman Church in Catholic countries, such as France.
Up to the First World War, as we have seen, religion was a major factor in determining whether a Frenchman would belong to one of the
parties of the Right or of the Left. But the "religion" was all on one
side. In the large, if one were Roman Catholic, he was also royalist and
antidemocratic. If one were democratic, he was also anticlerical. And
with this theological rancor added to political differences between the
"two Frances," the relation between the two wings was to be more bitter and violent than in the Anglo-American countries. Catholic countries were not in a position to appreciate a "loyal opposition" or genuinely democratic mutuality.

In England, by contrast, the "two-party system" rested on a two-
Church system, that of Anglicanism and Dissent. In both Church and
State there had been since the seventeenth century a recognized opposi-
tion within the constitution. The tension between Cavalier and Round-
head was the historical antecedent of that between Tory and Whig.
The Puritan taught Parliament its duty from the Word, while the High
Anglican agreed with James I that episcopal and royal prerogative
stood or fell together: "No bishop, no king." "Born of ecclesiastical

disputes, nurtured amid religious strife, the two parties, despite their eighteenth and nineteenth century developments, never outgrew their early religious associations." [1] As Trevelyan argues, this division between Church and Dissent remained into the twentieth century the basis of the party system. " Throughout modern history it has been the dominant factor in determining the political allegiance of Englishmen." [2]

These are consequences of the fact that, while France had revoked her Nantes Edict, England passed her Act of Toleration. They have made English political life both more vigorous and at the same time less violent than the French. Though they might refuse to admit it, both Anglicans and Free Churchmen knew that the other tradition was a part of the Christian Church, and perhaps even a part needed to complement their own witness. There was common ground here on the deeper levels, common ground on which discussion might proceed with mutual profit. The admission of a recognized opposition since the Glorious Revolution has saved England from the revolutions with which the history of Catholic countries is punctuated. It has also saved England from any significant anticlerical or atheist movements of the type common to Roman or Orthodox Catholic and Lutheran societies. When an Englishman reacted against clerical pretensions he could still do so as a Christian, and did. Atheism has progressed in the modern West in inverse proportion to schism. There is less of it in the English-speaking world than anywhere else. And in politics there have been in England more freedom, stability, and decentralization than in any of the great Catholic nations.

After the Glorious Revolution, Anglican Tories could no longer hold strictly to divine-right monarchy. Or at least the bulk of them accepted the Parliaments' Hanoverians rather than holding the romantic cause of the Jacobites. They could stand, and did, for the standing order, for king (in Parliament) and Church, for the duties of loyalty and submission, for the maintenance of the social caste system. It was Dissent that upheld the liberal theses and that had half won its battle by the establishment of the Whig party. In the American colonies the " three old denominations " far outnumbered Anglicanism in New England and the middle colonies, while even in the dominantly Anglican southern colonies Puritan Anglicanism set the tone. It was Whig Puritanism that won the American Revolution on the principles of the social contract and natural rights against Anglican Toryism.

Nonconformity and Anglicanism alike, however, were already launched on the internal revolution of Evangelicalism. Shortly before the middle of the eighteenth century there had appeared at various places independently, both in the colonies and in Britain, the startling evidences of the " Awakening." In the nineteenth century the Evangelical current quickly became the most vital force in Anglo-American religion, and established itself as the norm against which other conceptions of religion, such as the revived Laudian clericalism of the Oxford Movement or the American social gospel, must define and defend themselves. The most impressive single institutional result of the Awakening was the splintering off from Anglicanism of the Methodist societies. Presbyterians, Congregationalists, and Baptists, however, were perhaps even more profoundly penetrated and reconstituted by the Evangelical outlook.

The political aspects and consequences of Evangelicalism are not so obvious as those of earlier Puritanism. Seventeenth century Puritanism was politically minded and highly articulate in political thought. Evangelicalism, by contrast, had at first almost no interest in politics. John Wesley's colliers did not have the right to vote, and the provincial Americans converted by Whitefield and Jonathan Edwards lived on a politically inchoate frontier. The doctrine preached and the books recommended were in general those of the " experimental " Puritan writers of the seventeenth century, and in this sense Evangelicalism was a revival of Puritan Protestantism. The most obvious change is by omission. The Puritan urge to theocracy, the demand for a common life integrated by the Word, had been quietly dropped. If the Evangelicals were Puritans, they were Puritans of the radical left wing, sons of Lilburne and Williams rather than of Cotton or Milton or even Baxter. They had accepted the compartmentalization of religion from economics and politics and science, and in these latter areas even men like Jonathan Edwards and Wesley were rationalists, sons of the Enlightenment. Their political and economic thought and practice were no longer related to revelation, but to the laws of nature.

This peculiar compartmentalization of modern British and American culture must be viewed more narrowly. For while it was considered illegitimate to draw consequences directly in the political or economic sphere from religious teaching, in fact religion exerted a strong indirect influence by example and analogy. The findings of " reason " about " natural law " have differed markedly in Evangelical culture from comparable findings by French or German intellectuals. Rationalists such as Jefferson or Voltaire must be read against the background of concrete religions whose experience they are unconsciously formulating on an abstract level. Anglo-American democracy in the nineteenth century was to be religiously neutral in its theory, but in fact unmistakably Evangelical in spirit.

Even the religious and theological character of Evangelicalism, which was to be felt by analogy in politics, was different from that of Puritanism, at least in emphasis. The central conceptions of sin and salvation were the same, but were radically individualized. The doctrine of the priesthood of all believers to each other became increasingly " the right of private judgment." The immediate role of the Holy Spirit was stressed more than the guidance of God through Scripture. Church authority, order, polity, the sacraments were increasingly viewed as instrumental and even optional in relation to the crucial direct confrontation of the individual Christian with his Redeemer. Puritanism generally assumed that there were definite God-given institutional means for man's salvation that must be uncovered in their apostolic purity. Evangelicalism, however, was relatively casual, for example, about the differences in polity between Episcopalians, Presbyterians, and Congregationalists, so long as the goal of individual religious experience might be achieved in any of them. Congregational evangelicals would still hold to the church covenant, but not with the earlier passion, while Anglican evangelicals would similarly take their bishops for what they were worth in the cause. In frontier conditions Evangelicalism could even be reduced by emotionalism to near anarchy. All this tendency was to lead by analogy in politics to emphasis on the importance of the consent of each individual.

1. THE LIBERALIZING OF METHODISM

Where Evangelicalism worked within dissenting churches of a Whig tradition, such as the American New Side Presbyterians, the inherited political tendency was simply confirmed. It is more startling to watch the development of Evangelical religion within Anglicanism, where it acted as the solvent of an antidemocratic heritage. Eighteenth century Anglicanism was the stronghold of antidemocratic Toryism and social conservatism, even in those voluntary societies organized by John Wesley. Yet the liberal pressure within Anglican Methodism was to be sufficiently powerful, first to separate Methodism from Anglicanism, then to lead Methodism itself through a series of liberalizing ecclesiastical revolutions, until at the end of the nineteenth century Methodism was to have become both ecclesiastically and politically liberal, and several times larger than its parent body. And even that parent body was to pass through a development similar to what we shall observe in Roman Catholicism, toward social and economic, if not political, democracy.

For a typical Anglican Tory at this epoch we could do worse than to instance John Wesley. Wesley stood on the same side of the line as Bossuet or Hobbes. He recognized no natural rights. He mocked at the social contract and the idea of government by consent which it embodied.

Like Burke, he opposed Price on the notion of government's deriving its powers by delegation from the people. He accepted and idealized the Hanoverian system of government by a few great families in their private club, the British Parliament. He vindicated the right of that Parliament to expel Wilkes arbitrarily. While he had at first sympathized with the grievances of the American colonists, he turned against them when they revolted. He justified the right of Parliament to tax them at pleasure, popularizing Dr. Johnson's *Taxation No Tyranny* in his *Calm Address* (1775). The consistent opposition of Anglicans, Methodists or otherwise, to the French Revolution was fully in Wesley's spirit. Similarly, he had never favored a wider franchise and would probably have approved the monolithic opposition of the Anglican bishops to the Reform Bill of 1832, and the even more general condemnation of the Chartist movement by Anglicanism. On all the great political controversies of these two or three generations, Anglicanism and official Methodism steadily defended authority and privilege, leaving the cause of liberty and justice to Free Churchmen.

Wesley's political views were very significant up to his death in 1791, due to the autocratic authority with which he imposed them on his hundreds of thousands of followers. But after his death they were much less significant than the inner dynamic of the Methodist societies that he had organized. The analysis of that dynamic may carry us far toward the understanding of the relation of the whole Evangelical movement to liberal democracy, in the Free Churches as well as within Anglicanism. In Methodism, of course, the democratic tendency was thoroughly inhibited in contrast to the case in Presbyterianism or Congregationalism or with the Baptists. Notice first these inhibitions.

Even in church fellowship the democratic potentialities of Methodism were suppressed in Wesley's lifetime and remained latent only. In contrast to the self-government of Free Church congregations, and to the representative principle, Wesley's societies did not choose their own leaders, nor hold any authority over them. It was Wesley who installed all class leaders and stewards as well as local and itinerant preachers, and they were all responsible to him, not to their classes or congregations. And when from 1744 the Annual Conference was established, members attended, not by right, but by invitation. " I sent for them," said John, " to advise, not govern me." [3] In 1790 the old man reaffirmed his paternalist principles of church government. " As long as I live, the people shall have no share in choosing either Stewards or Leaders among the Methodists. . . . We are no republicans and never intend to be. . . . I have been uniform both in doctrine and discipline for above these fifty years." [4] This authority Wesley held, as he believed all political authority should be held, in trust from God, to whom alone he was responsible for its use. " It was merely in obedience to the Providence of God, and for the good of the people, that I at first accepted this power, which I never sought." [5] And to the end Wesley also did his best to preserve his own strong sense of corporate character and historical continuity in his societies by holding them within the communion of Anglican sacraments and the authority of the Anglican hierarchy. " When the Methodists leave the Church of England God will depart from them."

Within the Puritan denominations, meanwhile, the impact of the Evangelical Revival was strongly conservative. The first result of the Revival was to send thousands of converts to the Free Churches for several reasons. For one, the Revival had its independent leaders here. Even within Methodist circles also, there was considerable resentment against the condescension shown to Methodists by Anglican clergy. Many preferred to be honest Dissenters rather than second-class Anglicans. Some actually had to take out licenses for Dissenting worship to be free from Anglican persecution. Indeed, one of the strong reasons for the final break of Methodism from Anglicanism was the fear that otherwise great losses of Methodists to the Free Churches would be suffered.

For all these reasons the old Puritan Churches, especially the Congregationalist and Baptist, had a great ingathering of converts, some of them from Methodist societies, and most of them theologically and politically conservative. The old Dissenting academies, which had stood at the head of English education, now deteriorated intellectually as they increased in evangelical piety. The advantages of Methodist ecclesiastical " connexionalism " for home missions and for financing the clergy were so apparent that both Baptists and Congregationalists formed conferences and then national federations. The temporary alienation of the Free Churches from democracy toward conservatism was also apparent from the time of Wesley's death. In all these ways the Evangelical Movement brought Dissent closer to Anglicanism.

Immediately upon Wesley's death, however, controversy within Methodism showed that the commerce of ideas with the Free Churches was not all going one way. Despite Wesley's own political and ecclesiastical authoritarianism, it was seen how Methodism could also be interpreted in a strongly individualist and liberal fashion. For while Wesley was strongly " churchly " and sacramentarian, he had always maintained the primacy of those Evangelical principles which preclude the idolatry of institutions, namely, justification by faith, and the authority of the Bible and of the living Spirit. The Revival was characterized by a fundamental Protestant personalism; every man was to do his own believing and then to bear witness to his " calling " by serving God " in the world." In these respects even Methodism was a very individualistic form of Puritanism in a Tory setting. And the history of Methodism in the century after Wesley's death was to be the history of the conquest of the Tory Anglican framework by the individualistic Puritan spirit. It was to be the history of the concurrent gravitation of Methodism to nonconformity and to political liberalism. Nearly solidly Anglican and Tory at Wesley's death, Methodism was a century later the largest Nonconformist Church in England and the largest Protestant Church in the English-speaking world, predominantly liberal democratic in politics.

The influence of both Presbyterian and French Revolutionary types of democratic ideas was apparent in the controversy that led to the first Methodist secession, the " New Connexion " of 1797. Through the '90's even Methodists were bound to pick up some of the republican ideas of natural rights, liberty, equality, fraternity. And former Dissenters now Methodist brought with them expectations of Church order that would not be satisfied with benevolent despotism. Both these currents are to be discerned in Alexander Kilham, the first great " Liberal Methodist." Kilham was one of those compelled by persecution to take out a Dissenting minister's license. He belonged to the " Sacramentarians," who urged that Methodism accept the status of Dissent and administer its own sacraments forthwith. Within the Church he desired parity of ministers, congregational self-government, and representative presbyterianism in districts and circuits. Class leaders should be elected, not appointed. " We all have an equal right to vote in these matters as we are all redeemed by Christ, and have each a soul to save, equally precious in the sight of God." [6] In his *Methodist Monitor* he reprinted Watts and other Puritans on Church polity. He would also admit lay representatives to all Church courts, thus precluding Wesley's clerical control. And all these ideas of Church government were also applied to the State, where Kilham presented the spectacle of a Methodist Whig desiring parliamentary reform or, more colorfully, a " Tom Paine Methodist." He was a democrat, not only on Biblical grounds, but because democratic government is necessary for the fulfillment of citizens' vocations. " The cool dispassionate voice of the people is the voice of God." [7]

The next independent movements in Methodism, the Primitive Methodists and the Bible Christians, had less theory to them. They were popular lower-class revivalist movements of the American frontier type, stressing camp meetings and the exercise of the priesthood of all believers in the cell organization of the " class " meeting. They were strongly antisacerdotal and destined to play a very important democratic role by the end of the century in the political education of the lower classes.

Participation in the life of Methodist societies and classes was, despite clericalism, a democratic apprenticeship for thousands of men who had nowhere else to learn the disciplines of group life. The lay helpers and stewards especially learned to care responsibly for common funds and business, to speak persuasively before large audiences or in committees, to write, to organize, to discuss policy objectively, to become, in short, trained leaders for public affairs. The lower middle class, from which most Methodists came, was a class that just in this generation or two was also becoming politically self-conscious and concerned over socioeconomic policy. Dissent, with its democratic inclinations, was socially much closer to the Methodists than were the Anglican country gentry, and influenced the laity more in shop and factory discussions. The Wesleyan Conference, unlike the Dissenting clergy, stood aside from the Anti-Corn-Law movement, but thousands of Methodists attended its mass meetings against high food prices. The Conference condemned the democratic program of the " People's Charter," with its sixfold demand for adult male suffrage, votes by ballot, annual parliaments, abolition of property qualifications for M.P.'s, payment of M.P.'s, and equal electoral districts. But many of the Chartist leaders, such as Stephens, Lovett, Cooper, Barker, came from Methodist backgrounds. The Conference denounced trade-unionism, but " from the very beginning of the trade-union movement among all sections of the wage earners, of the formation of Friendly Societies, and of the later attempts at adult education, it is men who are Methodists and, in Durham County especially, local preachers of the Primitive Methodists, whom we find taking the lead and filling the posts of influence. From their ranks have come an astonishingly large proportion of trade-union leaders, from checkweighers and lodge chairmen up to county officials and committee men." [8] And the transfer of techniques was obvious from Methodism to social politics. " Its connexionalism, its large-scale finance and enterprise, its division into districts, circuits, and societies, its propaganda methods of itinerant preaching and Sunday open-air meetings, its society class and weekly penny subscription were all copied at some time or other by the political reformers." [9] Just so in America Jacksonian democracy took over the techniques of the revival meeting.

Wesleyan Methodist officialdom, meanwhile, was maintaining an unbroken antidemocratic front. Methodism grew enormously in the generation after Wesley's death, from 90,000 to 237,000 full members. The Wesleyan ministers were overwhelmingly Tory, as were the laymen in the villages and countryside. The general tendency was toward the strengthening of ecclesiastical authority, and especially the clerical conference. Jabez Bunting, the " Pope of Methodism," headed the " Conference Party." He would not admit that the Church collectively shared in the minister's "power of the keys," and he fought to keep Conference, as an order of clergy, completely sovereign in the denomination.

In politics, meanwhile, Bunting was similarly authoritarian. Like Wesley himself, he always relaxed the "No Politics" rule for Methodist clergy when it was a matter of defending the king or his ministers. He succeeded in forcing out of the Church, on the other hand, many who dared to support the Luddites, the Chartists, the Reform Bill, or the Corn-Law reformers. Some of them went to Primitive Methodism. The rising working-class movement hated the Methodist clergy more than the Anglicans themselves, since the latter were natural social enemies, but the Methodists were, it seemed, traitors to their class. Cobbett called the Methodists, in 1824, the "bitterest foes of freedom in England." The Wesleyan Conference of 1833 denounced all trade-unions and combinations.[10] "Methodism," said Bunting, "hates democracy as much as it hates sin."[11] In part, of course, the Methodist fear of politics was due to the despiritualizing consequences observed in rationalistic ("wide") Dissent. In part it was due to horror at atheist or unitarian spokesmen for radicalism. But most significant of all was the influence of Church polity, the political assumptions and practices learned in the Church before many of the members ever had any political experience at all.

The catastrophic controversies in Methodism from 1849 to 1857 proved that the unbroken front maintained by Bunting and the Conference did not represent the true spirit of the body of Methodist laymen. Nearly all these early schisms were over polity, and nearly all their leaders, significantly enough, were also political liberals. In the first half of the 1850's, at least a quarter of the membership broke away from Bunting's authoritarianism, and it became clear that not only were the various "minor Methodist" bodies prevailingly liberal, but that even Wesleyan Methodism had a significant liberal minority wing. The last quarter of the nineteenth century, after laymen were finally admitted to Conference (1878), was to see the liberalization even of Wesleyan Methodism. Around 1850 one of the most militant of the liberals was Griffith, who spoke quite in the tone of Kilham, or a Puritan democrat: "If I am a Chartist, my Bible has made me so."[12] And, indeed, Methodist universalism and free grace could be considered an argument for universal suffrage and disestablishment, just as well as predestination had earlier nerved Puritans in the struggle against earthly prerogatives.

Those Evangelicals who had followed Wesley's injunctions and remained within the Anglican Church also maintained his Tory paternalism in the first half of the nineteenth century. Like Wesley himself, who had "discovered the poor," they differed from the mine-run of Anglicans by their zealous and untiring charity, but not by any democratic sympathies. They were highly conscious of the duties of the upper classes toward their inferiors, and even sponsored State action for such purposes. Wilberforce and the "Clapham Sect," Hannah More, and Lord Ashley are famous representatives of this aristocratic pietism. Oastler, Sadler, Stephens, also belong here. Hannah More's antidemocratic propaganda in the 1790's (*Village Politics*) was as influential as Wesley's writing against the American Revolutionaries. She and Wilberforce argued against theories of natural rights that religion justified, and made less galling to the lower orders, the necessary inequalities of society. Wilberforce actively supported the Combination Laws of 1799 and 1800, which deprived the laboring class of any means to defend themselves from the atrocities of the developing factory system. Evangelicals also agreed with High Churchmen in opposing the wider suffrage of the Reform Bill or the Chartist movement. They feared "despotic democracy" and taught that poverty was ordained of God, honor was due the existing authorities, and submission was owed to the upper classes. Lord Ashley considered socialism and Chartism "conspiracies against God and good order . . . two great demons in morals and politics." A few Evangelicals fought for factory legislation and reform of the Poor Laws, again as paternalist reforms, and even these were not widely supported.

With all this paternalism, however, Evangelical charity contributed indirectly to democracy, or was a necessary preparation for it. The brutalized, gin-soaked, illiterate miners and factory workers to whom Wesley preached were no more ready for responsible participation in political self-government than the African captives whipped to labor in America or the West Indies. There could be no democracy here until the Negroes were emancipated, the bonds of alcoholism over the English poor broken, some hope of escaping poverty provided, some education given to the poor, and to the degraded that new self-respect that came with the message of God's concern for those whom society had forgotten. All these things the Evangelical Awakening accomplished in startling degree. We may glance briefly at each.

With regard to education, Wesley's antidemocratic and authoritarian conceptions were quite in evidence. He began with his mother's principle, " The first thing with children is to conquer their wills and to bring them to an obedient temper." And the monastic regimen he prescribed for his own schools should have been enough of itself to close them. Yet, with all his ineptitudes in method, no one in Georgian England did as much for popular education as John Wesley. The Evangelical Awakening brought education to thousands who would otherwise have had none, both adults and children. Wesley's activities in providing popular editions and translations of good literature and scientific works is well known. His preachers were also book salesmen. And the Sunday school movement, whether it is to be credited to Hannah Ball or Robert Raikes, made the rudiments of reading and writing known to hundreds of thousands otherwise illiterate. In 1854, for example, there were 400,000 children in Wesleyan Sunday schools. And the greatest growth came in the decades thereafter. All this met the steady opposition of High Anglican Tories, who saw from the beginning that " it is impolitic to give these children knowledge; it will but unfit them for their respective stations, make them bad labourers and mechanics, and raise them above their order in the community." [13] Roman Catholics on the Continent had proceeded on these considerations also. It was the very direct and personal concern for the responsible soul of every common man that Protestantism nourished which lay at the base of popular education. And this the Evangelical Movement possessed, even in its Anglican manifestations.

The issue of Negro slavery was the greatest triumph of the Evangelical conscience. By the Asiento clause of the Treaty of Utrecht (1713), England had gained the lion's share in the systematic raiding and kidnaping of Africans for sale as captive laborers in America and the West Indies. Until the middle of the century scarcely a voice was heard against this atrocious commerce. The American Quakers, led by Benezet and Woolman, began the reaction. Quaker slave traders were " disowned " in 1761. The agitation increased, and Wesley was brought into battle in the '70's, when antislavery views were still definitely radical. The American Methodist Conference of 1780 declared slaveholding contrary to the laws of God and man.[14] Wesley published tracts and wrote letters in this cause. His famous last letter to Wilberforce (1791) is often quoted: " Go on, in the name of God, and in the power of His might, till even American slavery (the vilest that ever saw the sun) shall vanish before it." [15] Perhaps the agitation might have succeeded in that decade had it not been for the French Revolution, which held up all social reform and democratic progress in England for a generation. In 1807, however, Fox and the Whigs finally passed the Act of Total Abolition of the slave trade. Thereafter British self-interest was combined with humanitarianism in the drive to win international action against the traffic. In the wars with Napoleonic France every French colony occupied by the English was lost to the trade. And the British pressure at the Congress of Vienna was to be crucial in 1815.

Methodists were to be more influential in the continuing struggle against the institution of Negro slavery itself than they had been against the slave trade. The latter crusade had been led, in both England and

America, by an alliance of deist humanitarians with Quakers and Evangelicals. In the period after the Napoleonic Wars the Methodists were perhaps the strongest Church group engaged in the struggle both in England and America. In the West Indies, moreover, Methodist missions were the greatest humanizing influence. By 1828, 22,000 West Indies slaves were Methodists. The Acts of Emancipation of 1833 settled for the British Empire the issue that aroused more and more bitter controversy in the following decades in the United States until the catastrophe of the 1860's. In both cases, the bulk of the antislavery support came from those Anglicans, Presbyterians, Methodists, Congregationalists, Baptists, stirred by the Evangelical Awakening.

The traffic in liquor was another social curse whose brutalizing effects, like those of slavery, permeated all society. In the eighteenth century, gin-drinking was a contributing cause and regular attendant of the slaver, of prostitution, of the atrocious abuse of children and animals, of political corruption and poverty. Wesley, who saw its consequences among those least able to protect themselves, became the chief temperance advocate of his day. He was ready, in fact, to make an exception here in his theory of the proper limits of governmental action, and urge legal intervention. He would have had distilling made a felony. His preachers were forbidden to touch spirits and the advance of the revival in general meant the conquest of alcoholism.

As to the conquest of poverty, and economic ethics generally, the Evangelical Awakening represented a wholehearted acceptance and encouragement of economic enterprise. Here was the actuality of the union of " Protestantism " with the " Spirit of Capitalism " which Weber and Tawney have found foreshadowed in Calvinism and Puritanism. Neither of these scholars has adequately indicated how the acceptance of the capitalist spirit, while a development from Calvinism and Puritanism, also meant their defeat.[16] Calvinist and Puritan attempted to regulate economic life for community and religious ends, as can be seen still in Baxter at the end of the seventeenth century. It is the Evangelical who gave up Puritan theocracy in both State and economics with complete optimism about the " natural " course of Providence in these spheres. It was John Wesley, and no Puritan, who gave economic enterprise full freedom, with only the obligation of individual " stewardship." The Evangelicals were individualists and opposed to collectivist legislation like the theorists of early capitalism. Individual economic enterprise was a moral responsibility, and by its means whole classes of men in England were raised from degradation.

Wesley himself recognized, however, that this process of releasing religious and moral incentives into " business " introduced new dangers:

" Wherever riches have increased, the essence of religion has decreased in the same proportion. Therefore I do not see how it is possible in the nature of things for any revival of religion to continue long. For religion must necessarily produce both industry and frugality, and these cannot but produce riches. But as riches increase so will pride, anger, and love of the world in all its branches. . . . Is there no way to prevent this — this continual decay of pure religion? We ought not to prevent people from being diligent and frugal. We must exhort all Christians to gain all they can, and to save all they can; that is, in effect, to grow rich. What way then can we take, that our money may not sink us into the nethermost hell? . . . If those who gain all they can, and save all they can, will likewise give all they can." [17]

Wesley's recipe is not impressive, and the whole Evangelical movement which dominated Anglo-American religion in the nineteenth century was to be conspicuously weak on this point. The individual would be trained to sobriety, faithfulness, industry, honesty, and in the large he would succeed economically. The guards against acquisitiveness were very weak, on the other hand, and criticism of the economic order itself was scanty. These weaknesses, however, will occupy us later. At the moment our concern is to see how Evangelical religion contributed indirectly to democracy by raising from indigence and hopelessness thousands of men with new initiative and discipline. " To this movement, in combination on the one hand with the old Whig political traditions, on the other with the new *ethos* produced by the industrial revolution, British Liberalism of the opening nineteenth century owed its distinctive character." [18]

2. DEMOCRATIC UTILITARIANISM

Democracy in the seventeenth and eighteenth centuries had found its chief religious support in the Puritanism of what became the " three old denominations," and its theoretical statement in the ideas of social contract and natural rights. Nineteenth century liberal democracy, in Britain and America, found a new footing in both respects. In regard to religion, we have remarked how the abolition of slavery, the widening of the franchise, the spread of popular education, and other democratic reforms were related to the new Evangelical phase of the Puritan tradition. At the same time the older Whig political language of natural law was being replaced by utilitarianism. Almost from the beginning of the new century utilitarianism became the dominant and characteristic social theory of Britain and America. And the peculiar affinity of utilitarianism and Evangelicalism for each other is also characteristic of the century.

" The appeal of the Evangelicals to personal religion corresponds with the appeal of Benthamite Liberals to individual energy. Indifference to the authority of the Church is the counterpart of indifference to the authoritative teaching or guidance of the State or of society. A low estimate of ecclesiastical tradition, aversion to, and incapacity for inquiries into the growth or development of religion, the stern condemnation of even the slightest endeavor to apply to the Bible the principles of historical criticism, bear a close resemblance to Bentham's contempt for legal antiquarianism, and to James Mill's absolute blindness to the force of historical objections brought by Macaulay against the logical dogmatism embodied in Mill's essay on government. Evangelicals and Benthamites alike were incapable of applying the historical method, and neither recognized its value, nor foresaw its influence. The theology again which insisted upon personal responsibility, and treated each man as himself bound to work out his own salvation, had an obvious affinity with the political philosophy which regards man almost exclusively as separate individuals and made it the aim of law to secure for every person freedom to work out his own happiness." [19]

Despite the fact that utilitarianism was the Anglo-American form of atheism, and aggressively antireligious, it was able to co-operate with, and even in part combine with, the Protestant revival, in philanthropy, in ascetic self-discipline, and in individualism. " British individualism is a moderate individualism, a mixture whose constituents are often mingled beyond the possibility of analysis, a compound of Evangelicalism and utilitarianism." [20]

Philosophically utilitarianism stemmed from men like Hume, Adam Smith, and Bentham, who were inclined to be sympathetic with enlightened despotism and went out of their way to mock at the social contract and natural rights urged by advocates of the American and French Revolutions. The founders of utilitarianism were either indifferent or actively hostile to the liberal democrats of their day. Yet these democrats themselves, Priestley, Paine, Goodwin, increasingly used utilitarian formulations. And under the leadership of James Mill, in the period after the Napoleonic Wars, the later utilitarians became the most conspicuous propagandists for universal suffrage and representative democracy. The Mills, classic spokesmen for Anglo-American liberalism, restated in utilitarian terms moral postulates drawn from natural rights theories which could scarcely be defended on utilitarian grounds. Why, for example, should " every one count for one, and one only," in politics? And similarly, the fundamental postulate of the free-market theorists from Adam Smith to Ricardo, the thesis of the natural identity of interests, was a secular formulation of the faith in a benevolent Providence. Such half-conscious recourse to theological and ethical principles, despite the prevailing antireligious tone of the leaders, made certain types of utilitarianism accessible to Puritan Protestantism, and "radicalism" became in time almost the official social ethic of such Protestants. Continental utilitarianism, by contrast, was a far more systematically egoist and materialist position, without points of contact with Christian ethics.

One wing of revivalistic Evangelicalism actually provided a bridge to the theory of progress of radical social reform. This was the perfectionist tendency, especially strong in Methodism. More often conceived in purely individual terms, it was also expressed in millenarian views that the new age of the Spirit was at hand. Especially around 1830 in both England and America was the expectation of the millennium very widespread. Out of this came the Seventh Day Adventists. Some of the perfectionist groups produced socialist communities. Of these the pioneers in America were the Shakers. After them came the great Owenite campaigns in the '20's and '30's, and the Fourierist propaganda of Brisbane and Greeley in the 1840's. The dozens of utopian communities left by these excitements were but partial indicators of the widespread faith in impending social revolution and the possibilities of ideal constructions of human society. Revivalistic perfectionism and millenarianism combined with utilitarian ingenuousness and social reform in a mighty surge of utopian idealism which bit deep, especially into the American mentality, and which was to rise in another climax in the social gospel and related currents of the 1890's.

The most militant Anglo-American democrats of the post-Napoleonic period were the antireligious Radicals, some of whom, like Mill and Comte, consciously endeavored to make a religion of "humanity," with full paraphernalia of cult, saints, symbolism, and the like. Both Bentham and Owen felt their kinship with Evangelical Christianity, while fighting its theology. Bentham would have been a Methodist, he said, if he were not what he was, and Owen, who had been raised by two Methodist spinsters, wished to dedicate his first book to Wilberforce. The extraordinary naïveté of these utilitarian reformers, who really thought that they could inaugurate a reign of harmony and justice by effecting certain reforms in men's social environment, is just the complementary half-truth to that of the otherworldly Evangelicals, who considered nothing but man's personal responsibility, his dangerous moral perversity, and his need of help for any moral achievement. Yet many, both Radicals and Evangelicals, did far better than their theories would prepare one for. Owen, for example, with all his extraordinary ignorance and ingenuousness, was one of the great philanthropists and democrats. Immediately after the Napoleonic Wars he sought to meet the problems of unemployment with his "villages of co-operation." He campaigned for factory legislation. He began a labor exchange. He was interested in kindergartens. His New Harmony experiment spread some of his ideas in America, through his son and Fanny Wright. Owen's influence for secularism and co-operatives, for trade-unions and the franchise, was important. As with Bentham, there were unrecognized moral and religious presuppositions that gave Owen's utilitarianism its democratic values and its moral discipline.

One social basis of the utilitarian philosophy lay in the new urban working class, for whom Radicalism was a theology. The London Workingmen's Association was the source of the famous " Charter " and its six points. In addition to the strictly political and franchise reforms, the workmen's movement supported universal and secular education, direct taxation, abolition of the death penalty, pacifism, teetotalism. There were even " Female Chartist Societies." On several of these issues they went beyond even those Baptists and Unitarians and Congregationalists who were for the Charter. Probably three fourths of this new working class had no relation to organized religion at all, and found some substitute in their unions and political clubs. Some of the leaders were particularly antireligious and acted as colporteurs for the writings of Tom Paine and D. F. Strauss. The majority of the workmen, however, while holding a low opinion of the Churches, considered themselves to be Christians. Christianity to them was strongly ethical and social, but involved little of developed creed or ritual. It carried still the theological and Scriptural sanctions for natural law which in higher social circles had gone out of fashion. In the 1840's " Chartist Churches " began to spring up in many places. Soon there were Chartist hymnals and sacraments. All the clergy were lay preachers. Ecclesiastical Christianity refused to lead in democratic politics, but the Christian people and the Christian faith were seen to be more than merely the High Priests and the Levites.

In the '30's and '40's Evangelical fervor began to flow through the nearly clotted veins of old High and Dry Anglicanism, and produced the twin phenomena of the Oxford Movement and Disraeli's " Young England." Both were romantic efforts at restoration of medieval chivalry or Laudian church order, and both were antidemocratic and antiliberal from beginning to end. Pusey begrudged the money spent to manumit the slaves. Ward preferred absolute monarchy to Russell's Reform Bill, and Newman even as a boy was scandalized by his father's admiration for Franklin and Jefferson. They did inspire new charitable zeal, much like the Evangelicals, especially in the second generation, with the slum priests. The Oxford Tractarians had little feeling either for Church or society as a community; their nostalgia was for authority and clericalism. The efforts made [21] to prove their social contribution produce a total less impressive than that of the Evangelical Tories. The new social and political contribution, which, to be sure, was taken up by the successors of the Tractarians, came rather from the followers of Coleridge, and found its chief focus in the " Christian Socialist" group around F. D. Maurice. Maurice himself said of the Tractarians, " Their error . . . , consists in opposing to ' the spirit of the age ' the spirit of a former age, instead of the ever-living and acting spirit of God." [22]

The first manifestations of a new social outlook in the Church of England proper, as apart from Methodism, made their appearance with the " Christian Socialists" under the leadership of Maurice. Neither in theory nor in practice did these men stand on the forefront of democracy, and they were far from agreed on its principles, but at least they stood where they stood as representatives of the Church of England. The only real democrat of the leaders was the initiator of the movement and its best-informed member on political and economic questions, the lawyer Ludlow. Maurice, to whose religious and theological eminence Ludlow, like the rest, habitually deferred, was a conservative who moved very cautiously toward democracy. These two men brought a Reformed heritage into Anglicanism, Maurice coming from a background of Unitarian " Political Dissent " and retaining much of his father's social and ethical attitudes even while he sought deeper religious underpinnings. Ludlow served his social apprenticeship with French Protestantism in Paris during the '30's. Kingsley, at first the most conspicuous of the lot, was simply a paternalist High Churchman, convinced of the duties of the ruling classes to concern themselves seriously for the needs of the lower orders. He was no democrat at all.

The concrete activities of the Christian Socialists, in furthering producers' co-operatives, friendly societies, settlements, workingmen's colleges, women's higher education, and preparing the Industrial Societies and Provident Act, were, of course, strictly limited in their effect. They did demonstrate a capacity, new to Anglicans, of working with the disadvantaged as well as for them. But the chief significance of the movement was the new theological basis which all these various projects expressed in one way or another. Maurice was reworking for new conditions the old Puritan theocratic conception of society, and finding the specifically Christian and religious sanctions for the principles of natural law which were wearing so thin in their secularist formulation by rationalistic Dissent. As against the mechanistic views of the political economists, or even of Wilberforce or Rev. Mr. Malthus, Maurice found the grounds of human community in God as the living power and presence in history. This did not mean any " simple humanitarian

Christianity," but new historical realism. He was concerned not to
" build " Kingdoms, but to dig; " to show that economy and politics
. . . must have a ground beneath themselves; that society is not to be
made anew by arrangements of ours, but is to be regenerated by finding
the law and ground of its order and harmony, the only secret of its existence, in God." [23] Thus when these Anglicans attempted to adapt to
England the ideas of Louis Blanc and consorted with Owenite socialists,
they did so because Christian socialism was " the assertion of God's order." In a sense Maurice lived too soon. A generation or two of church
people would preoccupy themselves with squabbles over ritualism or
Darwinism before the significance of his teaching would be appreciated. But from about 1890 he came into his own.

In America, meanwhile, there was as yet little or nothing like " Christian Socialism." The nearest thing to Tory Anglicanism was the Congregationalist Federalism of New England, trying to maintain a social
aristocracy and ecclesiastical privilege. Baptists, Methodists, Disciples,
and to some extent Presbyterians, were popular Churches, and both
democratic and individualist in their outlook. The two generations before the Civil War were the great age of revivals, and, as in England,
they resulted in moral crusades, especially those for temperance and
against slavery. As in England, a small group of rationalist intellectuals
found themselves often in alliance with the religious masses on reform
proposals. Thus Garrison and Theodore Parker joined their natural
rights philosophy of " Wide Dissent " to the evangelical humanitarianism of the Finney revivals in the Midwest. Both strains contributed to
Lincoln, who preached again the natural rights of the Declaration of
Independence, universalized beyond the intentions of that document by
evangelical concern for every soul, even that of the slave. Southern Presbyterians, meanwhile, as well as Methodists and Baptists, developed a
new apology for slaveholding from Scripture. In the '40's, after the cotton gin had made cotton the most valuable American export, feeling
grew so high that the chief denominations were split between North
and South. Episcopalians and Roman Catholics alone escaped this fate,
and the latter by frankly justifying slaveholding on scholastic grounds.
The greatest moral struggle of nineteenth century American society had
no help whatever from the Roman Church. While Roman Catholics
were concentrated in Northern cities, they should more appropriately
have been assimilated in the feudal society of the Old South, to which
their political ethic was suited.

Universal suffrage was also making its way from state to state in the
period, as religious and property qualifications were dropped from the
franchise. Universal public education took its real beginning in Massa-

chusetts with the work of Horace Mann. The conception had to make
its way both against the non-state-interventionists and the religious
groups who were not content to have merely the rudiments of non-
sectarian Christianity taught in school. The role of the popular as well
as the aristocratic Churches in these democratic developments, as they
passed from state to state, has scarcely yet been carefully explored. But
by the 1850's American democracy and evangelical religion had been inextricably synthesized,[24] both of them, to be sure, in a highly individualistic form which was to prove itself dangerously inadequate to the problems of the industrialized society soon to emerge.

Of this synthesis of Free Church Calvinism with " the humanitarian,
freedom-loving, and cosmopolitan ethic of liberalism " two great statesmen are representatives. Troeltsch considers Gladstone in this respect as
" the great modern representative of Christian politics. He was an Anglican, it is true, but he inclined more and more toward Nonconformity. Politically and ethically, his ideals were those of the Nonconformists. Thus for ethical reasons he supported Liberalism, extended the
franchise, and declared his conviction that in the settlement of problems
of foreign policy the method of arbitration was both possible and desirable. His policy was decidedly Christian, and in the secular sphere he
was just as decided that the basis was that of natural law." [25] Such was
the specific international ethic of Puritan Protestantism, the influence of
which is so tangible in the statesmen and colonial staff of the British
Empire, when compared to other modern colonial policies. " The humanitarian and ethical movement against war, which aims at substitut-
ing a system of covenants and courts of arbitration in place of war, is
pre-eminently at home among Calvinists and the sects. . . . Ascetic
Protestantism views imperialistic and nationalistic movements with a
good deal of misgiving." [26] In the case of international conflict, such as
the war with China, Gladstone appealed to " the highest ground of natural justice — that justice which binds man to men; which is older than
Christianity, because it was in the world before Christianity was born;
which is broader than Christianity, because it extends to the world beyond Christianity; and which underlies Christianity, for Christianity itself appeals to it." [27]

Abraham Lincoln was in early life no such churchman as Gladstone,
but he attained a depth of religious insight through bereavement and
his war experience such as to make him also one of the great Christian
statesmen of all time. His three most famous state papers expressed the
profoundly Christian basis of the American democratic faith with a simplicity and dignity rarely equaled. " Why should there not be a patient
confidence in the ultimate justice of the people? " he asked in his *First*

Inaugural. " Is there any better or equal hope in the world? In our present differences is either party without faith of being in the right? If the Almighty Ruler of Nations, with his eternal truth and justice, be on your side of the North, or on yours of the South, that truth and that justice will surely prevail by the judgment of this great tribunal of the American people." And at the dedication of the Gettysburg National Cemetery the President recalled, " Fourscore and seven years ago our fathers brought forth on this continent a new nation conceived in liberty and dedicated to the proposition that all men are created equal." And after referring to the men who had died on that battlefield to serve that cause, he summoned all hearers to resolve, " that this nation under God shall have a new birth of freedom, and that government of the people, by the people, for the people, shall not perish from the earth."

Just as Lincoln was convinced that the honest inquiry and discussion of the whole people into God's will was a surer organ of perception than any ecclesiastical functionary, so was his faith oriented, not to any general abstractions of natural law in themselves, but to the will of a living God. " If we shall suppose," he said in his *Second Inaugural,* " that American slavery is one of those offenses which, in the providence of God, must needs come, but which, having continued through his appointed time, he now wills to remove, and that he gives to both North and South this terrible war, as the woe due to those by whom the offense came, shall we discern therein any departure from those divine attributes which the believers in a living God always ascribe to him? Fondly do we hope — fervently do we pray — that this mighty scourge of war may speedily pass away. Yet, if God wills that it shall continue until all the wealth piled by the bondman's two hundred and fifty years of unrequited toil shall be sunk, and until every drop of blood drawn with the lash shall be paid by another drawn with the sword, as was said three thousand years ago, so still it must be said, ' The judgments of the Lord are true and righteous altogether.' With malice toward none; with charity for all; with firmness in the right, as God gives us to see the right, let us strive on to finish the work we are in."

As was observed at the time in a British paper, Lincoln's accents recalled the exalted faith of the great democratic leaders of the Puritan Revolution and Commonwealth. There are few if any of the motifs of Puritan liberal democracy which are not stated in these brief addresses in the full power of their metaphysical and theological sources.

The decade of the '60's provided notable statements and demonstrations of the political ethic of several Christian traditions. In German Lutheranism this was the time when Bismarck was exemplifying the traditionalist monarchist ethic urged by Julius Stahl and in his international policy displaying a complete innocence of that sense of the law of nations so fundamental to Lincoln and Gladstone. In Rome, meanwhile, the Syllabus of Pius IX condemned every essential principle of the Christian democratic faith stated in Lincoln's *Second Inaugural* within a twelvemonth of its delivery. Puritan Protestants remained convinced that the pope of Rome was a much less safe guide in Christian morality, as well as a less impressive representative of Christian faith, than President Lincoln.

IV

THE REVOLUTION OF 1848 AND THE
ROMAN REACTION

✦ ✦ ✦

IN THE obvious sense the pontificate of Pius IX (1846–1878) was the most eventful in the nineteenth century history of the Roman Catholic Church. Comprising as it does the third quarter of the century, with a little to spare by way of prelude and sequel, it corresponds to no very clearly marked equivalent period in the history of Anglo-American Puritan Protestantism. The Civil War and Reconstruction dominated this generation in America. For Britain there was the triumph of mid-Victorian liberalism. In both cases liberal democracy was the prevailing current. And the Puritan Protestant churches on the whole were so thoroughly in accord with this political ethic, and had so far triumphed with it that they no longer conceived it as particularly their peculiar ethic to be defended against real alternatives. Here we are dealing with a religious tradition intimately related to liberal democracy from its origin, and in a society permeated by its aspirations. In the Roman Catholic world, in contrast, there was a very different political climate and a very different political ethic in the churches. The three traditional Catholic powers, Spain, Austria, France, were all, with slight qualifications for the last, monarchical throughout this period. Within these states Catholic opinion, lay and clerical, was prevailingly at the conservative if not reactionary wing, while the policy of the Roman court in the '50's, '60's, and '70's was emphatically if not hysterically antidemocratic. Roman Catholic tradition and practice, political theory, hierarchical statements, and education made almost universally for authoritarianism and privilege and opposed government by discussion and consent.

1. THE REVOLUTION AND THE CHURCHES

But there is a very interesting story in that " almost." It is the story of " Liberal Catholicism." The first chapter of that story we have recounted in relation to the revolutions of 1830. A second and more impressive effort must now be narrated, an effort finding its focus in the revolutionary agitations of the late '40's, especially in France, the Low Countries, Germany, and Italy. We must attempt to find some causes for both the failures and the limited successes of this liberal Catholic effort in the several nations, and note the terms and finality of its repudiation by the Vatican. For, to look at this development from the other side, we are to witness in this generation the rise to sole orthodoxy of what had previously been only one party in the Church, the ultramontanes, the proponents of absolutism in the Church and clericalism in the State. Let us begin with the Revolution of 1848.

To appreciate the significance of this second adventure into " Liberal Catholicism " some comparison with contemporary Protestant orientations is helpful. In the predominantly Reformed and Puritan countries the interesting thing about 1848 was that there was no revolution. Holland provides an exception, but despite its Reformed churches Holland had become largely conformed to German Lutheran political ethics. For the English-speaking world the basic issues of divine right and feudal prerogative had been settled in principle in 1649 and 1689 when Whiggism and Dissent won the right to live. As an English Congregationalist remarked of the Continental Revolutions of 1848, they were being fought in the name of ideas " consecrated by us." The fact that the democratic revolutionaries of 1848 were no longer " consecrated " by any Christian tradition may have something to do with their consequent lapse into nationalistic imperialism.

When we turn from Puritan Protestantism to Lutheran societies, we find ourselves at the opposite extreme of the spectrum in terms of political ethics and Church-State relations. (Here again we must notice a divergence from the type in the case of Denmark and Sweden, just as we found Holland atypical among Reformed societies.) The type may be described from the model of Protestant Prussia, by far the largest and most influential of the dominantly Lutheran Churches.

Ernst Troeltsch argues impressively[1] that it was in the generation preceding 1848 that German society and culture decisively diverged from the dominant liberal trend of West European culture. Without disagreeing with this judgment, we may argue that it was the defeat of Liberalism in 1848–1850 that made this divergence of spirit definitive and unmistakable in the whole structure and spirit of German social and political institutions. In the '40's there were at least vigorous proponents of a free State, a free Church, and a free Christian manifestation of oppressed social strata. After the revolution it was clear that the Protestant Church would be held captive to the political, social, and economic interests of the bureaucracy and aristocracy. There would be no possibility of Prussian Lutheranism's finding any attitude but condemnation for either social or political democracy. The results of 1848 weighed heavily on German Protestantism down through the Weimar Republic and to this day.

Sympathy for constitutionalist or liberal ideas was not to be found among many of the representatives of the Protestant Awakening of the generation before 1848. Schleiermacher, to be sure, the greatest of the new theologians, had been a political liberal, but in the '30's and '40's the revival tended to harden both theologically and politically. Most of the educated laity and many of the old pastors of Prussia still lived in the tradition of the eighteenth century rational theology and were cool toward the orthodox revival in court circles. The results of this unsavory alliance of Protestant leadership with a reactionary government was that religious liberalism was increasingly forced out of the ecclesiastical structure, and that it found itself at once a nucleus of the multitude of miscellaneous opposition forces. The free religious congregations began to be organized in 1844, as pastors who did not measure up to Hengstenberg's orthodoxy were forced from their parishes. These free Protestant congregations were dominantly constitutionalist or democratic in politics and reached the peak of their influence in 1848 itself. Thus comprised, however, they were virtually wiped out in the consequent reaction of the '50's, suffering fines, censorship, prohibition of meetings, arrests of leaders, and similar governmental pressure. Thus were extinguished the beginnings of a Protestant Church which had made some progress on German soil in uniting a liberal or democratic political ethic with a positive Christianity, an enterprise which had long since been the dominant pattern in British and American Protestantism.

As we now turn to Roman Catholicism in 1848, we shall notice some startling innovations in the attitude of the Church to constitutionalism and civil liberties. Hitherto Roman Catholicism, like Lutheranism, had opposed liberalism and allied itself with absolutism, prerogative, social hierarchy. The liberal ideas of the French Revolution were generally related, by a true instinct, to Calvinist sources, and were condemned as satanic. Lamennais, de Maistre, de Bonald, Haller, Adam Müller, Gentz, all stood in Bossuet's great tradition of divine right.

The Lutheran type of political authoritarianism retained its hold on a significant section of Roman Catholicism in 1848. In Spain and Latin America, indeed, it has hardly been weakened to this day. The Austrian Empire was then the center of Roman Catholicism's political power, and in Metternich's neighborhood there was no suspicion of any flirtation of Catholicism and liberalism. After the Revolution, consequently, the new Austrian Government built its policy on a military and clerical repression. The Concordat of 1855 between Austria and the Vatican made Rome sole mistress, denying the liberty of conscience or the legal existence of Protestantism. The censorship of the bishops and the Index of prohibited books was enforced by the Government. All ecclesiastical lawsuits and matrimonial affairs were reserved to Church courts. The pope ruled in Austria as second sovereign with the sanction of the civil law as an engine of destruction against liberalism.

This had been the consistent tradition of Roman Catholic political ethics for at least two centuries, emphatically reaffirmed by the highest authority in *Mirari vos* and *Singulari nos* in the 1830's. The startling thing was the emergence in 1848 of a Roman Catholic-liberal alliance in France, Germany, Holland, and even, apparently at least, in the papal states in Italy. Just a century ago, thus, a significant portion of the Roman Church first took a positive attitude toward the political liberalism and applied natural law maintained in Christian circles hitherto by Puritan Protestantism alone.

This revolution in Roman Catholic political ethics had been preparing for twenty years. French liberals like Constant had found it highly entertaining when the group led by Lamennais first appealed as Catholics to liberty on the eve of the Revolution of 1830. But the Belgian Catholics followed Lamennais' program, despite the condemnation of Gregory XVI, and supported a constitutional government with civil liberties. Through the '30's and '40's, Lacordaire and Montalembert in France and Döllinger and Buss in Germany shared experiences across the Rhine in their endeavor to prod the hierarchy onto the liberal band wagon. They demonstrated the possibilities of clerical social control by the new devices of liberal democracy, the press, the franchise, electoral campaigns, political deals in parliaments. A Catholic lay opinion was created, molded by a Catholic press, led by Catholic lay politicians, and increasingly more aggressive than the hierarchy itself. The school issue in France and mixed marriages in Germany provided occasion for the crystallization of loyalties and organizations. With the example of Belgium and the United States, and with a functioning Catholic political machine in existence, these liberal Catholics, or ultramontane parliamentarians, were ready for the Revolution of 1848. When it came, an organized electorate and a Catholic parliamentary machine were at a high point of efficiency almost at once, in France, in Germany, and in Holland.

In dominantly Protestant Holland and Prussia these parliamentary ultramontanes contributed more to the Revolution, and profited more from it, than did the Protestant majority. In Holland, for example, the Roman Catholics joined the liberals in the '40's, demanding liberty of the press and abolition of the placet (the required approval of Government to Church pronouncements), liberty of association, liberty of education. They secured all these demands save those in education, and in the ensuing elections supported liberal candidates. This Roman Catholic-liberal alliance endured about a decade, during which it was for a time defeated by an anti-Roman reaction. Then the Catholics and the liberals themselves split, as they already had in Belgium, over the issue of control of the school system.

It was a similar story in Prussia, where Catholic interests were well represented in 1848 both at Frankfurt and at the Berlin convention. In the Prussian constitution, finally adopted in 1850, the Catholic Church was given all the advantages of a free Church together with public subsidy for its school, university, and seminary education. Freedom of communication abolished the placet; the Church could control the education of its seminarians; freedom of association was interpreted to permit the free settlement of religious orders and the conduct of popular missions. The bishops were given greater freedom in appointments and the administration of property. Some matters remained ambiguous, but the bishops now took a high tone and announced that, having assumed their rights, they were prepared to defend them. To maintain this position, the Roman Church must perforce take a quasi-liberal line.

In dominantly Catholic France and Italy, however, liberal Catholicism proved to be ephemeral. The activities of the French liberal Catholics had brought it about that the February Revolution was as friendly to the Church as that of July had been hostile. In 1830 it was not wise for a French priest to appear on the street in garb. In 1848 curés were asked to bless the "trees of liberty" everywhere. In 1830 some French bishops hid and others fled. In 1848 episcopal charges were friendly to the Revolution and the archbishop of Paris blessed the colors of the National Guard and sang a *Te Deum*. Lamartine related *liberté, egalité, fraternité* to the ideals of Jesus, and President Buchez of the Assembly was a practicing Catholic. The first exercise in universal suffrage was generously supervised by the Church, and when the new Assembly gathered, there were 250 deputies pledged to vote for Catholic schools. The clergy were more openly active in politics than they had been since the days of Charles X.

This devotion of the French revolutionaries to the Church was the last argument that ended the opposition of Pius IX to a constitution for his papal kingdom. The well-meaning, sentimental, superstitious, and ill-educated new pope had been moving step by step in this direction for nearly two years, charmed by the cheers he won from the Roman populace every time he made a liberal gesture. He had issued an amnesty for political offenders, removed the ban on heretical street lights and railroads, summoned a Council of State, opened several ministerial posts to laymen. Now he followed Naples, Piedmont, Tuscany, and France in promising a constitution. The latter, to be sure, turned out to be an even more preposterous document than the Prussian constitution, reserving all real powers to the autocratic curia while attempting to satisfy the liberals with a façade of constitutional machinery.

But as the fever swept on into the Austrian Empire in Italy, Venice, Milan, Vienna itself, sending old Metternich for refuge to constitutional Protestant England, the pope's nationalism got the better of him. He referred to these events as the work of God, and with some hesitation gave his General Durando permission to open hostilities against the Austrians. As Catholic Germany arose, scandalized, Pius perceived he had gone too far. But when he repudiated the national cause, his government collapsed and the papal troops fraternized with the populace in demanding an all-Italian constituent assembly and war on Austria. The pope and several cardinals fled in disguise to reassemble a considerable section of the curia at Gaeta. Never from that day did Pius entertain any liberal illusions. The able and unscrupulous Antonelli now ousted Rosmini and Gioberti from all influence and re-established the curia on the familiar obscurantist despotism of Restoration popes. The Romans were to refer to the remainder of the reign as that of "Pio Nono Secondo." Constitutionalism was simply incompatible with the ecclesiastical system of Roman Catholicism, at least at home base.

In France, also, the initial sympathy of the Roman Church for the Revolution had been radically revised in these months. Here the principal factor was the threat of socialism. General Cavaignac had put down the revolt ruthlessly, and a deep and permanent rift had been driven between social democracy on the one hand and the bourgeois liberals and Roman Catholics on the other. And the Catholic electorate, which a few months before had supported the republic, now swung almost to a man to constitute the "party of order"; the Catholic party became the conservative party. This party decided the elections that fall for the presidency, rejecting Lamartine and General Cavaignac for the unscrupulous adventurer Louis Napoleon. This party captured the Assembly the next spring and enabled Louis Napoleon to use the troops of the French Republic to put down the Roman Republic. And, most significant of all, this party carried the plebiscite which ratified the *Putsch* by which Louis Napoleon broke up the Republic, imprisoned 200 deputies, and established a dictatorship. Catholic clergy and laity alike groveled before the man on horseback. Pius himself winked at Napoleon's betrayal of his oath of office and was first to congratulate him. Montalembert swung countless votes by urging, on the eve of the plebiscite, that " to vote against Louis Napoleon is to support the Socialist Revolution." [2] And Veuillot, prophet of the Catholic rank and file, poured out scorn for months on parliamentary institutions and civil liberty. " France will reject parliamentarism," he wrote, " as she has rejected Protestantism, or she will perish in trying to vomit it up. . . . She has said [to Louis Napoleon]: ' My orators fatigue me; rid me of them. Govern me.' " [3]

Italy, like France, now showed how slight were the roots that liberal democracy had struck into its Catholic population. In Italy the crucial question was whether the situation could be stabilized by the powers of the peninsula, in particular Sardinia-Piedmont, or whether Austria or France, or both, would intervene. Louis Napoleon managed to occupy the situation and did nothing decisive until the new 1849 elections had given him a Catholic majority and he could send in the troops to break the Roman Republic. Pius wanted revenge and was irritated by the French attempt to press moderate measures on him. For a time he wanted to transfer the seat of his government to Loreto, where he might live beside the Holy House which he was convinced had been miraculously transported there from Nazareth as a sort of flying carpet. He was talked out of this and re-entered Rome in April, 1850, with French troops. He excluded all laymen from office now, restored various abuses, and, contemptuous of the suggestion of another amnesty, turned loose a clerical terror that soon filled his filthy prisons with 8,800 offenders.

Pius also sought to persuade the other Italian rulers to revoke the constitutional concessions they had made. He got Leopold of Tuscany, for example, to revoke the Fundamental Statute of 1848, and to revive the medieval law against Jews' practicing medicine. The reading or distributing of Bibles was made a penal offense, and even Muratori could not be reprinted. Sardinia-Piedmont alone hung on to its liberal constitution under the leadership of Cavour. His ideal of Church-State relations, " the free Church in the free State," had been shaped by Vinet, Britain, and especially the U.S.A. For Sardinia the pope could not find invective strong enough. Gregory XVI and the Jesuits had come home to roost, but this time only under the protection of French bayonets, whose departure they were not destined to survive.

Catholic liberal democracy thus proved itself a one-night blossom in the Revolution of 1848 in France and Italy. Only in the context of a dominantly Protestant society and State did it survive. But from there it was to extend its influence notably during the reign of the next pope, Leo XIII. Louis Veuillot's famous proposition about religious liberty can be extended for this generation to the Roman attitude toward liberalism and democracy in general: " Where we Catholics are in the minority, we demand freedom in the name of your principles; where we are in the majority, we deny it in the name of our principles." [4]

Since it is in this crisis of 1848 that modern political socialism first became a significant factor in Western civilization generally, we may pause here to compare the attitudes taken toward it by Puritan Protestantism in England, Lutheranism in Germany, and Roman Catholicism in France. As with democracy, we shall find that socialism found more points of contact with Puritan Protestantism, and in Anglo-American culture was generally less atheistic, less violent, and more humane and more liberal than was the case in dominantly Lutheran or Roman Catholic societies. " Socialism," " democracy," " liberalism," all had quite different significations in the English-speaking world in the second half of the nineteenth century from their meanings on the Continent or in Latin America.

So far as economic and sociological factors were concerned, England was the most industrialized of European countries and saw the first significant proletarian movement in Chartism. Here, one might think, communism and antireligion should have been strongest. Yet as with liberalism, British Christianity was to exert a more constructive influence over the labor movement than was to be the case of Catholicism with the French and Italian or Lutheranism with the corresponding German labor movements. Anglicanism, to be sure, made few compromises with democracy in Church or State or industry; it was the Baptists, the Unitarian-Presbyterians, and an important minority of Congregationalists and Methodists who supported the Chartist cause. A handful of Anglicans around Maurice and Kingsley, to be sure, maintained a contact between Church and labor and helped to prevent the development of a Continental-style dogmatic anticlerical socialism. While several of the workers' leaders inclined in this last direction (Holyoake, Hetherington, Watson, Cooper, Carlile), the great majority of Chartists considered themselves good Christians, but opposed to the Churches and especially to the Church of England for its political conservatism, its paternalism, its intolerance, its tithes. The characteristic expression of the spirit of Chartism, thus, was less the club of infidels than the " Chartist churches," with their lay preachers, their hymnals, and even sacraments. While the workmen repudiated organized Christianity as a whole, there were enough bridges so that they felt themselves Christian and were concerned to defend themselves from the charge of infidelity. This mentality was to affect the British labor movement significantly for the next two or three generations.

In the 1840's it might have seemed that the same outcome was possible for the new German proletarian movement of those years. The typical agitator of the '40's was not Marx, but Weitling, whose books are steeped in Biblical language and religious pathos. To be sure, Weitling, unlike Cabet and Fourier, was ready for violence to bring in the Kingdom of a communist Christ, a sort of Münzer redivivus. But others in the *Bund der Gerechten* deplored these extremes. In any case, the whole movement was attacked by police power at clerical instigation in Switzerland and Germany. No bridges were left, as in England, and the first proletarian movement in Germany, like the liberal Churches of the same years, was forced by the State Churches into the arms of the atheist left-wing Hegelians, the Feuerbachs, Bruno Bauer, Karl Marx. The year 1848 scared the churchmen enough to listen to speeches on their social responsibilities at the Wittenberg Kirchentag, but nothing was done except to organize charity. The fateful opportunity passed, and when the labor movement again surged forward in the 1860's, the men who had been initiated by Weitling into a Christian communism were swept up by Bebel, Liebknecht, and Lassalle into a dogmatically anti-Christian Marxism.

In Roman Catholic France, meanwhile, as in Lutheran Germany, social and economic democracy was killed in the absolutist reaction, and what survived of socialism as of democracy was henceforth to be systematically anticlerical and illiberal. And, on the other hand, a new alliance was struck between capitalism and Catholicism. De Melun, a liberal Catholic leader, was instrumental in the passage of some moderate protective legislation for workers in 1851 and 1852. But in general the Catholic leaders of social democracy were silenced by death or political opponents. Villeneuve-Bargemont and Ozanam died; De Melun was imprisoned; Lacordaire retired. A generation of individualistic laissez-faire social thought followed among Catholics, finding its spokesmen in Le Play and Périn. As Tocqueville put it, " the fear of socialism has produced for the moment an effect on the middle classes analogous to that produced in the upper classes earlier by the French Revolution." [5] And while the formerly anticlerical *bourgeoisie* now restrained public expression of such sentiments, the new working classes increasingly adopted them. Like the workmen of Germany, those of France turned to atheism, to Karl Marx and Proudhon. In 1855 the latter voiced the general resentment of French labor: " If ever democracy gets another inning, and I count for something, it will be all up with Catholicism in France."

In a symbolic if not absolutely accurate dating, the Revolution of 1848 is the birth time of two of the spiritual powers now contending for the soul of the Continent, Marxist socialism and " Catholic Action," while the Puritan ethos is still discernible in British and American democratic socialism and capitalism. Of all this constellation of tendencies, 1848 was the first clear revelation and epitome, and it is this group of relationships that will occupy us for much of the rest of this history.

2. TWO MANIFESTOES

But while the antidemocratic reaction reigned in the Catholic world through the '50's, '60's, and '70's, and even consolidated itself in the Roman administration and in new doctrines, liberal Catholicism was not exterminated. In France and Belgium, especially, there remained a Gideon's army of unrepentant Catholic liberals. Distrusted by the Catholic masses and hated by the Roman court, these men won a series of political advantages for the Church — advantages that, as is usually the case, were then exploited by the illiberal party in the Church. Chief among them were still Montalembert and Lacordaire, with support in the hierarchy from Bishop Dupanloup of Orléans. Their organ was the revived *Correspondant*. They were continually scourged in the virulent pages of the *Univers* by France's lay pope, Veuillot, while Bishop Pie of Poitiers now rose on the horizon as the most aggressive spokesman of the majority of the hierarchy committed to political absolutism.

The fundamental principles remain constant throughout. We may illustrate them by contrasting two manifestoes of the '60's, one for the liberal Catholics and one for the ultramontanes. The former was proclaimed at an international congress of liberal Catholics held at Malines in 1863 by the most distinguished spokesman and warrior of liberal Catholicism, Montalembert. With some reluctance he had agreed to come from imperial France, where he lived under the shade of the dictator, to deliver his " political testament." [6] It was received with rapturous applause and clearly represented the views of the bulk of the liberal Catholics at the Congress. What did Montalembert say?

While, as we have seen, the dominant Catholic opinion held as normative the type of absolutism existing in Austria or the French Second Empire or the papal states, Montalembert urged that the best model of a political system for all Europe was that of Belgium. Bishop Pie had written Pius that the papal autocracy in central Italy was " almost the only refuge of political orthodoxy." [7] Montalembert declared that the French Catholic political party of the years 1830–1850 had formed on the slogan " Liberty as in Belgium " and that its convictions and hopes could best be expressed by the slogan " A free Church in a free State," as realized in the Belgian constitution.

The Belgian constitution should be taken as a model primarily because it presented a successful adaptation of the Church to the modern democratic society. That society, said Montalembert, was spreading, whether one liked it or not. In most of Europe outside Belgium, Catholics were politically ineffective because they were unwilling to accept modern democracy, with its civil equality, political liberty, freedom of conscience, and sovereignty of the people. Catholics on the whole still yearned back to the *ancien régime,* to the divine right of kings, to legitimacy, and to the league of throne and altar. But whatever its virtues, the *ancien régime* had one great disadvantage. It was dead. Willy-nilly, the Roman Church must cut loose from its ancient supports and launch out, like Noah's ark, on the democratic sea.

But for himself, as a liberal Catholic, Montalembert welcomed the rise of free society and considered it progress. To be sure he gave modern democracy no unqualified support. The French experience with democracy had revealed serious dangers. Democracy exhibited a tendency to egalitarianism in a leveling sense, a mean jealousy of distinctions of any sort, of ability and character as well as birth and fortune. Democracy sometimes degenerated to the cult of mediocrity. Or again the egalitarian urge in French democracy had shown a recurrent tendency to socialism, to the confiscation of property. Or again, French democracy showed an irrational compulsion to centralization, to the creation of a vast bureaucratic State which threatened to reduce the individual to an odious servitude like that of ancient Egypt or China. French democracy had more than once collapsed before plebiscitary dictatorship, into "imperial democracy." Montalembert wished to be understood as defending liberal democracy, not mere egalitarian or imperialist democracy. Democracy, he said, must be corrected by liberty and must be reconciled with Catholicism. There must be genuine political liberty and genuine religious liberty, as well as civil equality, in the democratic State. He quoted Dupanloup: "You made the Revolution of 1789 without us, and against us, but for us."

This necessity of liberalizing democracy and reconciling it with religion could be seen from history. More than the *ancien régime,* democratic society requires moral effort and responsibility from its private citizens. How are these personal traits formed in a society? Historically it has been done by the Christian Churches. All the successful democratic revolutions, said Montalembert, had had religious sanctions, and he cited those of Holland, England, and America. To these Protestant democratic revolutions he could add that of Belgium in the 1830's. In a society like that of Belgium, the regime of liberty taught men self-reliance, self-control, and responsibility — qualities of character not produced by the Catholic system in its usual form. Those who deny liberty pay the price in loss of moral responsibility. Yet in the four cardinal virtues of the Catechism were the sources of such habits of the spirit.

Modern democracy, in Montalembert's definition, rested on two prin-

ciples. The first was political equality, the right of each to share in political decisions and power. Why should the Church fear universal suffrage? Surely it had notable means of influencing the masses. Equality
with regard to taxation and financial obligations would be no crushing
blow. Ecclesiastical immunities and tithes had been legitimate in their
time, but were no longer conceivable. With liberal democracy Catholicism had a common interest in the rights of property, the liberties of education, association, and the press, and common foes in absolutism, centralization, demagoguery.

The second principle, Montalembert conceded, was opposed by most
Catholics. That was the principle of the ecclesiastical neutrality of the
State, the reciprocal independence of Church and State, the suppression
of all religious privileges and constraints, the principle, in short, of religious liberty, liberty of conscience and liberty of worship. Montalembert did not mean absolute separation, which could signify denial of
religious liberty, but rather the free co-operation of two autonomous
communities. In contrast he lamented the system of Inquisition and Index as practiced in Spain, Portugal, and Italy. He did not mean to question in any way the principle of intolerance in dogmas, but in civil matters and in public law tolerance was permissible and indeed necessary.
The old system was increasingly unenforceable. Nowhere save in Latin
America could the Roman Church really invoke its canonical privileges
over other religions. Elsewhere, even in " Catholic " countries, full
liberty for the Roman Church was attainable only in the context of
equal liberties for all. Catholics must give up their dreams of clerical
theocracy and boldly, publicly, sincerely, renounce all hope of a regime
of privilege and all appeals to force.

Montalembert did not make this proposal, again, as a mere concession
to expediency. He alluded to the behavior of many Catholics, such as
those represented by the *Univers,* who would appeal to liberal principles in Catholic interests but deny them to others when in power.
Catholics must concede liberty to error in order to deserve the right to
claim liberty for their truth. The chief fears and the chief weapons of
anti-Catholics were created by this kind of Catholic liberalism-out-of-
expediency, liberalism with reservations and *arrières-pensées.*

For himself, also, Montalembert execrated the resort to coercion and
the principle of the Inquisition. Persecution was odious to him when
carried out against Catholics, and also when practiced by Catholics. Catholicism had prospered more by its spiritual power under regimes of
tolerance, such as that of the Edict of Nantes, or the July Monarchy, than
under the dragonnades of Louis XIV or the clericalism of the Restoration after the Napoleonic Wars. " The Spanish Inquisitor saying to

the heretic: ' the truth or death ' is as odious to me as the French terrorist saying to my grandfather: ' liberty, fraternity, or death.' "

Montalembert presented himself before the Congress as a defeated
man, but the spokesman of a victorious cause. The liberal Catholics, he
said, had been defeated severally and individually, but together they
had won. There was in fact a liberal Catholic opinion. He hailed a new
era in Church history, the era of the liberty of the Church. The ovation
of the Congress testified its " Amen."

The ultramontanes, however, were furious and the papal nuncio scandalized. Bishop Pie demanded that Montalembert be condemned, and
in due time the letter of repudiation came. Montalembert was told that
his addresses had been submitted to examination by the pope and found
to contain doctrine contrary to the teaching of the Church and the
popes. He praised the regime of tolerance under the Edict of Nantes,
but Pius VI had definitively esteemed it as *plane exitiosum et pestilens.*
Montalembert had appealed to the French constitution, but Pius VII had
in 1814 protested against the article providing for liberty of conscience
and worship. And in 1832 in *Mirari vos,* Gregory XVI had expressed in
the most unmistakable terms his horror and hatred for the liberties to
which Montalembert would appeal.[8] The pope's theological advisers
felt that Montalembert must at any price be prevented from ever again
urging such exhortations as, " Catholics, grant liberty [of the press and
of worship] where you are in power! " This might even mean Italy, or
Rome! And so the repudiation came with crushing force the next year.
The official brochure containing *Quanta cura* and the Syllabus of Errors
carried as an appendix a letter of unprecedented warmth and commendation to an insignificant Belgian who had written a refutation of Montalembert's addresses under the title *Free Error in the Free State.*

This brochure contained the ultramontane manifesto, which we must
now compare with that of the liberal Catholics. First, however, we may
note the character of the official condemnation of Montalembert himself. On the death of the old warrior, a few years later, Pius forbade the
customary memorial service in Rome. " He was a liberal Catholic," said
the pope, " that is, he was a half-Catholic." [9] By this the pope had no
reference to theology. In doctrinal matters, the French liberal Catholics
generally, in contrast to the German, were quite innocent of historical,
scientific, or philosophical criticism. They were uncritically orthodox;
Montalembert's liberalism was strictly political. Even there, in fact, he
compromised liberalism at various points, as in international policy, and
perhaps in education, in the ecclesiastical interest. There are issues
enough, as we have noticed, between this " ultramontane democracy "
and genuine liberal democracy. Montalembert had won more for the

Catholic Church in France than any other man of his generation, but he was only " half-Catholic." To be a full Catholic he would need to hold Catholic political principles as well as Catholic doctrine.

These Catholic political principles could be summed up as the political authority of the Roman hierarchy over states and governments. The denial of such clerical supremacy was to Pius IX the head of offense in the medley of errors which he felt called to condemn in his Syllabus. Speaking of such errors in his covering letter, he wrote: " These perverse and false opinions ought to be the more detested in that their principal object is to prevent and put aside this salutary constraint which the Catholic Church ought to exercise up to the end of time . . . not only in respect to individuals, but also as regards nations, peoples, and their rulers, and to destroy the union and mutual agreement of the priesthood and the civil power, so healthful always for the good of the State." [10]

Approximately the first quarter of the errors are theological. These we may lay aside and consider the three quarters that are primarily political. In terms of the ten paragraphs of the documents, this is to begin with the fifth.

The fourth paragraph might be noted parenthetically. It does not propound, as do the rest, certain theses, but condemns certain movements and organizations, " pests of this type ": " socialism, communism, secret societies, Bible societies, liberal Catholic societies." The " socialism and communism " here referred to are not the Marxist variety, but the nonpolitical Utopian varieties sneered at in the Communist Manifesto. The " secret societies " meant first of all the Masons, and the Bible societies were Protestant missionary organizations. To classify liberal Catholics with Protestants, Masons, and Utopian communitarians was a studied insult, even apart from the generic epithet " diseases."

The remaining six paragraphs carry the following titles: " Errors Concerning the Church and Her Rights "; " Errors About Civil Society, Considered Both in Itself and in Its Relation to the Church "; " Errors Concerning Natural and Christian Ethics "; " Errors Concerning Christian Marriage "; " Errors Regarding the Civil Power of the Sovereign Pontiff "; " Errors Having Reference to Modern Liberalism."

It will be seen at once that the bulk of the Syllabus is addressed to various aspects of the relation between Church and State. It is in effect a condemnation of efforts to evade the claim of the Roman hierarchy to exert a theocratic supremacy in political affairs. Among such efforts the most important, and the one that concerns us, was the movement of liberal democracy. We have already followed the process by which Anglo-American democracy was made possible by the renunciation or defeat of the right-wing Puritan theocratic program. And for nine-teenth century Europe, similarly, Montalembert had noted as one of the two foundations of liberal democracy the renunciation of theocratic clericalism. The Syllabus was the most elaborate and uncompromis-ing repudiation of any reconciliation between the principles and prac-tices of Roman Catholicism and those of liberal democracy. The specifi-cation of its antagonism to liberal democracy can be blocked out in the following heads, citing under each the relevant " errors."

a. *Clerical Supremacy in Politics.* In his Malines addresses Montalem-bert had clearly defined the first principle of a liberal democratic so-ciety as the mutual independence of Church and State. This was the Church and State theory of Puritan Protestantism, as it had been of medieval Catholicism before the papalist party developed the claim to supremacy over civil administration. But Pius condemned not merely the modern system but also what Lord Acton referred to as the clas-sical Catholic tradition. In cases where there was a conflict between the civil power and the Church, ruled the pope, the former must submit to the jurisdiction of the Roman hierarchy (42, 44, 54). Thus all Cath-olics are bound, on all questions of morals, to disobey the law and re-nounce their obligations to the constitution of the State at the behest of the papal court. This policy makes Roman Catholicism a political as well as an ecclesiastical organization in the modern world in a sense paralleled by no other important Church body.

b. *Separation of Church and State.* This constitutional arrangement must be condemned (55). If the State were separate from the Church, how could the pope exercise his " jurisdiction " over it?

Several of the theological theses of the Syllabus may also be seen as condemnations of that nonecclesiastical " natural law " on which the ec-clesiastically neutral state in Anglo-American democracy had been based (3, 56, 57). Moral law cannot be ascertained by men of good will; it can be defined only by the papal court. Policy could never be deter-mined by democratic discussion, consequently, but only on the basis of papal ukases.

c. *Religious Liberty.* The equal freedom of all religious bodies, liberty of conscience and liberty of worship — these were the implications of the separation and ecclesiastical neutrality of the State. The suppres-sion of all religious privilege and constraint, said Montalembert, is one of the two fundamental principles of modern democracy. The liberal Catholics had tried to make the distinction between intolerance in dogma and tolerance in the State, the distinction first exemplified by the left-wing Puritans like Lilburne and Roger Williams. Montalem-bert would have agreed with the condemnations in the Syllabus of latitudinarianism (15, 16, 17, 18, 21), that all religions lead equally to God, that Protestantism is but another form of the same true Christian religion. But the argument of his Malines addresses had been that by granting non-Catholic views freedom of expression Catholicism had in the past and would in the future prevail more against them than it could by using the police power to suppress error.

The pope, however, trusted the police power more than the power of truth. As Pius wrote Bishop Pie, when the latter solicited a condemnation of Montalembert, " The Church will never allow that it is a good thing, or right in principle, that errors and heresies should be preached to Catholic populations." [11] The liberty of worship and opinion, he decreed, conduces " to corrupt the morals and minds of the people, and to the propagation of the pest of indifferentism " (79). Not merely is it thus correct in principle, but it is also still expedient at the present day " that the Catholic religion shall be held as the only religion of the State, to the exclusion of all other forms of worship " (77). He specifically condemned laws " in some countries called Catholic," which permitted public worship to non-Catholic foreigners coming to reside there (78). Thus the Roman Church was flatly set to combat the liberties of conscience guaranteed in most modern European and American constitutions.

d. *The Right to Persecute and Coerce.* Roman Catholicism, ruled its infallible head, is committed to the principles of the Index and the Inquisition, that is to say, censorship and terrorism, as means of controlling all Catholic populations, indeed, all baptized Christians. He was serving notice that Catholics had no apologies to make for persecution, and would persecute again in more opportune circumstances. To make the point doubly clear, Pius in this year opened the proceedings to make a saint of one of Torquemada's right-hand men. Three years later Peter Arbues was declared a " saint " and commended to the devotions of Catholics. This character had been assassinated by desperate *Conversos* in 1485 in a campaign of counterterrorism against the bloody purge of the Spanish Inquisition. By elevating such a terrorist martyr to the altars, Pius meant to slap in the face such chickenhearted sentimentalists as Montalembert among the half-Catholics.

The Roman Church is a " complete " society, that is, a society that possesses the right to all organs and functions necessary to its welfare, economic, judicial, military, political. The Roman court has the right to political rule directly as a State, with all functionaries from diplomats and soldiers down to secret police and executioners, to use force where necessary, and also indirectly, by using its spiritual disciplines over Catholic citizens, to break laws, to coerce or overthrow governments

(19, 20, 23, 24, 27). Even in liberal and democratic societies, consequently, a Roman Catholic police officer may be required to take orders from the bishop.

We may now observe six different areas of political concern in which these clerical claims are to be made good: diplomacy, the judiciary, economic policy, education, marriage, moral legislation. In each the principle of clerical supremacy stands flatly opposed to liberal democratic principles and procedure.

a. *Diplomacy.* The liberal democratic State cannot consistently accord diplomatic recognition to the Roman court as a government over all Catholics. To do so acknowledges the jurisdiction of canon law over its own Catholic citizens, and it becomes in so far a clerical autocracy. Consequently it cannot enter into treaties or concordats with the papal court. It is the theory of the papalists, on the other hand, that since civil states are rightly subordinate to papal supremacy, concordats are papal concessions to states, binding on the latter, but changeable at the pope's pleasure (43). Needless to say, the papal court has not ordinarily been able to put this theory into practice with states of any description.

The papalist claim to supremacy over civil governments was illustrated in another thesis of the Syllabus which concerns international affairs. The pope condemned the principle of nonintervention by which modern states generally agree not to interfere in each other's internal affairs (62). He wished non-Italian Catholics to intervene in his interest in Italy, and all through the 1870's he continued his incendiary attacks on the kingdom of Italy and his attempts to persuade other states, such as France, to intervene even at the cost of their own ruin. In general, again, the papal court has not been able to make this thesis effective in international politics. But even where the principle is not in general recognized, Roman Catholic diplomats and statesmen are under pressure to subordinate political justice and national interest to the institutional interests of the Roman court. Intervention at the behest of the Roman court has been a recurrent subordinate and sometimes surreptitious tendency pushed by Catholic groups, in the diplomatic history of several nations, as the present generation of Americans know well.

b. *The Judiciary.* Pius defended what was left of the medieval system of a separate Church judiciary for certain classes of cases, and for all cases involving the clergy (31). He had no intention of submitting the Roman Catholic hierarchy to the democratic principle of equality before the law (30). The Roman clergy were to be outside the jurisdiction of the civil judiciary just as they were by right to be immune from the obligation of military service (32). There is no right of appeal to civil courts from the ecclesiastical government (41). Where a State refuses to recognize this judicial immunity of the clergy, the Roman court has often been able to make it good by requiring Roman Catholic judges to compromise their civil oath in favor of canon law and to dismiss suits brought against Roman Catholic clergy. Roman Catholic laymen who bring such suits are excommunicated. Extraordinary pressures are brought to censor the news of felonies and misdemeanors by the Roman clergy out of the means of public communication. By such devices the personal immunity demanded in the Syllabus is still in part secured even in democratic societies.

c. *Economic Policy.* Here again the Syllabus claims privileges for the Church beyond the rights established by law in democratic states. The Church has a peculiar "innate" right of acquiring and holding property, which cannot be limited by civil government (26, 19, 53). In virtually every State where the Catholic Church has been long established, the civil government has found it necessary for the general welfare, or for a more equitable distribution of the tax burden, to set limits to the amount or type of property accumulated under the ecclesiastical dead hand. The Roman court has been forced to yield in practice, but the denial of this right on principle in canon law frees Catholic consciences for subterfuges and evasions of laws on mortmain or taxation. Church property is not to be subjected to the same limitations and burdens as other property in a democratic society.

d. *Education.* The problem of education in a liberal democratic society was under great controversy at the time of the Syllabus, and indeed has been ever since. It would seem safe, however, to say that a liberal democratic State claims the right to require that its citizens be educated for participation in a community based on the common moral and philosophical tradition. That would be, in the West, an ecclesiastically neutral but generally Judaeo-Christian theistic or deistic world view and morality. It is only on the actual existence of such a community of conviction and morals that democratic society has been able to come into being in the first place.

But just as the Roman court denied that men of good will could be trusted to discern moral law without its legislation (3, 56, 57), so the pope denied to the civil State the right to conduct instruction in public schools free of ecclesiastical interference as to teachers, curriculum, discipline, and degrees (45, 47). He condemned the thesis that "this system of instructing youth, which consists in separating it from the Catholic faith and from the rule of the Church, and in teaching exclusively, or at least primarily, the knowledge of natural things and the earthly ends of social life alone, may be approved by Catholics" (48).

The Roman court requires that Catholic youth, even in a democratic society, be instructed only under the rule of the Church and according to the Church's antidemocratic principles. In Roman schools there is to be no academic freedom, and philosophy, science, and history are to be censored by ecclesiastical authority (10, 11, 12, 14). Catholic teachers and authors are subject to such authority, moreover, not merely in matters of defined dogma (22).

e. *Marriage.* As with education, the ecclesiastically neutral democratic State has been forced to legislate on the basis of an agreed minimum " natural " morality, with regard to marriage and divorce. Whatever further regulations religious bodies may set for their own members, there must be general dispositions in public law to establish matters of marital status, inheritance of property, and allied issues of public concern.

The contention of the Syllabus was that legislation as to marriage and divorce must be based on the Roman canon law and could not be binding in conscience otherwise (74). The State should not permit the marriage of parties where there were ecclesiastical impediments in Roman tradition (68, 69, 70). A merely civil contract cannot constitute a valid marriage among Christians (66, 73) and a civil divorce is invalid (67).

In democratic states, of course, these canonical principles are not legally enforceable. But as in the matters of property, or judicial immunity, Roman Catholic judges may be required under ecclesiastical discipline to enforce the canon law even in contradiction to the public law they are sworn to serve. The disparity between public law and canon law on marriage has not infrequently been utilized by Catholics for morally dubious ends.

f. *Moral Legislation.* There remained the indefinitely elastic category of morality, within which the Roman court claimed the right to issue directives for governments (44). Catholics in free societies have frequently tried to reserve for their independent judgment the area of " politics " as distinct from " morals." But only the Roman court can decide where the line falls, so that in practice the Roman court has the right to demand obedience of any Catholic on any political issue. As Cardinal Manning said, " Politics is a branch of morals," meaning, " Morals is a branch of Church politics." A democratic society on the most fundamental level is a society where policy is determined by free discussion of moral and political issues. It is incompatible with a society where such issues are determined by decree.

We may return from the detailed consideration of these half dozen areas of " mixed jurisdiction " between Church and State to consider once again the great contrasts between the clerical conception and the liberal democratic one. In the Syllabus two sweeping generalizations provided a blanket justification of all papal history on the one hand, and a blanket condemnation of free society on the other. By denying that the popes had ever " exceeded the limits of their powers " or erred in the definition of morals (23), Pius justified the deposition of princes, the burning of " witches," the tortures of the Inquisition, the massacres and murders of Protestants and " heretics," instigated or approved by his predecessors. Standing pat on this record and these principles as permanently valid, he condemned the suggestion that " the Roman pontiff can and ought to reconcile himself to, and agree with, progress, liberalism, and civilization as lately introduced " (80).

The Syllabus had little to say about Montalembert's second principle of democracy, political equality. It was almost exclusively a definition of clericalism, for if the pope could make that stick, democratic forms could have no meaning anyway. In three theses, nevertheless, he did condemn in a garbled form the principles of popular sovereignty (39), the right of revolution (63), and government by majority rule (60). In the formulation he gave them, to be sure, most liberal democrats might hesitate to defend them, but they would recognize themselves at least as slandered. Pius blessed a delegation of pilgrims from the embryo French Republic a decade after the Syllabus, expressing " the hope of seeing them again engaged in the difficult task of eliminating if possible, or at least of attenuating, a frightful disease which is afflicting human society, which is called universal suffrage. Yes, that is a disease which destroys the order of society and which deserves to be called ' universal delusion ' (lively applause)." [12] While he thus commissioned the Catholics of France to undermine their republican institutions, the pope did his best to cripple the new national state of Italy in the famous *Non expedit,* commanding a sit-down strike in which Italian Catholics might neither vote nor run for office. His primary concern in this case, of course, was the recovery from Italy of the former papal territories, but the nature of his action displayed his contempt for parliamentary procedure or democratic discussion. Pius not only hated the constitutional state in Italy, but the whole conception of parliaments and democratic ballots in general and anywhere offended his absolutist instincts.

3. The Problems of Enforcement

But despite the Holy Father's fulminations ex cathedra, and " off the cuff " on the subject of liberal democracy, the majority of the nations of Western civilization intended to keep their hard-won civil liberties and representative governments. The promulgation of the Syllabus in constitutional countries raised difficulties. Was such a document, issued with the sanctions of spiritual discipline, an act of sedition? The French Government not merely so interpreted it, but forbade its publication for a time as contrary to the French constitution. The Belgian Catholics, whose practice Montalembert had urged as a model, felt themselves even more seriously embarrassed. Unlike the Catholics of Britain and America, who were as yet too weak to do anything about such papal instructions, the Belgian Catholics possessed the power to shape the Belgian State. There where the Roman Church and liberalism had entered a generation before into a political compact, there was so great a commotion about the papal Syllabus that the *Civiltà cattolica* had to hasten to declare that neither the Belgian constitution nor the rights and duties of Belgian citizens were affected by the documents of December 8, 1864.[13]

In Spain, Spanish America, and Italy, of course, there was little doubt as to the meaning and authority of the Syllabus, but in the more progressive nations distress was intense. Three of the most distinguished Catholics attempted to " explain " the Syllabus. In England, where Ward would have been delighted to have a syllabus for breakfast with his egg daily, Newman wriggled and squirmed. He was not sure that the Syllabus came from the pope. He was very doubtful as to what the several condemnations might mean. Each would need to be studied in the original context from which it was cited, and the interpretation would require a battery of theological experts. In Germany, where Catholics had the most highly developed intellectual life, Bishop Ketteler embarked on similar qualifications. The condemnations cited in the Syllabus, he urged, referred only to very specific situations of which 999 out of 1,000 knew nothing. Hence their bearing was a matter for experts. Ketteler even dared to interpolate the papal statements. The pope had not meant to condemn progress and modern civilization, he said — only " so-called " progress! Bishop Dupanloup of France, again, made perhaps the most famous of all the minimizing interpretations when he wrote in answer to those who inquired whether they could still, as good Catholics, take the oath to the constitution. Of course they could, advised Dupanloup. Provided the Church kept the issues of principle clear (the " theses "), it could afford to make concessions to practical expediency (the " hypotheses "). Like Ketteler and Newman, he wished to restrict the relevance of the condemnations to the very concrete circumstances that had called them severally forth. He volunteered his own specifications as to what type of " liberty," " progress," and the like were really condemned. And while the *Univers* railed at Dupanloup's " anti-Syllabus," some 360 bishops wrote him in gratitude.

Such a demonstration forced the pope to swallow his bile and acknowledge Dupanloup's book. Pius was not pleased, however, with these interpreters. He did not care for these refinements as to which "liberty" and "progress" he condemned. He meant liberty and progress. And as to the necessity of understanding his condemnations in terms of the various concrete situations that had originally elicited them, he himself had taken them out of context and sent them out for the guidance of the universal hierarchy in their more general bearings. The most honest and accurate commentary on the Syllabus, by the Jesuit Shrader, who had himself served on the pope's drafting committee, made no such sophistical distinctions and was quite explicit about the crucial issue of persecution. Shrader informed Ketteler that it was only by special indulgence that the latter's book was not put on the Index. Similarly, when Newman later put his qualifications into print in the *Letter to the Duke of Norfolk,* the pope desired that he be informed that there were objectionable passages in the book. And Dupanloup never got his red hat.

A further aspect of the political significance of the antidemocratic manifesto can be illustrated from American history. Two generations after the promulgation of the Syllabus, a Roman Catholic campaigned for the Presidency of the United States. When publicly challenged in *The Atlantic Monthly* as to how he reconciled responsibility to the American Constitution with obedience to the Syllabus, Al Smith replied that he had not read the Syllabus and was not responsible to it. He is reported, in fact, to have turned to his political advisers in some perplexity: "What the hell *is* an 'enkiklika'"? In such an attitude Al Smith was doubtless representative of the American laity in general.

But the American hierarchy has no such casual attitude. *The Catholic Encyclopaedia* defines for Americans the force of the Syllabus as follows: [14] " Many theologians are of the opinion that to the Syllabus as such an infallible teaching authority is to be ascribed (whether due to an ex cathedra decision by the pope or to the subsequent acceptance by the Church). Others question this. . . . Even should the condemnation of many propositions not possess that unchangeableness peculiar to infallible decisions, nevertheless the *binding force* of the condemnation in regard to all the propositions is beyond doubt. . . . All Catholics, therefore, are bound to accept the Syllabus. Exteriorly they may neither in word nor in writing oppose its contents; they must also assent to it interiorly."

How, then, shall we understand the ignorance of American Catholic laity and of Al Smith as to their duties to oppose the American constitutional system? Much of the answer lies in certain principles and procedures of the confessional. According to the most approved Roman moral theology, the sin of an act, such as supporting religious liberty on principle, does not lie in the act itself, but in the conscious rebellion of the actor against the laws of the Church in committing the act. If he was in ignorance, he does not sin. A confessor who discovers such ignorance in his laity must consider carefully. If he informs the penitent that to do thus and so is against the Church's teaching when he is morally certain that the man will continue to act so anyway, he is himself guilty of leading the man into sin. Therefore, in normal circumstances, the priest should not inform his ignorant penitents of the wrongness of those actions that are likely to continue to prove too tempting to them.[15] If your penitent is apparently a convinced liberal democrat, and likely to stay so despite all " enkiklika," then do not convert his ignorant misdemeanors into conscious sin by teaching him how the Church has condemned liberal democracy.

In normal circumstances, that is. But when the penitent holds political power, such as to be able to serve the Church materially, then new considerations come into play. If Al Smith had won the election, it would then have been his confessor's duty to inform him of what Rome required of him, even at the risk of leading Mr. Smith into intolerable tensions and probably mortal sin.[16] It is on these highly rationalized principles that the Catholic population in a liberal democratic country are left with a minimal sense of obligation to such political principles as are taught in Rome, until they are in sight of the power to put them into effect.

Let us return, then, from this discussion of the immediate and the continuing political bearing of the Syllabus to the further developments of the reign of Pio Nono Secondo. The culminating act of the reign of Pius IX was, of course, the promulgation of the canons and decrees of the Vatican Council of 1870, and the revolution thus effected in the doctrines and government of the Roman Church. From the point of view of their significance for democracy, the theoretical definition of papal infallibility was less important than the new absolutist centralization in Church government, and the authority lent the program of the Syllabus. These considerations were also more important from the pope's viewpoint.

" Pius IX constantly asserted that the desire of obtaining the recognition of papal infallibility was not originally his motive in convoking the Council . . . apart from the doctrine of infallibility he had a strong desire to establish certain cherished opinions of his own on a basis firm enough to outlast his time. They were collected in the Syllabus, which contained the essence of what he had written during many years and was an abridgment of the lessons which his life had taught him. He was anxious that they should not be lost. They were part of a coherent system. The Syllabus was not rejected, but its edge was blunted and its point broken by the zeal which was spent in explaining it away. . . . Probably the pope would have been content that these his favorite ideas should be rescued from evasion by being incorporated in the canons of the Council. . . . More than once, addressing a group of bishops, he said that he would do nothing to raise disputes among them and would be content with a declaration in favor of intolerance. . . . The meaning of this intimation, that persecution would do as a substitute for infallibility, was that the most glaring obstacle to the definition would be removed if the Inquisition was recognized as consistent with Catholicism. Indeed it seemed that infallibility was a means to an end which could be obtained in other ways, and that he would have been satisfied with a decree confirming the twenty-third article of the Syllabus, and declaring that no pope has ever exceeded the just bounds of his authority in faith, in politics, or in morals." [17]

The *Civiltà cattolica,* the pope's quasi-official organ, gave the first frank statement of the hopes of the papal party when in February, 1869, it printed a prophecy that the council would both proclaim the dogma of infallibility and confirm the Syllabus in positive rather than negative form in less than a month. Such a positive statement of the Syllabus had already been made by Clemens Shrader, S. J., who was a leading member of the pope's dogmatic commission at the council as well as of the Syllabus commission, and the pope had given his approval to the book. But the pope had also felt constrained to give his blessing to Dupanloup's efforts at minimizing, so that it would be an advance in precision if a council published the theses in the positive and uncompromising form he and Shrader had in mind. In the event, of course, the Syllabus was not specifically mentioned along with the definition of infallibility in the canons of the council, but it was given new authority by the requirement of absolute obedience to the pope in matters of discipline and Church government even where he did not claim to be infallible.

In 1874 a debate was launched in England on the political significance of the Syllabus and Vatican Decrees which engaged some of the most distinguished minds of British religion, Gladstone, Newman, Lord Acton, and Manning (if the last may be called a distinguished mind). One of the chief motifs of this debate is highly relevant to the problem of this analysis. It is the question of how much weight should be attached to the official doctrine and policy of Rome, to its canon law and papal decrees, as a force shaping the actual political conduct of Roman Catholic populations. This is a query that in its most general form must set a question mark beside all conclusions on the political tendencies of ecclesiastical systems. If it be granted that the influence of the Roman court and the canon law was consistently for absolutism in the Church, and absolutism of the Church, one may still 'ask, " How significant is the influence of the Roman court and the canon law on the political conduct of the Catholic laity? " It might be that in England Catholics would still act as members of a liberal democracy, despite the hierarchy, due either to the influence of the general culture about them (shaped positively by other religious traditions, especially Puritan Protestantism), or, conceivably, due to certain tendencies in Catholic religion itself which make for democracy provided canon law and Roman absolutism are not allowed to stifle them completely. Up to 1870 the liberal political tendency of Britain and the United States had been shaped almost exclusively by Protestantism. The Catholic populations in these countries took their political coloration from a Protestant culture, and unconsciously read even their Catholicism in terms of political principle shaped by Protestantism. Politically they were not really Roman in fundamentals, and yet they were themselves hardly aware of the fact.

The discussion in public was launched by Gladstone, the leader of the Liberal party, but at the time not prime minister. In 1874 he issued a " political expostulation," the *Vatican Decrees in Their Bearing on Civil Allegiance.* He recalled that at the end of the eighteenth and the beginning of the nineteenth century, when there had been in Parliament discussion of releasing English and Irish Catholics from their civil disabilities, official inquiries as to the political loyalty of Catholics had been made and answered. Did the pope claim supremacy over civil governments? Did he possess power to depose kings and invalidate laws by releasing Catholics from their civil obligations? Did Rome still teach the doctrines of persecution, and of keeping no faith with heretics? Were all Catholics bound in conscience to a universal obedience to the pope, or to consider him infallible? The answers made then by English and Irish Catholics had been emphatic and indignant. English Roman Catholic bishops, clergy, and laity gave solemn assurances that they rejected papal infallibility. The Irish hierarchy declared that it was notorious within the whole Roman Catholic Church that papal infallibility could not be made part of their faith, and that the pope's claims of civil authority, direct or indirect, were rejected by them. They were free, even as Catholics, to serve as responsible members of a free society. And partly on the grounds of these assurances they had been granted civil liberties.

But now, observed Gladstone, all these protestations and assurances had been falsified. Some of the men who had sworn to the contrary principles had now submitted to the Syllabus and Vatican Decrees. The faith and government of the Roman Church had been radically changed over the heads of English and Irish Catholics and now consisted precisely of what they had denied it to be when they had been claiming the right of full citizenship in a free society. The pope now claimed absolute obedience from all Catholics, the right to depose, to annul laws, to absolve from oaths of civil obligations; the right to censor and persecute — rights which he still thought it wise to use wherever he could muster the force. Gladstone did not believe that English and Irish Catholics had changed their religion so radically as had Rome. He considered that under the circumstances they owed their fellow countrymen assurances that they would fulfill the engagements their bishops had promised on their behalf in 1826, that they would repel the claims of the pope in political affairs.

The replies to Gladstone on the part of English Catholics were numerous and varied, but in substance they satisfied him " that the loyalty of our Roman Catholic fellow subjects in the mass remains untainted and secure." But how, then, were they orthodox? To the vast majority of Roman Catholics the Syllabus and Vatican Decrees remained practically unknown. A very large class of Catholics supposed that they believed with Rome, and knew not what Rome stood for. As Lord Acton replied in a letter to the *Times,* " I think you will admit that your Catholic countrymen cannot fairly be called to account for every particle of a system which has never come before them in its integrity, or for opinions whose existence among divines they would be exceedingly reluctant to believe." [18] The great bulk of teaching in the Catholic parishes was simply common Christian morality and faith, and the ordinary layman had only the sketchiest notions of the more immoral and politically dangerous teachings of the papal court.

Even among that small minority who really understood the bearing of the papal political position, of the Syllabus and Vatican Decrees, their force was evaded in numerous ways. Newman's *Letter to the Duke of Norfolk* was a masterly instance from that " glorious sophist." The very ultramontanes themselves, men like Manning, perhaps even Veuillot or Pie, did not face the full moral consequences of their position. They were men who professed to follow the full teachings of the papal chair, as for instance the doctrine taught at Rome for over four centuries that no Catholic could be saved who denied that heretics should be put to death. They were peculiarly pledged to guide their lives by those of canonized saints as well as popes, such as that of Pius V, the first pope saint for centuries, who released English Catholics from allegiance to Queen Elizabeth and commissioned an assassin to take her life, or that of his next successor who, " on learning that the Protestants were being massacred in France, pronounced the work glorious and holy . . . and implored the king . . . to carry the work on to the bitter end until every Huguenot had recanted or perished." [19] Yet in practice these things which the pope and the ultramontane party justified and defended did not seem to lead often to action in the same spirit. " If they do not, then it cannot truly be said that Catholics forfeit their moral freedom, or place their duty at the mercy of another." [20]

With all his vast acquaintance through the whole Catholic world, Lord Acton wrote Gladstone, he had never met an informed and sincere ultramontane. " I do not know of a religious and educated Catholic who really believes that the See of Rome is a safe guide to salvation. . . . They will therefore deny, or conceal, or explain away the things that are its reproach, but they do not believe in or approve them. . . . Some are unwilling [even in confidence] to avow their disbelief in those things to which the papacy is committed; but even among those I know none who really entertain the convictions they wish to impose. . . . These men all accept the Pope with their own conditions and interpretations. I could scarcely imagine how it could be right or reasonable to argue with a professed ultramontane; it would seem an impertinence to ask him to put off his uniform and speak in his real character." [21]

Assuming that Lord Acton's reply was justified, it meant that Romanism as a system is hostile to liberal democracy, and that Catholics are free and responsible citizens of a liberal democracy only in so far as they are ignorant or inconsistent. " This means," said Gladstone, " that the poison which circulates from Rome has not actually been taken into the system." But while accepting the protestation of Catholic leaders of his generation, educated in other doctrines than those of the Syllabus and Vatican Decrees, to civil loyalty, he viewed the generations to come after 1870 with uneasiness. What was to be expected of the silent diffusion among Catholic laity of the authoritative principles of Pius IX? " An army of teachers, the largest and most compact in the world, is ever sedulously at work to bring them into practice." The tightening of papal discipline in the Church gave promise that these principles would gradually gain even in free countries, in the training of the clergy, in ecclesiastical appointments, in the Catholic school system, in the press, in the pulpit, in the confessional. " By undermining moral liberty they impair moral responsibility, and silently, in the succession of generations if not even in the lifetime of individuals, tend to emasculate the vigor of the mind." [22] We must inquire whether Gladstone's foreboding of the increasing hostility of English-speaking Catholicism to liberal democracy in the twentieth century has been justified by events.

V

PURITAN PROTESTANTISM AND
LIBERAL DEMOCRACY, 1865–1914

❖ ❖ ❖

IN THE course of a contrast between the spirit of British foreign policy and that of the chief Roman Catholic and Lutheran powers, Kantorowicz characterizes the political ethic of the whole group of nations primarily influenced by Puritan Protestantism.

" Common to all of them, in higher degree than to the rest of the Continent, are genuine democracy, the considerable influence of religion on politics, the urge for the moralization of public life, the belief in international organization, the contempt for militarism, the high estimation of woman, impartiality of justice, strict honesty in business, a sober sense of reality, and many other things, together with a relatively slight philosophical capacity and artistic and especially musical talent as well as less personal passion." [1]

In Roman Catholic countries, including even Ireland, and in German Lutheranism, Christian ethics is no such determinative force in public life. In England and other countries of this group, however, " the Christian ethos has been far more deeply influential, thanks, in part, to the Calvinist doctrine of election."

The countries of the Continent which Kantorowicz assimilated to this political ethic especially characteristic of British Protestantism were Holland, Switzerland, and the Scandinavian countries. Of these the last are particularly interesting, as being solidly Lutheran and as representing possibly that normal development of Lutheran Church life and political ethics which was stifled in the cradle in Germany. The reasons for this divergence of German and Scandinavian Lutheranism deserve more careful analysis than can be presented here, but certain factors leap to the eye. In Sweden, in particular, the Church retained an independence as against civil authority which was generally lost in Germany. The episcopate, while in the last analysis regulated by the Lutheran monarchy, nevertheless retained its own organs of administration and exercised in practice a considerable measure of independence.

In this respect the Church of Sweden had more freedom in fact than the Church of England and approached that of the Church of Scotland, which is the model of an established Church independent of the State in its own affairs.

A second manifestation of the relative freedom of the Scandinavian churches from civil control appears in the mode of their reception of pietist and dissenting tendencies. In most of German Lutheranism this pietism was shackled by social caste and political regulation of the churches, and became an affair of the aristocracy. In Britain and America, by contrast, the analogous movements often produced new denominations. Scandinavia (and to a degree Württemberg) exhibited a middle course. In Norway, for example, the "readers' meetings," which were comparable to English-speaking Evangelical revivals, gave new scope to the priesthood of lay Christians to each other, and their urge to form religious communities, but all within the State Church system. The Inner Mission, which in Germany was often forced into an anomalous extraecclesiastical position, could in Denmark actually form congregations in local parishes, call sympathetic clergy, and share in the use of the parish church. Similarly the Grundtvigian movement constituted religious communities within the one State Church. This extraordinary flexibility and comprehensiveness of the State Church contrasted with the Church of England, which out of snobbery and narrow-mindedness had ejected comparable movements into "nonconformity." In Scandinavia the democratic tendencies that in Britain had been expressed in dissent were able to work inside the inclusive Church. Their social and political influence was perhaps most dramatic in Grundtvig's movement, which revolutionized the Danish peasantry through the development of folk schools and co-operatives. The early history of the temperance movement, and even of the labor movement, in Scandinavia also showed an influence from the Church for the democratic development of State and society. Today one may read Scandinavian Lutheran discussions of the authority of the moral law over government which contrast completely with the characteristic position of German Lutheranism.[2] American Lutheranism, similarly, stands closer to the Puritan Protestant sociological type than to German Lutheranism.

1. ANGLO-AMERICAN INDIVIDUALISM, 1865–1890

The Protestantism of the English-speaking world, to which we will devote most of our attention, should be studied as a whole. Britain, the United States, Canada, Australia, and New Zealand represent one historical movement from such a perspective as this, and together consti-

tute the chief illustration of the political and social tendency of Puritan
Protestantism. We must limit ourselves to Britain and the United States.
Americans are usually irritated by the British habit of regarding them
as still British imperials, but there is more to it than most Americans
realize. Britain in the period we have under consideration was simply
the most industrialized and intellectually sophisticated corner of the
English-speaking world. Social conditions, cultural currents, and various institutions moved in successive waves from Britain across the Atlantic to New England and the urban northeast quarter and from there
filtered out into the rural three quarters of the states. The political traditions and the democratic faith of the Americans were largely British
in origin. The dominant churches of America in manifold ways still
took cues from their parent bodies in British Anglicanism, Presbyterianism, and the Free Churches. In both countries, in contrast to the Roman
Catholic countries of the day, the struggle for political democracy was
over in this period, and a liberal democratic State was assumed by all
parties. The problems were the achievement or maintenance of a democratic society and economy as conditions of such a State.

Notice the way in which the problem of democracy was now presented. As A. D. Lindsay has pointed out, all through the nineteenth
century, while the industrial countries of the West were becoming politically more democratic, the structure of their industry was becoming
more autocratic and oligarchic.[3] In such an increasingly urbanized and
industrialized society the majority of men came to spend most of their
lives under orders in an authoritarian and disciplined organization.
Most men most of the time were not in a position to make independent
and responsible decisions on issues of policy and they acquired the mental habit of not expecting to make responsible decisions, of a kind of
fatalism about the powers that rule the world of international industry
and finance in whose hands the masses of men are puppets to be ma-
neuvered. The old agrarian democracy of Jefferson, Jackson, and Lincoln assumed a citizenry of independent landholders and small businessmen. Modern monopoly capitalism was rapidly rendering such a
citizenry extinct and creating a society of more and more centralized control, where the vast majority earned a salary for doing an assigned job
under orders. By 1896 one per cent of American families owned over
half the nation's wealth. Two thousand men controlled half the nation's
business. In a society which had become autocratic and oligarchic it was
increasingly difficult to make democratic political machinery function.
There were not enough democratic people trained by daily living to
responsible initiative. Communism and monopoly capitalism are alike
in the tendency to crush out all independent centers of economic ini-

tiative by great bureaucratic organizations. And the attempts to arrest this process by antitrust legislation have had about as much success as the attempts of Mussolini to change by legislation the curve of the birth rate. The campaign talk about free enterprise in the American economy of modified monopoly is quite comparable to the talk about the New England town meeting as a contribution to democracy. They are both irrelevant to the present scene. Only the cultivation of workers' self-government and a wider participation in policy decisions could hope to contribute to a democratic solution.

When we turn to the Churches to examine their response to the challenge of industrial autocracy and bureaucracy, we have to do primarily with Anglo-American " Evangelicalism " and its liberal utilitarian ethic. This was the religion of the majority of Anglican laymen, and nearly all Methodists, Baptists, Congregationalists, and Presbyterians on both sides of the Atlantic. Evangelical Protestantism was a very live force in business and in politics, but its individualistic ethic, stemming from a preindustrial, early capitalist era, was particularly unsuited to cope with this new and unforeseen threat to democracy. We should recall first the positive thrust of this ethic.

The twin symbols of security in the America of a century ago were the village church and the county courthouse, representing together the God-given law of the universe in the two spheres of nature and of grace. "From Puritanism more than from any other source the American democratic faith of the middle of the nineteenth century derived its emphasis upon the fundamental moral law and upon the doctrine of the self-disciplined individual." [4] The goal of this society was the production of responsible free men dedicated to the service of this higher law. The theological expression of this moral framework of the free life was found in the almost universal American concept of God as the just Judge before whom all men should stand at the last day. [5] This period was indeed the second classical age in the development of the Anglo-American common law, and in both Puritan Protestantism was a controlling factor. " The age of Coke was the age of the Puritan in England and the period that ends with our Civil War was the age of the Puritan in America." [6] " Puritanism put individual judgment and individual conscience in the first place where the traditional modes of thought had put authority and the reason and the judgment of the prince." [7] Deliberate conscious contract became the focus of legal thinking, with great stress on individual freedom and responsibility, and great suspicion of legislation and equity. And common law rights were generally regarded as the specification of natural rights in the moral universe.

In economic affairs also this moral discipline pervaded the society.

R. C. K. Ensor's description of British business at this time would also pass for the American, *mutatis mutandis*. " If one asks," he wrote, " how nineteenth century English merchants earned the reputation of being the most honest in the world (a very real factor in the nineteenth century primacy of English trade), the answer is: because hell and heaven seemed as certain to them as tomorrow's sunrise, and the Last Judgment as real as the week's balance sheet. This keen sense of moral accounting had also much to do with the success of self-government in the political sphere." Of Victorian Britain in general he held: " Among highly civilized, in contradistinction to more primitive countries, it was one of the most religious that the world has ever known." [8] " There was no make-believe in the genuine piety of the English middle-class home. . . . It was the central core of life for a great body of men and women who represented between them the major portion of the wealth, power, and activity of the world. It gave them regularity of habit, a rule of sober conduct that made them invincible in their narrow achievement, and a certain intensity of purpose that lent dignity and even beauty to their otherwise monotonous and ugly lives." [9]

The eighteenth and early nineteenth century tradition of Evangelical humanitarianism continued and expanded in this period. Characteristic aspects of this tradition were its voluntarism and its ecclesiastical anonymity. Wherever an Evangelical felt a concern to meet a concrete human need, nothing seemed more natural than to organize a group of friends and acquaintances to meet it. Scores and hundreds of enterprises, philanthropic and humanitarian, came thus into being. But in contrast to the comparable initiatives of Catholic Action, which are to be described in our next chapter, these Evangelical societies were nonecclesiastical in basis and tended in time to become institutionalized and professionalized and to lose even their unecclesiastical Christian flavor. The human sensitivity and moral insight nurtured in the Evangelical congregations were thus poured out into the common life unstintingly. But where the Christian Evangelical pioneered, the second generation tended to professionalize and to sever any remaining ties to the religious parent. This is the history of countless American schools and colleges, orphanages, asylums, hospitals, social settlements, and the professional staffs that carry on their work. Such " secularization " usually meant increased efficiency and operation on a larger scale. The whole community profited significantly, but there was little recognition, to say nothing of institutional advantage, for the churches from which most of the initiative had sprung.

A characteristic instance in this later period of a voluntary, interdenominational, but in origin strongly Evangelical, undertaking for reli-

gious and social work, was the Y.M.C.A. From George Williams'
Bible-reading society of a dozen apprentices a remarkable expansion
took place, especially in America. And to the main work of conversion
were added several important auxiliary services, the provision of boardinghouses for young men, and schools. The Y.M.C.A. was very active
in the great revival of 1857–1858, and who was better equipped for
Christian work in the Civil War than this agency designed to minister
to young men? From it came the United States Christian Commission,
which was transformed after the war into the American Christian Commission. This Commission made the first important survey of the situation of Protestant work, evangelistic and philanthropic, in the new
cities. Its conventions in the '60's and '70's made the need more widely
known, and its studies into British experiences and the German Inner
Mission provided suggestions as to means of coping with problems so
new to America.

For two decades after the Civil War there was an increase in various
types of Protestant societies in the new cities, evincing in various degrees the same mixture of evangelistic and philanthropic concerns as
the Y.M.C.A. The most characteristic of these was the city " mission,"
of which New York and Boston had seen examples even before the War.
By 1880 there were some thirty of these city missions in operation, most
of them interdenominational but definitely Evangelical in character,
and usually with a strong interest in temperance. Like the Y.M.C.A.,
they often provided boardinghouses, served as employment agencies,
and supplied educational and recreational facilities in addition to their
presentation of the gospel.

From the '80's the mission was widely supplemented by two new
types of institution for accomplishing much the same work. The generation before the First World War was the great age, in both Britain
and America, of the " institutional " church and the slum " settlement."
Episcopalians and Congregationalists had been experimenting with
educational and social programs even earlier, as the best hope of avoid-
ing the death of their downtown churches and finding a use for them.
The inner city meant death to the old family-style Protestant congregation. From 1868–1888, for instance, seventeen Protestant churches
moved out of the Greenwich Village area of Lower Manhattan, while
two hundred thousand more people pressed in.[10] In America several
famous and very large institutional parishes were developed, Saint
George's and Saint Bartholomew's in New York, Berkeley Temple in
Boston, Baptist Temple in Philadelphia. By 1900 Russell Conwell, of
this Baptist Temple, the largest Protestant congregation in the nation,
listed one hundred and seventy-three " institutionalized churches," and

there were scores of others who had adopted some parts of the conception.[11] From 1894 on there was an " Open and Institutional Church League " in active operation.

Like the institutional church, the settlement went beyond the " mission " in attempting to root itself permanently in the community. The idea came first from the Anglican Christian Socialists, as a development of their endeavor to use able university teachers in their workers' education projects. From Toynbee Hall it was carried to America by Coit and Jane Addams, and in Britain its progress was pushed even more enthusiastically by nonconformists than by Episcopalians. No other Christian reform program of the period won more followers than the settlement movement.[12] By 1905, for example, there were over seventy Church-related settlements in the United States, twenty-four of them in New York and eleven in Chicago.[13]

The latest, but in some ways the greatest, new enterprise of Evangelical philanthropy was that last great secession from Methodism, the Salvation Army. While Dwight L. Moody and the Y.M.C.A. ministered to the needs of the middle-class people outside the rolls of the regular congregations, the Army, as Cardinal Manning said, was " the only considerable body of Christians who had a passion for sinners as such." [14] William Booth had a concern for the redemption of those broken in body and spirit by the new industrialism, and, despite " the hard conservatism of the Wesleyan cardinals," insisted that body and soul must be saved together. *In Darkest England and the Way Out* demonstrated the futility of purely " spiritual " religion in the slum. In America the Army had a slow beginning, but by 1900 it was gathering some two millions to its meetings. There were a score of " Army posts " in various slums, nearly as many rescue homes, and the system of city and farm colonies for rehabilitation was highly successful. The Army conducted labor exchanges and even a life insurance department. Few Christian movements in modern history have a comparable record.

In specifically political matters, as against the general social influence of such philanthropy, we have an index of the Evangelical political ethic in a familiar saying of Lord John Russell. " I know the Dissenters," he remarked. " They carried the [franchise] Reform Bill; they carried the abolition of slavery; they carried free trade; and they'll carry the abolition of Church Rates." [15] If Russell had added something about temperance, he would have hit nearly all the high spots. The Dissenters had been consistently liberal on the franchise, consistently laissez-faire in economic policy. The campaign against taxes to support the Anglican Church, which triumphed in 1866, was part of their long battle for religious equality. Their two most impressive social campaigns of the nineteenth century dealt with the ending of Negro slavery and the control of the scourge of liquor. The slavery issue was now over — not entirely happily in the United States. By the end of the century almost every British free church had a temperance society, and in America the Protestant churches were nearer unanimity here than on any other general social problem. For other issues the liberalism of the vast majority meant that the Christian should be active in politics, but only in his capacity as a private citizen, and that the functions of the State should be held at a minimum.

In Britain and in America the laissez-faire attitude of this Church tradition was influenced by various factors. For nearly two centuries in Britain Dissent had suffered under the galling disabilities imposed by politically dominant Anglicanism. Dissenters had also been excluded from government service by the barring to them of the universities. Thus their tradition of political responsibility was crippled and they tended to think of government as a nuisance which should be reduced to the smallest possible dimensions.

Again, nonconformity was predominantly a business group sociologically. Even the Methodists, formerly miners and laborers, were by the second half of the century increasingly middle-class. Self-made businessmen were more inclined to count on individual initiative in all matters than were the Anglicans, still strongly colored by the tradition of the landed gentry. While Free Churchmen were concerned with the growing indifference of urban labor to the Church in the first half of the century — a generation before American Protestants generally discussed the problem — nevertheless they were more opposed than Anglicans to the Factory Acts and Ten Hours Act. Such legislation was viewed as an attempt to change natural economic law by fiat.

The presence of the frontier conditioned all American thinking in the second half of the nineteenth century. Everyone acted as though resources were inexhaustible. It was not necessary to work hard over problems of equitable distribution or the structure of social relations so long as everyone was, or could be, on the escalator. The concrete experience of continual and amazing expansion of wealth and power accustomed Americans to a trust in the beneficent direction of unregulated social forces. Americans were a nation of self-made men, and saw no reason why everyone should not be expected to make his own way as they had. Political pacifism, isolationism, and the laissez-faire State are all manifestations of the nineteenth century faith in automatic progress, that a people can have democracy without working and fighting for it. The Puritans had known better.

As we have already remarked, English free churchmen were predominantly urban in the latter nineteenth century. The Primitive Methodists, however, who were generally workmen, had still a substantial following in the countryside and small towns, and in that resembled the majority of American Protestants. In both countries there was a significant stirring of Protestant agrarian agitation. In the first half of the '70's Joseph Arch, who had joined the Primitive Methodists in revulsion from the caste lines in Anglicanism, led the formation of the National Agricultural Labourers' Union. He had a wider following than any popular leader since Cobbett and Owen. The Nonconformists generally were more sympathetic than Anglicans. As H. F. Lovell Cocks suggests,[16] dissenters felt a common bond with the laborers they had known in their own country childhoods, and with whom they had suffered from squire and parson. When Lord Shaftesbury had described scandalous factory conditions, John Bright had countered with an account of life on Shaftesbury's own estates. The manufacturing classes were even ready to qualify the absoluteness of private property, when it was a matter of land monopoly. Despite the tradition of laissez faire, Henry George won a hearing from Evangelical Protestants, both in America and Britain. Anglican class interest worked the other way. Bishop Charles Gore recalled later: " The only time in my life when I was very strongly driven to desert the Church was at the outbreak of the agitation against Joseph Arch. The attitude of the Anglican Church towards Arch's movement was lamentable; the clergy and the well-to-do were deaf towards the almost inconceivable record of injustice which the movement voiced." [17]

In America the comparable movement came two decades later, in the '90's, and was strongest in the Midwest centers of Baptist, Methodist, and Presbyterian evangelicalism, in Kansas, Nebraska, Minnesota, and the Dakotas. Bryan, the " Great Commoner," carried the South and most of the trans-Mississippi states in the 1896 election, fusing rural discontent with popular Protestantism. It was the last great revolt of the old equality of opportunity of Jefferson, Jackson, and Lincoln against the mortgages and high freights and marketing deals of the new plutocracy. Herron's preaching tours rode on the tide of this current and Rauschenbusch acknowledged it as " allied to Christianity " in contrast to the Democratic and Republican party systems, which were merely allied with the money power. Most of the Protestant social gospelers were too provincially urban, however, to discern the meaning of the movement.

Protestantism could supply a moral backbone to populism and agrarian revolt on a very general basis because these risings were essentially conservative. They were an attempt to preserve the threatened values and customs of traditional British and American life. In another important respect the main thrust of Protestant democracy still had unfinished business which did not introduce new social questions. That was in relation to local government. In the '70's nonconformist councilors began to turn out Tory Anglicans in the Northern and Midlands manufacturing towns and to reform the whole administration. The famous Congregationalist minister Dr. Dale was as influential in politics as Bright or Chamberlain. He served on the Birmingham town council, the school board, the Guardians of the Poor. Of the Unitarian Joseph Chamberlain, J. S. Hammond observes: " He was the first statesman of commanding power to put the whole question of town civilization in its proper place in politics. His career as a reformer in Birmingham is a landmark in English history." [18] In America a somewhat similar campaign was launched against Tammany by the ministers Parkhurst and Newton in the '90's, and in Chicago by the British journalist W. T. Stead. From the agitation of *If Christ Came to Chicago* developed the Civic Federation. The " muckraking " of the Progressive Era carried on this municipal good government movement into the twentieth century. Although their urban concentration gave them the greatest opportunity for good in this way, American Roman Catholics left municipal reform almost entirely to Protestants and Jews.

The limitations of Evangelical individualism appeared at the points where the whole structure of society was called in question, and particularly when the State itself was summoned to effect social changes. The rise of organized labor is a case in point. Most of what was done to Christianize the British labor movement in this period was done by Free Churchmen. Methodists especially provided an amazing proportion of the personnel of labor leadership. They supplied sobriety and reasonableness and precluded the dogmatic atheism of the Continental socialists. But what they did not supply was intellectual leadership or a policy. The only significant intellectual leadership on the horizon came from the solid knowledge and precise thinking of the Webbs. The Fabians were impatient with such forms of preindustrial nostalgia as Ruskin's or the guild socialists' and ruled out Marxist violence as impossible. Theirs was an evolutionary democratic socialism, accepting large-scale industry, and arguing that nationalization was the only feasible form of democratic control of such a society. None of the Christian groups could provide any proposals of comparable solidity, and the Evangelicals were rather scandalized that any such radical proposals should be made at all.

The same psychology can be seen at work with regard to the proposal of public education. Free churchmen had led in popular education with their day schools and Sunday schools for the poor. They contributed substantially to mechanics' institutes and to the production of cheap literature. But when Miall, the leading nonconformist journalist, served on the education commission that demonstrated that voluntarism was incapable of solving the problem, he found a cool reception among his fellow churchmen. The younger men became " state educationists " but the older generation generally opposed it. The large public grants to Anglican schools not only represented improper governmental functions, but also seemed to be reinstating the Church rates they had barely been emancipated from. The old grievance against Anglican privilege dominated nonconformist thought on public education for more than a generation more, and appeared strongly in the row over the Education Act of 1902, when the Anglicans and Roman Catholics combined to put something over on the nonconformists. Very few nonconformists in this period were able to raise themselves above their ancient jealousy and take a statesmanlike view of the problem of maintaining any semblance of Britain's Christian heritage. In America, similarly, Protestant thought on public education and Christianity was strongly colored by defensiveness and suspicion of Roman Catholicism, and is still.

With this outline of philanthropic and reform activities are nearly exhausted the major sociopolitical undertakings of Evangelical Protestantism. With very few exceptions these proposals assumed the given economic and social order to be providential and sound, and were designed simply to aid individuals to find themselves a responsible role in it. On the latter point they were more constructive than Roman Catholic charity, for which the increment of the gift to the giver's spiritual credit was the ultimate criterion, rather than its effect on the recipient. The Evangelical wished every man to have a fair chance, even a second and third chance, to stand on his own feet and " make something of himself " as a responsible citizen. Every man should be freed from bondage, educated, protected from demoralizing conditions, encouraged to join with his fellows in voluntary associations for mutual aid. But every man should then fight his own battle and make himself one of the independent contributors to society. The notion that the structure of that society should be subject to Christian challenge would seem not merely to infringe upon the traditional separation of the jurisdiction of revelation from that of creation, but it also impugned the goodness of the Creator.

It should not be overlooked in this connection that the lack of constructive leadership with regard to a democratic shaping of the structure of society was even more conspicuous among Anglo-American Roman Catholics than among Evangelicals. In Britain and America alike the Roman Catholic community was slowest of all to recognize its political responsibilities. In the first half of the century there had been in both countries a small old Catholic community, oriented in Lancashire to the Tory landlords, in Maryland to the Southern aristocracy. In both cases the fight for full citizenship and religious liberty was enough, and for the rest Anglo-American Catholics were politically conservative and little inclined to public life. From the '40's came the great migration of half the Irish into England, Scotland, and the United States, which, supplemented in America by millions of Continental Catholics, raised the Roman Catholic section from inconsequentiality to a major religious body in both Britain and America by 1914. These Roman Catholic masses were poorly educated, politically inexperienced, and, in America, divided by language and nationality. They gave to Anglo-American Roman Catholicism its characteristic sociological position as a workingman's church, but up to 1914 their attitude to social and political questions resembled that of the most conservative and pietistic Protestant bodies, such as Baptists or Lutherans. On the whole, the Roman Catholics were the last of the large Anglo-American denominations to accept responsibility in social and political issues. Up to the First World War their chief social interest seemed to be opposition to "socialism."

The dominant pattern of Catholic social activity in these two generations was philanthropic social service like that of the evangelical Protestantism, with the difference in motive that we have already noted. Hundreds of hospitals, old-age homes, and orphanages were erected in the same years in which resources were taxed to the utmost to erect the great parochial school system of Britain and America. There were charitable societies, especially those of the Irish and Germans in America, while the Catholic Young Men's Society might be roughly compared to the Y.M.C.A. and the Society of Saint Vincent de Paul to the Protestant Salvation Army. Priests like Farelly and McGlynn in New York built up parishes that resembled in many respects the Protestant "institutional churches." Temperance, the chief reform of the more conservative Protestant Evangelicals, similarly marked the limit to which most Anglo-American Roman Catholics would go. There was an American Catholic total abstinence society, but Archbishop Gibbons never was an enthusiast. His friend Manning, however, was, with Sir Wilfred Lawson, the chief temperance agitator of Britain in his day, which gave Manning a hold on the Irish masses such as Wiseman and Vaughan never had, and which led to his summons to mediate the great dockers' strike of 1889.

With regard to such industrial problems, however, Manning and Gibbons were far over the horizon of most Roman Catholics. The American prelate Archbishop Bayley of Baltimore expressed the dominant opinion of the American hierarchy in the '70's and '80's. "The miserable associations called labor organizations," he said, were subversive of government and "communistic." "No Catholic with any idea of the spirit of his religion will encourage them." [19] While the Baltimore Council of 1884 ruled that clergy must not condemn such societies without " previous explicit authorization," the Synod of Cincinnati and the Provincial Council of Milwaukee two years later advised Catholics to abandon labor organizations because of their "violent, socialistic character." In the same year, however, Gibbons won the grudging approval of the archbishops' committee for his defense of the Knights of Labor. His strongest argument with Rome was the argument from expediency. A condemnation simply would not be obeyed, and the Roman Church could not afford to alienate the American workman.

The same kind of consideration was paramount in the policy of the hierarchy with regard to McGlynn, Henry George's chief clerical champion. Few groups would be naturally more susceptible to single-tax propaganda than the Irish core of Anglo-American Catholicism. In England it was their preoccupation with Irish home rule and land reforms that brought the Roman Catholic constituency into association with liberal and labor programs in contrast to the old English Catholic Tory line. Many New York Irish rallied behind Henry George in that mayoralty campaign of 1886 which awakened young Rauschenbusch. Archbishop Corrigan and his bellicose colleague McQuaid, of Rochester, were horrified at the proposals entertained by the reformers. Not only were the sacred rights of private property to be qualified with regard to land rents, but the State should regulate the liquor traffic, child labor, corporate monopolies, tenement housing. McQuaid was all for summary execution on such barefaced sin, but Leo's delegate Satolli overruled Corrigan and released McGlynn from the ban. Satolli saw that the intervention of the hierarchy on such matters would confirm the widespread American opinion that Roman Catholics were not permitted by their faith to be loyal to the democratic determination of social policy.

At the end of the '80's came the first widely influential Protestant conference on social issues, the meetings of the Evangelical Alliance in 1887, 1889, and 1893 organized by Josiah Strong. The impact of these meetings on public opinion was not lost on the liberal Roman Catholics. Gibbons' right-hand man, Archbishop Ireland, organized the first American Catholic congresses in 1889 and 1893, and here social issues were likewise treated. The regulation of Sunday labor, the liquor traffic, and child labor was advocated and co-operatives were commended. The

Roman Catholic Church was struggling against its identification in public opinion with saloonkeepers, corrupt city politics, the " Continental " Sunday, and a high incidence of crime.

In Britain, Roman Catholicism did not have so many unsavory connotations, but was not to be brought beyond the most elementary steps in social policy. Manning found support for regulation of Sunday labor and that of women and children, but met stubborn resistance when he talked of limiting hours and setting minimum wages. In his later years Manning felt increasingly isolated from the leading laity, who took no interest in the social and political questions so close to his heart. By contrast he recalled his Anglican days when " I had only to lift up my hand and forty men sprang to my side." [20] Looking back two generations, he wrote:

" All the great works of charity in England have had their beginning out [side] of the Roman Catholic Church; for instance, the abolition of the slave trade and of slavery; and the persevering protest of the Anti-Slavery Society. Not a Catholic name so far as I know shared in this. France, Portugal, and Brazil have been secretly or openly slave-trading or, till even now, slave-holding. It was a Quaker that made Fr. Matthew a total abstainer. Catholic Ireland and the Catholics of England, until now, have done little for temperance. The Anglican and Dissenting ministers are far more numerously total abstainers than our priests. . . . The Acts to protect children from cruelty were the work of Dissenters. . . . So again in the uprising against the horrible depravity which destroys young girls — multitudes of ours — I was literally denounced by Catholics, not one came forward. . . . There are endless works for the protection of shop assistants, overworked railway and tram men, women and children ground down by sweaters, and driven by starvation wage upon the streets. Not one of the works in their behalf were started by us, hardly a Catholic name is to be found on their reports." [21]

" All the great social and philanthropic reforms down to our own day were the work of nonconformists or Anglicans; but," Cardinal Manning added, " the names of Catholics, on the other hand, are to be found as opponents to almost every social movement or reform of the day." [22]

But while the humanitarian and philanthropic reforms of Evangelical Protestantism looked rather impressive beside the comparable Roman Catholic record, the activities of both systematically avoided any challenge to the economic structure in itself. At best they aided the disadvantaged individual within the assumptions of the competitive system. Most Christians doubtless supported this system on the general assumption of a providential harmony of egoistic enterprises, but there were other and grimmer theories abroad. The quarter century after the Civil

War was the age in America of the great influence of Darwin, Herbert Spencer, and Sumner, who were generally understood as demonstrating that society was destined to live on the principle, or lack of it, of Hobbes's state of nature. Darwin, Wallace, and Spencer had all come independently to the notion of the " survival of the fittest " from Malthusian studies into problems of population and economics. " Social Darwinism " was simply the return of the idea to social theory, whence it had started, with the added prestige of some analogous verifications in biology. The theory went through various stages of secularization. Spencer himself did not travel so far from his nonconformist background. Here was the source of his suspicion of the State, his defense of individual " rights," his faith in an automatic providential development to social perfection. And it was this last evolutionary optimism that brought peace to the troubled conscience of Andrew Carnegie and became a mainspring of the theology of Lyman Abbott. Spencer's disciple Sumner, however, although he had served briefly as an Episcopalian rector, pushed the philosophy of individualistic competition in a definitely antidemocratic and antihumanitarian direction. Similarly Justice Holmes carried Spencerian individualism to a position that at times sounded like Nietzsche in his repudiation of the higher law reference of pre-Civil War jurists. In many of his judicial decisions, to be sure, Holmes employed normative criteria which he refused to acknowledge in his theory of law. The influence of the general body of ideas urged by men like Holmes and Sumner, however, was toward the removal of all criteria except naked power, thus both anti-Christian and antidemocratic. As William Jennings Bryan prophesied of the *Descent of Man* in 1905, it would " weaken the cause of democracy and strengthen class pride and the power of wealth." [23] The American social scene, indeed, brutalized by the tremendous slaughter of the Civil War, and preoccupied with the ruthless exploitation of a continent, presented a living example of the theory of the survival of the most carnivorous. Social Darwinism had less to commend it to Christians than had Marxist Communism. And when capitalistic democracy was widely understood in these terms in the twentieth century, millions of exploited peoples, especially in colonial areas, would elect for Communism as morally superior.

2. The Solidaristic Tendency, 1890–1914

Not all the Protestants, however, were content with the individualistic humanitarian reforms of Evangelicalism. The year 1890 is the best date in round numbers, both in Britain and in America, for the rise to real influence of a new and more solidaristic social ethic. There had been notable pioneers, in Britain and in America, from before the middle of the century, and the '80's witnessed a very considerable number of rather scattered efforts at a new type of Christian social reform. About 1890 there was a consolidation of this social gospel movement. The Anglican " Church Social Union " appeared on both sides of the water, while the American " Church Association for the Advancement of the Interests of Labour " might be compared in some ways with the earlier British " Guild of St. Matthew." The American " Brotherhood of the Kingdom," surprisingly enough, was largely Baptist, while the American " Institute of Christian Sociology " was interdenominational. The whole movement was much stronger in Great Britain than in the United States, where it was largely confined to certain urban congregations in the Northeast.

The time lag between Britain and the United States was due in part to the higher degree of industrialization and urbanization in the former case, and to the psychological results of the American frontier. American reactions to the new economic and social distress were delayed by the continued predominance in the nation as a whole of the agrarian and small-town mentality. In Britain agriculture was virtually eliminated in the long crisis of the '70's and '80's. The general faith in laissez faire died then, as it was not to die in America until the Great Depression and the New Deal fifty years later. The British labor movement passed out of its " A.F. of L." state into " new unionism " and political organization forty years before the comparable developments in America. The social legislation of the labor-conscious liberals after 1905 was the British " New Deal," thirty years before Franklin Roosevelt. Paralleling these events occurred notable changes in the political and social thinking in the Churches, in which again it was the British who faced the problems first. We may glance at the Americans before considering the more advanced Englishmen.

The American social gospel was a form of liberal Evangelicalism. Its representative spokesmen were sons of individualistic Evangelicals and they retained in various degrees the fervor of their childhood faith. It was in large measure the Evangelical concern to save souls that plunged them into bitter experiences of economic and social distress and so prompted them to consider social reform. Ten years in an immigrant church near Hell's Kitchen in New York, for example, taught Walter Rauschenbusch that " Christian work " as conceived by pietistic Baptists was inadequately conceived. Henry George's mayoral campaign of 1886 wakened him to problems of social justice. In search of a social ethic, Rauschenbusch found no help in individualistic Evangelicalism. He turned to Bellamy, Tolstoi, Mazzini, and Ruskin, and garnered clues

for a social theory, but he still struggled long to relate the social program to Christian redemption. The unifying formulation, the "Kingdom of God," apparently came to him from Ritschlian literature in
1890, and he spent much of his time in Germany the following year on
the first draft of the book that was at length to establish him as the
chief spokesman of the new revelation, *Christianity and the Social
Crisis*. Even Ritschl's theological capacities, however, were unable to
fuse the idealistic moralism of the "Kingdom" with Evangelical doctrine, and among less sophisticated thinkers the divergence was more
apparent.

Washington Gladden drew more on indigenous sources, especially
the "progressive orthodoxy" of Bushnell, which was widely diffused
among American Congregationalists. Royce similarly furnished him
with a new message of community responsibility, the hope of the "so-
cialized individual." Another Congregationalist, George Herron, represents an extreme of ecclesiastical and political anarchism, based on
high faith in progress and the new era of the spirit, in which all the
oppressed and sufferers should be set free.

For Rauschenbusch a democratic, solidaristic structure was norma-
tively "Christian." Thus he rejoiced that four of the five major areas
of human common life were already successfully "Christianized" in
constitutional structure — the family, with new rights for women and
children; the Church, emancipated from clerical tyranny; education,
where methods were democratized; and, finally, the State, where all
men were free and equal before the law and shared in political responsibility. Only economic life was unchristian still, being organized on
the mainspring of avarice and with a most unjust distribution of economic power. And toward the Christianizing of this social and economic order Rauschenbusch recognized four promising movements —
co-operatives, the single-tax crusade, trade-unionism, and "socialism."
"God had to raise up socialism because the organized Church was too
blind." Viewing the whole, Rauschenbusch was confident. "The era
of prophetic and democratic Christianity," he wrote, "has just begun."
And so thoroughly did progress comprehend for him the whole activity
of God that he felt that the failure of this "social movement" would
impugn God's very existence. Yet devotional practice was stronger
than logic. Even apart from social progress, Rauschenbusch was in
prayer "conscious of touching God." He wrestled for years to establish
Biblical and theological bases for his democratic idealism.

The political content of the social gospel ethic was that of liberal
democracy now seriously wrestling with economic oligarchy. The
Marxist dogma of inevitable class warfare was not credited, but when

industrial conflict came, the social gospelers defended for labor the right to organize and to strike. The bureaucracy of State socialism was disliked, and business freedom was considered a moral value. Public ownership of natural monopolies was urged, on the other hand, and Government regulation of the great industrial empires. Protective labor legislation on the part of Government and profit sharing and co-operatives within industry were commended. Gladden's judgment on the "trusts" was proclaimed from the housetops when, as moderator of the National Council of Congregational Churches in 1905, he objected to a gift of one hundred thousand dollars from the president of Standard Oil as "tainted money."

Theologically considered, the difference from the ethic of individualistic Evangelicalism seemed slight at first. The characteristic left-wing Puritan and Evangelical demarcation of the spheres of natural reason and revelation was maintained. The continuity of tradition within the latter was unbroken. In the former sphere, that of State and society, the old assumption of the providential course of historical development endured more strongly than ever. Instead of leaving all to the mechanisms of survival of the "fittest," however, conscious shaping of society for humane goals was now conceived as part of the natural course of evolution on the human plane. Academic sociology in America was largely a by-product of this new recourse to reason for improving the structure of society. Henderson, Elwood, Ely, Commons, broke new paths in social science.

The new faith in social progress was so intense as to resemble the perfectionist millenarianism of the 1830's and 1840's. The realm of created nature, including man, was now invested with intrinsic tendencies to redemption and fulfillment, *independently* of grace through Christ. The moral idealism that should bring in the New Jerusalem was, to be sure, associated with the "teachings of Jesus" and "building the Kingdom of God." The very attempt to exploit Biblical ideas in this way, however, emasculated and moralized them, and instead of lending religious sanctions to social reform, confused and disintegrated the central Christian insights themselves. In practice, consequently, the old separation of nature and grace broke down, and a new faith in nature alone, in God immanent in nature and mankind generally, in evolution, in progress, increasingly dissolved and replaced the faith in special revelation, in redemption from sin and death. The process was gradual, largely unconscious, and very difficult to measure. From our historical perspective it now appears that the social gospel liberalism from the beginning was an unstable compound, predestined to early dissolution or absorption into something else. On the side of political and economic ethics, at least, it remained at the head of the movement of liberal democracy.

In Britain the leadership in Christian political and social thought if not action was taken from the 1870's by the Anglican Church. This was also the golden age of Free Church preaching, and one dare not slight the political and social activity of men like Dale, Paton, Chamberlain, or Hugh Price Hughes. But the Church of England was strongest among the classes with a tradition of service to the State. For the majority of Anglicans, no doubt, as for most Free Church Evangelicals, the role of Christianity was to inspire individuals to altruistic service to society. The forms this service should take would be defined by the problems themselves and the movements already in the field, on the assumption that the general structure and tendency were sound. Christian faith, sacraments, and community were resources for private individuals, but had no intrinsic relevance to social structure and purposes. And as in America, the general tendency was to identify the Kingdom of God with the full realization, in the not too distant future, of a peaceful and just democratic society. In contrast to Americans, however, or to British Free Churchmen, Anglicans were more prepared by long experience to accept the moral responsibilities of the State in industry, for example, and on the other hand were less naïve about the limitations of State action. While Britain and American Free Churchmen generally held to a naïve and increasingly irrelevant Lockian conception of the minimum policeman State, the great Anglican universities kept a vital tradition of the historic and organic ethical State from Burke, reinforced by T. H. Green with Hegelian elements. A man like Scott Holland, the chief animator of the Church Social Union, thus stood full in his Oxford tradition in urging legislation on industrial abuses for the good of the community.

The strongest social gospel organization on either side of the Atlantic was the Anglican " Church Social Union." Its leaders were university men and its work was largely educational, despite Henry Scott Holland's extensive knowledge of factory conditions, strikes, white lists, and the like. In addition to a long series of pamphlets on social and industrial issues, the C.S.U. published the *Economic Review* and from 1896 the *Commonwealth*. The Oxford branch was a chief source of literature and the center of influence on Anglican ordinands. In London and other cities the work was a matter of reading circles, lectures, sermons. By 1900 there was a membership of four thousand, and five years later the " Christianized Fabians " of the Church Social Union were at a peak of about six thousand. In America, with Bliss as traveling secretary, the Church Social Union reached over a thousand with its " progressive conservatism."

The Church Social Union was less effective in making any significant contact with, or effective impression upon, the labor movement. It did succeed, however, in convincing the Anglican hierarchy of its social responsibilities. The first two Lambeth Conferences, for example, in 1867 and 1878, had dealt only with specifically ecclesiastical problems. The restored Convocations and the new Congresses of the '50's and '60's confined themselves to education and temperance. In 1888, largely at Holland's prodding, Lambeth cautiously recognized the existence of social issues, but came to the conclusion that the best aid was " self-help." In 1897, however, the Lambeth bishops virtually adopted the Church Social Union manifesto, declaring that a " Christian community as a whole is responsible morally for the character of its own economic and social order." They suggested that social service committees should be established in every diocese.[24] By 1931 fourteen members of the Church Social Union had joined the bench of bishops. The Lambeth Conference of 1908 again worked over a Church Social Union agenda and affirmed a " living wage " as the " first charge " on any industry, a dangerously concrete proposal. And the famous Fifth Report of the Archbishop's Committee of Enquiry on Christianity and Industrial Problems (1918) was, as it were, the final matured fruit of thirty years of Church Social Union study and production. Since the First World War the Anglican bishops generally have been far in advance of the laity and lower clergy, and have included a few out-and-out agitators.[25]

The theological basis of this British social gospel was similar to that of the Americans, but kept more points of contact with a specific revelation and with a concrete historical community. The Anglicans tended to domesticate evolution in their " Incarnationalism " as the work of the Logos in all things. And among such Free Churchmen as Dale and Forsyth and Hughes, as well as among the Anglican followers of Maurice, there was a strong sense of the calling of the Christian Church to demonstrate its gospel by a peculiar community life and discipline even in political and social matters. Gore's primary concern, for example, was " the recovery of the idea of the Church as above all else ' the Way,' a visible symbol of the life of man as the Creator meant it to be lived." [26] And Stewart Headlam's little Guild of St. Matthew was conceived as a mission to make the Anglican clergy realize the democratic and social implications of a high conception of Church and sacraments. This current represented but a small minority before the First World War, but it colored the whole. America had nothing comparable in the way of a sense of the social significance of the Church itself as a pattern of regenerate humanity. The American Anglo-Catholics left social and political ethics to the liberal Evangelicals,[27] who conceived the

Church, on both sides of the Atlantic, as "the committee room of the Kingdom of God party."

The heyday came in the enthusiasm of the Liberal-Labor coalition in the decade before the First World War. The Church Socialist League now led the van, and Conrad Noel, its organizer, proclaimed that "Christianity is the religion of which socialism is the practice." [28] Noel was well known in every industrial area; no other clergyman was better known in the labor movement. Others like him appeared constantly on labor platforms. In 1909 came the first great demonstration in Trafalgar Square. Donaldson led a march of unemployed to London. In 1912, George Lansbury, then chairman, led a procession over Westminster Bridge to protest against the bishops' hesitation at taking the miners' side in the lockout. The group was soon torn apart, however, by political controversy within the socialist movement. Most were supporters of the Independent Labor Party, but there were points at issue between Fabians and Marxists. Then Hilaire Belloc's *The Servile State* converted many, and a considerable section rejected State socialism for guild socialism, a curious return to the original program of Maurice, Kingsley, and Ludlow. Theological tensions over churchmanship had also been increasing among the clerical leaders, and after the interval of the war, the old Church Socialist League split into three fragments in the postwar period.

The first dozen years of the twentieth century were the period when, in both Britain and America, the embodiment of the new sense of social responsibility passed from voluntary associations to official organs of ecclesiastical bodies. Hopkins has pointed out that the leadership in the '80's and '90's was primarily given by the Congregationalists (together with their offspring, the Unitarians) and the Episcopalians, the two Churches with the colonial tradition of an establishment and generations of responsibility for a class accustomed to political and cultural leadership. Congregationalists and Episcopalians were also the first to take official action toward incorporating new agencies for social service into their denominational structure. The Presbyterians actually beat them to it, being favored with the leadership of that "son of the Bowery," Charles Stelzle, the former machinist, who pioneered as a Church secretary in labor relations from 1903 to 1913. In 1910, the Congregationalists engaged Atkinson, and the Episcopalians Crouch, for similar work. In 1908, meanwhile, the Federal Council, representing some twenty denominations, took shape, adopting at once a statement of "Social Ideals" taken almost verbatim from the "Social Creed of Methodism" of that Church's new Department of Church and Labor. The first Federal Council Commission was designated for the Church and Social Service. Stelzle volunteered his services as secretary to this commission until, in 1911, it received a budget and secretary of its own.

In 1910 and 1911 the social concern of the American Churches was further stimulated. The great Bethlehem Steel strike of 1910 posed a challenge. On behalf of the new Federal Council, Stelzle studied the strike and issued a twenty-page report that startled the workmen and public alike with the vigor of its condemnation of the twelve-hour day and seven-day week. The evangelistic campaign of the " Men and Religion Forward Movement " the following year was dominated by the social concern. Stelzle was dean of its social service team and recommended co-ordinated social service groups in all the churches. Rauschenbusch told a conference that " the social gospel has now come to be one of the dogmas of the Christian faith." [29] Nearly all the denominations now fell into line with social service commissions and secretaries, including the Roman Catholics in 1911. Despite the views of Rauschenbusch's largely Baptist Brotherhood of the Kingdom, the Baptists and Methodists showed themselves more pietistic and less inclined to intervention in public affairs than the denominations organized earlier. All this new organization by no means meant general agreement by the rank and file in the churches, but it did argue that a social concern was officially conceded to be a possible legitimate interpretation of the faith.

In Britain the same institutional development had been taking place. The first of the Free Church " social service unions " was organized by Keeble among the Wesleyan Methodists in 1905. Paton was active in urging similar undertakings in the various Churches, and by 1911 the pattern was general. A new enterprise was undertaken together in that year, when the several denominational unions sent representatives to Birmingham where, under Bishop Gore's presidency, was organized the Interdenominational Conference of Social Service Unions (" I.C.S.S.U."). The I.C.S.S.U. organized common research and held a United Summer School nearly every year until 1925. Local councils were called into being and a Council of Christian Witness on Social Questions was devised to confer on the occasion of specific crises or problems. Anglicans and Free Churchmen worked together, and even for a time enjoyed the co-operation of Roman Catholics. The famous Conference on Politics, Economics, and Citizenship of 1924, which was to be the most important basis of the Stockholm World Conference on Life and Work of the following year, was the climax of I.C.S.S.U. preparation.

In comparison to Protestantism, the Roman Catholic interest in social issues had a relatively slow growth, about two decades later than such Protestant Churches as the Congregationalists, Episcopalians, or the Church of England. The famous "labor encyclical" of Leo XIII, *Rerum novarum,* came as a justification to Manning, Gibbons, Ireland, and Spalding in 1891, but one gains the impression that it was more sympathetically received in Britain and America by Protestants than by Roman Catholics. Lyman Abbott was enthusiastic, as was the *Andover Review.* In the Church Social Union *Economic Review,* Scott Holland noticed that Leo was not yet thinking in terms of such advanced industrialization as that in Britain and America. "A patriarchal simplicity is assumed throughout," he wrote. "It has nothing to do with the world in which we live; it is the voice of some old-world life, faint and ghostly, speaking in some antique tongue of things long ago." But while the main body of social Protestantism in Britain and America was at least as advanced as the school represented in *Rerum novarum,* for Anglo-American Catholics the most useful sections of the encyclical seemed to be those critical of socialism. The influence of Marxism in both Britain and America was negligible; the word was a conservative shibboleth. While the C.S.U. and C.A.I.L., the American Institute of Christian Sociology, the Brotherhood of the Kingdom, and similar groups were most active in the '90's in the formation of progressive opinion, Catholic public men boasted of their Church, with virtually no qualification, as a "great conservative force." John A. Ryan would still say in 1909 that on matters of social policy the bishops "who have made any pronouncements . . . could probably be counted on the fingers of one hand, while the priests who have done so are not more numerous proportionately." [30]

The tide of Anglo-American social Catholicism turned about 1908. At that time a new morale became apparent on both sides of the water. The Eucharistic Congress of 1908 apparently convinced British Roman Catholics of their own strength. Similarly the Missionary Congress in Chicago and the Eucharistic Congress in Montreal expressed a new vigor. Three years later came together the centennial of the Baltimore diocese and Cardinal Gibbons' jubilee. The American Church was now accounted of age. It was removed from control of Propaganda and turned loose with two new cardinals of its own. A new determination appeared in Catholic social action. In Britain, a Catholic Social Union had been stillborn in the '90's, and British Catholics were still generally absent from reform movements in the early twentieth century. But now the Catholic Truth Society began to publish an occasional pamphlet on social issues and individuals pressed for new ventures. Leslie Toke urged the organization of something as "intelligent and enthusiastic" as the *Sillon* (cf. pages 169 ff.). The young Jesuit Charles Plater urged workmen's study circles like the French and Belgian *cercles d'études* and retreats for workmen. He thought the German *Volksverein* the most remarkable organ of social education in the world. These two men became the leaders in the Catholic Social Guild, organized in 1909 as the pioneering body of British social Catholicism. The dominant social program was the " distributism " of Chesterton and Belloc. Plater was successful in bringing thousands of workmen to retreats every year and supplied a stream of articles on the methods of Continental social Catholicism. He carried the Guild with him into the I.C.S.S.U. and was active at several of the Union's summer schools and in planning sessions for Copec Rome forbade Catholic participation in the latter at the last minute.

In America, Peter Dietz was the chief organizer of social Catholicism, as John Ryan, the disciple of the Protestant economist Richard Ely, was the theorist. The first substantial support came from the midwestern German Catholic Central Verein from 1908. The Verein imported English Catholic Social Guild literature and found this its best material. Men were sent to Germany to study methods used there. Dietz launched the English section of the *Central-Blatt and Social Justice*. Impressed by Stelzle's methods, he organized the Roman Catholic " Militia of Christ " in the A. F. of L. The pattern of the Protestant social service commissions was adopted in 1911, when the American Federation of Catholic Charities set up a Social Service Commission under the chairmanship of Bishop Muldoon. The establishment of this program, in the opinion of *America,* marked " the general awakening of social conscience on the part of American Catholics." Bishop Muldoon was likewise to head the labor work of the National Catholic War Council. Postwar Catholic social action would be second to none in America.

One general contrast between this Anglo-American Roman Catholic social concern and that of the Protestants was the constant orientation of the former to expediency. In the Protestant discussion, positions were taken on issues on grounds of principle, of love and justice. All Catholic activities, by contrast, were constantly referred to the calculable effects on the position of the Church as an institution. In this instance, the Catholics got on the band wagon when the Protestants had proved it safe and even ecclesiastically profitable. In part this was because of the Catholic minority status and fear of criticism. Even deeper, however, was the attitude that always sets institutional advantage before principle, democratic or otherwise.

For Europeans, though not for Americans, the First World War killed that faith in automatic progress which had been the key to the social idealism of the preceding generation. Reckitt finds both their theology and their sociology judged by their complete failure to envisage the probability of war and to face its implications. Their error was "to regard war as a hideous and illogical interruption of the development of industrial civilization, rather than as an all too natural outcome of it, which is only by the most elaborate efforts to be forestalled while the moral and economic assumptions of that civilization remain unrepudiated and largely unrealized." [31] "It is but fair to remember," he continues, "that it is a great deal easier to see this now than it was then."

For a measure of the influence of the American social gospel one might leaf through the studies of the religion of American soldiers made during the First World War. To judge from these, the preaching of "social salvation" was still confined to a minority of Protestant pulpits and had not yet widely affected Christian education. For the bulk of the American soldiers, Protestantism meant pietistic Evangelicalism, with no essential modification of the prevailing individualist economic ethic. Salvation was strictly individual and primarily next-worldly. The social gospel had not yet gathered its harvest. Despite the efforts of men like Gladden, Ely, Rauschenbusch, the main body of American Protestants had swallowed the ambiguous lure of "free enterprise" and voted against Bryan for McKinley, the representative of the industrial oligarchy. The social gospel was an important element in the progressive movement behind Teddy Roosevelt and Wilson, and reached its climax after the First World War. At the end of our period the social gospel had at least put the older type of individualistic liberalism on the defensive in certain respects. And in any case liberal democracy in politics was taken for granted by both schools.

By way of summary of the political ethos of Puritan Protestantism in this period, we may again cite Kantorowicz. While directed specifically to England, his observations would hold for the Protestantism of the English-speaking world in general, and, with some modifications, for Switzerland, Holland, and Scandinavia:

"In England all parties are liberal, whatever they call themselves, and it is this which binds them all together in spite of everything. Everyone is liberal, in the first place, in the sense that the freedom of the individual must be protected against the authority of an irresponsible executive. Thus every Englishman, the king not excepted, is a republican at heart. . . . Liberalism, rather than democracy, also lies behind the rule of the majority. No one is a democrat in the sense that the majority could decide whatever it pleased. . . . The will of the state finds its limits in the inalienable rights of the individual. . . . And everyone is liberal, in the third place, in the sense that the state is to leave the individual to himself so far as possible in economic and spiritual affairs. On the degree of this possibility, to be sure, opinions do differ widely. Finally, almost everyone in England is an ethical relativist, believing in the free competition of ethical views and action, and that is the outlook appropriate to liberalism. For whoever believes he has absolute moral truth in his possession has the right, indeed the duty, to compel dissenters autocratically to his will. A practical relativism suffices, of course, which doubts that there is a criterion for establishing which of the many who claim it have discovered absolute value. This was precisely the Puritan position and modern political liberalism has developed out of the battles of these individualistic believers in revelation." [32]

Not merely was this Puritan Protestant ethic liberal democratic almost without qualification. It was also successful in far higher degree than any Roman Catholic or German Lutheran ethic. Kantorowicz contrasted the attitude of Anglicanism with that of French Catholicism and German Lutheranism as regards the First World War. The English, he argued, were the most Christian people of Europe in public policy.[33] The same superiority in moral influence was everywhere apparent in Puritan Protestantism. A series of European observers from Tocqueville to Bryce had been startled by the hold of Christian ethics on American political life in comparison with Catholic countries or German Lutheranism. At the time of the First World War, American life was more pervasively influenced by Christian ethics than was the case in any Continental power. The religion of millions, to be sure, meant some vague idea of God, immortality, a veneration for Jesus, and a respectable morality combined with indifference to, or impatience with, the Churches. Yet there was nowhere in the Puritan Protestant sphere of influence any such considerable segment of the people who had consciously broken with Christian morals as well as Christian faith as there was in every great Catholic country and in Germany. Puritan Protestantism, whatever its other failings, had humanized and moralized politics in absolute superiority to every other Christian tradition. And it had done so on the program of liberal democracy.

VI

ROMAN CATHOLIC DEMOCRACY
UNDER LEO XIII AND PIUS X

❖ ❖ ❖

THE long generation and a half of world peace (relatively speaking) that preceded the First World War was substantially comprised within the reigns of the two popes of our chapter title. For the Catholic Church it was a period that began in the doldrums of the senility of Pius IX, reached new and unexpected triumphs in the long reign of Leo XIII, and ended again in weakness and savage internal conflict under Pius X.

Pius IX lived seven years after the Vatican Council of 1870. He was an embittered refugee monarch, breathing forth diatribes from his self-elected Vatican " prison " against the kingdom of Italy and all liberalism, and attempting to rouse foreign Catholics to avenge him by war on the Italian State. He had become a die-hard monarchical absolutist, a survivor of the old Metternichian age, with only wrath and contempt for the political currents dominant in all the major states of Western civilization. Any attempt by Roman Catholics to accommodate themselves to progress and civilization " as lately introduced " was more hateful to him than actual revolutionaries or the leaders of the Paris Commune of 1871. " I have always condemned liberal Catholicism," he told a French deputation in 1871, " and I would condemn it forty times more if necessary." [1]

The result of this papal policy was that by the end of the '70's the Roman Church was launched in a Kulturkampf ("battle for civilization") with France, Italy, and Germany, while its influence on State and culture was at a minimum. Western civilization was not to be anathematized back into the age of Innocent III. As Czacki observed, " we condemn the separation of the Church from the State, but we are running the risk of separating the Church from society." [2] And Manning was deeply depressed by the stagnation to be found in the papal court, with the pope " old and garrulous "· " Six years have passed over the Holy See since 1870 and its organization has been dying out year after year. . . . Are we to shut ourselves in like Noah and wait? Or are we to act upon the world?" But by 1883 he was happy to observe a change. The "Abstentionists" were still dominant among the cardinals, but were increasingly recognizing the futility of their policy. "They see too that the past can never come back; that the temporal power may come but under new conditions; that the old dynastic world is dying out, and a new world of the peoples is coming in." [3]

A new wind had blown through the fossilized papal court with the accession to the throne of Leo XIII, a vigorous administrator and able diplomat. This accession marks a third notable stage in the accommodation of Roman Catholicism, at least in part, to liberal democracy. As we have seen, the Belgians first astonished the Catholic world by accepting constitutionalism and its civil liberties as recommended by Lamennais in 1831. They had some admirers, chiefly laymen, in France and the Rhinelands, in the following two decades, and at the Revolution of 1848 the second stage of Roman Catholic adjustment can be noted. A significant section of the episcopate in France, Holland, and Germany committed themselves cautiously to the external forms (at least) of political liberalism. And now, in the last quarter of the nineteenth century, the absolutist affiliation of the Roman court itself was qualified. Leo XIII was the first pope to develop and carry out a policy of friendly co-operation with republican and democratic parties and governments as well as with monarchist traditionalists. To justify this policy he developed a body of political and social theory in his encyclicals which is much studied today in the democratic countries, if not in the old-fashioned reactionary Roman Catholic strata of Spain and Latin America. We must outline both the theory of Leo's encyclicals and the practice of his administration. Then we may treat more briefly the policies of Pius X, his successor.

1. Political Thought and Action Under Leo XIII

The dominant motive of Leo's diplomacy for a quarter of a century was the recovery of the papal territories from the kingdom of Italy. The stream of protests from the Vatican against Italy did not weaken, nor did Leo during his quarter century of rule relax the prohibition on Roman Catholic participation in national Italian politics. He schemed and intrigued in Paris, Vienna, and Berlin through a series of war scares to build up alliances that would force the kingdom of Italy to cede him the former lands of the pope-king. This pressure was one of the major factors that led Italy to enter the Triple Alliance in 1881 in order to have some international security. And into the twentieth century the Government of Italy viewed all papal diplomacy with a well-grounded mistrust. It was these activities that cost the papacy a seat in the peace conferences at the end of the First World War.

This intransigence of Leo with regard to the Roman question and to Italy, while it failed completely of its primary aim, greatly strengthened the position of the papacy in other respects. The mere fact of the loss of the papal states aroused great sympathy among the Catholics of the world for the " prisoner of the Vatican." The sympathy was rather unnecessary, to tell the truth, for the papacy was not being persecuted, but it served to revive an income from Peter's pence which was soon greater than the papacy had formerly received from its territories. Morally, also, the papacy gained. When Leo addressed himself to public and ethical issues, he won more of a hearing generally than any previous Counter Reformation pope, for he had fewer private axes to grind than any of his predecessors. No longer was he the king of central Italy, with the political and international interests and affinities of such a statesman. As " prisoner of the Vatican," living on the gifts of Roman Catholics of many nations, Leo developed an unprecedented reputation for political disinterestedness and neutrality. This reputation was heightened by the very intensity of his one pre-eminent political ambition, for to prevail against Italy he needed allies, and it was to his private political interest as well as to the moral advantage of the Catholic Church for Leo to be friendly with States and societies outside Italy that were caught up on the stream of " progress, liberalism, and civilization as lately introduced."

For the first time in generations the papal court really thought in terms of international Catholicism and partially broke out of the hitherto regnant provincialism of Italian, Spanish, and Austrian conservative tradition. Leo set out at once to make his peace with the new Hohenzollern empire and to negotiate away the Kulturkampf with Bismarck. Quietly, at first, but steadily, his nuncio labored in France to cultivate the anticlerical leaders of the Third Republic and to dissolve the alliance of the Roman Catholics with the pretender Comte de Chambord. Similarly Leo gave Archbishop Gibbons unprecedented liberties in accommodating Romanism to American conditions, and was deeply impressed by the vistas opened to him by Gibbons and Manning of the future of Roman Catholicism in the liberal democratic English-speaking world. Leo also wooed the Eastern Uniats with concessions as to their liturgies, institutions, and married priests, provided only they would hold to Roman doctrine and jurisdiction. Leo had learned much as a nuncio in Brussels in the 1840's of the possibilities for Rome in using the new constitutional liberties, and his policy was to be pointed as much to the situation of Roman Catholics in countries like

Germany, Holland, Belgium, Britain, and the United States, as to the old " Catholic countries " like Spain and Italy whose traditions alone had seemed normative to his predecessors. Or rather the clerical police State of the Restoration and the Syllabus was still the norm, but in tactics and policy Leo was ready to make all sorts of expedient arrangements on the " hypothesis " of Dupanloup's famous argument. At the beginning of his pontificate Leo declared, " I desire that modern society should end by reconciling itself sooner or later to the Syllabus, by understanding all its aims." [4] And the tactic was, by using the liberties of liberal democracy, to end them.

In his own political theory the pope was apparently accustomed to the tradition of conservative absolutism dominant in Roman Catholicism through the nineteenth century. This conception of the nature of political authority was closely akin to that of Hegel and Lutheran monarchism. As we shall see later, Leo's social theory also found its closest counterpart with that of Bismarck and the largely Lutheran Hohenzollern empire. " In that encyclical which begins *Diuturnum* [1881]," wrote Leo, " we describe the ideal of political government conformed to the principles of Christian wisdom." According to Catholic doctrine, says *Diuturnum,* a people may choose whatever form of government they prefer so long as justice is respected. In certain cases, consequently, it is in the power of the people to choose who shall be placed over the State. The right of government, however, is not thereby delegated by the people, nor can it be revoked by the will of the people, as in liberal democracy. The example of the election of a pope makes this clear. " The ruler is designated but the rights of ruling are not thereby conferred. Nor is the authority delegated to him." [5] The authority comes from God and not from the people, and rulers hold it not as a trust from the people, but " as their own," beyond revocation by the people. It thus appears that the statement that people may choose their own form of government is subject to some limitations. As good Catholics, they could not choose one form, government responsible to the people. Congratulations came to Leo for the soundness of this encyclical, from the czar of Russia, the German Kaiser, Emperor Leopold of Austria, and, curiously, the French Government. [6]

When it was brought to Leo's attention that in this recapitulation of the dominant Roman Catholic conservatism of the nineteenth century he had apparently ruled out Suárez' version of popular sovereignty, he is reported to have made amends in a private conversation. He had not meant to reject any Catholic opinion, and apparently had not realized that there was a Roman Catholic school of popular sovereignty and delegated authority. He meant to condemn only those who held that political authority in no way originates in God, but from human wills. Just what Leo's better-informed views on this point were is still debated. The neo-Suárezians have tried to rescue both Leo and Thomas Aquinas from the absolutism defended by the main tradition of the nineteenth century Roman Catholic political theorists.[7] With a certain plaintive note Ryan and Boland object, " It is quite unfair and unscientific to read into two isolated sentences a condemnation of a doctrine which was taught by the great majority of Catholic moralists and jurists for upwards of seven [sic] centuries."[8] If we are to suppose that Leo might have wished later (had he not been so infallible) that he had so phrased *Diuturnum illud* as to leave room for the Suárezian version of popular sovereignty, we must do so in the face of the exegesis of his successor, Pius X, who, as we shall see later, leaves no ambiguities in his own assertion of the Roman Catholic decision for irresponsible authority in political life.

With this note taken of the homage paid by Leo to the " thesis " of absolutism, we may turn to the " hypothesis," his concessions to responsible democratic government, as in France and the United States. In France the great majority of episcopate and leading laity remained monarchists, and by their hostility to the Third Republic had provoked it to anticlerical legislation, especially with regard to the schools. Leo's nuncio, Czacki, had the assignment of convincing the legitimists that the Holy See considered their cause lost, and tried to bargain with Gambetta for terms on which the French hierarchy might be ordered to become supporters of the Republic. Cardinal Pie, according to his friends, was killed by the silence Leo imposed on him. He had been through the '70's chief counselor of the Bourbon pretender in the latter's mystical absolutism. When the latter heard of the papal line he, too, saw it as a mortal blow. " I thought that the Church forbade suicide! " But most of Leo's maneuvers with the politicians were behind the scenes, while in his episcopal appointments he tried to change gradually the die-hard political cast of the French hierarchy. He asked the statesmen, if they had complaints to make, to make them to him. Thus he might possibly both strengthen his absolutism within the Church and win concessions from the State.

In the latter half of the '80's Leo's encyclicals *Immortale Dei* and *Libertas humana* continued the development of his " hypothesis " tactic. We must return to them with regard to civil liberties, but here we may note Leo's prodding of Roman Catholics toward accepting democratic patterns where they seemed expedient. He repeats his thesis of *Diuturnum illud* that " no one of the several forms of government is in itself condemned," and adds, " neither is it blameworthy in itself, in any manner, for the people to have a share, greater or less, in the government; for at certain times, and under certain laws, such participation may not only be of benefit to the citizens, but may even be of obligation." [9] " Again, it is not of itself wrong to prefer a democratic form of government, if only the Catholic doctrine be maintained as to the origin and exercise of power." [10] " In matters merely political, as for instance the best form of government, and this or that system of administration, a difference of opinion is lawful." [11]

But this was indifferentism on one of the essential dogmas of French Catholicism. At the next chance of overthrowing the Republic, General Boulanger's projected *coup d'état* three or four years later, the French Catholics rallied overwhelmingly to the party of the would-be dictator, as they had a generation before at the *Putsch* of Louis Napoleon. The undignified collapse of the " Man on Horseback," however, gave Leo another opportunity to press his policy of reconciliation. The most distinguished French prelate was the patron of African missions, Cardinal Lavigerie, who fifteen years before had urged the Bourbon pretender de Chambord to attempt a coup. " There will be a street fight in some towns: but it will serve your cause and last but a day." [12] Leo now put the cardinal under orders to urge a definite Roman Catholic adhesion to the Third Republic. The result was Lavigerie's famous " Algiers toast " of 1890 to the Republic, which froze up most of the sources of contribution to his mission work. And as the pope found the bulk of French Catholics inclined to the policy of a mere armistice with the Republic, he released at last his strongest word on the subject, the encyclical *Au milieu des sollicitudes* (1892). " Whatever be the form of civil power in a nation, it cannot be considered so definitive as to have the right to remain immutable, even though such were the intention." Revolutions occur in history and " social need justifies the creation and the existence of new governments, whatever form they take; Civil power considered as such is from God. . . . Consequently, when governments representing this immutable power are constituted, their acceptance is not only permissible, but even obligatory." [13]

We may observe that in the very act of declaring himself most emphatically in favor of the democratic republic, Leo had betrayed his profound contempt of the whole spirit of the democratic process. The best analogy would be one of those directives from the Comintern, requiring all good comrades to adhere to some " united front." When Leo counseled Roman Catholics that they might accept a democratic form of government, what he really meant was that they might observe the formalities of ballots and parliaments in the sense in which these are observed in Soviet " democracy." In sharp contrast to Puritan State and society based on the consciences of private men, for Leo "the civil wisdom of private persons seems to consist entirely in the loyal execution of the precepts of lawful authority." [14] Having given their consent, if only tacitly, to certain rulers, citizens are expected to obey, not to contribute to the determination of policy. In particular, "the faithful should accept religiously as their rule of conduct the political wisdom of ecclesiastical authority." [15] The Catholic citizen, like the Soviet citizen, is expected to acclaim a party line, and in this procedure he is free, if he desires, to utilize certain "democratic" formalities. The Roman Political Committee, the bishops and the pope, are to be obeyed even when unrighteous. "Subjects are to be warned that they shall not arrogantly judge the life of their superiors; even should it be their lot to see such superiors acting blameworthily. . . . Should such superiors really have committed blamable actions, their inferiors, full of the fear of God, must not judge them, even in the mental blame, except in a perpetual spirit of respect and submission. The actions of superiors are not to be touched by the sword of speech even when they seem to deserve a righteous rebuke." [16] Without qualification Leo thus repeats the political maxims of Gregory the Great as advice to modern Catholics with regard to their political bosses, the bishops.

Perhaps the ultimate touchstone of the democratic character of a political theory is the way that most delicate point, the right of revolution, is handled. Anglo-American liberal democracy has tried to hedge revolution about with various safeguards and safety valves, but it has always held that in the last analysis and when all other means have failed private citizens are justified in taking up arms in the name of higher law against established rulers and authority. Human rights have precedence over State's rights or property rights, justice over prerogative and technical legality. Only if the ultimate sanction of force be permitted, can the appeal to the higher law from established injustices be made effective. And so the Anglo-American liberal tradition had maintained that effective respect for the moral law of nature which the Roman Catholic States had largely lost.

On this touchstone Leo ruled out democracy for Roman Catholics. "If it happen at any time," he ruled, "that the power of the State is rashly and tyrannically wielded by princes, the teaching of the Catholic Church does not allow an insurrection on private authority against them, lest public order be only the more disturbed, and lest society take greater hurt therefrom." [17] Leo's position was thus essentially Lutheran conservatism. To the signers of the American Declaration of Independence he would rather have counseled "the merits of Christian patience and earnest prayer to God." As models Leo praised the early martyrs, who died unresistingly rather " than oppose the public authority by means of sedition and tumult." Even under persecution, " they were so far from doing anything seditious or despising the imperial majesty " that " they had no thought of resistance " and " at no time omitted to conduct themselves obediently and submissively." [18] Similarly, he observed that while many Christian slaves passively resisted the law at the command of the Church, " history has no case to show of Christian slaves for any other cause setting themselves in opposition to their masters, or joining in conspiracy against the State." [19] And to the Irish revolutionaries of the 1880's, Leo gave repeated warning against violence.[20] Catholics appealed to medieval justifications of resistance to tyrants, but Leo's ruling was that that right of active resistance to tyranny is today " dormant." The Catholic hierarchy itself, of course, can at any time summon Catholics to take up arms for the sake of the law of God and nature as interpreted by the hierarchy.

When we turn from the issues of the democratic constitution of states and of responsible government to its corollaries in the separation of Church and State and the maintenance of civil and religious liberties, we find again that Leo displays the same contrast of " thesis " and " hypothesis." Here was the focus of much of the Roman Catholic opposition to liberal democratic constitutions all through the nineteenth century. Liberal democracy requires that the Catholic hierarchy renounce some of the political functions which they exercise in canon law under the Syllabus. And it concedes to other religious groups than the Roman hierarchy equal rights to worship, propaganda, and education. Roman Catholics had gravely doubted whether they could conscientiously take an oath to the Belgian constitution in the 1830's, or the Sardinian from 1848, and here the Catholic-royalist case against reconciliation with the Third French Republic found perhaps its most telling argument for Roman Catholics.

On these issues Leo set forth thesis and hypothesis especially in *Immortale Dei* and *Libertas humana*. In them he made it clear that his most fundamental objection to the modern democratic state was that it refused on principle to respect the Roman claim to have a monopoly of truth, and to have a directive and veto power on political actions. The great fault of liberal democracy was " the rejection of the holy and august authority of the Church, which presides in the name of God over the human race." " States have been constituted without any count at all of God or of the order established by him." [21] On the contrary, the State must " act up to the manifold and weighty duties linking it to God, by the public profession of religion," as is evident to natural reason. " It is a sin in the State not to have any care for religion, as if this were something beyond its scope, or of no practical benefit; or else out of many forms of religion to adopt that one which chimes in with its fancy." [22] It is one of the first obligations of all States consequently to give official privileged status to the Roman Catholic hierarchy, since, as "is evident," this religion alone is established of God, the others being human inventions. First principles thus laid down, Leo proceeds to the hypothesis: "The Church indeed deems it unlawful to place various forms of divine worship on the same footing as the true religion, but does not, on that account, condemn those rulers who for the sake of securing some great good, or of hindering some great evil, tolerate in practice that these various forms of religion have a place in the State." [23] Even this concession seems to fall far short of the liberal democratic principle of separation, and, rather, to sanction, under extenuating circumstances, the system of toleration and conjoint establishments as found in Germany or France under the Napoleonic Concordat. Separation as embodied in American fundamental law would not even come under Leo's hypothesis, once Roman Catholics were in a position to abrogate it.

Corollary to the separation of Church and State are the civil and religious liberties of various democratic constitutions and bills of rights. With reference to such liberties Leo reaffirmed specifically the condemnations of *Mirari vos* and the Syllabus. Liberty of worship, of conscience, of thought, of the press, are all contrary to the Catholic doctrine of society.[24] "If unbridled license of speech and of writing be granted to all, nothing will remain sacred and inviolate. . . . A like judgment must be passed upon what is called liberty of teaching . . . which the State cannot grant without failing in its duty." [25] Leo does not merely mean here to rule out pornography or incitation to violent revolution, as would be done by those liberal democratic States that insist on civil and religious liberty. Leo means that no Catholic can consider ideal any State that does not by law enforce the thought police of the Inquisition and Index. The papal critique of the Bill of Rights is not concerned merely to protect public morals and public safety; it includes a demand for the suppression of all sorts of political, historical, and philosophical opinions and facts that the Roman hierarchy regards as unedifying or, by its own private criteria, untrue. A Catholic State in short could never admit the democratic process on any of the wide and elastic range of issues on which the hierarchy has a principle or an interest, temporary or permanent. On these issues citizens could not be allowed either to know all the facts, or the various opinions proposed, or to express their own judgments, save when the last coincided with those of the hierarchy. We shall have occasion later to notice some of the devices by which the Roman hierarchy can in practice abrogate a bill of rights even when it remains the law of the land.

But again, once the principles of a Romanized society are laid down, Leo has a hypothesis: While " it is quite unlawful to demand, to defend, to grant unconditional freedom of thought, of speech, of writing, of worship, *as if these were so many rights given by nature to man* . . . , it likewise follows that freedom in these things may be tolerated where there is just cause, but only with such moderation as will prevent its degenerating into license and excess." [26]

Leo's concessions and adjustments to democracy, as we have traced them, were primarily shaped by his desire to cultivate the Third French Republic. But in these decades the tremendous post-Civil-War immigration of Roman Catholics into the United States was taking place, and soon the number of practicing Catholics in the United States was greater than that in France. These American Roman Catholics had apparently accommodated themselves thoroughly in political matters to the Puritan democracy in which they had settled. With an occasional exception, such as their self-appointed intellectual leader Brownson, the American Catholics were republicans and democrats by conviction. To the minority of French Catholics who were similarly inclined, consequently, American Catholicism was a working demonstration, just as the Belgian Catholics had been to the French liberal Catholic pioneers of the days of Louis Philippe. Thus it happened that French Catholic democrats of the 1890's became involved in " Americanism," which was as much a French as an American heresy. It was the heresy of those French and Americans who took a little too enthusiastically Leo's " hypotheses " in the direction of democracy.

Leo had developed a particular interest in this startling Roman Catholic growth in the United States. Many of the officials of the court were somewhat scandalized by " the pope's Americanism." The democracy of these traditionless Americans, their positive acceptance of the separation of Church and State, seemed to most to be matters that needed correction. " This people aroused a feeling of bewilderment, if not also of fear, among many in Rome." Even their patron, Prefect Simeoni of Propaganda, was " not quite sure of them." But Leo, who took the long view, was rather indulgent to Gibbons' audacious oration in Rome in 1887, on the advantages of the American separation of Church and State over European establishments, as well as with his readiness to cooperate with heretical Protestants. Leo was in particular profoundly impressed by the contention Gibbons and Manning both urged, that the " Church has no longer to deal with parliaments and princes, but with the masses and with the people." [27]

In certain respects, however, Leo found it necessary to rebuke Gibbons gently. The archbishop had always opposed the sending to America of a resident apostolic delegate. He feared that such a move would be widely understood as an entering wedge for full diplomatic relations between the Vatican and the American Government. Such relations, he considered, were incompatible with the constitutional separation of Church and State. Leo overruled him, however, and the majority of the American episcopate, and sent Satolli as apostolic delegate in 1893, without raising the issue of diplomatic accreditation. And two years later he set up a caveat against the views of the American liberal Catholics led by Gibbons. Leo conceded that the American Roman Catholic Church " unopposed by the Constitution and government of your nation, fettered by no hostile legislation, protected against violence by the common laws and the impartiality of the tribunals, is free to live and act without hindrance. Yet, though all this is true, it would be very erroneous to draw the conclusion that in America is to be sought the type of the most desirable status of the Church, or that it would be universally lawful or expedient for State and Church to be, as in America, dissevered and divorced." [28] While Gibbons had held that if he could change the American Constitution, he would not alter a word, Leo would prefer privilege for the Roman Catholic Church before the American fundamental law. The Roman Church in America, he continued, " would bring forth more abundant fruits if, in addition to liberty, it enjoyed the favor of the laws and the patronage of the public authority." [28] Leo was serving notice that it was the program of the Roman Church to win a political and social authority for the Roman hierarchy in the United States which was incompatible with the Constitution as it stood, and with the liberties for which America was a symbol.

We have traced the policy and doctrine of the Roman court toward political democracy through the first half of Leo's reign. This policy has been analyzed in three aspects: first, the policy toward responsible democratic government; second, that degree of separation of Church and State which leaves the democratic process free of arbitrary clerical intervention; third, the civil and religious liberties which are a condition of government by discussion. There were still important doctrinal definitions to be made by Leo on these matters, most significantly in *Graves de communi* (1902). And Pius X likewise was still to lay down some highly important definitions of the Roman Catholic attitude to liberal democracy. But these developments will be better understood if one or two related aspects of the whole social and political practice of the Church are first dealt with.

We may first delay briefly to notice how the canonical theories of the rights of the hierarchy to control the political decisions of Roman Catholics worked out in some concrete instances. With regard to certain problems, such as education and marriage legislation, the Church claimed jurisdiction on principle. In Leo's reign there were bitter conflicts over the control of education in Belgium, France, Germany, Italy, and even the United States. As we have had occasion to observe earlier, the Roman Church had shown no enthusiasm for the education of the common people until other agencies began to provide it. Left to its own devices and without an educational rival, Roman Catholicism historically had always tended to a minimum of education for the lower classes. They are easier to control when they are ignorant and simple. Only when first Protestantism and then liberal democracy pressed for a fuller development of each person did Roman Catholicism, in self-defense, become concerned. Rome delayed general education in Catholic countries like Belgium, Italy, and Spain far behind the Protestant peoples. And it fought any suggestion that the State, as representing the interests of the community, had any right to teach the young. In most countries, of course, a public-school system was inaugurated sooner or later, to do what the Roman Church had not done but still claimed was its exclusive right to do. The Church everywhere continued the struggle, attempting on the one hand to penetrate and control the public-school system, and on the other to build a confessional school system wherein Catholic children could be reared in insulation from dangerous thoughts. The whole Catholic population was regularly put under penalty of ecclesiastical discipline to support Church schools financially and to send children only to them. Policy in this area was quite beyond the scope of laymen. There is some evidence, for example in the United States, that the whole parochial school program was forced down the throat of the laity. A democratic decision would probably have led to a very different outcome and possibly a much more extensive amount of teaching of religion in the public schools than is now the case.

The range of issues on which a Catholic discovers his own opinion from the bishop's pastorals is seen to be indefinitely elastic when we observe the bargains struck in politics. A notorious illustration here is seen in the action of the Catholic Center Party in Germany at the time of Bismarck's pressure for military appropriations. Leo bargained with the chancellor, offering the Catholic vote for the appropriations in return for the removal of some of the Kulturkampf legislation. Beyond the deal in hand over the May laws, Leo wished to cultivate the gratitude of the German emperor for possible future support toward remedying his own territorial situation in Italy.[29] Put more generally,

Catholics have perfect freedom to make up their own minds on purely "political" matters, but almost any purely "political" matter can cease to be such overnight as the hierarchy discovers a direct or indirect interest in it. The Catholic citizen can never determine the scope of his own independence; only the hierarchy can say how far the interests of the Church extend into what would seem to the uninformed eye to be "purely political" matters. This type of bargaining became the settled strategy of the Center Party in the decades before the First World War, and it is also familiar in municipal and state politics in the United States. Such local and recurrent manipulation of the democratic process by episcopal bosses is even more corrupting to democracy than the more conspicuous instances of Vatican intervention in national affairs.

The contrast between the methods of liberal democracy on the one hand and canon law on the other may be seen in two famous controversies of the 1880's in the United States. This decade saw two striking social developments, the very rapid expansion of trade-unionism in the Knights of Labor, and the propaganda, especially around New York City, of Henry George's single tax on land rents. Here were two issues of social policy that were of particular concern to the American Catholics. How were they to be settled? The upholders of Roman methods in the hierarchy, led by McQuaid and Corrigan, demanded that the hierarchy simply deliver ukases and enforce them on Catholics by ecclesiastical discipline. The Catholic democrats, led by Gibbons, Ireland, and Keane, urged that the condemnation by the Index of *Progress and Poverty,* or of the Knights of Labor by the Inquisition, or the severe discipline of Father McGlynn, George's clerical supporter, would all seem to American Catholics and the American public generally an unwarranted short-circuiting of democracy.

The Canadian hierarchy had already condemned the Knights of Labor for Canadian Catholics, and the Inquisition had sustained them. The American President Cleveland, however, was opposed to repression of trade-unionism. Gibbons feared that this condemnation would show that the Roman Church was less American and less just than the Government, and that since it would be largely disregarded, it would in any case only injure the authority and prestige of the hierarchy. " In our age and in our country obedience cannot be blind. . . . Condemnation would be considered both false and unjust and therefore not binding." [30] He also pointed out that Peter's pence would be affected. Rome had presented a stone wall at first, but, apparently at Leo's personal intervention, reversed the Inquisition decision, to the amazement of the Catholic world. And similarly, with Manning's support, Gibbons managed to hold off the Indexing of Henry George. Not that either Manning or Gibbons were single taxers; both considered the scheme impracticable and unsound. But Gibbons did not think it was wise for prelates to intervene authoritatively in the free determination of economic and social policy. He trusted the American democratic process to find the weaknesses of George's proposals. Gibbons recognized that Corrigan was quite within his canonical rights as a Catholic bishop, and the Canadian prelates likewise, in the several condemnations. It was an issue, not of rights in Roman canon laws, but of policy. The hierarchy had the canonical rights to forbid all Catholics to join trade-unions, or the Odd Fellows, the Knights of Pythias, and all the rest of the fraternal societies. But Gibbons saw that if Roman Catholics were to be in any sense politically democratic, the hierarchy would have to restrain itself voluntarily from exercising many of its prerogatives in canon law. He did his best to establish such a tradition of reducing episcopal adventures in political authoritarianism to a minimum. Unfortunately the American hierarchy in the twentieth century was to abandon the democracy of Gibbons for the autocracy of McQuaid and Corrigan, and American democracy was to be faced with the problem of an unassimilable absolutist State within its society.

Besides France and the United States, the country should be mentioned in which Roman Catholicism first confronted the problem of adjusting to liberal constitutional government — Belgium. " The example of Belgium proves that in a Catholic and religious country, the clergy succeed, at the end of a longer or shorter time, in controlling the elections and consequently the government also." The chief political device that is unique to the Roman Church is, of course, the confessional. " The constitutional regime which has been developed in Protestant countries evidently suits them only: in a Catholic country confession spoils all its machinery, for it destroys the independence of electors, of representatives, of functionaries, and of the sovereign." [31] The Belgian hierarchy could threaten Leopold II with spiritual penalties through his confessor, and the bishops were disrespectful to him because he was not subservient. Absolution was refused to judges who refused to render the judicial decisions desired by the hierarchy. Parliamentary legislators were in the same vulnerable position, and in a Catholic population there is no such thing as a secret ballot. Priests would go electioneering for or against lists of candidates, especially with women voters, threatening them with spiritual penalties. And Leo, of course, advocated for the world-wide Catholic Church the practice of blackballing political leaders who were offensive to the hierarchy. " The Church cannot give either patronage or favor to the men at whose hands she knows only oppression, who in the broad day refuse to respect her rights, and who strive to tear asunder civil and sacred polity." [32]

At its very source, meanwhile, the democratic process was stifled by the exercise of censorship and the silencing of discussion. Much was done simply by forcing parents to send their children only to Church schools and colleges, where they could be kept in ignorance of many awkward truths and unsettling opinions. The means of political discussion could also be controlled by economic pressure. Absolution would be denied to all who subscribed to newspapers or periodicals that the bishops wished to punish. A café that subscribed to a disapproved journal might be denounced by name from the pulpit as a place of bad reputation. No good Catholics would dare patronize it thereafter, and the owner would soon discover that in a Catholic community his livelihood depended on subservience to the priests.

More frankly than the American prelates at this time, the Belgian episcopate indicated that it did not intend to exercise that self-restraint which was necessary to free a sphere of democratic self-government of imposed authority. In France and Belgium the hierarchy refused any such compromise; they meant to rule the State. One must submit to them or fight. But fighting political Catholicism, as it had been done in France, Spain, Italy, and Portugal, meant spreading Voltairian skepticism and weakening morality. Here was the tragic choice of Catholic countries, posed by the clerical lust to rule: to be priest-ridden or to be de-Christianized. " If the country preserves its faith like Belgium and Ireland, it will fall into the hands of the clergy. If it forsakes its faith, it will fall into anarchy, like Spain and Mexico." [33] The middle way of a free Christian society was possible only in Protestant societies. " Protestantism resting on free inquiry and individual interpretation [sic], the constitutional and representative regime is the political form which best suits the reformed nations. Catholicism realizing the ideal of an absolutist organization, absolutism is the natural constitution of Catholic nations. This is what Bossuet maintained, and he was right."

2. Catholic Social Ethics and Democracy

We have been considering the impact of Roman Catholic teaching and methods on politics, especially in relation to responsible representative government, to separation of Church and State, to civil liberties, to the determination of policy by discussion. But other issues came increasingly to the fore in the generation before the First World War. The crucial problems of internal governmental policy, as we have already seen in the dominantly Puritan Protestant Anglo-American world, were the unforeseen social consequences of the industrial revolution. Political democracy came to seem formal and irrelevant to the new laboring classes in the rapidly expanding urban concentrations, men whose lives and livelihoods were ruled despotically by the holders of absolute power in financial and industrial empires. It was due primarily to this situation that faith in political democracy lost its momentum in the generation before the First World War, and in the period between the World Wars yielded the initiative to the other movements. These nondemocratic movements with their new social policy must now occupy our attention. With regard to the Christian Churches we shall observe a startling reversal. Precisely those Churches that had most opposed liberal democracy, the Lutheran, Anglican, and Roman Catholic, now disclosed new possibilities of dealing with " the social problem," while Puritan Protestant Churches, which had best supported liberal democracy, were relatively uncertain and ineffective.

When we estimate Roman Catholicism from this perspective, we must distinguish various areas. American and British Roman Catholics, as we have already seen, were overwhelmingly capitalist individualists in social policy, and noticeably slower to respond to the ethical challenge of industrial society than were the Anglicans and even most of the Puritan Protestant denominations. In social as in political thought, these Catholics took their color from their Protestant environment and provided no important leadership or new initiatives. The same is true to a slightly less degree of the industrialized democratic countries of the " Catholic World," France and Belgium. Certain exceptions to the rule must be considered later, but in both these countries the great bulk of Catholic clergy and laity were capitalist individualists, and quite opposed to any major political intervention toward the solution of the social problem. Catholics in all these Western and democratic countries were generally devotees of that same " gospel of wealth " we have already characterized in relation to American Protestantism.

There were other Catholic countries, such as Spain, Latin America, and Poland, that were neither democratic nor industrialized and hence do not concern us here. The phenomena that interest us arise out of the industrialization of nondemocratic societies, and here the prime instance is Germany, and to some degree Austria. A few decades later Russia and Japan were to provide further illustrations. In all these cases the authoritarian bureaucratic system of modern industry was imposed on peoples long accustomed to absolutism, and touched by neither the aspirations nor the disciplines of liberal democracy. In certain respects the authoritarian political traditions proved more resourceful in dealing with the social problems of industrialization. We can observe a return movement from these countries. Modern industry had been created in the democratic Puritan Protestant West and moved from there out to non-Protestant and nondemocratic societies. Some of the political and social devices elaborated in the nondemocratic countries then made their way back into the lands where the technology and its social consequences had first appeared. The Nazi and Soviet programs of the twentieth century may be seen as a violent climax of this countermovement from industrialized nondemocratic societies.

In terms of social classes this new counterdemocratic offensive may be partly seen as the result of a political alliance of the old landed aristocracy with the new urban proletariate against the middle class of industry and finance. Such a league often seemed indicated by class interests. Both might find a certain plausibility in the Marxian theory that liberal democracy was merely the "ideology" of the middle class. And at any rate, as we have already observed in the case of the Anglican gentry, the landowner was often readier to hear the cries of injustice from industrial workers, and come to their assistance, just because his own interests were not involved as were those of the Puritan Protestant businessman or banker. Very similar ventures were undertaken by Lutheran and Catholic aristocrats on the Continent in the same generation. Let us begin with Germany, our prime instance, and with the Lutherans.

Politically the Hohenzollern empire was an authoritarian monarchy, akin to the Hapsburg dual monarchy, or to Romanov Russia. Liberal democracy was a distant and distasteful rumor in all these empires. Yet first of all the powers of Europe to deal positively with the social problem for the benefit of the working classes was antidemocratic Germany. And the venture was conceived as based on Christian ethics and the long tradition of the house of Prussia. Bismarck would have preferred to describe his policy as that of the "Christian State." He consciously opposed it to laissez faire, and the Manchester school of social thought, which meant "the abandonment of the weak to their own resources and to private help." He recalled the social and economic policy of Frederick the Great, who liked to call himself "the poor man's king," and he hoped to accomplish for the new factory workers something of what Frederick William III did for the German peasants. Paternalistic Lutheran monarchy had a tradition of the welfare state, and Bismarck could not be moved by protests of "socialism" or "communism," which he called catchwords. "For my part I confess openly that my belief in the consequence of our revealed religion, in the form of moral law, is sufficient for me, and certainly for the position taken up on this question by the emperor. . . . I, the minister of the state, am a Christian, and as such am determined to act as I believe I am justified before God." [34]

Bismarck's charitable impulses were not solely responsible for the new social legislation. The imperial reforms were admittedly undertaken to steal thunder from the Marxists. Bismarck recognized that the misery of the working classes made them susceptible to revolutionary propaganda, and he intended to convince them that they had a future within the existing State and social structure. He was a thorough conservative; he believed that nobleman and peasant, rich and poor, were natural, necessary, and permanent divisions of society. All his reforms were designed to make political and social inequality and authoritarianism more palatable and more paternalistic.

The chancellor himself was notoriously impatient of theory, but he did have theoretical support at hand. The powerful group of economists headed by Adolf Wagner and Gustav Schmoller provided a rationale for this " State socialism." The German " historical school " had maintained against the English " classical " economists that economics was not an exact science with quasi-physical laws, but rather a branch of ethics and social policy. To permit human labor to be treated simply as a commodity in the free market was inhuman and unchristian. And since there were no fixed principles as to what the State might or might not do in the economic field, labor legislation, social insurance, and regulation of industry were all to be considered on their merits.

German State socialism involved many things, from tariffs and subsidies to tax policy and government ownership, as of railroads and forests. It is the legislation directly affecting the workman that most interests us here. Protective industrial legislation had begun in nearly all countries for children and women workers and for the provision of Sunday rest. In this the Germans were not pioneers or otherwise remarkable. It was in social insurance that Bismarck set the pattern for all the Western States. He based his proposals on the principle stated in the Prussian fundamental law of 1794, that the workman has a right either to a job or to relief. The State was obligated to find him one or the other, if private industry could not. On such a conception of the State's duties was erected the system of insurance whose three chief elements were the Sickness Insurance Law (1883), Accident Insurance Law (1884, 1885), Old Age Insurance Law (1889). Voluntary agencies of various sorts supplied many of these needs in Britain and America, as we have seen, but it was to be decades before any democratic government was to follow the lead of Lutheran absolutism.

The German attitude toward guilds exhibits the tradition of State regulation of industry. In England the old privileges and monopolies, the old restrictions to certain locations and occupations, or the prescriptions as to the amount and quality of goods to be produced had long since been forgotten. But German economic development had lagged far behind that of Britain, France, or Belgium. Trade had been retarded by the political fragmentation of the country until the customs union of 1834. Germany remained largely landlocked until the coming of the railroads in the middle of the century. The old guild and manorial regulations kept the peasants as serfs and the artisans bound to certain trades and localities until well into the nineteenth century. From 1811 there was a steady whittling down of the monopolies and restrictions that maintained the traditional static economy. In 1850, however, Germany was still more largely agricultural than England had been in 1750, and was still controlled politically by a squirearchy. Peasants and workmen did not dream of political liberty or the vote. And while the tendency to industrial freedom reached its climax in 1869, with the North German Trade Law, thereafter reaction set in. The conservative parties sponsored a revival of guild regulation in the effort to protect the artisans and handicrafts against the fatal competition of the new machines and factories. In the '80's in particular, the Trade Law underwent a series of amendments in the interest of the guild system. The guilds were given power to license employers, and to limit the number of workmen they might employ. All employers, members of the guild or not, were compelled by law to contribute to training schools, hostels, and labor offices for journeymen and apprentices. Many of these provisions, of course, were destined to be but temporary measures to ease the transition to the factory system. Some, however, such as the Board of Arbitration for industrial and trade disputes, composed half of employers and half of employees, gave promise of enduring value in the new economic society. Similarly, boards that might set hour and wage limits, as well as health and moral standards in the several industries, would be continuing functions of the old guilds.

In this whole current of social thought, there appears a close parallel between Lutheran and Roman Catholic aristocratic paternalism. Indeed, despite the confessional bitterness of the Kulturkampf, Lutheran and Catholic conservatives could sometimes even agree on legislative proposals as against the economic liberals. They were both anticapitalist and antidemocratic. The patron of the " social Catholics," Bishop Ketteler, was an ultramontane and a conservative aristocrat, yet he appropriated not merely the analysis and proposals, but also the incendiary tone of the socialist agitator Lassalle. It is significant, in fact, that both Bismarck and Ketteler took counsel of Lassalle, and that both seriously experimented with his scheme of subsidized workers' producing cooperatives. Feudal Catholic and Lutheran noble could strike hands with socialist proletarians more readily than any of the three could come to terms with capitalist individualism. The lesser nobility and country gentry were jealous of the new power of fluid capital and industry. The Catholic Center Party generally stood for protective industrial legislation for women and children, for legal sanction for guild regulations on production and wages, and for measures to regulate the "tyranny of capital." The fact that most of the "Catholic socialists" were large landowners made them particularly sensitive to the evils of usury and heavy taxes on land.

Certain hesitations or deviations on the side of the Catholics are readily understandable from their experience of State persecution in the Kulturkampf. Bishop Ketteler for a time entertained the romantic notion that Catholic charities rather than the State could support the cooperatives Lassalle proposed. Similarly many or most Catholics opposed the social insurance legislation as putting too much in the hands of the State. Some feared the guilds again as interconfessional and likely to dilute Catholic morale. Considerations of this sort were the qualifications set by special ecclesiastical interests to a social policy which in general they supported. In contrast to Catholics in countries like Belgium, or America, German Catholics generally were convinced that the social question was definitely the Church's business, and that the Church should request the State to do something about it. The convergence of Evangelical and Catholic social policy was again illustrated in 1890, when the International Congress to standardize protective legislation for child and women workers and to assure Sunday rest was invited to Bern. The Swiss Catholic Decurtins had been the chief moving agent in this project, with the approval of Leo XIII. When the German emperor was approached on the subject, however, he at once welcomed the idea on the ground of the responsibility of the Christian State for the welfare of its weaker subjects, and invited the assembly to meet at Berlin. What is more, the Kaiser wrote to the pope, hoping for his support on the same grounds. Protestant Prussian *Junker* and Catholic nobleman shared a sense of paternalistic *noblesse oblige*.

Outside Germany, in France and Austria especially, the Catholic landowning aristocracy were displaying the same "socialistic" and antidemocratic tendencies. Austria-Hungary was overwhelmingly agricultural, and Austrian Catholics represented the agrarian interests, landowners and peasants. There was very little of a Christian middle class; the banks, the press, the stock exchange of Vienna were to a high degree Jewish. The agrarian "socialist" reaction, consequently, was also an anti-Semitic program, and anti-Semitism gave the feudalist leaders a popular basis among the peasants which they might otherwise have lacked. The peasant and the landowner were natural enemies of the mortgage companies, while the artisan found himself at a disadvantage against the capitalist employer. From this Austrian anti-Semitic Catholic " socialism " was to spring Adolf Hitler.

The Catholic feudal party found its focus around the journal *Vaterland*. Its two chief leaders were both converted Prussian Protestants, Rudolf Meyer the economist and Baron von Vogelsang. The program, like that of German Catholic socialists, was largely borrowed from the German State socialist economists, together with the guild program of controlling prices and production and the freedom of occupation. The first great victory of the feudal socialists was the Industrial Laws of 1883, by which guild membership was again made compulsory, at least in the smaller industries. A Catholic Congress in Vienna in 1889 urged extension of guild regulations to factory workers as well as craftsmen, and more sweeping regulation in the interest of limitation of production. Von Vogelsang had meanwhile sponsored a public investigation of labor conditions and the party had worked for legislation for an eleven-hour day and the protection of women and children in industry. But with all this, the feudal socialists opposed universal suffrage, representative government, and the parliamentary system, and stood for authoritarian rule by monarch and aristocracy.

In France, again, while most Catholics were opposed to State intervention in business affairs, a similar movement was under way among Catholic monarchists. Two legitimist Army officers, Comte de Mun and Comte de la Tour du Pin, came back from the Franco-Prussian War with the notion of adapting the clerical and politically reactionary social interest of Ketteler to France. These monarchist reformers struck most French workers as somewhat quaint, with their program of restoring the Bourbons, enforcing the Syllabus, and restoring the medieval guilds. In the Chamber of Deputies, however, de Mun often struck a curious alliance of the extreme right with the extreme left, joining the socialists in support of legislation such as the regulation of child and women labor, of Sunday work, the legalization of trade-unions, and the support of social insurance. Mgr. Freppel spoke for most of the clergy and laity of France in repudiating such " socialist " proposals. But while de Mun used the Chamber of Deputies as his rostrum, his party, like its German and Austrian counterparts, really opposed the whole pattern of liberal democratic government. The notion was that legislative bodies should be constituted by the groups controlling the guilds, rather than on a democratic suffrage, much as Mussolini substituted his " corporative state " for the Italian parliament in the 1920's. The title of a pamphlet by Comte de la Tour du Pin was *Le Parlementarisme, voilà l'ennemi!* The alternative of the clerical conservatives was representation by guilds or professions.

In the middle '8o's the " social Catholics " began to consolidate internationally. The French and Austrian feudal socialists found common ground readily. The tension between French and Germans, which was the heritage of the war of 1870, was successfully bridged over by the Swiss, and an organization, the Fribourg Union, met at the home of the Swiss Cardinal Mermillod. The Union studied industrial problems, working conditions, wages, protection of child and women workers, and sought to build up a body of social and economic ethics. Leo followed this movement closely, receiving its results through Cardinals Mermillod and Jacobini. He was convinced of the strategic political significance of the new laboring classes and deeply impressed by the evidence of an international consensus on a coherent Catholic social program. He encouraged the great workers' pilgrimages to the Vatican which Leon Harmel organized in the late 1880's, and, contrary to his usual custom, he never refused collective audiences to workmen. In 1887, there were fourteen hundred pilgrims, led by de Mun and Cardinal Langénieux. In 1889, de Mun, Harmel, and the archbishop of Rheims brought four thousand. One year Harmel brought no less than twenty thousand to Rome. In his discourses to these deputations Leo indicated his adoption of the views of the central European social Catholic school, in contrast to the capitalist individualism dominant among French, Belgian, English, and American Catholics. Leo caused comment by affirming the duty of the State to undertake social legislation, and by urging the guild program of " professional representation." He considered that " professional representation would one day be the salvation of society." [35]

These two theses were again the most striking aspects of *Rerum novarum,* the famous encyclical of 1891 in which the pope laid down a Roman Catholic theory of social politics. On both points Leo repudiated the capitalistic rugged individualism of the bulk of Catholics in Western countries, and affirmed a paternalistic conception substantially equivalent to that of Lutheran monarchism. The Fribourg Union now dissolved, considering that its purpose was accomplished. Count Blome, its president, announced: " We have the joy of finding in the encyclical the sanction of the theses that this Union has adopted since its foundation. . . . We are now given a definite line to follow regarding the value, even the necessity, of a guild system. We have a fixed line regarding the duty of the State to protect the worker, not only women and children, but adult men, to limit hours of work, and, if necessary, and by suitable measures, to ensure a sufficient wage." He could not, however, suppress a certain disappointment on one point. " The encyclical is limited to the observation that rapacious usury, often condemned by the Church, is still practiced under various disguises." [36]

The first principles of *Rerum novarum,* like those of Lutheran conservative paternalism, rested on the acceptance of the existing social and political structure. Humanity must remain as it is; " there will always be differences and inequalities of condition in the State." [37] The Church concerns itself to incline the rich to generosity and the poor to resignation, and labors for the reconciliation rather than the conflict of classes. The " first and most fundamental principle " of social policy must be the inviolability of private property. " The chief thing to be secured is the safeguarding, by legal enactment and policy, of private property. Most of all, it is essential, in these times of covetous greed, to keep the masses within the line of duty." [38] Property must also be protected from excessive taxation by the State. The class structure of rich and poor is divinely ordained and unchangeable.

Standing on these age-old privileges of the aristocracy, oriented to land, Leo permitted himself strong language with regard to abuses among the new financial and industrial aristocracy. " It has come to pass that workingmen have been given over, isolated and defenseless, to the callousness of employers and the greed of unrestrained competition. The evil has been increased by rapacious usury, which, although more than once condemned by the Church, is nevertheless, under a different form but with the same guilt, still practiced by avaricious and grasping men. And to this must be added the custom of working by contract, and the concentration of so many branches of trade in the hands of a few individuals, so that a small number of very rich men have been able to lay upon the masses of the poor a yoke little better than slavery itself." [39]

Leo justified social legislation within carefully defined limits, taking a position, as we have seen, about equivalent to that of the more moderate group of Protestant social reformers in the English-speaking world. He advocated Sunday rest, the regulation of the work of women and children, and maximum hours for at least some types of men's labor. He urged the ideal of a living family wage instead of " free " wage contracts, but he did not suggest actual legislation for a minimum wage. The regulation of hours and working conditions, generally, he considered, could be better handled by boards within industry than by the State directly. Here, of course, he was setting forth " guild " conceptions. He defended the association of workmen as a natural right which the State could not abrogate,[40] and he especially commended the type of association in which both employers and employees were members.[41] Such corporations should provide for religious duties. They should also attempt to prevent unemployment, and should create funds for emergencies such as sickness, accident, and old age.

The encyclical *Rerum novarum* can thus be seen as a landmark in the countermovement we have already described from the nondemocratic countries. Leo's manifesto of aristocratic paternalism, while founded on central European traditions, seemed startlingly " progressive " to the dominantly individualist capitalistic Catholics of Belgium, France, and the English-speaking world. To the more advanced social thinkers among the Anglicans, on the other hand, as we have already seen, *Rerum novarum* seemed naïvely impractical, reflecting a less developed stage of industrialization. In any case, it gave great stimulus to the social interest and activity of Catholics. In particular it was a major factor in the rise in the 1890's of a new school of " Catholic democracy."

Before describing the activities and the fate of " Catholic democracy," however, we should characterize the antidemocratic aspects of this countermovement of Catholic paternalist " socialism." The contrast of the rigid Central European caste system with the social fluidity of democratic countries is obvious enough. Two other points deserve mentioning, the maintenance of the theocratic principle throughout social life, and the preference for massive coercive organization over localized and voluntary associations.

With regard to the last, it is particularly significant that the pioneer and model of modern " Catholic Action " in the social and economic sphere was authoritarian Germany. Catholic Action and Marxist socialism arose together in the Revolution of 1848 and both achieved their fullest maturity and power in the period up to World War I in imperial Germany. This was no accident, for their common features correspond to the expectations and temper of German social organization, with its disposition to militarism, bureaucracy, disciplined obedience to authority.

The contrast with the democratic patterns of English society was sharpened by the attempt to transplant English institutions to Germany. In the middle of the century a very popular scheme in Britain was that of co-operative production, as of groups of tailors or builders. Maurice and Ludlow urged them, as had Louis Blanc in France. Huber tried to carry them to Germany, but he met a cold response. Lassalle, however, found a mass enthusiasm as soon as he combined the idea of co-operatives with State subsidies. The German workmen had no confidence in local initiative; they looked to the bureaucratic State. It was the same story with the quest for security. The workmen of Britain built up a vast network of locally organized " Friendly Societies " to insure themselves against various contingencies. In Germany, however, as we have already seen, this was from the beginning regarded as the business of the State. The English type of trade-union, again, with its goal of specific gains by bargaining, won little support in Germany. The so-called "Hirsch-Duncker unions" of this type were quickly outdistanced by the Marxist unions, which proposed to capture or replace the State as a means to economic improvement. All these social patterns show, on the one side, the pervasive trust in the initiative and voluntary association of private men, and on the other, the reliance on the coercive powers of the centralized State. The ecclesiastical parallels to these contrasting conceptions are already familiar to us.

Marxist socialism and Catholic Action expressed in their social pattern this reliance on coercive Statelike authority, but in the nature of the case could not accept the existing State. They were conceived as Counterstates, as states within the State, as machines of rebellion when necessary. Bismarck tried to break both the Red and the Black Internationals, but both proved too strong for him.

When we consider the social character of the clerical State of Catholic Action within the Hohenzollern empire, another antidemocratic aspect is striking. Catholic Action not merely absorbs all democratic voluntarism and localism into a massive authoritarian bureaucracy; it also embodies in a new form the old theocratic idea. To the Anglo-American, a striking aspect of German social organization is the prevalence of political and ideological affiliations. Every sort of society, vocational or cultural, seems to be also an instrument of social and political control and an agency for a *Weltanschauung*. In this sense Germany is theocratic, or, a group of theocracies held together by the external framework of the State, but with no real social or spiritual bonds between them. Marxism and Catholic Action are one in their refusal to acknowledge an ecclesiastically neutral sphere where men of various theologies may meet on common pragmatic and moral ground. Just as the democratic State was based on ecclesiastically neutral moral or "natural" law, so democratic society generally is organized innocently of ecclesiastical or ideological interests. In a democratic society a trade-union, a consumers' co-operative, a boys' camp, a farmers' association, is normally just that and nothing more. In the scheme of Marxist socialism, however, or Catholic Action, comparable organizations are viewed as something to be captured and manipulated as proselyting agencies and means of social control and political pressure. The Marxist and Catholic theocracies accept no limits to their imperialism, no nonideological spheres.

In a series of illustrations of this theocratic penetration of the common life in the economic sphere by Catholic Action we might begin with the organization of rural life. Back in the '60's, when the European agricultural crisis hit Germany, the Catholic cavalry officer von Schorlemer-Alst made himself a defender of rural interests and culture. The ostensible endeavor was to maintain an independent peasantry on the land. Co-operative buying, credit unions, mutual insurance companies were all developed, as well as education in improved farming methods, and legislation beneficial to farm interests. Gentry and peasants found a common interest in this program, which was comparable to the influence of the Grundtvigian movement in transforming rural life in Lutheran Denmark. But the Peasants' Unions of Westphalia, the Rhinelands, and Bavaria also served confessional interests, and as auxiliaries of the Catholic Center Party were used as political pressure for such interests.

The pattern spread across the Rhine into Belgium, where the *Boerenbond* was founded in 1890. This Belgian Peasants' Guild began with co-operative buying of seed, feed, fertilizer, machinery. The Raffeisen banks were introduced from Germany. Periodicals were developed. The league was organized by parochial and communal units, each with its chaplain and patron saint. The whole social, economic, and religious life of the peasantry was shaped by the Peasants' Guild, and at the same time it was a chief instrument of clerical control and increasingly the main basis of the Belgian Catholic Party. In the twentieth century the pattern was to be adopted in Italy, again, and then after the World War to be transferred to the United States as a method of penetrating the Protestant countryside.

Among industrial workers, similarly, local priests began in the '80's in Germany to organize Catholic labor unions. The purpose was largely defensive at first, to combat the antireligious propaganda in the flourishing Marxist unions. These Catholic trade-unions won their chief strength in the strongly Catholic Rhine provinces and in Westphalia, among miners, textile operatives, and iron and steel workers. They were much more submissive than the socialist unions, which were eight or ten times their strength. The Catholic unions emphasized benefit programs and voted strikes only on extreme provocation. For a time the Lutheran monarchist and anti-Semite Stoecker attempted to emulate this confessional trade-union effort, but most of the Catholic unions took in Protestants also. They could afford to so long as Catholic control was retained, and they remained tied to the Center Party as the Marxist unions were to the Socialist Party.

Closely associated with the Catholic labor unions was the Catholic League, the *Arbeiterverein,* founded by Canon Hitze at the end of the '80's as a political organization of Catholic laborers. The chief activity was education and propaganda on Catholic social policy to counter Marxist socialism. A particular function was the development of secretariates to furnish expert information to workers on all social problems and legislation relating to them. The People's Union, *Volksverein,* similarly developed a widespread system of secretariates and information bureaus for all classes of the population, on both religious and social subjects. München-Gladbach was the central office from which pamphlets, articles, lectures were sent out in all directions. The organization represented the permanent activity keeping continuity between the great annual Catholic congresses of Germany which had been meeting since 1848.

In Italy a similar congress was first tried in 1874 in Venice, and a permanent committee, the *Opera dei congressi,* emerged to remain the nerve center of Catholic Action in Italy until 1904. Regional, diocesan, and parish committees of the congresses were organized. Professor Toniolo, of Pisa, was instrumental in the founding of a *Unione popolare* to serve the functions of the German *Volksverein.*

In France the comparable developments came only in the twentieth century. From 1904 the French also developed annual congresses on Catholic social ethics. These "social weeks" migrated from city to city in France. A new development was to confine each congress to one major issue, treating it with considerable thoroughness, and thus over the years building up a solid body of information and opinion on the group of central problems. Belgium and Holland also took up the "social weeks," and they have since become almost universal in Catholic countries.

The French counterpart of the *Volksverein* and the *Unione popolare* was the *Action populaire,* a sort of permanent bureau of social Catholicism. Among a profusion of pamphlets, plays, study courses, and the like, the annual *Guides socials* from 1904 were most impressive. From 1910 appeared an *Année sociale internationale,* which was unrivaled even in Germany.

Of the actual Roman Catholic political parties which integrated and made effective these manifold clerical penetrations of social life, the most important were the German Center and the Dutch and Belgian Catholic parties. The Catholic Church was at such odds with the State in France and Italy through most of the period from 1870 to 1914 that political action within the parliamentary structure was never effectively developed, although France had a "Popular Liberal Party" from 1902, and Italy a "People's Party" under Pius X. We have already commented on the methods and problems of clerical direction of these parties in connection with the political theory and practice of Leo XIII (see above, pp. 145 f.). From our present point of view they are simply the most inclusive and explicitly political of the whole hierarchy of organizations of Catholic Action by which a theocratic control can be injected into the machinery even of a democratic society. In fact, the methods and techniques were first worked out in authoritarian Germany, and transplanted from there to the West.

This much of a sketch must suffice to suggest the system of institutions by which the Catholic Church mobilized and disciplined its whole population, relating all sorts of economic, vocational, and cultural societies to a frankly political organization, knitting the whole together by clerical chaplains and the constant strategic oversight of the bishops. The sharp contrast with the nonpolitical and nonecclesiastical parallel social institutions of Puritan societies is everywhere apparent. The twentieth century would see the attempt of the Roman Church to use this clerically disciplined social organization as a means to penetrate and capture the strategic centers of the hitherto free and nonideological social structures of Britain and America. This outline must also suffice for the sociopolitical organizations of Roman Catholics in dominantly Protestant Switzerland and Holland, which followed the German pattern with variations. The vast philanthropic activities involved in each case are beyond our scope here, which is to sketch the sociological pattern of the massive machinery of social control developed to extend the political power of the Roman hierarchy.

Within this structure of social Catholic Action — in Germany, the country of origin, and in Belgium, France, and Italy — the decade after *Rerum novarum* witnessed heated controversies over " Catholic democracy." A marked increase in social and political activity of both clergy and laity was evident. Leo had advised: " Recommend to your priests not to shut themselves up within the walls of the church or presbytery, but to go among the people and busy themselves cordially with the worker, the poor man, the lower class. In our time above all it is necessary to fight prejudice and bridge the gap between priest and people." [42] Leo was encouraging Catholics to put themselves into situations where they might be affected by the contagion of democracy. In his inexperience, both of political democracy and of industrialization, the pope did not foresee this consequence.

One might found co-operatives, savings banks, workmens' Catholic clubs to forestall the Marxists, but in talking with workers it was not so easy to refute the democratic demand for equality of opportunity with two or three " Replies to Objections " from the *Summa Theologica*. Some of the younger clergy progressed to outright democratic views, to the horror of conservatives. The consequence, for which the pope himself was largely responsible, was that for the third time in the nineteenth century there was a significant upsurge of Catholic political liberalism and democracy.

In Italy, Belgium, and France, especially, the small handful of democratic militants ran into such bitter conflict with traditional Catholic monarchism and aristocracy on the one hand, and Catholic capitalistic individualism on the other, that the unity of political and social Catholic Action was injured. In Italy, Don Romolo Murri became the national leader of the Christian democrats and the best-known priest in Italy. There were soon one hundred and fifty Christian democratic associations in operation, developing an increasingly forthright position. Leo encouraged this development, hoping perhaps that with this new political power of the workers he might gain a weapon in his fight to win back the former papal states from the kingdom of Italy. Within the *Opera dei congressi,* however, the aristocratic conservatives, led by the president Count Paganuzzi, objected strenuously to the democratic wing. The controversy became so bitter that in 1904 Pius X dissolved the *Opera dei congressi* entirely, seeking to put Catholic Action directly under clerical control, where discipline would be absolute and instantaneous. We shall record later the rebellion of some of the Italian Catholic democrats to this repression.

In Belgium, similarly, the unity of the Catholic social congresses held at Liége in 1886, 1887, and 1890, and the discipline of the Catholic Party itself, were dangerously strained. The bulk of the clergy and laity, as with English and American Catholics, opposed the demand for State intervention for social justice. While Belgium was the most highly industrialized Catholic country, and the homeland of Catholic political liberalism, its social conscience was markedly slow to develop. Wages were low, illiteracy high, and working conditions generally appalling in contrast to comparable Puritan Protestant countries. In 1893 the limitation of the franchise to the well-to-do classes was dropped when manhood suffrage, qualified by plural voting, was introduced. The result was nearly to eliminate the old liberals, greatly to strengthen the Socialists politically, and to strengthen the popular element within the Catholic Party. In 1891, Helleputte had organized the Catholic progressives in the *Ligue démocratique belge.* The workers' groups grew increasingly restive under the control of the Catholic Party by the social conservatives, led by Woeste, and the general orientation toward the Flemish peasantry. In the industrial centers there was a strong movement to form a separate party. The hierarchy managed to hold the democrats in line at Liége, but at Alost the abbé Daens organized a separate " Christian Democratic Party." As with the Italian Christian democrats, there was a rebellion from the hierarchical discipline in the reign of Pius X. The controversy over " Catholic democracy " was most violent of all in France. A vigorous Catholic democratic movement took the initiative from de Mun's paternalistic monarchism in the '90's. All through the provinces, and especially at Paris, workmen's study groups and discussion circles were organized. The Christian democratic periodicals, conducted by journalist priests such as the abbés Naudet, Dabry, and Six, kept up enthusiasm. The *Ligue démocratique belge* served as a model for regional and national congresses. Credit unions and consumers' co-operatives were employed. A particular project in North France and Belgium was legislation to make the workman's patrimony of house and garden untaxable and indivisible. The most conspicuous proponent of this scheme was the abbé Lémire, the first Catholic democrat to get elected to the Chamber of Deputies. Harmel was assembling Catholic workmen's congresses, meanwhile, and in 1896 at Rheims it was decided to organize politically as a Christian democratic party. Local groups were to be free to decide whether or not to engage in politics, but those that did should declare themselves " democratic republicans." [43] In 1897 the party set up an executive committee, with Harmel president and Lémire secretary-general. But France was already involved in its disastrous Dreyfus affair, and the Christian democrats had reached their apogee.

It is necessary also to indicate the share of the Catholic democrats in preparing the Dreyfus scandal. As with the Catholic feudal Socialists of Austria, French Catholic democracy was disfigured by vicious anti-Semitism. The French anti-Semite agitator in chief since about 1885 had been Edouard Drumont. He combined Catholic fanaticism with the economic resentment of workers and clerks against the Jewish capitalists. At the end of the '80's, similarly, General Boulanger had sought to capitalize on this device to win support from both reactionaries and revolutionaries for his projected coup. In the '90's the Catholic democrats became the most vigorous anti-Semites. A congress of Catholic democrats in Lyons in 1896 was organized by the anti-Semitic *France libre*. Drumont was chosen honorary president, and Abbé Gayraud, assuring the congress that the Catholic Church had always been anti-Semitic, called for " the expulsion of all the excrements of society, and especially of the Jewish excrement." [44] Catholic anti-Semitism was, to be sure, not at all limited to the Catholic democrats. Several of the leading representatives of some of the religious orders in France, especially Jesuits, Assumptionists, and Dominicans, were at this time preaching hatred and violence, and thoroughly earned the legislative penalties laid against them after the Dreyfus affair. Even the Vatican's quasi-official

Civiltà cattolica was at this time printing virulently anti-Semitic articles, articles that were to be gleefully reprinted by the Fascist Farinacci forty years later when the pope rebuked Fascist anti-Semitism. The French Christian democrats, however, made themselves peculiarly the champions of the anti-Semitic propaganda in the '90's.

Anti-Semitism, however, was not the chief ground of hostility toward the Christian democrats. They were most bitterly hated for that for which the pope valued them most highly, their effort to break the identification of Catholicism with monarchism in France and to come to terms with the Third Republic. In arguing that democracy, the satanic and atheist creed of '89, could be Christianized — indeed, that it was in essence Christian — these men were flying in the face of the French Catholic convictions of three generations. Yet they could well claim that their cause was the pope's. With the encyclical *Au milieu des sollicitudes* (1892), Leo had advised French Catholics to give up the cause of the pretender and the series of conspiracies to overthrow the Republic, to accept the Republic and work within it to prevent the de-Catholicization of France. While some royalists, La Tour du Pin, for example, simply refused to obey the pope, a considerable group " rallied " to the Republic out of obedience and without conviction. De Mun and the *Univers* took this position. The minority of French Catholics who accepted the Republic out of conviction and enthusiasm thus became the chief targets of the monarchist reactionaries, who did not often dare to attack the pope openly. De Cassagnac referred contemptuously to the " democratic priests," the " vagabond priests," who were preparing the way for Communism. Harmel and Fonsegrive, of the *Quinzaine,* were called heretics and disguised freemasons by the bishop of Nancy. Every speech and article of the Catholic democrats was combed for an unguarded phrase by heresy hunters like Barbier and Fontaine, who fastened with unholy glee on every hint of error. It was in this atmosphere that the American bishop Ireland made his enthusiastic confession of faith in democracy while on a visit to France. The repercussions led to the papal condemnation of " Americanism," which was Leo's first move toward repression.

3. The Purge of Catholic Democracy

The definitive repudiation of Catholic democracy came with Leo's last major encyclical, a sequel to and commentary on *Rerum novarum,* the *Graves de communi* (1901). All through the '90's Leo had refused to yield to the pressures to condemn the Catholic democrats, pressures that even included several of the crowned heads of Europe.[45] At the last, however, he made it clear that while Catholics might call them-

selves " democrats," they must in no way identify the Church with democracy in fact. Catholic democracy must henceforth mean simply
" Catholics devoted to the amelioration of the working classes." Such
Catholics " can never be actuated with the purpose of favoring and in-
troducing one government in place of another." [46] There was to be no
" intention of diminishing the spirit of obedience, or of withdrawing
people from their lawful rulers." So far as political forms were concerned, Leo's personal preference was for absolutism. " If there is such
a thing as a perfect democratic form, this is undoubtedly to be found in
the Church." [47] Leo thus redefined " democracy " to mean, as it does
for Marxists, a movement in behalf of the people. It specifically could
not mean the advocacy of government of the people *by the people,* nor
the opening of the class hierarchy by the equality of opportunity. He
emphasized the social role of upper-class philanthropy. *Rerum novarum*
was to be understood in the spirit of paternalism, not as the Christian
democrats had interpreted it. And in particular Leo repudiated the
alarming tendency Christian democracy had shown to seek to define a
sphere of political action in which laymen might shape policy independently of clerical direction. " Whatever projects individuals or associations form in this matter should be done with due regard to episcopal authority and absolutely under episcopal guidance." [48] The
condemnation of these three democratic errors made it clear that Leo's
flirtation with democracy had never been seriously meant. His reign
ended as it had begun, with a clear definition of the antidemocratic political and social doctrine of the Roman Church.

The political line to be followed by Leo's successor was, in contrast,
unqualified and brutal. Back in the '90's Cardinal Sarto of Venice had
issued a series of discourses and letters on social and political issues distinguished by their hatred for the Christian democrats. He would not
let his priests even read Murri's publications, and made insinuations
about Murri's personal morals, to which the latter replied indignantly.
In 1896, Sarto reminded the " Socialist Catholics " at Padua of that
" inequality which is necessary and inevitable " and warned them
against the " hateful and pernicious doctrines and subversive principles
of liberalism and its worthy offspring, socialism and anarchism." He
urged his clergy to earn the epithets of " intransigents " and " clericalism." " Liberal Catholics," he agreed with Pius IX, " are wolves in
sheep's clothing." [49] While Leo lived, Sarto could not get his knife into
the Catholic democrats, but when he became Pius X, it was patent that
heads would roll.

The new pope defined his political direction at once in a *motu proprio*
of December 18, 1903, on " Popular Catholic Action." This *motu pro-*

prio laid down nineteen principles to guide all Catholic social action. They were to be published in all Catholic papers, read frequently in all Catholic societies, committees, unions, and the like. They were all culled from Leo's pronouncements on the subject, but emphasized only the negative aspects. There was none of Leo's critique of capitalist irresponsibility, his recommendation of guilds and even labor unions, his qualified endorsement of protective industrial legislation, his policy of co-operation with republicans. Pius rather selected all the antidemocratic and reactionary aspects, which were, of course, the stronger: the sanctification of existing social classes and inequalities, the inviolability of private property, the denial of a claim in justice to change these conditions, and the basing of Catholic Action on charity instead of justice, the injunction to Catholic writers on social issues not to take a tone displeasing to the upper classes, the denial of any political significance to Catholic " democracy," and the strict submission of all Catholic social action to the direction of the bishops. Journalists in particular were to be subject to prior censorship in all matters by the hierarchy.

In the campaign of repression that followed, Pius X made himself the agent of *L'Action française*. This organization was the focus of the intransigent monarchists in France who had refused to follow Leo XIII and come to terms with the Republic. French Catholicism as a whole had been dishonored by the Dreyfus affair, but *L'Action française* shamelessly proposed that a judicial murder was easily justified for *raison d'état*. From 1900 the organization pushed a steady propaganda for counterrevolution. While its chief leader, Charles Maurras, was an atheist, *L'Action française* devoted most of its propaganda to Catholics. It occupied a position of extraordinary influence in the French hierarchy and among Catholic intellectuals — young Maritain began here — and at the Vatican was the most effective agency in securing the condemnation of Catholic democrats.

Maurras supported Roman Catholicism as an instrument of social control, although he personally felt only contempt for Christian faith and morals. " Catholicism is an attenuated Christianity filtered through the happy genius of France," or, at other times, and as Mussolini preferred, filtered through the political tradition of the ancient Roman Empire. Maurras hated the Reformation because it had released the Christian gospel from the imperial organization, and had set it free over Europe. As an atheist Catholic, he took the imperial organization without the gospel and cultivated that large group of Frenchmen who, in the tradition of de Maistre and Veuillot, had praised the Church for the same reason. As a disciple averred, " There is a whole Church of such persons in France."

Maurras was thus a Machiavellian Catholic. " In case of necessity," he held (and strictly he did not observe even this qualification), " there is no morality." To destroy democracy, one may " buy women, buy consciences, buy treason." Or one might simply use murder: " Let us revive our Sand and our Orsini." [50] It was Maurras and his *Action française* who first taught the Fascists the effectiveness of a private army of roughs (sometimes from upper-class homes) to intimidate democratic governments.

As soon as Leo's death had released the pressure for the reconciliation of French Catholicism with the Third Republic, Maurras leaped to take up the slack with a revival of counterrevolutionary monarchism. A group of periodicals, *La Gazette de France, Libre parole, Autorité,* campaigned against Catholic democrats, and especially their most impressive leader, Marc Sangnier, of the " *Sillon."* Many such articles were written by legitimist priests like Barbier, arguing from divine right. Maurras used these legitimists and defended the Syllabus enthusiastically, for his own reasons. Politically he thus fitted Pius X to a T: Pius had formed his political thought in general and his opinions of the Third French Republic in particular from Bishop Pie, the fanatical adviser of the pretender de Chambord, and the mortal foe of Montalembert. For long, Pius forgave Maurras his atheism. He even called him a " fine defender of the faith."

With such advisers Pius initiated his great purge of Catholic democrats. In Italy, as we have seen, he began by dissolving the *Opera dei congressi* and putting all Catholic Action under direct clerical supervision. Romolo Murri, however, did not take the hint. With the approval of some Italian bishops, he called a congress which launched the *Lega democratica nazionale* (1905). The Catholic democrats used as a campaign document the novel *The Saint,* written by the most distinguished Catholic layman of Italy, Senator Fogazzaro. The pope was enraged. In 1906, *The Saint* was put on the Index, and Murri and the Catholic democrats were savagely attacked in the encyclical *Pieni l'animo.* There was no theological issue here; Murri was a good scholastic. Yet the pope was more violent than he was to be in the later encyclical against theological modernism. *Pieni l'animo* attacked Murri and his associates with cowardly libels, as men of " degrading corruption of morals," who " defile their flesh." Priests and seminarians were forbidden to enroll in the *Lega democratica nazionale* or to give their names to any other societies that were not under the control of the episcopate. Clergy were forbidden all lecturing, preaching, and writing, even on purely technical matters, save under episcopal censorship. All newspapers and periodicals were forbidden to seminarians except for

DEMOCRACY AND THE CHURCHES

one that might be designated by the bishop. In Catholic papers there was to be no more talk of " new orientations of Christian life, new directions for the Church, new aspiration of the modern soul, a new social vocation for the clergy, a new Christian civilization." The Church and " Christian civilization " were, it seems, beyond improvement.

The pope clearly intended to leave no middle ground between clerical reaction and secular socialism. Many priests, confronted with this strait jacket, went socialist, along with the majority of the members of the *Lega*. Murri was suspended *a divinis* for his political and social activities. The series of " modernist " periodicals that sprang up in Italy were silenced. In 1909, Murri at last decided to cross the Rubicon. He came out of retirement, entered politics, and was elected to parliament. Thereupon the pope finally excommunicated him. No single act of Pius X occasioned more universal condemnation in moderate Italian opinion than this systematic persecution of such sincere Catholics as Murri, simply because they were democrats.

In France, meanwhile, a struggle of greater proportions was under way, in which Marc Sangnier was to be the comparable martyr to absolutist venom. Pius had inherited a tense diplomatic situation in France, due to Combes's inquisitorial and unrelenting administration of the Associations Law. Pius himself was equally truculent, being coached on French affairs by the reckless *Action française* intransigents. Diplomatic relations were broken in 1905 between Rome and the Third Republic. In the ensuing Church-State conflict those Catholics who, following Leo's lead, had sought to co-operate with the Republic, and especially those who were republicans and democrats by conviction, came under merciless attack by the adherents of *L'Action française* and by the Vatican. The law of separation, initiated in a spirit of hostility to the Church, was so modified in the legislature as to emerge a rather statesmanlike proposal. The majority of French bishops agreed at first to try the *associations culturelles* proposed by the law. Nearly all the Christian democrats and Catholic liberals favored accepting the law, many of them anticipating a religious invigoration from the new independence of the Church. But Pius would have none of it, and overrode the French episcopate to condemn and " invalidate " the law in his encyclicals, *Vehementer nos* (1906), *Gravissimo officii munere* (1906), and *Une fois encore* (1907). Not until 1924, with a certain amount of face-saving, did the Vatican accept the legislation of the period of separation and in effect admit the factitious nature of the issue blown up by Pius and his secretary of state Merry del Val.

In the heat of this war between Pius and the Third Republic, the Inquisition turned on the Catholic democrats. Pius cleared the field of all periodicals that might rival the *Action française* press. Despite the fact that bishops vouched for the orthodoxy of *Justice sociale* and *La Vie catholique,* both were "reproved and condemned" in 1908. *Démocratie chrétienne* went the same way. *Quinzaine* and *Demain* closed down voluntarily to forestall condemnation. The surviving press, which took its cue from Maurras, campaigned mercilessly against the Catholic democrats, particularly the most impressive and profoundly religious manifestation, Marc Sangnier's *Sillon.* The bishops also sensed which way the wind was blowing and favored the *Sillon* with as many censures after 1907 as they had with compliments before.

The *Sillon* had grown out of a Catholic student movement in the 1890's. Its leader, Marc Sangnier, was perhaps the most charismatic personality of his generation among French Catholics. Sangnier resigned his military commission in 1898 to devote his full time to his vocation as a lay apostle of a new religious fellowship. His ardent personal religion and tangible sincerity won unprecedented success among the intellectuals on faculties, among soldiers, and among workmen and clerks in the Paris *patronages.* Sangnier was from the beginning frankly a democrat. To his mind democracy was that form of social organization which tends to develop to the maximum the conscience and civic responsibility of each person. And politically, "the republic (not the caricature which we have today, which is only a decapitated monarchy, but the true republic) seems to us to be the form of democracy as we have defined it." [51] The *Sillon* proposed to bring about such a true democracy by creating an elite in every level of society of members profoundly transformed and dedicated as Christians. Bishops had lavished commendation and Leo had sent his warmest encouragement. In 1905 fifteen hundred delegates represented a thousand local *Sillons* in a congress. But from 1907, as we have seen, the *Sillon* was under attack.

There were various reasons. Capitalist individualists who had tried to break the rising trade-union movement with a system of company unions, the *syndicats jaunes,* had crossed lances with the *Sillon* in various localities. A personal row within the *Sillon* itself had led to scandalous public polemics and discredited both Sangnier and the movement in the eyes of many. And most important of all, *L'Action française* monarchists must deprive this all too appealing democratic movement of the right to call itself Catholic. Maurras hammered away at the thesis that by claiming to be both a democrat and a Catholic, Sangnier had put himself in a "hopeless dilemma."

It was not hard to show that the *Sillon* did not conform to Pius' regulations for Catholic Action. There was no denying that its spirit was republican in politics, and socially democratic. Furthermore the *Sillon* resisted clerical control in conformity with its democratic idealism. It was not integrated into the regular ecclesiastical machinery of parishes and dioceses, with priests for chaplains and episcopal oversight. Where priests were members of local *Sillons,* they were accepted on a basis of equality as comrades. Similarly when the *Sillonists* met workmen at the *patronages,* it was not as lecturers on the *Summa* of St. Thomas, but as friends and equals. Soon these workmen and clerks became the most zealous of apostles of the *Sillon.* All this was incompatible with the *motu proprio* on Catholic Action.

Sangnier had tried to escape from his " dilemma." For a time, up to about 1906, he argued that the *Sillon* was not really pressing for political democracy since it was not active in politics. Then he turned to the other alternative, seeking to give up the character of a Church-based group. In 1906, the ranks of the *Sillon* were opened to non-Catholics. In 1907, Sangnier announced that he was now engaged in politics simply on a platform of " idealist democracy." Religion became less evident in the *Sillon's* publications. A new daily, *La Démocratie,* was decided upon. In 1909, Sangnier, like Murri, himself contested a seat in the Chamber. But all was to no avail. After various warning shots from minor prelates, Pius released in August, 1910, his broadside against the last important democratic movement in a Catholic country.

The grounds of Pius' condemnation are worth some attention as the fullest twentieth century articulation of the authoritative papal rejection of democracy. On the first principles of political democracy Pius supported his condemnation by citing the *Diuturnum illud* to which we have already referred. Government of the people and by the people, government responsible to the people, is contrary to Catholic truth. Christian democrats like those of the *Sillon* hold that political authority derives from God, but is by him vested in the people, who then may delegate it to officers responsible to them. Catholics, however, may not so hold, for " it is abnormal for the delegation of power to ascend." [52] Authority and ruling power is not delegated anyway, as Leo pointed out, but only in certain cases the personnel to fill the offices are elected. The democratic theory that power is delegated and rests on consent is opposed to the Catholic theory that power is independent of the people and imposes law on them externally by authority. " If the people are holders of power, what becomes of authority? " Democracy vests sovereignty under God in the people, which, says Pius, is opposed to Leo's teaching. Catholicism insists on the inherited privileges of ruling castes and dynasties, the " natural and traditional bases " on which the " Christian states " actually rest. So God built society. It does not need democratic reform; at worst it needs restoration. None can say that any form of government is better than that of the Catholic Church itself, namely, absolutism.

The economic basis of this un-Catholic political democracy is the program of economic independence for the masses of the people. The ideal of the *Sillon* democrats here was not State socialism, but that every workman should have the " soul of a master." The technique chiefly advocated had been co-operatives.

Such a conception of a society of economically independent and politically responsible men, ruled the pope, is based on un-Catholic views of the dignity of human personality, of the equality of men, and of human brotherhood. This notion of the self-determined responsible conscience is false. The human ideal is found in the monk or priest-whose life is founded on obedience to another's conscience. Were the saints, who were the most obedient of men, slaves and degenerates? Are the humble of the earth who plow their furrows in Christian patience and obedience less than full men? And as for equality, as Leo has pointed out, it is un-Catholic to appeal to justice against the divinely ordained system of caste. Catholic " justice " is justice within the latter system. To praise democratic equality is to insult aristocracy and royalism. And the democratic appeal to brotherhood, last of all, as the sanction and impetus of moral initiative and responsibility, is chimerical. " There is no true fraternity outside Christian charity "; [53] natural fraternity cannot resist the disintegration of covetousness and passion. Pius would have none of Bergson's emphasis that the central core of democracy, as of the Christian life, is fraternal love.

This emphasis on democratic fraternity had also led the *Sillon* into culpable tolerance and co-operation with non-Catholics. The pope deplored the development of 1906 by which it had become the " greater *Sillon*." This attempt to draw in all sorts of denominations on a common moral basis involved an attitude of respect toward error that was very dangerous for young Catholics. It could only lead to a promiscuous democracy more catholic than Roman Catholicism, and was thus part of a movement of apostasy. What scandal to agree not to press the interests of the Church in such a united front, as if it were a selfish end! What blasphemy to attempt to find points of contact between the democratic tradition of the Revolution and the gospel! The energies of Catholics, moreover, were thus dissipated in the interests of the larger community and were not confined to strengthening the Church.

The practice of the *Sillon* was also contrary to Roman Catholic practice with regard to the nature of the Church. The *Sillon* had attempted to claim a certain freedom for Catholics in the purely political sphere, arguing that there, at least, they were not subject to orders from the hierarchy. But Pius agreed with the opponents of the *Sillon,* who pointed out that democracy as understood by the *Sillon* was ethical as well as political, involving a theory of man's nature and fulfillment. But all such ethical matters are the sphere of the Church, and no Catholic can claim liberty there from clerical directives. It is within the sphere of the Catholic hierarchy to decide whether democracy as understood in the *Sillon* (and in the English-speaking world) is sound. The hierarchy has decided. It is erroneous and contrary to Catholic truth. And Catholics like Sangnier are not entitled to defend it on the ground that it is merely political and hence not subject to prelatical jurisdiction.

In practice also the *Sillon* had acted on this assumption of the independence of the laymen in political affairs. Whenever priests had been members of the *Sillonist* groups, they had always been treated simply on their merits as men, without special regard for clerical status. They had not lectured, but discussed as comrades. The dignity of the clergy had thus been injured and proper docility had not been shown to the hierarchy. Clergy had been expected to discuss with laymen issues of policy just as if the laymen might have significant insights into Christian morals to contribute. The *Sillonists* had not, like the modernists, applied this organic conception of the Body of Christ to dogmatic issues, but they had been " modernists " in political ethics, trying to distinguish the latter from the religious sphere.

With a touch of unconscious humor, the pope concluded that of course a Catholic might with a clear conscience still be a democrat, provided he did not hold any of these erroneous conceptions of democracy characteristic of the *Sillon.* But " the true friends of the people are neither revolutionaries nor innovators, but traditionalists." [54]

To the disappointment of *L'Action française,* whose influence was probably primary in engineering his condemnation, Sangnier submitted promptly. There were Catholic democrats to whom humanitarianism had become the substance of religion, who saw the Church only as its instrument. When their views were condemned, they renounced Christianity with little pain. The majority, however, considered a democratic ethic the fullest expression of the Christian life in modern conditions, but held to the essential Christian faith as true and the communion of the Church as integral to that faith. When such men were condemned — men like Murri, Sangnier, Tyrrell — a terrible crisis of conscience was occasioned. Pius and his wretched Gestapo, however, cheerfully excommunicated many of the most dedicated Christians of the generation at the behest of the atheistic and viciously immoral *Action française,* with whose politics they agreed. It was more important for the Vatican's purposes to be antidemocratic than to believe in Christ. The condemnation of the *Sillon* was aimed at all French democracy, and perhaps, as Loisy thought, was the most dangerous blow given French Catholicism in his generation by Roman authority. It "was a crime against morals and religion, perpetrated solely in the interests of reckless despotism." [55]

We have followed to the end the chief moves in the campaign in which Pius and Merry del Val and Benigni's clerical Black Hand and Maurras hunted down the Catholic democrats whom Leo had summoned from the Catholic subsoil. Some of them under attack left the Church altogether. Others joined the moderately conservative Catholics. But while the paternalist social Catholics were absorbing some of the refugees from the scattered battalions of Catholic democrats, they were not themselves wholly exempt from the fury of the witch hunt. Modernism and Christian democrats disposed of, the "integral" Catholics turned their attention to the social Catholics. P. Fontaine opened the campaign the year after the imposition of the antimodernist oath with a book against "social modernism." Abbé Barbier was one of the most indefatigable inquisitors and did not spare even Leo himself. De Mun and Goyau were attacked. There were no formal condemnations, but the sycophants of Maurras and the spy system of Benigni at least secured some restraining pressure from Rome. [56] None were beyond suspicion. Count Sforza reports that when Benedict XV took office in 1914, he found among the old business on the papal desk accusations against his own orthodoxy! But with Benedict the black terror at last played out, and after the war social Catholicism at least would again flourish.

What is to be said of the permanent significance of the tragic career of Catholic democracy in the "Catholic" countries in the generation before the First World War? Was it all for nothing? One may doubt how thoroughly it was stamped out. Great numbers, at least of the "Generation of the Exodus," who went to seminary in the last dozen years of Leo's reign, were at heart unconvinced by the scholasticism, obscurantism, and political reaction to which they outwardly submitted under Pius X. In Italy in 1911, it was said that "of a hundred clerics from forty years of age onwards, no less than sixty keep most jealously in their private desks the best products of the Modernist literature." [57] In France clergy submitted with the public explanation that it was against their conscience and only by constraint. And if this was true of theological liberalism, what are we to suppose happened to all the thousands of young men once fired with the noble faith of the *Sillon* and *Lega democratica nazionale*? The Christian gospel, Christian community, and a democratic spirit have not been wholly crushed out of the Roman communion by its canon law and despotic politically-minded Church government. But they were weak, especially in Latin countries. There was not enough real faith in Italy to make possible the sort of heresy trials Protestant America was then carrying on. The collapse of the modernist movement was due to religious indifferentism. It would revive whenever a genuine religious concern would stir the Latin peoples.[58] But so long as the vast majority were Catholic only in etiquette, the ecclesiastical police could always stamp out any breath of new life within the tiny religious elite. And the authoritarian structure of the Roman Church that Maurras admired would triumph over the ethical consequences of the captive gospel that he hated and feared.

VII

FASCIST COUNTERREVOLUTION AND
ROMAN CATHOLICISM

❖ ❖ ❖

IN EACH of the earlier epochs of the history of liberal democracy we have begun our comparative analysis with the societies shaped by Puritan Protestantism and then turned to Roman Catholic cultures. This order was dictated by the nature of the historical materials themselves. For the century and one half, or more, before the First World War, the initiative in Western civilization in general came from Protestant peoples, especially in politics, industry, technology, science, and scholarship. Liberal democracy in particular arose earliest and rooted itself most deeply in Puritan Protestant societies. From them it passed, as we have seen, partially, and against bitter resistance, into Continental Lutheran and Roman Catholic countries in the two generations after the revolutionary ferment of the 1840's.

For the period opened by the cataclysm of the First World War we shall find it more convenient to reverse this order of discussion. This is not because the political orientation of the chief religious traditions altered. On the contrary, they remained remarkably consistent. But in this period the initiative passed to antidemocratic movements. Although the war was nominally won by the liberal democracies, its consequence was a widespread reaction against liberal democracy. Against only half-hearted resistance by Britain, the United States, and France, a series of authoritarian revolutions wiped out, or at least suppressed, the liberal and democratic movements in Germany, Italy, Austria, Spain, Russia. The period after 1914–1918 proved to be a " Restoration " like the generation after the Napoleonic Wars just a century before — an attempt at " archaism," in Toynbee's terms. The result was that virtually all the countries that had received liberal democracy as late as the revolutions of the 1840's now again repudiated it and returned to their earlier absolutist habits in new guises. The map of liberal democracy had receded in 1930 to almost the exact positions it had recorded in 1830. There still remained, in 1930 as in 1830, a democratic toehold in the " Catholic countries " of France and Belgium, but the rest of European and Latin-

American Catholicism had swung back to the Restoration politics of Gregory XVI and Pius IX. The strongly Roman Catholic flavor of the Fascist counterrevolution is indicated summarily by the great predominance of dictators of Catholic origins: Mussolini, Hitler, Franco, Dollfuss, von Schuschnigg, Salazar, Tiso, Pétain, Perón. We shall then consider first this antidemocratic counteroffensive in Roman Catholic culture, and only then turn to Puritan Protestant democratic cultures, now on the defensive.

The new form of political authoritarianism was in part a product of war. In societies shattered and brutalized by years of organized massacre and starvation the only enduring social bond for many was military camaraderie and discipline. A considerable if not dominant element in the early following of Mussolini and Hitler consisted of veterans, unemployed or otherwise disillusioned. The preference of "action" to programs and the appeal to the old wartime nationalist enthusiasm were characteristic of the mentality of frustrated veterans. From this point of view the Fascist dictators were repeating the pattern of the officers of the Praetorian Guards of the dying Roman Empire, or the *condottiere* captains of late medieval Italy. They were unprincipled professional soldiers and terrorists, to be had for a price, and yet quite capable of double-crossing employers and seizing the State for themselves. And the totalitarian State, as they shaped it, was simply the State completely mobilized for war, which was all most of them knew how to prepare for or conduct.

One group of employers who gave direction to some of these *condottieri* were the monarchists of Europe. Mussolini and Primo de Rivera were called to power semilegally by the kings of Italy and Spain and ruled in their names. Dollfuss, von Schuschnigg, Tiso made capital of the hope in a Hapsburg restoration, as did Franco of the aspiration to restore the Spanish Bourbons. Hitler was shoehorned into power by the Catholic monarchists of Germany. Pétain incarnated the Catholic monarchism of the French officer. It was a degenerate monarchism that employed such agents, and the sincerity of the agents was often questionable. But the aura of a once honorable political tradition gave the new dictators a certain plausibility, especially in Roman Catholic countries, which they would never possess in Puritan Protestant societies. Here was the chief link to the main stream of Roman Catholic political ethics, from Bossuet to Pius X.

The other important group of employers were the industrialists, bankers, and landowners, who contributed lavishly to the *condottieri* in employing them as strikebreakers and anti-Communist private police. In few if any cases was there serious danger of Communist revolution on the Russian pattern, but all the new dictators claimed to be saving their respective countries from the Bolsheviks. What they really did was to suppress by violence movements for agrarian reform, trade-unionism, and democratic reformist socialism. In fact, by refusing all democratic discussion on social issues and by driving the under-privileged to desperation, the Fascist movements of this period created a Bolshevik danger where there had been none. A distinguished Catholic may be quoted on this point. " When violence is given the first place and one depends upon it before all else, it turns on those who use it, carrying its own weakness with it. . . . The triumph of these reactions in Germany and Italy has not succeeded, even in these countries, in suppressing the Communist danger. . . . On the contrary, that triumph has aggravated the danger everywhere. . . . If there is anyone in Spain who has really worked successfully for international Communism it is Señor Largo Caballero, who desired it, and also General Franco, who desired the opposite." [1] We may add what M. Maritain did *not* say, that if there is anyone in Europe who really worked successfully for international Communism, it is Stalin, and also Pope Pius XI and his secretary of state Pacelli, of whose whole policy of backing Fascists in this period General Franco is a fair sample.

The most successful defense against Communism in this period was maintained in the English-speaking world. The Puritan Protestant societies maintained the same unique immunity to Marxism that we have already observed in the period from 1865 to 1914. Despite a certain hesitation about State intervention in economic affairs, the democratic procedure permitted a flexibility to the " class war " that could not be found in the caste-bound social hierarchies of Catholic Europe and Latin America. There was enough " equality of opportunity " here so that industrial workers in general shared " middle-class mentality " to the despair of Communist agents. Where " socialistic " proposals could be debated one by one and on their merits, no revolutionary proletarian movement could win support. New Zealand, Australia, Great Britain demonstrated that it was quite possible to go " socialist " by democratic and constitutional means without benefit of castor oil, concentration camps, or civil war. And while such issues could be settled on evidence and by discussion rather than by encyclicals and censorship, it was even possible to go back again without conducting a White Terror. But while the strongest and most convincing answer to Communism was a successful democratic solution of social conflicts, the Roman papacy in this period made the deliberate choice of Fascism over liberal democracy.

This successful defense of the Protestant liberal democracies was only a defense. It began to appear that liberal democracy was no longer an article for export, and in their foreign policy in particular the leading democratic powers, Britain, France, and the United States, did much to weaken democracy in Europe and Asia. This was in part simply incompetence. Even more, perhaps, it was due to the fact that foreign policy and state departments were disproportionately influenced by those strata of society terrorized by the fear of Communism into the same shortsighted ruinous cultivation of Fascism that Pius XI had embarked upon. In fact, as we shall see, the state departments of the democracies were disproportionately influenced by the direct pressure of Roman Catholicism, especially with regard to Mussolini, Franco, and Latin America.

In our survey of the relation of Roman Catholicism to democracy (and Fascism) in this generation between World Wars, we must be rigorously selective. Italy is important as the first experiment that set a pattern. Germany proved to contain the most dynamic force of all these counterrevolutions. Austria is crucial as the key to Vatican policy in Central Europe, and as representing the tradition of the last Catholic power. For the Hispanic cultural area we must be content with Spain. France and Belgium require at least brief mention. The dozen or more smaller countries that illustrate with variations the same conflict of forces must be left aside. In a later chapter we shall consider the political tendency of the new power of Rome in the English-speaking world. We shall find, with few qualifications, a consistent collaboration of Roman Catholicism, and especially the Vatican, with Fascism and Nazism against democracy.

1. The Execution of Italian and German Catholic Democracy

Let us turn then first to Italy, the host of the papal court and source of most of its personnel. Italy came out of the war disillusioned and poverty-stricken. After long and inglorious bargaining its leaders had managed to elect the winning side, but secured few prizes to offset war losses and the suffering of the economic dislocation. Demobilization was followed by unemployment. The peasants and workers, who had been promised the moon during the war, now turned to socialism, which had opposed the war throughout. There were strikes and riots. And in the postwar elections of 1919 the Socialists gained enormously, polling over half the vote and securing the largest group of deputies, though not an actual majority in the Chamber. Here was a prospect that caused certain privileged groups to have second thoughts about democracy. What if a democratic Italy should mean a socialist Italy? Was democracy worth it?

The second party in the Chamber was not wholly reassuring to those who took this point of view. It was a new party, a " People's Party," whose real character was that of a Catholic party. Now this was a startling development in Italy. In Germany, of course, there was the great Center Party, and there were long-established Catholic parties in Belgium and Holland. But the papacy had enforced a boycott of national Italian politics since the consolidation of the kingdom of Italy in 1870, the famous *Non expedit*. If Catholics were allowed to engage in the political structure of constitutional Italy, to vote or to hold office, this implied a recognition of the regime. And the Vatican was still formally protesting against the annexation by Italy of the states of the Church. How, then, could the pope relax the *Non expedit* and permit the organization of the " Popolari "?

The *Non expedit* had proved itself a failure. Even before the death of Leo XIII it was evident that Catholic obedience to it was too partial to make it effective, and the net result was not to cripple the kingdom of Italy but only to weaken its conservative parties. Pius X from 1905 permitted the bishops to allow local Catholic political activity at their discretion to combat the growing power of socialism and anarchism. The " Roman Question " was really no longer a major issue. A *modus vivendi* had been stabilized even while the theoretical difficulties remained. And within this *modus vivendi* Italian Catholics pressed to be allowed to take their full share in political life. Especially in the war was this reconciliation hastened. Clergy and laity supported the national war effort enthusiastically, and a " clerical," Meda, actually served in the Ministry. After the Armistice the Vatican quietly gave the nod to the organizers of a national Catholic party, which took shape in January, 1919.

Pius X doubtless shuddered in his grave. The People's Party was in a measure a new version of Murri's *Lega democratica nazionale* or of Sangnier's *Sillon,* and was guilty, as they had been, of disobeying his *motu proprio* on Catholic Popular Action. It was a frankly democratic party, and not merely in the Pickwickian sense of " democracy " defined by *Graves de communi.* Its leader, Don Luigi Sturzo, had served his apprenticeship under Murri and Toniolo back in the days of Leo XIII, and really believed in political democracy as well as social and economic reform. The Popolari also stood for a high degree of local self-government and decentralization. They were strong internationalists, perhaps Wilson's most fervent European supporters. As with the German Center, the backbone of the party was made up of the various organizations of Catholic Action, " white labor unions," farmers' co-operatives, clubs of youth, in which the clergy directed policy. Sturzo tried to make the party function, however, as a genuine democratic party independent of hierarchical control. For the time being, Benedict XV indulged this repetition of Leo's experiment. The *Non expedit* was publicly and formally withdrawn on the eve of the elections in 1919, which under the circumstances was taken as a papal blessing on the People's Party. In their first contest, the Popolari gained one fifth of the seats in the Chamber, and became the nation's second great party.

The year after the elections was a turbulent one. Social disorder spread, while the Government seemed unable either to restrain violence on the one hand or on the other to undertake constructive reform. Disappointed in the long overdue agrarian reform, peasants seized land in some areas. In September, 1920, the socialist agitation in northern industrial cities reached a climax with actual seizure of factories. A modern industrial society, however, is scarcely to be reorganized by such tactics, and many socialists realized the futility of them. The party split in the following months, a small minority electing for the new Russian Communism, while a right wing which was strong in the General Confederation of Labor moved toward responsible participation in government and a program close to that of the Popolari. The elections of 1921 showed the conservative reaction as the Popolari gained and the Socialists lost a fifth of their seats. A workable grouping of moderate responsible opinion seemed to be crystallizing.

Such a crystallizing, however, was precisely what was feared by another group on the political horizon. As the Socialists split, the gangs of Fascist thugs which preyed upon them increased in strength, and at a congress in November, 1921, a Fascist party was consolidated around an imperialist and anti-Marxist program. The ablest leader was a one-time small-town schoolteacher, Benito Mussolini, who had been expelled from the Socialist party in 1914 for his opposition to its antiwar stand. The experience of the war and its mass emotions had convinced him that nationalism was the most effective means of swaying the masses and that socialism must become nationalist to be successful. After the war he directed his appeal chiefly to veterans and their families, seeking to exploit the pathos of the cause for which so many had died. He developed the myth of the betrayal of Italy at Versailles. This would have been just another disgruntled veterans' organization, however, if the frightened landowners, bankers, and industrialists had not begun to subsidize the Fascist gangs in 1921 to terrorize socialists. Mussolini only reluctantly adjusted himself to this conversion of his movement for socialism into a strikebreaking private police for the rich, but agreed in time to retain his leadership. For a larger program Mussolini was dependent on the nationalism of D'Annunzio, with his black shirts, fezzes, salute, songs, cheers, his " march on Fiume," and his abortive corporative state there. The movement centered in Milan, where the local archbishop, Ratti, was sympathetic. Archbishop Ratti and Mussolini shared the hope that the Popolari and reformist Socialists would be unable to form a vigorous democratic government in Italy. And while one would scarcely have guessed it in 1921, they were to become the two men most responsible for killing democracy in Italy.

The motives of these two personalities are interesting. With Mussolini the question was how he could bring himself to collaborate with ecclesiastics. Before the war he had published *There Is No God* and the *Cardinal's Mistress,* and after it had demanded the confiscation of all Church property. In 1921, the *Civiltà cattolica* had been able to find nothing to choose between him and the Communists. Yet in his maiden speech in the Chamber of Deputies that year Mussolini startled his followers by taking a new line, the atheist Romanism of Maurras. " Fascism does not preach and does not practice anticlericalism," he announced. " The only universal idea which today exists in Rome emanates from the Vatican." [2] With his cult of the ancient Roman Empire, Mussolini was moved to deference before the ghost sitting crowned in its grave. He hoped to be able to exploit it in his own imperialist schemes.

Archbishop Ratti of Milan, on the other hand, was elected pope in February, 1922, to succeed Benedict XV. As Pius XI, he was to be primarily responsible for the antidemocratic policy of the Roman Church from 1922 to 1939, and contributed notably to the gains of Fascism and Communism in this period. This was in part personal; he was temperamentally an irritable, obstinate autocrat himself. He derived from that lower middle class which furnished the bulk of adherents to Fascism. And his brief diplomatic experience in Warsaw in 1920 during the counterattack by the Russian army left him with an obsessive fear of Communism. " He believed that democracy was too feeble and incoherent to serve as a dam against the Communist tide, and a strange irony made him turn to the new form of authoritarian government as offering the only hope of successful resistance. . . . Nor had he at the time of his election any real appreciation of the forces that give democracy in the hour of crisis a strength and toughness far greater than the most rigid authoritarian system can command. . . . Perhaps too he was not free from the delusion which is even still common, and to some extent excusable in ecclesiastical minds: that the authoritarian form of government which is indispensable to the Church should also be most beneficial for the State." [3] In this last view Pius merely maintained the spoken conviction of his predecessors Pius IX, Leo XIII, and Pius X.

In his immediate Italian situation Pius XI faced the choice between democracy and authoritarianism in the form of the struggle between the People's Party and the Fascists. It was in effect the same choice Pius X had made as between Sangnier and Maurras. Both popes preferred the atheist reactionary to the Christian democrat. On three occasions in particular Pius XI intervened gratuitously in Italian politics to cripple the democratic defense against Mussolini's violence.

The first occasion was the preparation of the Fascist "march on Rome" in October, 1922. This *Putsch,* justified at the time in Fascist propaganda as saving Italy from the Bolsheviks, was, as Mussolini himself admitted later, nothing of the kind. The Bolshevik danger, if any, was well past in Italy by the middle of 1921, and through 1922 the Socialists were perceptibly losing ground. The danger in 1922, from the Fascist point of view, was that Italy was at last settling down to peaceable and democratic government. A coalition of reformist Socialists and the People's Party seemed indicated, and such a coalition with a working majority of Italian voters behind it would soon make Fascism appear something of a luxury. The Fascist slogan of 1924 was significant for the mentality of 1922 also: "Better the Communists than the Popolari." Mussolini and Pius XI had to act quickly.

A circular of October 2, 1922, from Cardinal Secretary of State Gasparri paralyzed the People's Party. All priests (and the great majority of them, of course, were in this party) were summarily ordered to withdraw from politics. In the consequent consternation among the democratic forces, Mussolini staged his "march." The Cabinet urged a decree of martial law, but, against the counsel of his military advisers, the cowardly king refused to suppress the demonstration and instead made Mussolini prime minister.

The following four years witnessed a virtual civil war in Italy, a war in which the constitutional and democratic forces sought to free themselves from the creeping totalitarian blight. In this war hundreds were murdered and tens of thousands jailed illegally by the Fascists. The core of the democratic opposition remained the Popolari and the moderate Socialists. Communism was still insignificant, comprising not more than one in six of the Italian socialists. The pope feared this democratic opposition as much as did Mussolini, worrying especially lest the bulk of Catholic Action should gravitate to alliance with democracy and socialism. When Mussolini attempted in 1923 to force the Popolari to coalesce with his own party and eliminate all political opposition, Pius again pulled his chestnuts out of the fire. He undertook a reorganization of Catholic Action along the lines urged by Pius X in 1903, forbidding any democratic political activity. It was not neutrality on the part of the pope. It was active support of Fascist revolution to prohibit Catholic organizations to oppose it.

Another specific intervention by the Vatican occurred in June, 1923. In the spring the Fascist attempt to maneuver the Popolari congress to vote for unqualified support of the Fascist ministry had been frustrated chiefly by Don Sturzo. Thereafter the Fascist press concentrated its attacks on him as their most dangerous opponent. In June, at the height of this campaign, Don Sturzo suddenly resigned as general secretary of the party. The resignation, however, was first sent to the Vatican, for it was the pope who had requested it. Whether Mussolini had put Pius up to it with threats of legislation against Catholic schools and congregations, as was then suggested, is not known certainly. In any case the pope had forced the retirement of the general of the democratic forces at the height of the battle. And the impossibility of full and responsible participation in democratic politics by a Roman priest was again illustrated.

After Sturzo's resignation the Fascist campaign to wipe out the " white " trade-unions, co-operatives, and youth organizations increased in violence. The characteristic device of heroic doses of castor oil was applied to priests and laity. In the summer Father Minzoni was brutally clubbed to death, but all the Fascists involved were acquitted and the Vatican did not protest. Matteotti listed over two thousand outrages, murders, clubbings, castor oil purges, burnings, and lootings for the year after the march on Rome. In June, 1924, Matteotti himself was murdered at Mussolini's personal instigation. Indignation was intense throughout the country. Nearly all the opposition groups, including the People's Party, left the Chamber in protest and requested the king to dismiss the criminal prime minister. This was the last crisis in which there seemed real opportunity of re-establishing constitutional government. But once again Pius intervened on behalf of the murderer.

The only alternative to Fascist rule in Italy was a coalition between Popolari and democratic socialists. This, the pope now warned, was precluded by the moral law, which forbids " collaboration with evil." When Catholic democrats protested that just such a coalition was the basis of Catholic policy in Germany and Belgium, the Vatican replied evasively. The Catholic parties of Belgium and Germany, to tell the truth, themselves faced no promising future in Vatican tactical calculations. Pius followed this with a circular to the bishops obliging all priests to resign from the party. This was the *coup de grâce* to the People's Party and to Italian Catholic democracy. As the best Catholic historian of these events writes, " Fascism reached agreement with the Church over the grave of Catholic democracy." [4] Or, as Mussolini described the achievement for which the credit must be divided between him and Pius XI, "Fascism has marched to victory over the rotting corpse of liberty."

In 1926, the year in which the last survivors of the People's Party were mopped up by the Fascists, Mussolini began negotiations with the Vatican for a settlement of the "Roman Question." Benedict XV and Pius XI had made overtures in this direction with the constitutional government before Mussolini, and it would probably have been settled in these years if a democratic government had been in power. It would have been settled, however, on very different terms. Neither Pius nor Mussolini liked the type of separation being urged by some Catholic democrats. Both preferred an agreement consisting of privileges and controls. Negotiations continued from 1926 to 1929, when the Lateran pacts were at last published. Both leaders had difficulty in convincing their constituencies of the wisdom of the deal. The bulk of the Fascist leadership was still contemptuously anticlerical, and only to be restrained with effort. And the best Christianity of Italy sympathized with the long, slow martyrdom of the Popolari. The pope did his best. Knowing well that Mussolini was a heretic and a murderer and that Fascism was inculcating violence and statolatry, he announced in a speech of December, 1926, that the *Duce* was nevertheless "the man sent by Providence." Cardinal Merry del Val, three months before, had, in his role of pontifical legate, described him as "visibly protected by God." The Anglo-American Catholic press repeated these diplomatic honorifics with nauseous ingenuousness. Newspaper debates, meanwhile, prepared the public for the necessary concessions; the Catholics to give up all but Vatican City and to make the pact without international guarantees, the Fascists to concede outright sovereignty over Vatican City instead merely of usufruct. This treaty might well have been drawn up with a democratic Italy, but never the accompanying Concordat which Pius did his best to make indissoluble from the Treaty. The antidemocratic character of this Concordat must be noticed.

Least significant of the three pacts was the financial convention by which the papal court was compensated for the loss of its former territories to the Italian state. Certain aspects of these payments, however, were significant. They consisted of a billion lire in Fascist bonds, and three quarters of a billion in cash. The Vatican agreed to withdraw the latter only gradually and to reinvest much of it in further Fascist securities. Apparently it was also agreed that the debentures should not be sold for some years. The effect of the whole operation was to make the Holy See one of the largest investors in Fascism. To be sure, the greater part of its income still came from the United States.

The Concordat did much more to commit the Roman Church to the Fascist cause. The Fascists were given control of the management of by far the greater part of Church property in Italy, in return for the generous subsidies to the Roman clergy.[5] And even more significant, the Fascist government was given a veto on episcopal appointments, which it sought to use to secure the promotion of pro-Fascist clergy. This was of more than local interest, for the great bulk of the administrative staff, if not the future cardinals of world Romanism, was to be selected from these prelates sifted by the Fascists. With regard to minor benefices: " In addition to the Government's right to object to a parish priest on the occasion of his appointment, it may appeal for his removal at any time, ' should grave reasons arise which render the continued presence of an ecclesiastic in a particular benefice undesirable ' (Art. 21). . . . In general the threat is quite sufficient to prevent any signs of a dangerous independence, although the Government has in fact secured the removal of a few ' troublesome ' clerics *pour encourager les autres*." [6] Mussolini was quite accurate in telling the Chamber that under the Concordat the Italian Church was not free. Pius and Pacelli had given him powers to force the adherence of the Italian clergy to the Fascist program. They had preferred this to democratic liberty.

What did the Vatican negotiators win in return for this Fascist control over the personnel of the Roman clergy? Mussolini was willing to make concessions to canon law on marriage and divorce. He cheerfully placed further restrictions on the liberty of Jews, Protestants, and ex-Roman Catholics. As with atheist Catholics generally, he was ready to persecute nonconformists to his kept Church as threats to national uniformity. In place of equality before the law, the Concordat conceded special treatment for felonious clergy (Art. 8). And Article 23 gave civil force to ecclesiastical penalities upon apostate priests. Mussolini discharged about a thousand of them from the educational system to satisfy the rancor of the Vatican. The religious orders were given full juridical personality and the right to hold property, although within certain limits. The chief gains of the Church, however, at least on paper, concerned education and Catholic Action. We must see what each of these was worth.

Mussolini feared Catholic Action as the former basis of the People's Party. He had attacked the Boy Scouts as survivors of *popolarismo* even before the Lateran pacts. The Catholic youth and university students were ordered suppressed in the consequent row of 1930 and 1931. The pope protested to world opinion in *Non abbiamo bisogno* and then a deal was worked out. The Government announced that measures against Catholic youth were revoked, but they were denied all athletic and professional functions, as well as all lay control. The result was that, despite the pope's protest, the system of Catholic Action which he had built up as an improvement on democratic action was assimilated, just as were the clergy, to Fascism. From 1931 to 1938, Catholic Action was obtrusively Fascist, despite its constitution as " outside and above politics." Yet even the servility of its leaders did not save it from renewed attacks in 1938 on the pretext of the racialist controversy. At best Fascism would permit strictly devotional practice and the teaching of private morality to an organization that would sanction its own pagan ethical policy on public issues.

A similar adjustment was worked out in education. In accordance with the Concordat, the rights of conscience were denied and Roman doctrine made compulsory in both primary and secondary education. The religion class was set beside that in reading, where violence and militarism were commended. Class opened with prayer and a Fascist song. The Fascists " integrated " Catholic teaching with the philosophy behind the rest of the curriculum, the glorification of violence, militarism, nationalism, truculence. Children could study the prayer book so long as they were taught how to use it in good Fascist fashion.

Politically speaking, Pius XI had deliberately sabotaged democracy, the strongest opponent of Communism, for the politically and morally ruinous experiment of Fascism. In Mr. Binchy's opinion he had also made the most dangerous choice for the Church. The " cold pogrom " of Nazism was more insidious than the massacres of Bolshevism as more adapted to the laxity of the average man.[7] Even more dangerous than Hitler's " cold pogrom," however, was the Fascist system of incorporating and neutralizing homeopathic doses of Christianity. The pope had led the Church as well as Western civilization into mortal danger because he so hated democracy. And the Catholics of democratic countries generally applauded. The leading English apologist, Hilaire Belloc, gloated: " The anti-Catholic and Masonic organizations have been effectually got rid of by the happy suppression of Parliaments and all their sham authority, which is but a mask for a few rich men controlling a corrupt machine."[8]

The sharpest attack Pius ever published against Fascism came in his *Non abbiamo bisogno,* smuggled out of Italy by Cardinal Spellman. The substance of this encyclical was a protest against the ferocious campaign of the Fascists against the youth groups of Catholic Action in 1930 and 1931. The pope repudiated the charges that these groups were political in nature, or nuclei for political opposition to the regime. He had done his honest best to silence all anti-Fascist Catholic activity. The real motive of this persecution, he charged, was " to monopolize completely the young . . . for the exclusive advantage of a party and of a regime based on an ideology which clearly resolves itself into a true, a real pagan worship of the State." [9] This revolutionary regime sought to inculcate into young people " hatred, violence, and irreverence."

The pope was thus at last declaring the moral judgment on the Fascist program which democratic Catholics had been urging for ten years. As he looked back over this period Pius recalled how, despite all pressure, he had " always refrained from formal and explicit condemnations, and had even gone so far as to believe possible and to favor compromises [compatibilità e cooperazioni] which to others seemed inadmissible." [10] And now what — a tardy condemnation of this political system committed to violence and statolatry? On the contrary: " We have not said that we wish to condemn the [Fascist] party and the regime as such. Our aim has been to point out and to condemn all those things in the program and activities of the party which have been found to be contrary to Catholic doctrine and Catholic practice. . . . We have fulfilled a precise duty of our episcopal ministry toward our dear sons who are members of the party, so that their conscience may be at peace." By this the pope meant that he recommended subscription to the Fascist oath with a silent mental reservation. " We believe, then, that we have thus at the same time accomplished a good work for the party itself." Acknowledging thus " perennial gratitude " for all that Mussolini had done for the benefit of religion, Pius indicated that essential Fascism was still acceptable to him. It needed only to be pruned of those two or three elements which Mussolini had consistently maintained *were* its essence, violence, statolatry, amorality.

The full moral implications of the kind of " collaboration with evil " in which Pius XI had felt able to indulge were conspicuous at the time of the Abyssinian outrage. He had known from the beginning that the Fascists made a cult of war and violence, and the crime statistics of the country seemed to indicate some success in this teaching. He had known also the Fascist denial of any moral judgment on the State, which should have a " conscience " of its own. Knowing these things, he had yet deliberately entered into a concordat which gave these Fascists new powers of control over the Catholic clergy, and had himself agreed that Catholics should engage in no political actions save as they supported Fascist policies. Not until 1931 did he publicly attack these ideas which had been taught and exemplified for a decade. Even this condemnation was emasculated by illogical attempts to separate the Fascist party and regime from the Fascist program. There still remained a possibility of a certain minimum moral dignity in genuine abstention from politics, a real neutrality. This possibility, however, the Roman Court did not realize; on the contrary, the teaching Church went out of its way to put itself in the same moral category as the Fascists, and to lend the sanction of Roman Catholicism to actions condemned by the moral consensus of the civilized world.

In 1935, the Fascist propaganda preparation for imperialist aggression in Ethiopia was followed by an outright attack. The Fascists now collected their profits from the rights of selection and control which Pius had given them over the Italian clergy. A large number of the lower clergy still retained the democratic and internationalist views they had expressed openly in their Popolari days, and some suffered imprisonment or worse for refusing to play the Fascist game. The hierarchy, however, led by Cardinal Shuster, the first appointee under the concordatory system of a Fascist right of veto, displayed astonishing servility. Many actually contributed episcopal rings to the Fascist war chest. Salvemini tallied up a score of seven cardinals, twenty-nine archbishops, and sixty-one bishops who became notorious for connivance with the Fascists.[11] In Binchy's language, " Perhaps the most nauseating feature of the whole oratorical campaign was the attempt to represent this cowardly aggression against the weak as a just, nay even a holy, war; a twentieth century crusade by the forces of Christian civilization." [12]

In August the pope had expressed himself on the alleged issues of the war. He referred to the Fascist case for colonies. " The need for expansion is a fact which must be taken into account; the right of self-defense has its limits and must observe a certain moderation in order to be itself blameless." [13] In September, again, as the League debated the Abyssinian problem, the pope again urged recognition of the Fascist case, desiring that " the hopes, the rights, and the needs of the Italian people . . . be satisfied, recognized, and guaranteed with justice and with peace." This was just what Mussolini was saying, while the Italian troops were still en route to Africa. On their face these were unexceptionable sentiments, but spoken when they were and in consideration of the use that would be made of them, they put the infallible director of Catholic morals in a most ambiguous position. In October, Abyssinia was invaded in flat defiance of the Covenant of the League and the Kellogg Pact. Practically without exception the whole world condemned Mussolini, all except the pope.[14] He now subsided into a dignified and correct silence. According to a Catholic writer, the diplomatic machinery of the Vatican was now used in Latin America to prevent the application of sanctions by the League against Mussolini.[15] The Catholic press in Britain and America, as usual, was the center of the attempt to mobilize opinion in democratic countries against international law and democracy.

The following spring the poison gas and bombs of the Italians had done their work on the Abyssinian villages. In May the pope broke his silence and expressed his jubilation along " with the triumphant joy of an entire great and good people over a peace which, it is hoped and intended, will be an effective contribution and prelude to that true peace in Europe and the world." [16] While Mr. Binchy felt that the Fascist acclamation of this statement as " a knock-out blow to the plutocratic League Powers " was extreme, he was forced to concede that " even if we accept the whole of the Fascist case at its face value, the notion that the military triumph of a country which had been formally proclaimed a lawbreaker and an aggressor by the votes of over fifty nations was a hopeful prelude to ' true peace in Europe and the world ' was not likely to carry conviction." [17]

Pius' policy of collaboration with Fascism in Italy had thus involved not merely the knifing of Catholic democracy, but also support in the Fascist defiance of international law and morality. In order to pursue this latter development we must now turn back and trace the Roman Catholic contribution to the rise of Hitler, who from the time of the Abyssinian War took the lead in international banditry away from Mussolini.

In Germany under the Weimar Republic was played out much the same drama as in postwar Italy. A democratic Catholic initiative was betrayed by Catholic reactionaries within Germany and finally sold out to the Nazis by the Vatican. There was no outstanding leader of Catholic democracy in the crisis, like Don Sturzo in Italy. Matthias Erzberger, who gave promise of becoming one such, was assassinated in 1921. The antidemocratic Catholic politicians, Brüning, Kaas, von Papen, aided and abetted by the nuncio Pacelli, were able to dominate the boards from the middle '20's on and to make the Catholic Center Party the midwife to Nazi dictatorship. German Lutheranism, consistent with its history, was at least as antidemocratic as the Catholics.

The end of the Hohenzollern empire in the war gave considerable advantages to German Catholicism. In its new freedom the Roman Church effected a national organization, acquiring a Catholic bishop for Berlin and a nuncio, Pacelli (now Pius XII). In the general disorganization of the '20's, German Catholic Action profited by its effective discipline in manifold institutions for all classes. With the new freedom of association, the number of monasteries and monks doubled under the Republic. Artists and writers were active among Catholic intellectuals, constituting in some ways a revival of modernism, especially in the liturgical movement. A " new Counter Reformation " seemed in progress in Germany, but of a different type. The laity here were freer of hierarchical control than anywhere else in the Catholic world, and intellectual life was freer and more creative. And the political organ of German Catholicism, the Center Party, held the balance of power and determined the course of the Weimar Republic.

Holding the balance of power, indeed, seemed to involve an oscillation in political orientation which was absolutely unprincipled. But in fact the Center contained within itself great divergences, ranging from monarchist and militarist conspirators against the Republic to genuine democrats. The only real unity lay in the interests of the Church. In consequence the Center reversed its political alliances ten or a dozen times between 1918 and 1933, joining now with the socialists and now with the nationalist and conservative parties. Catholic workers were more sympathetic with the former, and increasingly voted for them, while Catholic industrialists and intellectuals, as in France and Italy and Spain at the same time, were drawn by militarist and absolutist movements. In Bavaria particularly, the Catholic party was predominantly antidemocratic.

Erzberger, the Catholic politician who negotiated the Armistice, did not carry the Center with him. The party as a whole accepted the Armistice and the Republic with the same contempt that French Catholics had shown for the Third French Republic in the nineteenth century. The leaders of the party had been convinced monarchists and imperialists and were not now converted. Men like Brüning would have preferred not to sign the Armistice. Cardinal von Faulhaber, who had considered the First World War as " the perfect example of a just war," told the Munich Catholic Congress in 1922, " The Revolution was perjury and high treason, and will go down in history branded forever with the mark of Cain." [18] These Bavarian Catholics were in close touch with the legitimist conspiracies of Mgr. Seipel and his friends in Austria and Hungary. They subscribed to the new German and Austrian constitutions with mental reservation of the Catholic doctrine that political power cannot be delegated by the people or responsible to them.

After the murder of Erzberger, Wirth seemed to come the nearest to a successor as leader of the democratic wing of the Catholic party. But Pacelli, who had supported Erzberger's efforts under Benedict XV, treated Wirth coolly after 1922 and cultivated the reviving reactionaries. The elevation of Pius XI in 1922 and his collaboration with Italian Fascism had given a decided turn to Catholic politics. In Germany the policy from 1924 to 1928 was to lend support to the nationalists against the socialists in return for legislation favoring the confessional rather than the religiously mixed public school. Even Wirth followed Pacelli's lead in this policy, while Brüning now appeared for the first time in the

Reichstag as a representative of the militarist reactionary wing of the party.

In the 1928 elections the Pacelli policy showed its failure. The school bills had not succeeded, and a large section of Catholic voters, disgusted with the new party line, voted Socialist. Pius XI was faced with the frightening possibility he had sought to preclude in Italy, that the bulk of the Catholic party would ally itself with democrats and socialists. The development in this direction must be checked, and soon a new type of leadership emerged under Pacelli's patronage. At the end of the year Professor Kaas of Bonn became chairman of the party, a man who had recently distinguished himself by supporting the nationalist efforts of Hugenberg and Hitler to hamstring Stresemann's negotiations with the Western powers. The military clique around von Schleicher and Groener embarked on a conspiracy of Hohenzollern restoration and picked the right-wing Catholic Brüning as their parliamentary front. He became head of the parliamentary group of the Center at the end of 1929, with intentions very similar to those of Mgr. Seipel in Austria. Thus the Vatican reaction to the democratic and socialist tendency in the German Center Party was to install a leadership conspiring for a monarchist restoration. The democratic wing was carried along, for were not Kaas and Brüning sharing in a coalition government with the socialists? The mark of an able statesman, in Brüning's opinion, was that " one should not let either one's contemporaries or posterity see the ultimate motives of one's policy." [19]

In 1929, Pius completed his Concordat and treaty with the dictator of Italy, and the Catholic Fascists in Austria made an abortive effort to seize power in Mussolini's style. The German clericals and militarists were prepared for similar adventures. In March, 1930, the Socialist chancellor was forced to resign, and old Hindenburg at once summoned the clerical Brüning. On April 1, this spokesman for the new " Government of Front-Line Soldiers " served notice on German democracy. He announced that he would make " the final attempt " to govern " with the assistance of the *Reichstag*." In June, when the French evacuation of the Rhineland freed him from immediate external pressures, Brüning provoked a quarrel with the parliament over a financial bill and dissolved it. He then proceeded to launch a series of decrees, ruling as a personal dictator, representing not the German people, but the army clique.

For the next two years the Catholic chancellor developed his policy. He carried on large-scale secret rearmament, some of which was exposed by the Nobel prize winner von Ossietzky. He greatly increased subsidies to the large estate owners and set enormous import duties on foodstuffs to produce *autarkie*. At the same time shameless price-fixing by the cartels was permitted. The cost was paid by consumers and workers, for wages were cut twice as much as the standard of living, and unemployment rose from two to six millions. The world depression hit Germany hard, but the " Hunger Chancellor " was out to heighten its effects in order to show the Western powers that " reparations could not go on in this way." He was cultivating the economic catastrophe desired by the great industrialists and the Nazis they were financing. As Hitler's " angel," the Catholic industrialist Thyssen, had said in 1929: " I need that crisis now. It offers the only chance of settling wage and reparations questions at one and the same time." [20] An economic newspaper calculated that the economic losses Brüning's policies produced in his two and one half years would have paid reparations for fifty-five years. But Brüning was successful. He had made a joke of parliamentary government, had extensively rearmed Germany, and won the Hoover Moratorium on reparations in 1931. And the social and economic conditions so induced raised the Nazis to the strongest political force in Germany.

To the Nazis, and the nationalist group led by Hugenberg, Brüning offered a deal. If they would give him a year to conclude his campaign to get rid of reparations, he would then admit them to the Government with him. His ultimate goal was to re-establish the Hohenzollern crown prince with a ministry drawn from the nationalist and reactionary parties. But the Nazis, the Nationalists, and Hindenburg all declined. For their various purposes they no longer needed him, and intended to have no obligations to the Catholic Center Party whom he still represented.

Brüning made one more surprising reversal before he went under. Disdained by Nazis, he turned the Center for the last time toward the Socialists with the slogan, " Elect Hindenburg and defeat Hitler." They did elect Hindenburg, but the old marshal rewarded Brüning by discharging him in May, 1932. Again the military had their Catholic front man ready, the sporty millionaire with the shady past, von Papen. Von Papen had given his word to Kaas not to accept the chancellorship, and when he did head up the new " Cabinet of Barons," he was expelled from the Center. But neither von Papen nor the Vatican intended any future for a Catholic parliamentary party anyway. Von Papen made his deal with Hitler and entered the first Nazi government with him as vice-chancellor. He then went off to Rome to cement a treaty between the papacy and the new dictator of Germany. Despite his quarrels with Fascism, culminating in *Non abbiamo bisogno,* Pius still preferred a deal with a dictator to Catholic democracy.

But there was still a little help Brüning and his Center could give the Nazis in the way of providing the Nazi coup with a semblance of legality. In March, Brüning and Kaas agreed to deliver the Center's votes for Hitler's " Enabling Enactment " giving dictatorial powers. A small minority of the demoralized Center still wanted to vote " No," but in the event all voted for this suicide of the *Reichstag*. The same day the Catholic bishops released the ban they had imposed the previous year on Catholic membership in the Nazi Party. Both the Center and the German episcopate were thus forced unwillingly to come to terms with the Nazis by Pius and Pacelli.

The Vatican thus acted as Hitler's executioner on Catholic democracy in Germany, as it had done for Mussolini in Italy, and still hoped to do in Austria and Spain. It proceeded to build up a system of concordats with the new postwar dictators. Hitler sent von Papen to Rome in April to confer with the Italian *Duce* and to negotiate a concordat. It was completed in July and Brüning announced the dissolution of the Center. In the meantime the Nazis had exerted severe pressure on Catholic Action, confiscating funds, arresting leaders, breaking up meetings. Brüning had retired to a monastery. Kaas got out of the country, but from Rome praised Hitler's " high ideals " and " clear thinking." Cardinal Faulhaber rejoiced in the " change of mentality." Pacelli did his best, meanwhile, to reassure the disarmed regiments of the Center that they were not being abandoned.

The Concordat was modeled in many ways on that with Mussolini. There was the same agreement Pius had there urged, that the Church would avoid all political activity (save that in favor of the dictatorship, Art. 32) in return for assurances as to its rights in education, family affairs, and youth activities. As in Italy, the totalitarian party was to be given in practice a veto right over new episcopal appointments. In fact the Nazis continued their terrorism against the press, Boy Scouts, trade-unions, workers' clubs, and similar organizations of Catholic Action. By the end of 1933 there were not a few Catholics among the hundred thousand in concentration camps. Yet to the persecution against the Jews, socialists, and Communists which aroused protest around the world, the Vatican had nothing to say. For the next two years Hitler was chiefly preoccupied with his parallel endeavor to take the German Protestant Church into camp, and it was only from 1935 that the Catholics began to receive his attentions again on a large scale.

The further controversies of the German Catholic Church with the Nazi dictatorship after 1933, for all their interest and importance, have no part in the history of the Churches and democracy. They belong with the centuries-old story of the conflict between absolute States and an absolutist hierarchy. The Catholic Church has many martyrs against Hitler, but they are not martyrs for democracy. The leaders of political Catholicism in Germany, with the support of the Vatican, deliberately preferred Hitler to democracy. They discovered that Hitler was dishonorable and criminal, and intended the elimination of Christianity. There was ample evidence for all this when they made their choice. They had thought they could control him as a tool in installing a monarchy, but they found that they were not even to be junior partners. They protested. *Mit brennender Sorge* is stirring reading for any Christian, Catholic or Protestant. But the protest was for adherence to the Concordat of 1933, a concordat that, like all the other concordats of Pius XI, assumed a dictatorship, just as did the corporative state of *Quadragesimo anno*. As a Catholic writer pointed out, " Pius XI issued in 1937 the encyclical *Mit brennender Sorge,* in which, with considerable skill, the extravagances of German Nazi doctrines are picked out for condemnation in a way that would not involve the condemnation of political and social totalitarianism." [21]

So far as internal affairs are concerned, the papal concordats with Mussolini and Hitler complete the history of Catholic democracy in Italy and Germany between the World Wars. For the fourth time in a century the papacy had authoritatively and devastatingly liquidated Catholic democracy. In international affairs, however, the Roman Court wrote still another chapter in the '30's by its covert or open support of lawlessness against what was left of the League of Nations and international law. In virtually every successive blow to this structure, from the invasion of Manchuria in 1931 to the final outbreak of the Second World War, Vatican diplomacy was friendly to the aggressors. We have already noticed the Abyssinian War of 1935–1936. In 1936, the Nazis remilitarized the Rhineland, with the expressed approval of the Catholic hierarchy. And in the plebiscite of this year on Hitler's total record, the German episcopate instructed Catholics that they might vote for him with reservations. Then came in succession Hitler's conquests of Spain, Austria, and Czechoslovakia, in each of which political Catholicism was the chief vehicle of his penetration. In all these countries the Catholic parties were conspiring with the Vatican to break the constitutional regime for a less democratic one, and in every case they were persuaded that Hitler was the man to speed them to their goal. Let us consider Austria and Spain.

2. Clerical Fascism in Austria and Spain

While with Italy and with Germany there were vigorous Catholic democratic movements, effective through Catholic political parties in constitutional regimes, Austria and Spain, the two ancient pillars of the

Counter Reformation, were still almost innocent of Catholic democracy in the twentieth century. Spanish and Austrian Catholics were by
definition antidemocratic and antiliberal, as French Catholics had been
a century before. In these countries, consequently, we do not have to
describe the betrayal and suppression of democratic by authoritarian
Catholicism as in Italy and Germany. Here we have simply a story of
civil war and massacre launched by counterrevolutionary Catholics
against democratic and socialist groups. The betrayal here, for there was
betrayal here, was betrayal by the Vatican and hierarchy to Nazism.
Having embarked on the slippery path of alliance with terrorism and
dictatorship, Pius XI and Pacelli found themselves gravitating steadily
from the milder clerical Fascism of such as Dollfuss and Salazar, the
" ethical " State of Mussolini, to the full and frank brutality of Nazism.
The Vatican served as middleman to arrange the betrayal of Austria to
a dictatorship on Mussolini's model and with Mussolini's aid, and then
to sell, in turn, von Schuschnigg's Fascist Austria to Hitler. For by the
late '30's Mussolini and Franco and all the little clerical Fascist " fueh-
rers " were being *gleichgeschaltet* by the largest operator in the racket.
The Catholic projects of a Hapsburg Mittel-europa or a Latin bloc were
now absorbed or replaced by Hitler's New Order, for only Hitler was
really powerful enough to undertake the Vatican's·" crusade " against
the U.S.S.R.

The treaty of St. Germain (1919) defined a preposterous Austria. It
was reduced from a State of thirty millions to six and one half, of which
the capital, Vienna, now constituted a third of the population. The
Wilsonian principle of self-determination for nationalities was economic and political insanity east of the Oder, ensuring starvation and
political instability in a Balkanized area. The treaty makers were not to
be blamed overmuch, to be sure, for this fragmenting was the demand
of the nationalist minority movements of the old Austro-Hungarian
empire, and the treaty was simply recognizing their pressure. But with
regard to Austria, for example, the postwar settlement meant that a
State that could not be self-supporting would be dependent indefinitely
on the charity of the Western powers. " League of Nations Austria "
lived on loans which could never be repaid on the condition that she
would not cement the economic ties with Germany or the Danubian
countries which alone could make her a functioning economy.

There were in postwar Austria two rival political programs to meet
this situation.

The strongest single party in Austria, as in Italy, was Socialist. In the
revolution which ended the Hapsburg rule at the end of the war, the
Socialists of Vienna played a major role. They saved Austria from Com-

munism in 1918–1919 and consistently offered the strongest resistance
to Communism in the following decades. Their policy was peaceful,
democratic socialism, not dissimilar to that of the British Labor Party.
The revolution itself, unlike others we shall have to describe, was blood-
less. The old aristocrats were allowed to leave peacefully. There were
no concentration camps, no hangings, no deprivation of civil or economic rights. The Socialists had a large stake in Austria, where, after
losing the first place, they polled steadily forty per cent of the total vote
so long as there were free elections. And internationally in the early
years of the Weimar Republic they hoped for some kind of rapproche-
ment with a democratic Germany.

The second party and program was that of the Catholics, who held
the countryside, and, by a slight margin, the national government. The
Catholic program was, or was later disclosed to be, restoration of the
monarchy and the traditional privileges of the Roman Church in the
Austrian State. The leader of the Catholic party in the '20's, Mgr. Ignaz
Seipel, was frank to state that he found intolerable the limitations
placed on the power of the clergy in a republican constitution. Their
candidate for the Hapsburg throne was the Pretender Otto, son of the
deposed Empress Zita.

Internationally the Catholic monarchists ·had a bold and sweeping
scheme, worked out by Mgr. Seipel. It amounted to legitimist revolution over Austria, Hungary, Yugoslavia, and Czechoslovakia, by which
the strongly Catholic sections of each should be detached and reformed
eventually in a new Hapsburg Holy Roman Empire. Mgr. Seipel had
close relations in these schemes, as we have noted, with Bavarian reactionaries like Cardinal Faulhaber. Czechoslovakia must give Slovakia;
Yugoslavia, Croatia; and Hungary and Rumania, Transylvania. Such a
restoration could not come all at once, of course. Customs unions and
similar arrangements might prepare it first with a Danubian Confederation. And since such a reorganization against the wishes of the bulk
of the populations concerned would not be easy to effect with internal
resources only, Mussolini, sent by Providence for the Italian hierarchy,
might also solve difficulties in Austria, Hungary, and Yugoslavia. Mussolini, of course, had his own ideas about who should head up a Danubian Confederation.

Any such program also involved the necessity of finding some alternative to democratic government. In a country where forty per cent of
the voters were socialist republicans, Seipel had virtually no chance of
a restoration of monarchy and clerical privilege by democratic means.
His answer was to imitate Mussolini and build up an illegal army for a
coup d'état, headed by Prince von Starhemberg. The clerical Fascist

Heimwehr was recruited among Catholic peasants with the aid of the clergy and was given free rein by Seipel's government in its outrages against the Socialists. Mussolini subsidized them, as did some industrialists such as the munitions maker Mandl.

The domestic policy of the clerical Fascists was the "corporative State." The Austrian Vogelsang, it will be recalled, had been a chief theoretician of the guild idea in the preceding century. In the 1920's Mussolini and Seipel adapted the device to new purposes. Back in Leo's day it was the program of economic traditionalism, of the crafts and artisans against the factory and the machine. In the hands of Mussolini and Seipel it was inverted to form the mechanism of rule of a clique of industrialists through a dictator without the inconveniences of trade-unions or parliaments. Mgr. Seipel was asked to advise Pius XI in the drafting of an encyclical on this subject, the famous *Quadragesimo anno* of 1931. In this encyclical the pope expressed some qualifications about Mussolini's exploitation of the guild system as possessing "an excessively bureaucratic and political character." [22] In general, however, the pope felt that the Fascist corporative system had proved its ability to settle industrial conflicts by state action and in the "repression of socialist organizations and efforts." Virtually every Fascist revolution of the next decade was to fly the flag of *Quadragesimo anno* and its corporative State.

Mgr. Seipel, however, was a Moses who was never to lead his people into the Promised Land. In 1927 he thought that his hour had struck. A protest march was organized in Vienna in July, when for the fifth time in two years the courts had acquitted *Heimwehr* Fascists for the shooting of socialists. Seipel provoked a bloody battle by sending mounted police against the marchers. Eighty-five were killed and hundreds wounded in the rioting. A general strike was called, and broken by the *Heimwehr*. Seipel now made the famous statement that earned him the nickname of "Cardinal No Mercy," and in protest twenty thousand left the Roman Church. In April, 1929, Seipel resigned from the government, declared himself a Fascist, and put himself at the head of the *Heimwehr*, which had been shouting for months: "Away with Parliament! We need an authoritarian State!" But the British and the French were paying the bills, and, despite the encouragement of Mussolini and Pius, Mgr. Seipel could not make his "march on Vienna" stick. The Western powers served notice that they expected a constitutional government. And the spiritual father of Austrian Fascism died in 1932 before he could realize his goal. Dollfuss and von Schuschnigg were to be his executors.

In the spring of 1933, as the Nazis came to power in Germany,

Chancellor Dollfuss of Austria followed Brüning's technique. After a visit to Italy to take counsel with Mussolini and the pope he began to rule by decree. He was determined to silence the socialists who had exposed, despite his efforts to bribe them, the arms traffic among the Italian, Austrian, and Hungarian Fascists. "I announce the death of Parliament," he proclaimed. The equipment of the corporative State was installed — concentration camps, censorship, anti-Semitism, abridgment of civil liberties, and the substitution for trial by jury of "Lightning Courts." But now Austrian Fascism became aware of a dangerous rival. Nazi agents began to work openly in Austria with murders, bombings, and anti-Semitic outrages. They intended to terrorize Austria into *Anschluss*. Little Dollfuss, however, sought to keep Austria for Austrian Fascism. After a series of murders in June he outlawed the Nazis. He spurned, however, the repeated offers of the socialists to co-operate with him in defense of the country. He rather took this moment to attack them. Papal nuncio Sibylla, according to Otto Bauer, "pushed the government into Fascist extremes, saying now is the time to destroy socialism forever." [23] And at last the day dawned for which Mgr. Seipel had labored so long. In February, 1934, the Catholic *Heimwehr* seized the provinces and attacked socialist Vienna in frank civil war. Major Fey, who commanded the slaughter, boasted that he refused all offers of negotiation. The victory was achieved by the use of artillery against the world-famous municipal housing of Vienna. Nearly two thousand were killed, and some five thousand wounded, many of them women and children. Only a portion of the defenders had even small arms; the Fascist losses were only a tenth as great. One result of this *Heimwehr* St. Bartholomew's Massacre was that the hitherto negligible Communists of Austria multiplied tenfold, an epitome of the effect of the whole pontificate of Pius XI.

Such were the birthpangs of the new "Christian, German and Federal State on a Corporative Basis" whose constitution, claiming to be the first based on *Quadragesimo anno,* was promulgated in May, 1934. In fulfillment of the slogan, "Restore Austria to Christ," it deliberately turned its back on democratic principles, universal suffrage, civil liberties, and substituted the autocracy of the *Führer* principle for responsible government. By the end of 1934 nearly 20,000 political prisoners languished in jail without trial and incommunicado. The trade-unions were dissolved as well as the socialist party. The school system was put in the hands of the clergy and deteriorated. The great housing project was stopped. A new concordat with the Vatican was completed, and the Roman clergy were instructed to support the dictatorship. But when everyone was required by law to belong to a church, the population expressed its resentment in a mass movement from Romanism, one hundred thousand in Vienna alone. Austrian Protestantism mushroomed to a third of a million, overwhelming the handful of Protestant pastors still at liberty.

The leader of Italian Catholic democracy, Don Sturzo, described the achievement as follows: " The Austria of Dollfuss and Schuschnigg pretends to be a Catholic State founded upon the Encyclical *Quadragesimo anno,* but in reality it is a dictatorial State with a Catholic and Fascist predominance; the Government represents only a minority and is staying in power only on the ground of martial law. The social measures inspired by papal encyclicals are not realities. . . . The masses of the workers have not forgotten the bloody repression of February, 1934." [24]

While the Nazis had temporarily restrained their outrages to watch those of the Catholic *Heimwehr,* they soon resumed them, and in July they killed Dollfuss. They were not yet strong enough, however, to exploit the murder. The Austrian troops were called out and remained loyal. Mussolini, who intended to dominate the " corporative States " aborning in old Austria-Hungary, rushed Italian soldiers to the Brenner Pass. Von Papen arrived to explain everything from Hitler's side, and Fascist Austria held on its way with a von Schuschnigg instead of a Dollfuss.

But when Mussolini had committed his forces in Abyssinia and Spain in 1935 and 1936, the situation altered. Hitler's price for supporting the Italians in Abyssinia was Austria. When von Schuschnigg appealed to Mussolini against increased Nazi pressure, *il Duce* referred him to Hitler. In 1936, an Austro-German-Italian pact was signed, according to which Nazis were taken into crucial posts in the Government and Austrian foreign policy was subordinated to that of the Nazis. Then after a year and a half of further Nazi consolidation Hitler gave von Schuschnigg his ultimatum. Cardinal Innitzer now counseled surrender as the desire of the Vatican. Hitler promised him special favors for his support. When the storm troopers marched in, they found the Catholic churches decorated with swastikas. Cardinal Innitzer and the episcopate released a pastoral letter urging all Austrians to hearken to the voice of their blood and vote for annexation, concluding with the episcopal salutation, " Heil Hitler." Thus was Hitler welcomed back to his native land and the Catholic party which had taught him his anti-Semitism.

Spain, Portugal, and Latin America, to which we now turn, form a common cultural unity, whose political and ecclesiastical traditions bear the stamp, even more than Austria, of the " austere immorality " of the Counter Reformation. Theirs is not the Catholicism of the Middle Ages, as is so often said, but something far narrower, more sectarian, and more corrupt. In this preserve of the Counter Reformation there is little or none of the social Catholicism, the modernism, the liturgical movement which have given Catholicism in Protestant countries religious and moral stature. Theirs is the most despiritualized and unchristian of the major types of modern Christianity, and that form of Christianity which has most bitterly opposed liberal democracy to this day.

It was not always so. In the great days of Las Casas and John of the Cross, of Theresa, Luis de Leon, Suárez, and Mariana, Spanish Catholicism was a deep and profound faith, and a faith that made for a high degree of social equality and political justice. But sometime in the seventeenth century the soul went out of this Catholicism, and from the eighteenth century it has been intellectually contemptible, morally corrupt, and politically reactionary. In contrast to his earlier intellectual and humanist leadership, the Spanish and Latin American priest now became an " African medicine man." [25] For this development the Inquisition doubtless bears a major responsibility. In any case there was here a degeneration unique in Western Christianity. No other form of Western Christianity has earned and received such active and bitter hatred from those to whom it was called to minister.

Certain symptoms are striking. Latin America, for example, provides the one major area of the world in Latourette's survey of the expansion of Christianity that in the course of the nineteenth century witnessed no major gains but even possibly a decline. The temperature of Latin American Catholicism has been chronically so low that it has never produced enough vocations to maintain its own clergy. Down to this day it has constituted a missionary establishment, maintained only by supplies of clergy from Europe and the United States.

In Spain, again, every popular revolution since the days of Napoleon — and there have been several — has been disfigured by mob attacks and burnings of churches and convents. This has been done, not by middle-class Liberal anticlericals, but by the people, poor, illiterate, and in the great majority till the end of the nineteenth century, practicing Catholics. Churches were burned and priests were killed by a devoutly Christian people, a phenomenon not to be seen elsewhere in nineteenth century Europe and one to be considered thoughtfully by churchmen. Disdaining " the slow work of example and persuasion," the Spanish hierarchy, however, concentrated on political alliances with reactionary forces, drawing on itself " the hostility of every decent or progressive force in the country." [26] " Behind every act of public violence, every curtailment of liberty, every judicial murder, there stood the bishop, who either in his pastoral or in a leading article of the Catholic press showed his approval and called for more. When one remembers that this political intransigence often covered the greatest laxity of conduct and a more or less total absence of the Christian virtues, one cannot be surprised that the Church became to large sections of Spaniards the symbol of everything that was vile, stupid, and hypocritical." The consequent dechristianization of the Spanish people was more thorough than in Italy or France, despite the illiteracy by which the Church protected them from dangerous thoughts. Even the peasants lost their faith, and even before the anarchist and Marxist propaganda reached them. And the feeling of the middle classes and workers was not the indifference so widespread in Western civilization generally, but anger and active hatred. The famous declaration of the president of the Spanish Republic of 1931 was simple fact: " Spain has ceased to be a Catholic country." Only one Spaniard in five was a practicing Catholic.

Portugal is so small as scarcely to justify discussion on the scale set for us. Nevertheless, as with tiny Austria for its whole region of Central Europe, it supplied for the Iberian peninsula and Latin America a working model of papal as against liberal and republican politics. Dollfuss' Austria and Salazar's Portugal were the examples of the " good " dictatorships frequently cited by Catholic publicists in democratic countries. They illustrated the corporative State recommended to Roman Catholics in *Quadragesimo anno*.

Portugal had been a Republic from 1910 to 1926. This meant ecclesiastically that the anticlericals were in power. The State was separated from the Roman Church and diplomatic relations with the Vatican were broken. The State salaries of the Roman clergy were discontinued. Religious orders were expelled. The usual pattern of " liberal " regimes in Latin America and Spain was observed.

Then came the clerical Fascist revolution. To the usual general, here Carmona, and the usual prelate, here Cardinal Cerejeira, was added the Catholic intellectual, Professor Salazar. As intellectual, however, Salazar had no intention of making any contribution toward the education of the Portuguese people, a majority of whom were illiterate. " Education and undesirable literature," he said, " these are our enemies." [27] Nor was there any intention of improving the economic condition of these illiterate masses, whose standard of living was, with that of Mussolini's Italy, the lowest in Europe in 1931. In the new constitution of 1933, strikes and threats of strikes were absolutely prohibited, since all economic issues were to be settled authoritatively by the State, guided by the " corporative chamber."

Politically, " partisan politics " and parties were abolished. Portugal was a one-party State. To prevent adverse criticism a huge police and espionage system was built up, with a budget four times that required for the whole British Empire. And the heritage of the Inquisition in the peninsula appeared in the methods of torture used on political prisoners by the clerical government. The ministers were responsible, not to the people or their representatives in parliament, but only to the head of the State. Salazar expressed his admiration, not merely of Mussolini and Dollfuss, but also of Hitler, of whom he declared, during the Spanish Civil War, " Gratitude is due to the head of the German Government and State for the defense of civilization, achieved by him in his victory over Communism in Germany." [28] Needless to say, Salazar's Portugal supported the Spanish Rebellion in 1936. The leader of the rebellion, General Sanjurjo, was killed in a plane accident on his way from Portugal to take command, and Franco succeeded him. Franco received military and financial aid from Salazar, as well as from Mussolini and Hitler.

In the generation between the World Wars, Spain attempted, for the second time in its history, to constitute itself as a democratic republic. But after five troubled years (1931–1936) the Republic was attacked by a military conspiracy, aided by the Spanish Church, the Vatican, Mussolini, and Hitler, and after an atrocious civil war of almost three years, was at last supplanted by a clerical Fascist dictatorship under General Franco. The alliance of Roman Catholicism and Fascism was here so obvious and confessed that it needs no documentation. The deeper problem, however, is the same one exhibited over a century before at the French Revolution, namely, that " liberals " and " democrats " in Catholic countries know little more of liberal democracy than does the Church. In the French Revolution the Rousseauist democrats were as intolerant, as doctrinaire, as authoritarian, as were their Catholic monarchist opponents. Where would they ever have had experience of finding new truth through discussion, of honoring minority opinion, of holding civil liberties sacred, and law above the executive? In all these things the anticlericals were but inverted Romanists and far from liberal democracy. It was so again in Spain in the 1930's. As Mendizabal remarked, " the great difficulty in Spain has always been to find a man who is genuinely liberal." [29] At the beginning of the Republic there was a group that gave promise of genuine leadership in this direction, the Liberal Republican Right, led by Zamora and Maura. But in a short time the absolutists of the Left, Socialists, Anarchists, Communists, and the absolutists of the Right, monarchists, Fascists, ground the handful of liberals as between millstones. Violent seditions were attempted by both sides before Franco's, and on neither side was there much honesty about the constitution. It was apparent that if Spain ever was to have a democratic republic, it would probably back into it as a *pis aller,* like the Third French Republic, devised without enthusiasm as the government that would " divide Frenchmen least."

The majority of Catholics together with that section of the propertied classes whose interests the Church represented were still monarchist. The complete Church Catechism issued in 1927 taught that liberty of conscience, of assembly, of education, was heretical, that it was generally a mortal sin for a Catholic to vote for a liberal candidate. In its parochial or convent schools, the Church taught all children that they would go to hell if they had to do with liberals. The whole religious educational system was a political agency for the monarchy and dictatorship. In the elections of 1931 the Catholic press and pulpit had identified the Church with the monarchist cause. And two weeks after the Republic was proclaimed, Mgr. Segura, cardinal archbishop of Toledo, released a violent pastoral against the Government, referring to the triumph of the " enemies of the Kingdom of Jesus Christ " and summoning the faithful to " prepare to fight " for the restoration of the monarchy. The voice of the Catholic hierarchy declared in the Cathedral of Toledo, " May the Republic be cursed." Then he fled to the Vatican, where the pope declined to receive the new ambassador of Republican Spain. The majority of the prelates maintained a more correct attitude, but this was generally understood to represent prudence rather than good will. And a month after the municipal elections attacks on churches and convents had swept over Spain in a spontaneous conflagration. The damage was estimated at five million dollars. The new constitution, drafted in the swell of these emotions, was so anticlerical as to alienate many lay Catholic intellectuals and poor parish priests who had hitherto supported the Republic. Despite their traditional " housekeepers," the latter were, on the whole, conscientious and worthy workers.

The provisional draft of the Republican committee for Church affairs might well have satisfied most Catholics. It declared a separation of Church and State which the hierarchy would have decried, but many good Catholics felt that a release from the control and patronage of the State would invigorate the Church. And the Church was still to remain a corporation of public law, with the right to conduct its own schools, to satisfy legal requirements by canonical marriage, and to conduct public ecclesiastical functions under certain safeguards. The Cortes, however, balked at these provisions of the draft constitution. The Church was obviously the chief focus of reaction, both in its teaching and in its direct political activities. By an overwhelming majority the

Cortes voted to disestablish and disendow the Church, to exile the Jesuits and nationalize their goods, and to forbid the Church to continue education, save for the priesthood. Full religious liberty for non-Catholics was decreed for the first time in the history of Spain.

Some of this legislation was unworkable, as well as imprudent and illiberal. The Jesuits, for example, with their enormous wealth and antirepublican interest, were a serious problem for the Spanish State. In 1912, according to Joaquin Aquilera, Secretary of the *Fomento,* they already controlled, " without exaggeration, one third of the capital wealth of Spain." [30] But the Jesuits, with their old skill in aliases, were not to be caught by any such simple device as this law. When the law came to be enforced, the Jesuit wealth all proved to be held by somebody other than the Jesuits, and when the order was dissolved in Spain, the same personnel continued their activities just as if they were still Jesuits. The annual subsidy, on the other hand, was a debt of honor, and the Republic legislators might well have concentrated on getting it past the prelates into the hands of the parish clergy who earned it.

Again with regard to education the new legislation was impracticable. The education given by the Church had been of very low quality and politically crassly antiliberal and antidemocratic. The ignorance of the Spanish clergy was almost incredible. " Though medicine was taught, it suffered from the suppression of that erroneous Lutheran notion upon the circulation of the blood, whilst if one touched on physics one had to remember that the Copernican system was still a *cosa del inquisición.* In the elementary schools the children of the poor were deliberately not taught to read, but only to sew and to recite the Catechism." [31] What the Catechism inculcated in politics we have already noticed. To maintain its monopoly the Church worked through local political bosses in the second half of the nineteenth century to keep down the budgets of the new public elementary schools. In 1901 education was put on the national budget, but the amount was still scandalously small. At the time of the Republican legislation on education in 1931 the provision for public education was still pathetically inadequate. Half the children who were in school at all were in Church schools. The only enduring answer to the Catholic school system was not to close it by fiat, but over a period of years and with considerable outlay to build up a public-school system which was conspicuously more effective as well as loyal to the constitution.

The anticlerical legislation, as we have already said, precipitated the resignation of such conservative Republicans as Prime Minister Zamora and Minister Maura. It threw the Republic toward the working-class parties. The latter are worth a moment's attention as illustrations of the effect of Roman Catholicism on the political mentality of the Spaniards. Of these working-class parties the Communists were the least significant, despite the anti-Republican Catholic propaganda abroad about the "Bolsheviks" and "Moscow gold." There were less than three thousand of them, and they had not elected a single member to the constituent cortes. The Socialists and the Anarcho-Syndicalists, on the other hand, were strongly organized and numbered about a million and one half each. The Socialists, centered in Madrid and the West, followed the general pattern of the Second International. The Anarchists were especially significant and characteristic of Spain. They had no trust in a centralized Marxist dictatorship of the masses. Like the Russian peasants of the late nineteenth century, they were fired with wild idealism and a naïve millenarian hope in "the Revolution" and the age of liberty beyond it, and were capable of the most ruthless violence to achieve it. The characteristic lack of constructive thought on the part of Spanish revolutionaries grew from the peasant experience that if only one could break the hold of a dozen landlords and the priest, the commune would run itself naturally. The general strike as a weapon was taken over from French Syndicalism and became the theory of the peasantry which had been sucked in as industrial labor to the Barcelona factories. But the interesting aspect of the movement was its moral and religious character, its moral asceticism, its uncompromising idealism, its love of liberty. It was a *mystique,* an anti-Catholic heresy, and in fact responsible for practically all the church-burning and most of the priest-killing. To the Spanish Anarchist the Roman Church was the Antichrist, the fount of evil, the blasphemer of the great ideal of human solidarity. Wholly unsuited to the conditions of modern society, anarchism reflected the Christian training of centuries in its violent rejection of the caricature of Christianity in the Roman Catholic Church. Its strength in Latin America rested on the same reaction to sanctification of intolerable agrarian injustice by a hierarchy kept by the landlords.

On the Right, and in opposition to the Anarcho-Syndicalists, Socialists, Communists, and Republicans, there grew up a new form of Catholic political action in Spain. After two years of Republican rule the Right gained strongly in the elections of 1933, and for the following two years the dominant power in the Republic was Gil Robles and his *Acción popular.* This was the new Jesuit bid for power within the conditions of the Republic. With the collapse of the monarchy it had become necessary for the clericals to appeal to the masses in Spain. To learn how to do this young Robles was sent by his sponsors, first to Hitler's Nürnberg rally in 1933, and then on to Austria, where Dollfuss was consolidating his "corporative state" by decree. From the election of 1933, Robles was in a position to carry out his schedule of revolution from within. Once in the government coalition he would widen his power until he was alone, and then by a managed plebiscite gain sanction for a rejection of the constitution for a corporative state and perhaps a restored monarchy. It was Robles who had a particularly ruthless soldier brought to the War Office as Undersecretary and this General Franco used the savage Moors of the Foreign Legion to terrorize the Asturias in disproportionate revenge for the rising of the miners there in " Red October." In 1936, as in 1933, the order went down the hierarchy from the nuncio and Cardinal Goma to every priest to get out the vote against the republicans on pain of hell-fire. Yet only a third of the electorate voted the Roman ticket. During the course of 1936 two hitherto inconsiderable groups grew to major significance on the Right and on the Left. They were the Communists and the Falange. The circumstances favored their frank and revolutionary violence. The Falange was simply Mussolini's Fascism oriented to a Spanish Empire, over Morocco, Portugal, and Latin America. They assimilated Gil Robles' Catholic Action Youth, as the Communists similarly annexed the Socialist Youth shortly after. What particular responsibility is to be charged for the final and irrevertible precipitation of the terrible civil war is unquestionably to be divided between the Spanish military and the Roman Church.

In the following two and one half years of war the victory was decided by foreign help. The morale of the Government forces was conspicuously higher, and their humanity and decency unquestionably far nearer the rules of war than the behavior of the clerical Fascist armies. There were terrible atrocities on both sides, but only the Government side publicly denounced those committed in its name and tried to control them. Terrorism was a fault of the Government forces, but it was the systematic policy of Franco's. As to foreign aid, Hitler and Mussolini helped Franco from the beginning, having been in on the plot, while Stalin's arms arrived only from November and on a much smaller scale. Pius, who was flying Franco's flag at the Vatican, repeatedly appealed to the whole Catholic world for aid to Franco and the Axis. The Catholic Church was apparently the decisive factor in influencing the United States and Britain to deny the Spanish Government access to arms to defend itself. Due to their organizing capacity and to Russian help, the Communists came to be the leaders of the Republican effort for two years. Yet in the last months of the war, as Stalin withdrew his aid, their influence diminished and the far more numerous Socialists and Republicans asserted themselves again. The outcome represented the conquest of the large majority of the Spanish people by the Axis coalition under Vatican blessing.

In 1939, with the surrender of Madrid, Franco could organize his version of the clerical Fascist "corporative state." It was inaugurated with a stupendous proscription, herding into prisons a million or more, and executing thousands. All political parties save the Falange were destroyed, and freedom of speech and the press ended. The country was reduced to semistarvation and ridden with disease. To preserve his position the dictator had to maintain and continually enlarge a police and Gestapo system as expensive as his army of a million men. Most of the schools were closed. The Catholic Church was re-established, its subsidies and properties restored. Protestant schools, college, and seminary were closed, together with four fifths of the Protestant churches. Two thirds of the Protestant leaders were murdered, imprisoned, or exiled. But while Falange would cheerfully persecute dissidents, like Mussolini it did so without religious conviction. In the schemes of the Falange in Spain and Latin America, Catholicism was the means and not the end. Franco quarreled with the pope as had Mussolini over control of education and the selection of bishops. He even suppressed the publication of *Mit brennender Sorge* in Spain. The quarrel ended as it had with Mussolini, by giving an atheist party the right to claim such oaths of allegiance from the bishops as made them Fascist party agents.

In the meantime the Second World War had been launched. Franco had been instrumental in preparing the betrayal of France through the French ambassador to Spain, Marshal Pétain. Now he was eager to take Gibraltar, with Hitler's help, and close the Mediterranean to the democracies. From 1940, in conformity with the " unchangeable and sincere adherence " to Hitler personally and to the Nazi cause, which he repeatedly declared, Franco made available U-boat bases against England and built submarines and trained crews for Hitler.[32] This was about as much as his impoverished and disaffected nation permitted him to contribute. He similarly congratulated the Japanese for their successful blow against the United States at Pearl Harbor and sent his regards to the head of the Japanese puppet regime in the Philippines. In this again he was following the lead of the Vatican, which joined the Axis powers in recognizing the similar regime in Manchukuo.[33] And when at last Hitler's death was announced, Catholic Spain expressed official and unofficial condolence. Through all this period the hierarchy and the Falange of Latin America were the pipelines for the Nazi propaganda and intrigue flowing across the sea from Spain. From the disaster of the World War for the Fascists, Franco, Salazar, and Perón were to be the most important survivors.

3. FRANCE AND BELGIUM

France and Belgium provide our last instance of the conflict of democratic and antidemocratic Catholicism. These were the countries where Jocism originated and had its greatest development in this period, a type of democratic Catholic Action among industrial labor. And while the Catholic democrats did not put up so much of a political struggle as did Sturzo and his Popolari in Italy, they were the most articulate in the Catholic world. One might have expected English and American Catholics to speak up boldly for the democratic cause. While here and there someone was discharged from a Catholic school for having dangerous thoughts about Franco, the bulk of Anglo-American Catholic laity displayed a degrading servility to their pro-Fascist episcopate and press. The best Catholic democratic comment came from a group of distinguished French writers and intellectuals, Bernanos, Mauriac, Maritain. These men carried on the tradition of Sangnier and the *Sillon,* of Péguy, speaking up against the Abyssinian and the Spanish conquests, the absorption of Austria and Czechoslovakia, the whole policy of encouraging every kind of viciousness which would make a show of being " anti-Red." They illustrated the truth of the Protestant conviction that the Holy Spirit, who guides the Church, speaks in the laity as well as the clergy, and that in every branch of the Church the clergy and hierarchy need upon occasion to be taught and rebuked in faith and morals by believing laymen. Yet in France and Belgium also, despite this witness, influential leaders of political Catholicism threw their weight against democracy and for dictatorship. What is more, they betrayed their own countries to Hitler's type of dictatorship.

The heritage of *L'Action française* appeared in the various clerical Fascist groups springing up in the 1930's in France. The Hooded Men and Fiery Cross were a French Ku-Klux Klan in a more violent form. Camelots du roi, *Jeunesse patriote,* were street-fighting and terrorist gangs on the Nazi model, hoping to panic the parliamentary government.

More significant was the old anti-Republican tradition among the Catholic officers of the Army. Marshal Pétain, Weygand, and Giraud belonged to this group who felt only contempt for the Republic they were sworn to serve. Pétain took new hope in 1933 when he saw Hitler seize power and Dollfuss begin to rule by decree. When Franco attacked the Spanish Republic, he had himself made French ambassador to Spain and began to mature plans featuring Pétain as the Franco of France. As in Spain, it would be necessary to have the help of foreign intervention to conquer the constituted republic, and Pétain, the " hero of Verdun," began to conspire to aid Hitler to conquer his own country. He would rather see France lose than see her victorious with democratic or Socialist states. He and Laval, that unsavory knight of the papal court, kept relations with Hitler and Göring, especially through von Stohrer in Madrid, and with Pius. He did not want Germany actually to conquer France if he could help it, but he undertook to keep France from opposing Hitler if war should break out.

Apparently the Vatican served to reconcile him to the necessity of this unpleasantness. Pétain and the papal Secretary of State both knew beforehand the date of the German attack on France. When it came, Pétain was called to aid by Reynaud and became vice-premier. He arranged for his fellow conspirator, Weygand, to be made commander in chief. Working in collusion with Laval in the Chamber, and all together with the nuncio, Pétain and Weygand bent every effort to have France surrender. When Mussolini announced that he too intended to "conquer" France, the generals were embarrassed, but neither the pope nor Hitler could dissuade *il Duce*. Instead the pope requested Pétain to accept the bitter pill.[34] The Nazis had invaded the Low Countries, and Weygand persuaded King Leopold to surrender without warning his allies. Pétain resigned in the crisis in France similarly, urging that only surrender could save the country. Weygand also demanded surrender, and when Reynaud ordered the evacuation of half a million men to Africa, he disobeyed the order. Finally, when Reynaud resigned, Pétain became premier and on June 17 asked for an armistice.

Thus ended the Third Republic, and thus was founded the Vichy version of the corporative state of *Quadragesimo anno*. Pétain announced that he had asked Hitler's permission to act as his ally in building the New Order. The *Osservatore Romano* enthused over "the dawn of a new radiant day."[35] A new charter of labor dissolved the trade-unions and organized the Christian guilds of de Mun and La Tour du Pin. Democratic parliamentarism was scorned and the "family vote" was introduced. Hopes were entertained of a Latin bloc of clerical Fascists, Pétain, Mussolini, Franco, and Salazar. Anti-Semitism and the Gestapo were organized. The public schools were handed over to the Jesuits for supervision and censorship, while Church schools were given equal subsidy from public funds. History texts were rewritten to play up the *ancien régime,* and show how the Republic had brought the moral ruin of France.

The higher clergy supported Vichy Fascism enthusiastically. Cardinal Suhard and Cardinal Baudrillart, in particular, were conspicuously pro-Nazi. *L'Action française* and *La Croix* denounced the resistance and the De Gaullists. Some of the lower clergy and many of the Catholic laity, however, gravely questioned the right of the Vichy regime to loyalty. They were not at all convinced with Mgr. Piquet that it was God who had installed Marshal Pétain as Hitler's satrap. These men were to provide the French Church with its martyrs and heroes of the resistance when the De Gaulle whom the Church had rebuffed in exile proved the winner. Then bishops were arrested and Cardinal Suhard confined to his palace and the nuncio was withdrawn. Ways were found, of course, of settling these matters out of court, but Pétain, Laval, Doriot, Maurras all received their sentences.

Space forbids more than the mention of the very similar Catholic betrayal of Czechoslovakia.

In 1939, Pius XI died, to be succeeded promptly by his Secretary of State Pacelli, who had been the manipulator of most of the Vatican support of dictatorship for at least the decade preceding. Pius XI did not live quite long enough to see the disastrous results of his policy for two decades. By this hostility to democracy he had weakened the strongest foe of Communism. By his encouragement of Fascist reaction and injustice he had heightened the appeal of Communism to the less privileged groups everywhere in the West, sowing a new crop of dragons' teeth. The bankruptcy of his labors was indicated by his successor, who had to drop his scheming of two decades and reorient himself to the Anglo-American democracies. But even this was a dubious compliment to democracy, for, having climbed on the democratic victory train at the last possible minute, the Catholic hierarchy intended to run it.

By way of summary, we may commend again the judgment of the most distinguished English-speaking Roman Catholic historian of culture, Christopher Dawson, whose observations on the relation of liberal democracy to Puritan Protestantism we have earlier cited. "There seems no doubt," he writes, "that the Catholic social ideals set forth in the encyclicals of Leo XIII and Pius XI have far more affinity with those of Fascism than with those of either Liberalism or Socialism. . . . Against the Liberal doctrines of the divine right of majorities [sic] and the unrestricted freedom of opinion the Church has always maintained the principles of authority and hierarchy. . . . The ruler is not simply the representative of the people; he has an independent authority." And the principle of hierarchy "is, of course, diametrically opposed to the liberal democratic ideal of absolute equality which ignores the very idea of status" regarding society "as a collection of identical units" [sic]. "These ideas correspond much more closely, at least in theory, with the Fascist conception of the functions of the 'Leader' and the vocational hierarchy of the Fascist State than they do with the system of parliamentary democracy. . . . Nevertheless it would be a mistake to conclude from this that the political ideals of Catholicism and Fascism are identical or that Catholics can support the Fascist program without reservation. There still remains a wide gap between the Catholic and Fascist ideals of the State, although both of them are authoritarian and hierarchical." [36]

To put it in another way, Roman Catholicism still yearns for the absolute monarchy of the seventeenth and eighteenth century *ancien régime,* in which it crystallized in its present Counter Reformation form. That type of government is no longer a real alternative, even in Spain or Austria. Fascism offers a substitute for it which is more congenial than liberal democracy. "Catholicism is the Fascist form of Christianity, of which Calvinism represents the democratic wing. The Catholic hierarchy rests fully and securely on the leadership principle with the infallible pope in supreme command for a lifetime. . . . Like the Fascist party, its priesthood becomes a medium for an undemocratic minority rule by a hierarchy. . . . Catholic nations follow Fascist doctrines more willingly than Protestant nations, which are the main strongholds of democracy. . . . Democracy lays its stress on personal conscience, Fascism on authority and obedience." [37]

It is also to be noticed that these Catholic principles of politics — authority, censorship, the leadership principle, social status, and hierarchy — are exemplified in Soviet Russia. In the midst of the present Roman Catholic crusade against Communism the fact that, politically speaking, this is a family row, should not be obscured. Communists can come to an understanding with Roman Catholicism far more readily than they can with Puritan Protestantism. Pius XI made repeated efforts to come to such an agreement with Moscow. The nightmare that haunted Dostoevsky cannot yet be wholly exorcised. Natural affinity may yet one day unite these two most deadly enemies of man's freedom.

VIII

THE PROTESTANT SOCIAL GOSPEL
AND AFTER

❖ ❖ ❖

THE First World War shattered the English-speaking world less
than the Continent. Britain lost as much perhaps as some of the
Roman Catholic countries that renounced democracy for dictatorship,
but in the United States and the British Commonwealth the war was
no such crisis for liberalism and the belief in progress. Liberal democracy still constituted the context within which social policy was to be
determined. In the course of the postwar generation, however, the
spectacle of Continental dictatorship and lawlessness, and the home experience of grave economic and social dislocation, brought about a
gradual but radical revision of the prevailing view of society and history. In 1914 the war had appeared to most respectable Britons and
Americans as a horrible and irrational intrusion upon the orderly
peaceful development of society. When it was resumed on a full scale
in 1939, however, after some years of localization and a fitful truce, it
no longer bore the guise of an irrational intrusion, at least to the more
thoughtful. " We recognize that the war is not a mere clash between
rival national ambitions but it is a crisis of civilization," declared the
spokesman for the Malvern Conference in 1941. " Hitler is as much a
symptom as a cause of that disease from which European civilization is
suffering and of which the war is itself one phase." [1] In some ways war
was more tolerable and more humane than the " peace " that had
reigned in the interval. The democratic section of Western civilization
was also sick with this common affliction.

In the Anglo-American countries between wars this disease of civilization was manifested chiefly in the form of unemployment and the
apparent impossibility of making the system of financial industrialism
produce the goods for which the masses of men were urgently asking.
The utter spiritual desolation of millions of able-bodied men denied
any prospect of meaningful lives was a poignant condemnation of the
economic system. Beside unemployment stood the scandal of deliberate

waste, the limitation or actual destruction of badly needed goods, the substitution of shoddy or short-lived quality for better products, all " to keep up prices." And most significant of all was the fact that the Anglo-American democracies were able to recover from the depression, in so far as they did, only by the development of vast armaments industries. All through the '30's, from the invasion of Manchuria in 1931, the threat of war grew steadily more ominous and increasingly paralyzed efforts at fundamental social reform. And yet preparation for war was a relief from the heartbreaking task of attempting to organize peace. In much more gradual and less dramatic form, the experience of the Continent seemed to be repeating itself, that the only basis of ordering a community morally disintegrated by financial industrialism was to militarize it.

The militarization of Fascism, Bolshevism, Nazism had provided a means by which the anarchy of financial industrialism could be mastered for social ends. All these systems ended unemployment and gave to the lives of men a spiritual significance which the chronically unemployed in free countries could never know. Up to the First World War the system of capitalism had apparently, on the whole, served social ends. It had produced goods of variety and abundance unknown to man before. It had provided useful tasks for most of those who desired them. But now it became apparent that these social ends were only accidental by-products of the system, which might disappear altogether. The motive of the system was not to produce either useful work or goods; it was to produce liquid profit. Left to itself, the system tended to reduce the purchase of goods needed by the community in favor of investing in further production which could return financial profit. From the point of view of the banker or salesman or advertiser scarcity is better than abundance, cheap goods than quality, slums than new housing, and best of all are armaments. Armaments are the ideal product from the point of view of the investor, financier, and salesman; one can never have enough of them, they are always obsolescent, they keep up prices all through the economy. And in the system of financial industrialism the point of view of the banker, the salesman, the advertiser with his "trader's values," predominates over the point of view of the consumer and community needs, and over that of the craftsman and manufacturer who seek fulfillment in creative work. It was against the trader's mentality that the new totalitarianisms arose, insisting that economic life must be subordinated to the spiritual needs of the community. To be sure, the "end of economic man" meant the violent substitution of Moloch for Mammon, but the free countries were troubled with the uneasy suspicion that on the negative side the judgment on Mammon had good grounds also in their case. The Marxian analysis of " capitalism " is a profound interpretation of the power conflicts of a society in which the search for profit is architectonic, and in which the Christian does not allow his faith to pass judgment on his social and economic practice.

The psychological basis of the old liberal society had been the security of the middle class based on its personal property. Industrial labor, of course, had never had security, but, in an expanding economy, it had some hope of rising into the middle class. The war and consequent inflation on the Continent generally ended this type of security. The middle class increasingly became simply the salaried class, and nearly as directly dependent as the industrial worker on the trade cycle, on the balance of exports and imports, on unemployment, on monetary policy, on the possibilities of new war — all very hazardous contingencies. The former middle-class mentality of self-dependence evaporated. What could the individual do " to better himself " ? The crucial decisions were now matters of mass policy, if they could be described as policy at all. Even the middle-class man sought to find status and security in some realm other than business, where neither is to be had. The tendency was to assimilate business to politics and politics to new secular religions giving direction and meaning to the whole. As Demant suggests,[2] the new totalitarianism finds its focus in a political party that is also a business, and also a Church.

It was the pressure of the First War again that had first revealed the possibilities of this spiritual coercion of modern man. Totalitarianism is simply the regularization of war as the normal condition of man. The new and unholy arts of propaganda were first used widely on the political and cultural levels in the First World War to mold men's minds, just as military and economic resources were mobilized. The State was trying to unify and co-ordinate the interests of life which Christianity had ceased to try to co-ordinate. Everywhere the fact of war and threat of war, as well as the anarchy of " peace," pressed toward more control of public opinion as well as economic life. " The steadily growing submission of citizens to public education and services, the unifying influence, often unconscious, which the ruling social group exerts over the whole society, lead in fact to a uniformity of spirit and behavior."[3]

Christopher Dawson has pointed out subtler forms of the process in Anglo-American countries. " It is not likely that the Western democracies will ever become either Communist or Fascist, but I think it is very probable that they will follow a parallel line of development and evolve a kind of democratic étatisme, which, while being less arbitrary and inhumane than the other two forms of government, will make just as large a claim on the life of the individual as they do, and will demand an equally wholehearted spiritual allegiance. We can already discern the beginning of this paternal-democratic regime in England and can see how all the apparatus of the social services — universal secondary education, birth control clinics, antenatal clinics, welfare centres and the rest — may become instruments of a collective despotism which destroys human liberty and spiritual initiative as effectively as any Communist or Nazi terrorism." [4]

While Christopher Dawson thus continued the polemic against the dangers of the welfare state, which Hilaire Belloc had initiated in England with his *Servile State,* similar tendencies appeared in America. The movement associated with the name of John Dewey and particularly prevalent among teachers and administrators in the American public schools might be compared for its role in the society to that of *L'Action française* in Catholic cultures. In each case a movement fundamentally hostile to Christianity succeeded in gaining wide influence among Christian intellectuals by posing as the chief exponent of the traditional political ethic of the society — monarchism in the one case and democracy in the other. In contrast to the authoritarianism of *L'Action française,* the American Deweyites believed in discussion and the political responsibility of the common man. But the " religion of democracy " of the Deweyites dogmatically opposed all ultimate metaphysical and theological affirmations, including those of Christianity and the " higher law " within which the " discussion " of democracy had historically been set. They staked out large claims as the only authentic interpreters of " democracy " and won wide influence not only in the public schools but also in the " religious education " movement in Sunday schools. A specific brand of pragmatic metaphysics was thus especially characteristic of the American drift to " totalitarian liberalism."

Toward the end of the '30's a new threat to liberal democracy came into prospect. Since the Civil War in America the chief danger had been bureaucratic industrialism. Now for the first time the militarization of the whole society, in reaction to European totalitarian war, presented grim possibilities. We have already observed how these European totalitarianisms could be understood as the normalization of preparation for totalitarian war. The military ethos and habit of mind is by nature anti-democratic and authoritarian. The more widespread and longer-sustained such a discipline may be in a democratic society, the less likely the society is to remain democratic. This whole subject, however, carries us beyond the limits of our present period.

Since these increasing pressures on the liberal democracy of Puritan societies did not, in this period, do more than weaken the tradition, our history of the Puritan churches in this aspect is far less dramatic than the concurrent narrative of the political activities of Rome. Here there are no civil wars, *coups d'état,* clerical intrigues. We are confined to statements of views on various controversial issues from the Churches and to some attempt at estimating the influence of the political thought and ethos of Puritan Protestants. We may conveniently begin with the American Churches and follow with the British, since the American development tended to follow the British with a lapse of some years.

In terms of such a history of opinion our period divides rather sharply into halves. The first is a continuation of the prewar liberal social gospel. The new currents of the post-social-gospel era can be most easily defined by contrast to what preceded, although a future historian may discern other more important tendencies in them. The watershed between these two periods may be approximately located in Britain at the half decade 1920–1925 and in America at 1930–1935. We begin thus with an account of the political ethics of the American Churches in the fifteen years or so between World War I and the Great Depression and add to this some notice of the comparable British developments reaching their climax in the Birmingham conference of 1924.

1. The Liberal Social Gospel

From about 1890 to 1930, for forty years, American religion worked out the problems of one distinct period: theological debates over science and religion, ethical controversy in the Churches between the social gospel and the pietist individual gospel, and various efforts at co-operation and federation to remedy the conspicuous inadequacy of the inherited denominational pattern. All these issues of the prewar period came to a culmination in the 1920's. And an account of the relations of the Churches to liberal democracy in that decade is simply the sequel to our earlier discussion.

Perhaps a half of American Protestantism in the '20's continued the pietist evangelical tradition. This was the old evangelicalism of small-town America, strongest in the "Bible Belt" of the South, Midwest, and Pacific Coast, and in the lower educational and income levels of the cities. The denominational leaders, on the whole, were no longer of this camp, whose strength lay in the laity. This old American Protestantism rebelled in the '20's, rising against the new city culture increasingly dominating the nation, a culture of foreigners and Roman Catholics, of Sabbathbreakers, drinkers, and mockers of the Bible. The attempt was made, not only to legislate teetotaling and "monkey bills" into public law, but to capture ecclesiastical machinery and unchurch the " higher critics " and social gospelers. With few exceptions both attempts failed; organized Protestantism as a whole rejected mere traditionalism. The denominations refused to submit to the kind of purge Roman Catholicism had undergone in the decade before World War I, and the Federal Council likewise held its ground. " Fundamentalism " then turned to create its own ministry in a system of " Bible schools " founded to replace the suspected older theological seminaries. For the generation between the wars the deepest cleavage in American Protestantism was this controversy, which cut right across nearly all the major denominations and was more significant than the differences between them. In most cases a mediating party labored to prevent schisms within the denominations.

In political economy this pietist and fundamentalist current was predominantly for a restoration of " free enterprise." Conservative business groups contributed liberally to the movement as a means of attack on the social gospelers and their " industrial democracy." In international affairs, similarly, this section of opinion was trying to restore the irresponsible isolation of the nineteenth century. American tariff and immigration legislation of the '20's made a major contribution to the rise of the dictators. In these questions of political and social ethics, as well as in Biblical studies and theology, mere ignorance and defensive traditionalism were more evident than responsible Christian leadership.

Despite the dead weight of the pietist individualist outlook in its various forms, the leadership of the Churches, the Federal Council, and the educated clergy generally, were committed to some degree of Christian responsibility for the democratic direction of international and social politics. While the overwhelming predominance in this movement of the clergy as a class set restrictions on its influence and its competence, which we must later analyze, it was significant enough to justify a summary here. In the decade before the Second World War, it will be recalled, the chief denominations had given the social gospel its most important institutional expression in their respective boards or commissions on " social service." No denomination as a whole was committed to the social gospel, but nearly all were ready to account the movement one possible and legitimate expression of their Christian faith. In the postwar years these denominational agencies continued and expanded their work, supplemented by various unofficial organizations of churchmen, and increasingly paced by the more and more potent Federal Council of the Churches of Christ in America.

The Congregationalists, Presbyterians, and Episcopalians represented the dominant social and economic strata in America and were prevailingly Republican and opposed to State regulation of business. They did produce, on the other hand, the most progressive leadership among the clergy of all the Protestant denominations, possibly because of their high educational standards. The Congregationalist Council for Social Action was given an adequate staff and budget at the Oberlin National Council in 1934 and remained probably the most successful and important official department among the denominations. Its periodical, *Social Action*, was the best of its kind. The scope of the Council's educational program was blocked out by the " Statement of Social Ideals " of 1929, in the five major divisions of education, industrial and economic relationships, international affairs, race relations, and agriculture. As was characteristic of such social gospel manifestoes, these ideals were a list of specific reforms that might appeal to any idealistic American group, Christian or otherwise, and Church people were simply exhorted to support them as individual citizens. Even so, the Council was barely tolerated by the laity in some congregations and was frequently challenged in denominational assemblies.

Among the Episcopalians and the Methodists this same tension between a politically progressive clergy and a conservative laity led to the development of voluntary groups that were not subject to the restraints exerted on the official denominational boards. The Methodist Social Service Federation stood for a sort of democratic Christian national socialism, a planned society with a large amount of public ownership of industry. The Federation was perhaps the most militant Church organization of this type. Only a small minority of Methodists, however, even of those socially concerned, supported the Federation. After all, three fourths of Methodist churches were rural. The strongly urban and socialist mentality of the Federation spoke to problems other than those of the bulk of Methodists, and in an alien vocabulary.

Among the Episcopalians, similarly, the episcopate supported the work of the official Department of Social Service, while the bulk of the laity exhibited little sympathy or understanding. The two prewar voluntary societies, the Church Social Union and the Church Association for the Interests of Labor, passed out of existence as the denominational department took over their functions. They were succeeded, however, by new voluntary societies. In 1919 a Church League for Industrial Democracy was founded in America with a High Church and Socialist cast. C.L.I.D. activities, or those of its secretary, were similar to those of the considerably larger Methodist Federation for Social Service. In Britain similarly the Industrial Christian Fellowship replaced the old Church Social Union. Unlike the latter, or the American C.L.I.D., the Fellowship reached a genuinely working-class constituency, especially through the great " crusades " in industrial areas, animated by the passionate evangelism of "Woodbine Willy," G. A. Studdert-Kennedy. Anglican laymen in the established parishes, however, were not significantly affected, and in any case the Fellowship had no clear-cut social philosophy with which to challenge the structure of industrial society.

Before the First World War denominational boards had constituted the chief channel of political and social thought and action among the Churches. The war, however, proved a major spur to interdenominational co-ordination of effort, and in the period between the World Wars such organizations came to the center of the stage. In America, the chief body of the sort was the Federal Council of Churches. The war itself had raised the Federal Council from its feeble beginnings. Its budget expanded tenfold, from $32,000 in 1913 to $325,000 in 1920, and its wartime activities established it firmly in the national consciousness as the most representative Protestant Church body. Federal Council sessions, usually attended by senior churchmen of various denominations, were often more cautious than denominational bodies, and for that reason provide us with the best index to the main thrust of social thought and action among the Protestant ministry between the wars. While there was a significant wing of politically and socially conservative opinion within the Federal Council, for our purposes its popular identification with the social gospel is sufficiently accurate. We must sketch the political and social ethic represented by the Federal Council, then, as our central thread.

The social ethic represented by the leadership of this movement was substantially that of theistic humanitarian democracy, asserting the dignity and worth of personality, brotherhood as the bond of society, and "service" as a primary motive. These postulates were identified with the "ideals" of Jesus. As the postwar manifesto, *The Church and Social Reconstruction,* put it, "The teachings of Jesus are those of essential democracy, and express themselves through brotherhood and the co-operation of all groups." On these principles the social gospelers undertook to erect the good society, "to build the Kingdom of God." The means was to be primarily education, developing the innate moral capacity and good will of men, which were estimated at a very high level. More concretely, the Federal Council leaders worked for these ideals of brotherhood and personalism primarily in four areas. Industrial relations, the chief preoccupation of the prewar social gospel, remained probably the most critical realm. It was now joined, however, by a new realization of international tensions. In the '30's, also, the racial question came increasingly to the fore and rural life was seen more clearly in its full strategic significance. We may consider each of these four areas briefly.

World War I provided the first stunning shock for most American believers in the optimistic humanitarianism of the social gospel. Most of them had supposed right up to the outbreak of the war that the whole course of history was making irresistibly for international organization and perpetual peace, conditions that were sometimes equated with " membership in the Kingdom of God." Christians in every land were called " to realize the Golden Rule in international relations," " to establish the Kingdom of God on a world-wide scale." And then as the actuality of war forced itself upon them, American churchmen reacted with extraordinary indignation and patriotic self-righteousness. After all, only remarkably vicious and malevolent forces could have so interrupted the irresistible progress of evolution toward a warless world. The war was widely conceived, in short, as a crusade. There was in 1916 comparatively little of the attitude dominant in 1940, that war was a morally ambiguous necessity and in part the result of, and God's judgment on, American failings.

Toward the end of the war, Protestant churchmen similarly rallied to President Wilson's League with acclamation, thus fitting the whole episode of the war into the scheme of progress as earlier conceived, and giving it meaning. " Now is the time," the Federal Council declared, " when all men and women of good will without as well as within the Church should join in a supreme effort to build and secure an enduring structure of national and international life founded on the life and teachings of Jesus. . . . The call for our nation to enter this League . . . is the greatest moral call that has ever come to the Church in all history." [5] This campaign for the League as " the Christian international order " reached a climax in 1920, and then fell off rapidly as it became apparent that the American Senate was not going to respond to the summons of the social gospel.

There were other actions that invited the energies of those who believed that reason and the " ideals of Jesus " could build a warless world. From 1923 the Federal Council steadily campaigned for adherence to the World Court. Later we shall have occasion to notice the European reaction at the Stockholm Conference to the American social gospel. In 1928 the Kellogg-Briand Pact enjoyed practically unanimous support from the Churches, while Europeans wondered at American naïveté in supposing that it meant anything to " renounce " offensive war. The Federal Council canvassed Church support for disarmament at the Washington Conference in 1921, and at London in 1931, and on various occasions between. Compulsory military training was similarly opposed. Opinion was divided, or perhaps oscillated, between the two conceptions of securing peace by world government or by just refusing to fight. A questionnaire sent to fifty-three thousand American ministers in 1931 found that three fifths of those replying believed that the Church should refuse to support any future war, while over ten thousand declared their own purpose neither to sanction nor to participate as combatants in such a war. The British Peace Pledge Union deliberately sought such commitments.

No other social issue so divided Anglo-American Christianity in this generation as the ethical justification of modern totalitarian war. Two pacifist organizations drew the support of individuals from a wide range of denominations, the Fellowship of Reconciliation and the American Friends Service Committee. Both joined to the effort to heal international hatreds a concern for racial and class conflicts, and particularly the problems of American Negroes, Mexicans, and, in the Second World War, nisei. The work camp, which revived in a new form the old conception of the university settlement, was very successfully used by both. Both groups also attracted numbers of idealistic humanitarians who felt uncomfortable with Christian theology. A Tolstoyan revolt against industrialism and militarism often produced local attempts at self-sufficient co-operative colonies and "ashrams," sometimes interracial in character. On the fundamental premises of these movements, however, no attempt at a reorganization of the existing power structures of society was likely. American Protestantism, and particularly the Protestant ministry, was deeply influenced by this pacifist idealism. It may even be that reports of the strength of this movement, and especially its British counterpart, helped Hitler to decide that he could risk aggression without Anglo-American interference. In the event, of course, the popular strength of this pacifism proved to be simply idealistic innocence about political realities, and only a hard core rested on real religious conviction. All through the '30's, as war with the dictators drew visibly nearer, social gospelers were engaged in a painful process of rethinking the basis and form of their Christian political ethic on war.

Another and related critical situation in the postwar generation imposed like strains on social gospel democratic idealism about brotherhood and the dignity of personality. This was the world-wide rise of colored peoples against the imposition of caste by the whites. Americans generally had been very slow to admit the implications of their democratic faith for Negroes, Indians, Mexicans, Orientals. The cancer of outright slavery as practiced by the founding fathers had at least been painfully cut out of the tissues of American society, but caste determined political and social and economic relations still. After the great crisis and disillusionment of Civil War and Reconstruction the race issue was not a central concern until World War I suddenly forced it to the fore. The postwar race riots led to the formulation of the first Church pronouncement on the subject, " A Crisis in Democracy," adopted at the Federal Council meeting in 1920. *The Church and Social Reconstruction* also laid down a program of economic, educational, legal justice for Negroes.[6] A Commission on Church and Race Relations was established in 1921, and at the Federal Council quadrennial in Atlanta, Georgia, a " Program of Applied Brotherhood in Race Relations " was officially adopted. The manifesto declared " the assumption of inherent racial superiority by dominant groups around the world is neither supported by science nor justified by ethics." [7] This was enough to identify the Federal Council with " Communism " in certain circles, especially in the South. The Roman Catholics were afraid to touch the issue at all.

The Commission's work was merely educational in its first decade, but in the '30's began to include economic and political action of various sorts. From 1933 the Executive Committee urged the Churches to work for Federal laws against lynching, asking of them also penitence for this " national sin." Charity was replaced by justice as the ethical rubric within which this problem was to be met. It must be confessed, however, that in this period neither the Protestant nor the Roman Catholic Churches dared to speak against segregation as such, or, even more striking, to repent of their own complete acceptance of the Jim Crow system *within the Christian Church.*

While dealing with the role played by the social gospel in the international and racial tension of the day, we should notice the American contribution to the first of the great ecumenical conferences of world Christianity held in the postwar period. The desire of witnessing to the international bonds of Christianity had been voiced repeatedly during World War I by the Swiss, the Swedes, and the Americans. As soon as the war was over, plans were set afoot for an international Christian conference to seek a common Christian approach to the social and ethical problems of the West, especially war. Bitterness among British, French, and German churchmen ran so high in the years just after the Versailles treaty that initiative in planning could not be carried by them, and a Zurich preliminary meeting just missed a breakup. The tireless efforts, particularly of Archbishop Söderblom, however, overcame all obstacles, and in Stockholm in 1925 some 500 delegates, representing 300 millions of Christians from twoscore countries, met in what was probably the most inclusive assembly of Christians since the Council of Nicaea sixteen centuries before. The only major division of the Church that declined representation was Roman Catholicism. From the character of the conference the social issues that were foremost were those of international relations, war, the League, immigration, and race problems.

The significance of Stockholm lay less in what it did than what it was. Its statements on social issues were of a high generality with little bite, and many of the addresses, particularly of the Americans, are to-day incredible in their optimism and social naïveté. Even the noble Bishop Brent was talking seriously of ending war within a generation. This was the first large-scale confrontation of American theological liberalism with Continental Lutheranism and Barthianism, and on both sides the shock was considerable. Stockholm got the benefit of the unchastened American social gospel at its most ingenuous, three or four years before the floods came. Beyond this theological contrast the political cleavages cut deep. From the French the Americans might have learned why mere disarmament was no panacea, and from the Germans why the League of Nations and world government schemes in general represent the ideology of satisfied powers. China and India and Japan, moreover, had their say about white supremacy and immigration legislation, a word that had been stifled by the Anglo-Americans at Versailles, but was calculated at Stockholm to make Americans redden with shame. The message, however, still formulated the Christian's social duties in terms of the isolated individual's work for " God's Kingdom," with no grasp of the role of the Church. Nevertheless, the *fact* of the universal Church, as symbolized and actualized in personal relations at Stockholm, was to count for more than what was said there about it.

Stockholm also dealt with the duties of the Christian in the economic and especially the industrial order. This had been the point of origin for the American social gospel as a whole, back in the nineteenth century, and in the period between wars the problem attained new dimensions of menace. In America the first crises came with the postwar readjustments of the early '20's. The issue with the leadership of the Churches was produced by the " open shop " drive of some of the great industries against the whole labor union movement. Now the Federal Council had been on record ever since the " Social Creed " of 1912 for the right of workmen to organize. This position was reaffirmed at the end of the war. The American Roman Catholic hierarchy took the same stand, hoping " that this right will never again be called in question by any considerable number of employers." A very considerable number of industrialists, however, launched a national drive after the war for the " American plan " of shops closed to labor unions. They were shocked and irritated when they discovered that the drive was flatly opposed by the Federal Council, the National Catholic Welfare Council, and the Jewish rabbis.

" Industry awakened to the presence of a new force and of what seemed at first to most businessmen an alien, uninformed and unfriendly force. Leaders of great industries found themselves called to account by their spiritual advisers, and their amazement and indignation were naturally unbounded. A violent controversy ensued which, while regrettable, was inevitable and necessary if the Church was to have permanent influence. An unfortunate effort was made to stifle the new voice by the use of personal influence, by the financial boycott and by striking at the co-operative leadership of the Protestant denominations." [8]

It is difficult to know what consequences actually resulted from the industrialists' counterattack on the Churches' democratic leadership. The bitter controversy over the twelve-hour day in the steel industry was materially influenced by the report of the Interchurch World Movement, which was associated in the popular mind with the Federal Council. U.S. Steel in turn attacked this Protestant leadership, which had been instrumental in pushing them to the triple eight-hour shift which they had previously resisted. Very likely the financial failure of the Interchurch campaign was seriously influenced by this controversy, although it is hard to see how it could have succeeded anyway. Judge Gary, of U.S. Steel, circulated a volume libeling Federal Council leaders until challenged by them. Professional " patriots " and Red hunters in and out of Congress have recurrently attacked the Council ever since but usually have not cared to attempt to substantiate accusations in court.

In sharp contrast to the British situation, where unionism was taken for granted, a significant section of American industry still cherished the hope of destroying American unionism and collective bargaining all through the '20's and '30's. The prevailing inadequacy or unfairness of the American press on industrial conflicts made the continuance of Federal Council surveys and reports on strike situations a valuable function. Similar services were performed by the (Episcopalian) Church League for Industrial Democracy and the Methodist Federation for Social Service. In 1930 the Executive Committee of the Federal Council criticized the practice of crippling labor union action and precluding collective bargaining by court injunctions. Again in 1934 the Committee commented: " When labor is denied the right of free choice of representatives and when employers refuse to deal with representatives so chosen, the spirit and purpose of justice and democracy are thwarted." [9] The annual Labor Sunday Messages have reaffirmed this position in various connections, as when in 1937 the Wagner Labor Relations Act was validated by the Supreme Court. While urging from the beginning the moral value and stabilizing effect of labor unions, the Federal Council steadily opposed the all-too-frequent recourse to violence by both labor and management, and contended against the thesis of the necessity of class war and proletarian revolution. As we have seen, the Council contributed directly to arbitration and conciliation in hundreds of industrial conflicts.

In addition to collective bargaining, the postwar social gospel movement has generally urged that industrial democracy also implies some share in management by labor. Various experiments were made in the '20's in profit-sharing devices under Church stimulation.[10] A sharing in ownership and control was urged on grounds of principle in the Federal Council statement of 1920. "The various movements toward industrial councils and shop committees have not only an economic but a spiritual significance in that they are, or may be, expressions of brotherhood and recognize the right of the worker to full development of personality."[11]

The social gospelers also consistently urged that the State should contribute to protect the conditions of "industrial democracy." From its beginning the Federal Council had rejected the "rugged individualist" theory of economic life as held by the majority of Protestant and Roman Catholic businessmen. The Council stood consistently for some form of accident, old-age, sickness, and unemployment protection for labor. From the beginning the Council urged protective legislation for women and children in industry. After 1922 the Federal Council, as it actively promoted the proposed child labor amendment to the Federal Constitution, found itself fighting the Roman Catholic hierarchy.

Far more radical still was the postulate in the Social Creed of 1912 of "a living wage as a minimum in every industry." The postwar manifesto, *The Church and Social Reconstruction*,[12] laid on the State the responsibility for securing to the worker an "adequate family wage." To be sure, we must not credit the leaders of the Federal Council with very radical intentions with regard to the social and economic structure. Like Americans generally, they assumed an expanding economy and rising production, and merely intended that the workman should get a little more of his share.

The implications of this minimum family wage as the first charge on industry were more clearly seen in hard-pressed Britain, where businessmen flatly rejected the whole conception. "The real and ultimate test," stated the Federation of British Industries, "must always be what industry can bear. . . . It may be necessary . . . for the workers to be prepared to accept a money wage which may, till trade revives, give them a lower standard of living . . . even than their prewar standard." [13] This was a challenge that set certain alternatives before the churchmen. What did they mean by a living family wage? Did they mean only that it was a good thing if you could get it? Or that if industry could not pay it, the State should make up the difference from taxes? Or that if industry could not pay it, industry must be reorganized? And just how would that be done? In America, at least, the meaning was that a living family wage was a good thing and industry could surely pay it. In the second half of the '20's, indeed, the Christian social movement in America found itself engulfed in the general mood of expansion and speculation, with little reason to look for reform. Out of this intellectually debilitating atmosphere it was then suddenly plunged at the beginning of the '30's into the whole problem of the very survival of capitalistic industrialism.

The Great Depression, we have already suggested, initiated the greatest shift in American thought and attitudes for half a century. For the first time Americans generally began to sense the mood of cultural crisis nearly universal on the European Continent since the war. And the American Churches responded in their own way with a new social and political awareness. The Episcopalian General Convention of 1931, the Congregational General Council and the Presbyterian General Assembly of 1934, the Federal Council sessions of 1932 all displayed for the first time a sense of " national repentance " on a scale at all comparable to that of the British Anglicans half a generation before. And the social and political thought of churchmen began to exhibit new precision and realism.

In Britain there had long been a great deal of " socialism " among churchmen, but now even Americans, at least American clergymen, supported it in large numbers and with awareness of what they were doing. In 1932 the Federal Council was explicit in support of a planned economy. The long-hallowed " profit motive " should, according to the 1932 edition of the Social Creed, be subordinated " to the creative and co-operative spirit." " The principle of competition," declared the Report of that year, " appears to be nothing more than a partly conventionalized embodiment of primeval selfishness . . . the supremacy of the motive of self-interest." [14] By contrast, " the Christian ideal calls for hearty support of a planned economic system." " Industrial democracy is a goal comparable to that of political democracy. . . . In one stage of development . . . the right of workers to organize and to be represented by counsel or agents of their own free choice must be recognized as fundamental. In another stage, participation of workers in management may be possible and desirable; in another, workers might provide their own capital and assume full responsibility; in still another, the Government might assume and exercise the powers of ownership, control, and management for the public good." [15]

The outlines of a substantial social philosophy of economic democracy are here clear, and a European observer [16] is inclined to credit the social gospel movement with a major responsibility in shifting the thought of the American people from nineteenth century individualism to a more organic conception. In considerable measure the New Deal of the 1930's incorporated and expressed this body of social thought, as was pointed out more than once by President Roosevelt. Members of the Federal Council staff and Executive Committee also observed this convergence and declared substantial agreement with the general philosophy and many of the objectives of the National Recovery Program. But while the social gospelers acknowledged a Daniel come to judgment in F.D.R., the Protestant vote in the North was still dominantly Republican. The New Deal was better supported, among the rank and file, by the Roman Catholics. Even at the end of the '30's, it was probably still only a minority of Protestant Church members who supported the philosophy of economic democracy we have been sketching.

The sort of social thought characteristic of the American Protestant clergy in the 1920's was much less evident in Great Britain. Before the war, as we have seen, British churchmen had been considerably in advance of the Americans in the realism with which they faced the problems of industrial society. After all, they had been facing them considerably longer. Britain was also much more industrialized and its churches were much less colored by the small-town ethos so influential in American Protestantism. And for the Americans the First World War was incomparably less of a strain than for the British. The Americans entered late and experienced in comparison only trifling losses. A difference was perceptible even at the beginning of the war. The Americans were full of outraged indignation and made a scapegoat of the Kaiser. The Church of England, on the other hand, initiated a National Mission of Repentance and Hope in 1916. It was no sensational success, to be sure, and was criticized by those patriots who thought that the Church should be acclaiming the heroes of the war effort rather than calling them to face their sins. The Mission revealed, however, a sense of independent Christian perspective on the nation's cause which was not then evident in America. And the Church was admitting a responsibility for a corporate witness going beyond the mere production of good Christian citizens as individuals. "There is a real difference," the Mission declared, "between a converted nation and a nation of converted individuals. All these citizens of a nation might be individually converted, and yet public life be conducted on principles other than Christian." [17] The C.S.L. acclaimed that Mission as "the first real attempt on the part of the Church of England, as a Church, to face the social question in the light of the faith, and to envisage a Christian nation." [18]

Two years later the effect of the National Mission was strengthened by the famous Fifth Report of the Archbishop's Committee of Enquiry on Christianity and Industrial Problems. Drafted in considerable measure apparently by R. H. Tawney, this report passed severe ethical judgments on British economic society, comparing some features of it to slavery, calling for a fundamental change from the motives of private gain, with its treatment of workers as hands, and affirming a family living wage as "the first charge upon every industry." [19] This report was widely disseminated, especially by the study groups of the Student Christian Movement and the Industrial Christian Fellowship, the heir of the old C.S.U. The American Federal Council attempted a similar action through its War-Time Commission, which produced a report, *The Church and Industrial Reconstruction,* which Tawney acknowledged in very generous terms. But the influence of this report was not comparable to that of the British; the mind of the Churches was less ready for it.

The contrast between British and American Christian thought endured and was even heightened in the 1920's. In Britain social discontent and distress were more general, and the Churches readier to accept responsibility. The war left Britain in a radically weakened position in world markets. Her financiers tried to meet the problem by devaluation in 1920, an action that left the nation with the shocking prospect of chronic unemployment for one or two millions of her workers. Much of the bitterest suffering was concentrated in certain blighted districts which came to be known as "special areas." The coal industry was particularly hard hit, and from 1921 to 1926 unrest was constant, with various Government commissions making studies and proposals. A climax came in the latter year, variously described as a "strike" or "lockout," which, by virtue of the sympathetic action of the transport workers, gained something of the appearance and the popular description of a "general strike."

In this strike, incidentally, Church leaders intervened conspicuously. Prime Minister Baldwin had called for unconditional surrender by the workmen. Archbishop Davidson, while describing the strike as "mischievous and unfortunate," nevertheless called upon the Government in the name of the Churches of England and for the common good, to reopen negotiations. The Government newspaper would not carry the plea, nor would the radio for some time. The archbishop was referred to in Parliament as an " irresponsible agency." With the laboring classes, on the other hand, the spectacle of the Churches of England standing over against dominant upper-class opinion and the Government had a startling effect. " Perhaps for the first time in English history poor men cheered an archbishop in the streets." [20]

The lockout dragged on, however, and the Government was not to be budged. A group of Free Churchmen and Anglican bishops now formed a committee to attempt mediation again. This committee met with miners and owners' representatives and with the prime minister. They were unsuccessful, and were later even accused of having delayed agreement on certain independent proposals that had been winning ground in negotiations of which the churchmen were not informed. In any case, inexpert as it may have been, the intervention staked out a new independence for the Churches.

While the preparatory work was being done for the Stockholm conference in the first half of the 1920's, similar efforts were being made in Great Britain to organize co-operative study and a conference on Christian social ethics. The enterprise was launched in 1919 at a meeting of the I.C.S.S.U. (cf. above, p. 129), building on the work of the study organ, the *Collegium,* of that body. Four years were assigned to study and discussion in a great variety of groups on the meaning of God's will for the common life in politics, economics, society, education, the family. The whole was to culminate in a great conference. While the Conference on Christian Politics, Economics, and Citizenship (Copec) actually met in Birmingham the year before the world conference in Stockholm, it marked a greater maturity in the social gospel movement, and can serve as a conclusion of our treatment of the latter. In some respects it already pointed beyond the social gospel to that new stage which Reckitt describes as the " quest for the autochthonous," a stage which, as we shall see, began to be apparent in some American circles a decade later, and was explicit at the Oxford Conference of 1937.

The quadrennium of study was the outstanding contribution of Copec. The great proliferation of study groups stimulated by the questionnaire and by various public meetings on particular questions involved more, and more varied participation, than any such previous undertaking, including college students, workmen, ministers' associations, girls' clubs. The whole process made known to each other hitherto isolated enthusiasts for social Christianity.

At the actual conference in 1924, fifteen hundred delegates met for a week, debated the Reports and accepted them, voting some 170 recommendations on a very varied range of issues. All the Churches of Britain were represented, save the Roman Catholic, which withdrew on orders. Penology, education, housing, leisure, politics, and citizenship were all reviewed in their own terms without much reference to the theological issues disposed of separately under " the nature of God and his purpose." Differences were sharp on birth control and divorce and a divided report came in on pacifism. " Industry and property " challenged the basis of British economy, contending that the concentration of wealth in the hands of some, and the unemployment of others, was affected slightly if at all by character or ability. The right to property was not to be considered absolute and the primacy of the profit motive in economic life was deplored. The living wage as the first charge on industry was asserted, as also the right of labor, not merely to organize, but to share in management.

One of the best Reports of all dealt with " The Social Functions of the Church." The problems of adequate thinking and education in the Church and the restoration of discipline were here reviewed. With the last came over the horizon the problem of the contrast that would then appear between the morality of the Church and that of the whole national community, and the resultant relations of Church and State. In protest against this line of thought, on the other hand, were to be discerned three emphases: first, the desire to limit social ethics strictly to individual responsibilities; second, the desire to keep the Church purely " spiritual " and not soiled with worldly matters; and, lastly, the realization that much of the best of Christian intelligence and devotion was already responsibly engaged in political and social organizations in actual operation which had no specific Christian character, but to which they lent much stability and humanity.

The continuation organs of Copec and of Stockholm in Britain were incorporated in 1929 in the Christian Social Council, on which the various Churches were directly represented. The representatives were drawn chiefly from the various denominational social service unions and the I.C.F. Principal Garvie and the Bishop of Winchester were joint chairmen. The most fruitful work of the Council was performed by its Research Committee, directed by V. A. Demant. The work of the Christian Social Council and then that of the Oxford Conference committees in Britain and America belong to the new phases of Protestant social ethics, to which we must now turn. In this new phase the emphasis shifts from natural morals to Christian theology and Christian sociology.

2. AFTER THE SOCIAL GOSPEL

The post-social-gospel leaders in Puritan Protestantism had no intention of repudiating the political ethic of their fathers. They considered the " democratic way of life " at least as " Christian " and more practically relevant than the political norms derived by Roman Catholicism from pagan Greece and feudal Europe. But they also considered that this democratic faith had been rested on inadequate and obsolescent sanctions, on faith in progress and the moral perfectibility of man through education. " It is a valid criticism of this liberal social Christianity," wrote a Federal Council scholar, " that its philosophy, its ideals, and its programs as commonly stated have little distinctive character in terms of Christian postulates. Many of the social pronouncements of Church bodies in this country might have been made by any high-minded group of educators or social workers claiming nothing other than a secular sanction." [21] " This recourse to a general principle of social utility makes the Church indistinguishable from secular agencies." [22] " The task of deriving ethical mandates directly and irresistibly from Christian assumptions about man's relation to God, about sin and redemption, about love and sacrifice, about the Church, and implementing these mandates in the corporate life of a Christian community — this task we have not done in any effective way." [23] This was the task undertaken by the new movements. Protestant theology and the Protestant Church were being reborn at the very time when the secular humanitarian tradition was disintegrating. And some of the ablest Protestant spokesmen doubted whether the case for democracy was as thin as its secular and social gospel defenders made it out to be.

What was involved in this revolution was a reconsideration of the nature of the compartmentalization of the ecclesiastical and the secular spheres of life which had first been devised in the Puritan revolution of the seventeenth century. In this Protestant parallel to Thomism, as we have already seen, the conduct of public affairs in government and business was regulated by " the moral law " as known to all men of good will. American life had been organized on common convictions supposedly independent of all positive theological and ecclesiastical traditions. Pietists, rationalists, creedalists, fundamentalists, and social gospelers had agreed on this; they were all simple theists or deists in public affairs (for that was the real " national religion ") whatever they might be ecclesiastically. And for generations the system had worked with conspicuous success in comparison with alternative patterns in Europe. The Puritan churches were vigorous enough in the society so that their peculiar urge to pass judgments and set goals for

State and society in the name of a " higher law " seemed the " natural " attitude to Americans in general. And there was still reason to hope that this generalized reflection of the Puritan theocratic urge would make American society more resistant to cynical violence or State absolutism than the chief Continental Christian traditions had made their societies. Nevertheless this conviction of obligation to the " higher law " seemed ever less " natural " from the Civil War on even to men of good will. Writing of the American democratic faith in the twentieth century, Mr. Gabriel observed: " One of its doctrines, nationalism, is magnified almost beyond recognition. All of the others, those of fundamental law, of the free individual, and the philosophy of progress, are challenged. It may be that they are on the way out." [24] It was time to reconsider how and why this faltering democratic faith had originally been related to Puritan convictions about the Creator, Judge, Redeemer, and sole Head of the Church. Let us review some schools of thought on these long-dormant but now revived issues.

In his various and valuable accounts of Anglican social thought, Maurice Reckitt has described the most striking manifestation of this tradition between World Wars as the " quest for the autochthonous." In contrast to the social gospel, which typically confined itself to urging that Christians as individuals should support the best " secular " programs and agencies on the horizon, the Anglo-Catholics thought they could present an " autochthonous," a specific and unique " churchly " sociology. A guild structure of production should be able to fix " just prices " and widen the distribution of private property. It was substantially the same appeal to a clerically controlled civilization on the medieval pattern which the Roman Catholics were making, although it was elaborated with more freedom and intellectual power than English-speaking Roman Catholics could command. A group manifesto, *The Return of Christendom,* appeared in 1922, and the League of the Kingdom of God continued this propaganda thereafter, finding its most effective expression in the Anglo-Catholic Summer School of Sociology, which met annually from 1924 throughout the period. The journal *Christendom* also appeared from 1931 on, and it was to " the *Christendom* group," as the proponents of the most coherent and developed body of social thought within Anglicanism, that the larger share of the papers for the Malvern Conference of 1941 were assigned. The contrast of this Malvern " quest for the autochthonous " with the social gospel of Copec can be stated in the terms of Archbishop Temple, who presided over both assemblies. While Copec had sought a Christian remedy for specific social evils, Malvern and the *Christendom* group generally raised the deeper question of the structure of society as a whole. This analysis of structure, moreover, was founded on a theological or philosophical conception of a " right rela- tion of the various functions of society — financial, productive, distribu- tive, cultural, spiritual, to one another. . . . There was a more pervasive belief that the evils of society arise from our desertion of an ascertaina- ble order for society which springs from and coheres with Christian faith in God as Creator, Redeemer and Sanctifier." [25] And thirdly, Mal- vern was more concerned with the function of the Church itself, as a community that should embody and exhibit the quality of life desired for society as a whole.

A second post-social-gospel school of Christian ethics was more defi- nitely Protestant in character. The Christian Socialist Fellowship of Britain and the Fellowship of Socialist Christians (now the Frontier Fellowship) in America embodied this current. Reinhold Niebuhr was the most influential thinker in both countries, and, while not without honor at home, was probably more widely understood in Britain. The American group was given added distinction by the accession of two refugees from the Nazis, Paul Tillich and Eduard Heimann. Their organ was *Radical Religion;* later, *Christianity and Society.* In the latter half of the '30's the influence of the group became sensible in other organizations, such as the Methodist Federation for Social Service and the Congregational Council for Social Action.

The quest here was not for the " autochthonous," in the sense of Christian tradition as against extraecclesiastical currents, but for the " theonomous," the recognition of the living God in every aspect of his creation, whether or not under ecclesiastical insignia. Thus a cer- tain continuity with the older social gospel was retained, of laying em- phasis on the sovereignty of God rather than the jurisdiction of the Church. The tendency of that older social gospel to identify God's will with certain moral standards, the " teachings of Jesus," was now re- jected. The vivid sense of God's unapproachable holiness was now matched by an equally vivid sense of the taint of " rationalization," of " ideology," of original sin, in all man's morality and religion. The " natural law " of the Catholic moralists, viewed from this perspective, dissolved into a series of historically conditioned compromises, unified only on a safely abstract level. The religious responsibility to use reason and conscience in every concrete situation was vigorously enjoined, but always with the warning that no formulations of moral law could be at once unambiguous and absolute, and that even the Church must always stand under judgment of God. Even Temple, sympathetic as he was to the *Christendom* group and the tradition of natural law, felt the unreality of the scholastic categories for actual Christian politics.

Comparing a work of Jacques Maritain to one of Niebuhr, he noted that it was the latter and not the former that gave " the impression of a deeply Christian mind grappling with the realities of today; and this is due to the fact that Niebuhr's whole mind is possessed by the sense of that aboriginal sin of man . . . which is the source of power politics." [26]

This general sense of man as a sinner was understood particularly, as by the Marxians, in terms of power structures of society and the devious ways in which all men are affected by them, consciously and unconsciously. The struggle of the socially disadvantaged for justice was read as one means used by the living God in contemporary history. And political action in collaboration with the labor movement and with parties New Dealist or Laborite commonly was practiced — less in America, to be sure, than in Britain. In 1931, for example, several Labor M.P.'s were drawn into the " Christian Socialist Crusade," which merged with the old Society of Socialist Christians under the presidency of George Lansbury as the Socialist Christian Fellowship. Here was a hope that collectivism might be qualified and informed by a self-disciplined Christian initiative, in contrast to what was happening in these years on the Continent.

The conception and method of this Protestant Christian socialism was also democratic in ways closed to the Catholic movements, Roman and Anglican alike. The evangelicals knew that only God was wholly trustworthy, that their own political and moral insights were always subject to ideological taint and in need of criticism. When pressed, they had to concede that the Christian Laborite was no more trustworthy than the Christian Tory, and that each needed the other in a continuing process of clarifying debate within the common loyalty. As Niebuhr repeated after Calvin, the nature of man is sufficiently corrupt so that government by many is " safer." The different varieties of Catholics, however, knew men not subject to such corruption, whose political-moral judgments were not to be touched by vulgar scrutiny or debased by discussion, namely, the spokesmen of the clerical hierarchies. There is no room for a " loyal opposition " to them. The Anglo-Catholics, to be sure, showed themselves far more affected by the democratic environment than the Roman Catholics, and, being largely limited to an esoteric coterie of intellectuals, were scarcely in a position to become a serious threat to democracy. Such expressions of Anglo-Catholicism as T. S. Eliot's *The Idea of a Christian Society*, however, indicated the common Catholic tendency to prefer social hierarchy and authoritative rule to responsible government by discussion and equality of opportunity.

For a comprehensive summary of the position of the best leadership of the Anglo-American churches at this point, we may conclude with some review of the significance of the Oxford Conference of 1937. Both the schools of thought that we have identified contributed materially to the Oxford discussions, at which, for various reasons, 300 of the 425 delegates were from the English-speaking world. The Oxford Conference represented the application of the study program of Copec on a world-wide scale. From the time when the date was set, in 1932, and the main topics outlined, a vast network of discussion and study was organized. Some three or four hundred scholars or specialists all over the world were engaged in a process of writing, circularizing, criticizing, and rewriting papers on various aspects of the relations of Church, community, and State. Six volumes of these essays were the result, and from 1937 they served as study manuals for thousands more Christians in various countries. Contributors of these essays, moreover, were not merely clergy; they were Christians of competence and experience in their several vocations. At Oxford, finally, the delegates met in five sections to draw up reports on as many main divisions of the conference theme. As with Copec, consequently, the work of the conference itself was but the visible portion of the iceberg in comparison to the engagement of the churches, both before and after, in its discussions. In the words of J. H. Oldham, the organizer of this project, " What the Conference was able to do was to co-ordinate, extend, and amplify the results of much preliminary thinking and in a series of tentative formulations to provide a promising starting point for future thought and study." [27] With these qualifications, the authority of the Oxford reports was unprecedented, at least in Protestant social ethics, and their competence enabled them to rank with the best of secular thought, a phenomenon scarcely seen since the seventeenth century.

The year after the preparations for Oxford were begun, the Nazis took power in Germany, and by the time the conference convened, German Christians, save for Methodists and Baptists who had made their peace with Hitler, were denied passports. The first and second Five Year Plans in the U.S.S.R. had developed new techniques of religious persecution and the Russian Orthodox were conspicuously absent. Japan was launched in an imperialist attack on China. Fascists had dropped gas on Ethiopians and were now using Spain as their training ground along with German military units. The Oxford Conference bore the signature of this setting.

In contrast to the social gospel of the '20's, Oxford was incomparably more realistic in sociology and psychology, more profound in theology, more daring in its criticism. " In this instance ethics gained immeasurably by being placed in a wider and deeper theological context." [28] No longer was hope oriented to secular progress and to man's educability. In a dangerous world these were too flimsy to live and work by. Christians must again learn to live " theonomously," out of the joy of God's mercy and faith in his redemption. No longer was the Kingdom to be simply identified with any social structure, achieved or proposed. " Every tendency to identify the Kingdom of God with a particular structure of society or economic mechanism must result in moral confusion for those who maintain the system and in disillusionment for those who suffer from its limitations." [29] " Much of the disillusionment about international affairs to be found among Christians is due to the fact that the hopes vested in specific schemes for international betterment were of an almost religious quality and it was forgotten that to all human institutions clings the taint of sin. On the other hand it is erroneous to hold that our hope in the Kingdom of God has no bearing upon the practical choices that men must make within the present order." [30]

With regard to positive proposals and strategy, a second striking change in the dozen years since Stockholm was the new conception of the function of the Church. At Malvern, Maurice Reckitt recalled his experiences with the Copec commission on international relations in 1923. It had not occurred to any of the members, he said, that there was anything for Christians to do other than to devote all efforts to the cause of the League of Nations. No one seemed to recall that the unity of Europe had been called into being by the unity of Christians in the Church, " that the mission field of today offered clues to us at least as significant for Christians as the working of secular international institutions; and that the Church had responsibilities for the spiritual leadership of the world which she could not devolve." [31] At Oxford, in contrast to Copec, a central motif in the consideration of every issue was the peculiar function of the Church.

Take the example of racialism. The sin of men asserts itself in " racial pride, racial hatreds and persecutions, and in the exploitation of other races," says the Report. Against this in all its forms " the Church is called by God to set its face implacably and to utter its word unequivocally, both within and without its own borders. . . . Especially in its own life and worship there can be no place for barriers because of race or color. . . . In such a world the Church is called to be in its own life that fellowship which binds men together in their common dependence on God and overleaps all barriers of social status, race, or nationality."

Or consider the Report on war. " The universal Church, surveying the nations of the world, in every one of which it is now planted and rooted, must pronounce a condemnation of war unqualified and unrestricted. . . . If war breaks out, then pre-eminently the Church must manifestly be the Church, still united as the one body of Christ, though the nations wherein it is planted fight one another. . . . This fellowship of prayer must at all costs remain unbroken. The Church must also hold together in one spiritual fellowship those of its members who take different views concerning their duty as Christian citizens in time of war."

With regard to the economic order, similarly, where the Report was most extended and circumstantial, reviewing, with a boldness that would startle most American laymen, the achievements and corruptions of the dominant capitalist system, there were again suggestions for the Church as such. The financial autonomy of congregations, e.g., was a denial in practice of Christian solidarity. On the international scale likewise mutual Church aid must be continued and increased. All the economic practices of the Church must be consonant with their purposes.

In education, lastly, while working for equality of opportunity and the highest standards for all, the Church has a " special responsibility to realize its own understanding of the meaning and end of education in the relation of life to God. . . . The Church must claim the liberty to give a Christian education to its own children. It is in the field of education that the conflict between Christian faith and non-Christian conceptions of the ends of life, between the Church and an all-embracing community life which claims to be the source and goal of every human activity, is in many parts of the world most acute." The weaknesses of the Church in Christian education in the home and with adults, in theories and techniques of education, must be repaired.

In sum, " the first duty of the Church, and its greatest service to the world, is that it be in very deed the Church — confessing the true faith, committed to the fulfillment of the will of Christ, its only Lord, and united in him in a fellowship of love and service. . . . Notwithstanding the tragedy of our divisions and our inability in many important matters to speak with a united voice, there exists an actual world fellowship. . . . The unity of this fellowship is not built up from its constituent parts like a federation of different states. . . . The source of unity is not the consenting movement of men's wills; it is Jesus Christ, whose one life flows through the Body and subdues the many wills to his."

The year after the Oxford Conference Austria fell, and then came the turn of the Czechs and the Poles. All thinking men were primarily preoccupied with the drift to a new and terrible war. And few of them placed any hope in the Christian Church in this emergency. The great reshaping of thought about the Christian Church and gospel of which Oxford was the symbol only highlighted the actual irrelevance of the Churches to the centers of power and the crucial decisions of Western civilization. Despite the high claims of the theologians at Oxford, the world at large "assumed that the Church is concerned with another world than this, and in this with nothing but individual conduct as bearing on prospects in that world." [32] Despite the prophetic vision of Christian thinkers, the average churchgoer and even the run-of-the-mill cleric were not convinced that the Christian community had a regular and normal witness and responsibility for the direction chosen by State and culture. "The Church fails in leadership," wrote J. M. Murry for Malvern, "because it shows no signs of having known despair: no evidence of having been terrified by its own impotence." [33]

This impotence and irrelevance of the Churches can be discerned in the whole range of their activities, their ethical discipline, the scope of their fellowship and organization, their worship and sacramental life. And with regard to our specific concern for democracy, we may venture the judgment that the Puritan Protestant Churches were no longer making any such contribution to democracy as they had done in the generations from Roger Williams and Cromwell to Lincoln and Gladstone. The relation between Christian faith and political decision was no longer evident in worship, no longer habitually the exercise of the whole Christian community to determine, no longer subject to the discipline of that community over its individual members. On the contrary, individual Christians were disciplined and constrained in their political decisions by practically every other kind of organization than the Church, and the effective scope of Church fellowship itself was so largely determined by social and economic forces as to deny in practice the right of the Christian gospel to shape the Christian community.

By ethical discipline we do not mean the enforcement of moralistic or ascetic duties on Church members, but rather the regular measuring of the Christian community by its own highest insights into the will of God. The Quaker "Queries" are an illustration of how a Christian fellowship may be maintained in a lively sense of the judgment of God upon the corporate life and public activities of its members. Yet such a Church discipline had become the exception rather than the rule in Puritan Protestantism. Two pietist and rationalist centuries had accustomed the bulk of Protestants to measuring themselves only by the better standards of market-place ethics in their business and political decisions. They would be startled and perhaps offended by any breaches in the wall of segregation between the spheres of natural law and Christian grace, by the suggestion that their Christian faith should be brought into direct relation to public life. The organs for exercising such discipline were notoriously atrophied. It was many generations since Calvinist sessions of elders really fulfilled any serious role in the leadership of the moral witness of the congregations. Baptist " covenant meetings " were still effective in private ethics, but the Methodist classes were gone. And the congregational meetings of such Puritans as the Congregationalists no longer really sought the guidance of the Holy Spirit on great questions of public policy. They had become miserable committee meetings on potluck suppers and the color of a new paint job in the Sunday school rooms. Such meetings contributed about as much to training in democracy as those " civics " classes in the schools where the children behave like Congressmen, or organize a school government, but are not allowed to deliberate on any issues of real importance to themselves, all these being reserved to the administration. The Puritan Churches had a precious heritage of corporate discipline under the Holy Spirit, and without it their contribution to democracy would be far less.

This decline of Church discipline, at least in the larger relations of life, is the crucial question to be raised in estimating the significance of the pronouncements of Protestant leaders in this period. In reviewing the statements of Federal Council spokesmen and denominational leaders we often had occasion to note divergencies from the current of opinion among the laity. In the absence of any corporate discipline involving both clergy and laity in the common waiting upon the will of God and in obeying it, all such pronouncements simply represented the opinions of groups of clergy. They had the recommendations of relative disinterestedness and of a concern for the total good, and often a fair degree of somewhat abstract educational preparation. But Protestant laymen in government, business, labor, social welfare, education, and the arts, tended to distrust clerical opinion as without concrete experience. Such laymen tended to professionalize their activities, and increasingly to replace philosophical grasp, and the concern for human values and the larger community by technical or mechanical standards of efficiency and a more or less rudderless pragmatism.

It was also evident that any effective revival of corporate discipline in these matters would involve a major reorganization of ecclesiastical patterns, in America at least. Corporate thinking and experiment by Christians competent in the business or professions of the modern world could never be carried on effectively on a parish or congregational basis. The social communities in which these activities took place were universally far larger than a congregational neighborhood. The discovery and actualization of Christian discipline in these several areas and vocations would be achieved only over large areas and on an intercongregational and, indeed, interdenominational basis. This did not mean that the local congregation and its " general practitioner " parson were to be scrapped, but it did mean that the theory and practice of congregational "autonomy," as held by perhaps one third of all American churches, must be abandoned altogether. This theory of the Baptists, Disciples, and Congregationalists (in so far as the last ever held it in America) had been adequate to the practical needs of a popular church in preindustrial generations. The isolated settlements and small towns of agrarian America had nourished it to unprecedented strength. But in the twentieth century it was to be defended only by those who intended to disqualify Christians from their responsibility to the larger communities of industry, commerce, State, and culture. A structure designed to discipline only the immediate neighborhood to Christian living was simply obsolete.

In similar fashion the inherited pattern of denominational autonomy could not survive any serious endeavor to realize the Christian mission to America as envisioned by the Oxford Conference. There were perhaps four large divisions in American Protestantism, separated by serious religious and theological convictions. Those Baptists and Disciples who held the separatist and sectarian view of the Church on principle could not agree with the ecumenical program in ethics or ecclesiology. The Lutherans had a long process of internal discussion and co-ordination ahead of them before relations with non-Lutheran bodies could become general or profitable. The Episcopalians would refuse any unions that would disaffect that section of their denomination which attached metaphysical necessity to postulated tactual successions of ordaining bishops. The Orthodox set similar value on another such succession. The rest of the Puritan denominations, however, especially the Congregationalists, Methodists, and Presbyterians, constituted a theological unity within which co-operation and unity must progress in proportion as the common witness should be seriously served. As each of the denominations within these major divisions tried to do everything independently, there were not enough first-class men to provide staff leadership, and when there were such men, their sphere of leadership was restricted to the narrow bounds of their own confraternity. Despite the Federal Council, there was no effective, regular, and constant communication and discipline under the Spirit across these denominational barriers. The visible unity and the effective reconciliation of Christ's Church were obscured and impeded. The very considerable resources of American Protestantism were strained to the limit to maintain an obsolete and mid-Victorian ecclesiastical structure, which could not even instruct the youth for whom it admitted responsibility, much less cope with the task set before the Church by the Oxford Conference.

It became increasingly apparent that the scope and divisions of Christian fellowship in America reflected the power of other than religious forces in American life, and that submission to them represented in part a denial of the Lordship of Christ in the Church. In the ages of creative faith when Puritanism had helped to mold democracy, devotion to that Lordship had created community across class lines, a community where reconciliation was brought about under a common discipline. But in the twentieth century barriers were admitted within the Church of Christ which testified to the power of mammon in the Church as well as the culture. More than Puritanism was shaping political democracy, the social hierarchy of capitalism and color caste was shaping the Puritan's Church.

The new realization of the ecumenical reformation that the Christian gospel itself involved a community of reconciliation, the Church, which was to hold in creative tension members of various classes and races, threw a new and harsh light on American ecclesiastical organization. For the extraordinary diversity of denominations was fully as sociological and cultural in its bases as it was theological, if not more so. That is to say, the very tensions that it was the mission of the Church to comprehend and reconcile within itself had been allowed in fact to divide the Church's fellowship and to triumph over its gospel. The typical American church, Protestant and Catholic, was really a religious club of a definite racial, cultural, and class character. Most of the critical issues of the society to which the Church was called to minister were thus extruded into the no man's land *between* churches, and never directly faced by the Church. This was true between individual congregations, and between the denominations, as well as between the Christians of the several nations.

This betrayal of the gospel by means of compartmentalization within the Christian community can be illustrated from analyses made at the end of the Second World War.[34] It is unlikely that the pattern had radically changed in the preceding generation. These studies seemed to indicate that while American Roman Catholicism was a definitely one-class Church, that American Protestantism as a whole was not far out of line with the national distribution of class, occupation, and education. As soon as one looked more closely at individual congregations and denominations, however, it became clear that the effective religious fellowship of American Protestants was also sharply segregated by class lines.

Of the seven chief denominational families, three were definitely middle and upper class, the Presbyterians, Episcopalians, and Congregationalists. The churches of these denominations had the highest proportion of business and professional people and the lowest of labor union members and the lower income group in general. Their educational level was the highest, with two thirds of their members at least high school graduates. These were the churches, by and large, of the more cultured and well-to-do strata in America. Their political preferences reflected this class and occupational character. Members of these groups were the most generally Republican and anti-Roosevelt of all the religious bodies.

The Methodists, Lutherans, and Disciples of Christ were more diversified in class make-up, with a higher proportion from the low income levels and only about half so great a proportion from the upper level. Only about half their constituency were high school graduates, and college graduates were markedly fewer among them. The Disciples were the most agrarian group, while the Lutherans followed, with one quarter of their membership farmers. The Lutherans and Methodists also included a very substantial group of urban manual workers, and the Lutherans had the highest proportion of trade-union members of any Protestant group. Politically these groups were also near the median, with the Methodists about equally divided, the Disciples favoring Roosevelt, and the Lutherans inclined to Republicanism.

The largest single Protestant denominational family in America was the Baptists, comprising perhaps one third of the total. By income levels the Baptists paralleled almost exactly the Roman Catholics, two thirds of the membership in each case being lower class. Similarly these two bodies had the smallest proportions among business and professional people and the upper and middle groups generally. Over half the Catholics were urban manual workers, and over one quarter of them were trade-union members. Similarly over half the Baptists were urban workers, but with only half so great a proportion of union members. They had nearly three times as many farmers as the Catholics, who were much more exclusively urban. The two groups were the least educated among American Christians and had the least influence on the higher culture of the nation. Archbishop Cushing boasted at the end of the Second World War that he did not know a single bishop or archbishop of the American Roman hierarchy who came from a cultured home. They were all sons of working people without higher education. Politically, again, Baptists and Roman Catholics were as predominantly Roosevelt Democrats as the Episcopalians, Congregationalists, and Presbyterians were anti-Roosevelt Republicans.

To save its soul the Christian Church must affirm its mission of reconciliation against this tendency to be fragmented into an anarchy of ideologies. Yet the subjugation of the corporate life of Christians to the divisions of secular society was painfully clear in regard to some of the great issues of these years. Anti-Semitism, for instance, swept in and out of the churches in accordance with social and cultural pressures. The gospel of Christ apparently had no power over it. But socialism, in contrast, displayed a real and significant resistance to anti-Semitism. Marx had discerned, better than the churches, at least some of the devices of Satan and learned to exorcise them.

In the face of the transformation of Western civilization into collectivist militarized masses manipulated from opinion-control offices by the means of mass communication, radio, television, movie, and newspaper, the relative position of Puritan Protestantism and Roman Catholicism was suddenly reversed. Just in the degree to which Protestantism had succeeded in penetrating, disciplining, moralizing the democracy, industry, technology, science, education of the Anglo-American world, it had become inextricably involved in the corresponding social and institutional structures of that world and assimilated to them. Just in the degree to which Roman Catholicism had made less contribution to the Christianizing of modern civilization, had held itself aloof psychologically and in its institutional structure, it was in a better position to take an independent line and exert leadership in the demoralization of that civilization. And while things still hung in the balance, as in the Anglo-American world in the '30's, Rome enjoyed already a superior freedom from inhibitions. With less sense of responsibility for the larger community, it could pursue its private institutional advantages more ruthlessly. Protestantism, on the other hand, was reluctant to retire to defensive positions when this would mean weakening still further the threatened structures of political democracy, for example, or the public school.

The whole constitutional structure and jurisprudence of America was Puritan Protestant in its presuppositions. Yet in the reaction against "natural law" after the Civil War, Puritan Protestantism no longer seemed to supply its metaphysical sanctions. Roman Catholics, however, built up law schools, and maintained a distinctive jurisprudence, which, while it had clerical and antidemocratic implications, at least combated the tendency to mere relativism and "realism." Puritan Protestants created the American school system, similarly, and provided generations of selfless and devoted Christian teachers. Yet when pragmatist, nationalist, and secularist movements made large inroads into this system, no considerable Protestant opposition was registered. The Roman Catholics had created a separate confessional school system, undemocratic in its influence, but at least they proposed one coherent and more or less Christian philosophy of education. In industrial life there were more Protestant than Catholic leaders of labor as well as of industry, but how did the Protestant Church help them to discover together their social duty? Roman Catholicism trained specialists for labor union work, ran labor schools, organized Catholic workmen. This Roman program, again, involved an antidemocratic system of clerical direction, but a discipline Christian in intention. Other realms of public life might be similarly analyzed, such as charities and social welfare, or the press, but these illustrations probably suffice. The Protestant constituency in America was twice as large as the Roman Catholic, yet by 1940, in terms of the conversion and shaping of society, State, and culture, Roman Catholicism may have been exerting more influence in American life than all Protestantism.

The fundamental difference lay in Church discipline. The Roman type of discipline is more external and superficial, easier to maintain. It rests on clerical authority over laymen. The self-interest of the clergy is thus enlisted in the effort to maintain discipline. Rome wants its own schools, hospitals, welfare agencies, press, lawyers, diplomatic agents, judges — all the organs of a *societas perfecta,* down to executioners. And in this bureaucracy the discipline is often materially antidemocratic, as well as in method. The Roman Catholic hierarchy, for example, overrode a majority of the American Catholic laity on the Franco issue, and persuaded the President and the Congress that it could deliver the votes against the stated convictions of the majority of Catholics. Again, the majority of Catholic women, to judge from several polls and their participation in birth control clinics, believe that doctors should have the legal right to give birth control information. But the hierarchy convinced the legislators in several states that it could deliver the votes overwhelmingly to the contrary. There is some reason to think that the situation was similar on several other political issues on which the hierarchy intervened, such as the child labor amendment and the parochial school issue. All this we must examine more closely in our next chapter. Here it is of interest to show how a disciplined Church has more influence than a Church that does not seek to shape its corporate witness by the will of God, whether the discipline be democratic or antidemocratic. What was left of Protestant discipline was democratic, but some had so long avoided measuring their decisions in prayer and discussion together under the judgment of the living God that there was fear that in putting their professed faith to the test they would discover that it was no longer there. To the new influence of English-speaking Romanism we may now turn.

IX

ANGLO–AMERICAN DEMOCRACY AND ROMAN CATHOLICISM

❖ ❖ ❖

IN THIS postwar situation of Anglo-American Protestant political confusion and indecision, the Roman Catholic Church, now well organized and strategically concentrated in the major American cities, suddenly took a new initiative. Until 1908 the Roman Propaganda supervised American Catholicism as a mission field, and at the time of the First World War half of American Catholics were still in foreign language churches. Only in the period between the wars, with mass immigration ended, did the Roman Church gain sufficient ground in the struggle to unify and organize its vast invasion of America, to be able to turn from internal problems and seek to shape the larger culture toward Roman goals.

The significant development of American Catholicism has taken place under Pius XI and Pius XII since World War I. The tremendous expansion of so-called " Catholic Action " under these leaders has made American Catholicism a stronger sociopolitical force than any other American denomination. The earlier anti-Catholic crusades are now banished to the cultural backwaters, and the Catholic Church holds such control over the means of communication — press, radio, and screen — that it is unlikely that much will henceforth be heard through them against the Roman Church. Non-Catholic America is now silent on the subject of the Roman Church and somewhat apprehensive of this new leviathan squatting in the Puritan heritage. No other Church or group of Churches exerts such influence on American education, popular culture, labor, or even possibly American politics, local and national. The Catholic Church looms up less as a religious than as a cultural and political force, because of the new quasi-political character of Catholic Action. This type of mobilization of the laity builds on a high proportion of people who are not at all devout, but merely social and political Catholics. They are willing to accept the hierarchy as their bosses in constructing an efficient power bloc. In no country in Church history has Roman Catholicism been so rich — in few since disestablishment, so influential and so politically effective — as it is today in the United States. And because of America's world position, the influence of American Catholicism is doubly significant. This is in many respects the greatest Catholic country as well as the greatest Protestant country. And it has all happened in one lifetime.

The new epoch began with the conversion of the emergency National Catholic War Council to the National Catholic Welfare Conference in 1919 as the co-ordinating administrative general staff of American Catholicism. Hitherto policies on social issues, for instance, or the press, had varied from diocese to diocese. Now an integrated nation-wide policy was possible. Annual meetings of the hierarchy date from the same year. The results of these developments are not to be gauged in numbers. Roman Catholics and the forty-three largest Protestant bodies gained in almost exactly the same ratio from 1926 to 1941–1942, with a shade of Protestant advantage. Similarly the evidence shows that Protestantism gains more converts from Roman Catholicism than vice versa, despite the impression given by the press.

The significant results of the American Counter Reformation are, rather, strategic. With the techniques learned in supporting or fighting European totalitarianism, Roman Catholicism in this generation made a systematic attack on the ganglia of American culture and social control, the schools, press, radio, movies, courts, police, military, labor movement, foreign service, as well as political parties, especially on the municipal and state level. With many of these new developments Protestantism had not come to terms and had neither a policy nor agencies to influence them. Rome had both.

In itself this effort to influence American society and culture was legitimate and natural. It concerns us only in its effect on liberal democracy in America, and, through America, in the world. As we found to be the case with Protestantism in this generation, the influence of Roman Catholicism was a mixed one politically. In social and economic internal policy as a whole there was little difference between the positions urged by the Roman hierarchy and by the Federal Council in this period. Because of the superior organization of the Roman communion, however, and because of its sociological location among the less advantaged groups, the Roman leadership found much more popular support among its laity and exerted more actual influence in political and economic life. This was true in legislation and also in such voluntary social organizations as trade-unions and co-operatives.

There was a sharp contrast, however, between the dominant Roman Catholic and Protestant policies in international relations. While Protestantism was prevailingly liberal democratic in foreign policy, but intermittently plagued by its inexperience into unrealistic forms of isolationism and pacifism, the American Roman hierarchy was realistically and competently working against liberalism and democracy and for American aid to Fascism. In this way, we have already seen, it also strengthened the cause of international Communism against democracy.

In the course of controversy over foreign policy there was also revealed a profound difference between the two traditions in their attitudes toward the most fundamental principle of democracy, the determination of policy by discussion. The chief agencies of political education and discussion in a modern democracy, the public school, the press, the radio, and movies — all were in various ways attacked and inhibited from their proper role in America by the Roman episcopate. The jugular vein of democratic life was constricted in a degree truly remarkable when the size of the Roman bloc is considered. We may survey the influence of American Romanism in each of these three respects — social and economic organization, democratic freedom of expression and discussion, and foreign policy.

1. Social Policy

Typical of the new attitude of Roman Catholicism toward the larger culture was its newly progressive social policy. As we have seen, the English-speaking Roman Church had lagged behind the Protestant social gospel before the First World War, manifesting no general interest in Leo's social encyclical. As late as 1926, the latter was comparatively unknown also in Great Britain.[1] But by 1922, Ernest Johnson, of the American Federal Council, conceded that the Roman Church had the initiative in the States. After all, Roman Catholicism in America was 80 per cent urban, while Protestantism was predominantly small-town or rural. A good half of American industrial labor was Roman Catholic, as against only one sixth of the general population. Rome was better situated than all other religious bodies put together to champion industrial labor and rise with it, or to make itself useful to management in controlling labor for meet considerations. The Al Smith candidacy in 1928 showed which way the wind was blowing. Cardinal O'Connell, dean of the hierarchy through the '20's, was a thorough snob and *nouveau riche* reactionary. But Al Smith's views on labor, utilities regulation, farm relief, the tariff, showed the substantial possibilities of the new Roman Catholic urban force for the democratizing of an industrial society. (To be sure, Smith had to repudiate the authority of the papal encyclicals to stay in the running.) A few years later American

Catholicism was more responsible than Protestantism, at least in the North, for Roosevelt's success, and Roosevelt apparently counted on the Catholic bloc as a socially progressive force in the American future.

The most notable positive contribution of the American Roman Catholic Church to democracy between wars was its work in the field of industrial relations. Its acknowledged leaders were John A. Ryan — whose seventieth birthday fell in 1939 — and his assistant, R. A. McGowan. The organization of the National Catholic Welfare Conference Department of Social Action, of which these men were respectively director and assistant director, gave them an agency that lent them more influence perhaps than all the Protestant social action secretaries put together. Ryan was the author of the " Bishops' Programme for Social Reconstruction " in those postwar days when Tawney was performing a similar service for the Church of England, Sydney Webb for the British Labor Party, W. A. Brown for the American Federal Council of Churches. The militancy of the Programme was chilled in the following decade of prosperity and materialism, but was revived in the '30's, especially after Pius XI sounded the tocsin with *Quadragesimo anno* in 1931.

Quadragesimo anno, the fortieth anniversary revision of the doctrines of Leo XIII, really launched American Roman Catholicism on a new campaign with a new program. The new program was the proposed revival of guilds, as already partly exemplified in Mussolini's " corporative state " and as further attempted in the '30's by Dollfuss in Austria and Salazar in Portugal. As now urged in America, however, if not as elaborated by Mussolini, the guild program at least served as a vehicle for the democratic principles of labor organization and collective bargaining, as well as opening vistas for employers of the elimination of competition within a given industry. The N.R.A. embodied much of the conception, and indeed General Hugh Johnson estimated *Quadragesimo anno* as a document " unsurpassed by the mind of man." The *Christendom* group in Britain also welcomed this authoritative affirmation of their triune program: the guilds, the " just price," and widely distributed property. " No pronouncement of equal profundity and vigor on our contemporary economic order," wrote Reckitt, " has been uttered by the official spokesmen of any Christian communion." [2]

More striking than the program itself was the technique with which the Roman bureaucracy set out to control the shaping of American labor in the '30's. Roman Catholic seminaries had been markedly slower than Protestant seminaries in offering training in social ethics. But Pius now instructed that all candidates for the priesthood must be adequately prepared " by intense study of social matters." [3] Similarly, there must always be provided specifically Catholic associations for Catholic union members, in which they would receive Catholic moral training in its social and political bearings.

In 1937 the Association of Catholic Trade Unionists (A.C.T.U.) was organized in America to form a disciplined elite within the labor movement. Chapters soon appeared in many industrial cities, each supervised by a priest. Labor schools were conducted, which performed notable educational service in the practices of union government, public speaking, economics, and, of course, Roman Catholic social doctrine. The influence of this co-ordinated penetration was soon apparent, especially in the C.I.O., where the Catholics made themselves the loudest spokesmen of the war with the similar Communist organizations. Between these two authoritarian disciplined minority pressure groups it began to be increasingly difficult for the American labor movement to have any genuine liberal democratic development. Catholic Action was using the anti-Communist issue and Communist methods to establish itself in the strategic centers of American labor, and from there to propagandize its whole antidemocratic "corporative state" program. Rome was effectively fighting Communism in American labor and providing leadership in widening labor's share of industrial control. In both regards Protestanism was quite ineffective. But on the other hand democratic unionism suffered, and Rome was also using the position so gained to campaign against liberal democracy in politics, both domestic and foreign.

The educational work of the N.C.W.C. Social Action Department included a great variety of conferences as well as publications. After 1922, for example, the "traveling universities" of the Catholic Conference on Industrial Problems opened for scores of two-day sessions in a variety of cities. At these conferences theologians, economists, employers, trade-unionists, Government experts engaged in discussion on concrete problems. The clergy were provided with more extended courses, usually of a month, in the priests' summer schools of Social Action, which were organized in ten dioceses. An immense transformation in the attitude of the Roman Catholics on social action was effected within a generation.

American Protestantism could make no such display, either of popular interest or of competent progressive leadership. The denominations strongest among urban labor, the Baptists and Lutherans, had by and large the least effective leadership in social ethics. The contrast in social and economic literacy between Protestant and Roman Catholic clergy was sharp by 1939.

Even in areas where Protestantism seemed as thoroughly established as did Roman Catholicism in industrial labor, namely, in rural life and among Negroes, Protestant leadership was newly challenged in the '30's. Until very recently American Catholicism showed only dislike and contempt for the Negro. The Catholics did not campaign against slavery, but rather tended to justify it. After the Civil War, when Congregationalists and other Protestants were contributing substantially to schools and colleges for Negroes, the Roman Church had no interest in them. Even after World War I, when the Federal Council and many denominations had departments on race relations, the N.C.W.C. had none. At the end of our period there were five and one half million Negro Protestants, but only a little more than one quarter of a million Negro Catholics. Against hundreds of Protestant Negro clergy, there were less than twenty Negro Catholic priests. In both communions segregation was the practice.

Yet in the '30's it was noticeable that the ratio of Negroes in the converts to Roman Catholicism was higher than their ratio to the general population. These conversions were taking place chiefly as Negroes moved into Northern Catholic-dominated municipalities, such as New York, Chicago, and Philadelphia. The chief instrument for conversion seemed to be the parochial school. The Jim Crow system still held in most Catholic churches, but through the '30's one Catholic college after another followed the pattern of Protestant Church colleges in admitting Negroes. An increasing minority of Catholic intellectuals demanded justice for the Negro. The Jesuit periodical *America* atoned in part for its continual subtle anti-Semitism by standing vigorously for Negro rights. In the urban situation the Catholic leadership for social justice began to reach the Negro also.

That leadership was even more conspicuous in rural life, where the experience of European Catholicism, with its success in organizing peasant culture in Belgium, Germany, Italy, could be drawn upon. Rural Protestantism, by contrast, was still dominated by the nineteenth century tradition of pietistic individualism and revivals. The latter, as we have seen, had no social philosophy, and when American agriculture began to slip into large-scale tenancy and create a new peasant class, rural Baptists, Disciples, and Methodists were unequipped to face this kind of social and moral decay. The social gospel, on the other hand, was city-centered, and calculated to scandalize small-town Protestants both socially and theologically. And even where Protestantism could produce leadership for healthy rural life, the tradition of denominational competition and congregational autonomy fettered every effort and restricted its outreach.

With Protestantism so handicapped by its ethical tradition, or rather the loss of it, and by its institutional anarchy, Roman Catholicism was able to start almost from scratch and still exert a notable influence. While the Catholic population was overwhelmingly urban, and from those centers of cultural influence exerted a force disproportionate to its numbers, the hierarchy was well aware of the liabilities of urban life for the future Catholic birth rate. Roman Catholicism must be planted in the high-birth-rate Protestant countryside if it was to maintain its position in America. Consequently the hierarchy supported a N.C.W.C. Rural Life Bureau in 1921, and has since given more effective support to this work than have the Protestants who were earlier in the field. By the early '30's there was a trained director of rural church work, with a staff, in every diocese. These directors were organized into state groups, and also into the National Catholic Rural Life Conference, headed by Mgr. Ligutti, who adapted to America the experience of the Italian People's Party. The pattern was one of rural community culture, and into the parish organization were integrated social and economic functions, such as credit unions, co-operatives for buying and marketing, and even for controlling real estate, as well as the basic parish school. Perhaps the most brilliant example of this kind of religious transformation of a sodden peasantry had been provided in Danish Lutheranism by the followers of Grundtvig. But in America no Protestant work rivaled Ligutti's. The Catholic Rural Life Conference at Peoria in 1943 drew an attendance of five thousand while the comparable Protestant assembly at Columbus totaled five hundred.[4]

In social and economic life, rural as well as industrial, Roman Catholicism was thus making a more effective contribution to democracy than was Protestantism. There were some distinctively Roman Catholic debits, to be sure. We have already referred to the contrasting positions of the Federal Council and the Catholic hierarchy on the child labor amendment of the mid-twenties. This same confessional opposition is to be observed in the case of other legislation for the benefit of the underprivileged. All through this generation the Roman episcopate was the chief opponent of Federal aid to education, and contributed in no small measure to the appalling deterioration of the American public school in this way and in others. Public health legislation was similarly blocked. And the fact that the Catholic Church had the worst criminal record of any white American denomination is probably not wholly unrelated to the hierarchy's reckless campaign to raise the Catholic birth rate irrespective of family resources for nurture and upbringing. In all these aspects of social policy the Protestant record was more responsible and democratic. Yet, on the whole, and due primarily to its sociological location among the urban poor, the Catholic record for social democracy probably outweighed the Protestant.

2. EDUCATION AND THE IDEA INDUSTRIES

More significant, although less conspicuous, than the Roman Catholic social program were the tactics used in advancing the social and political ambitions of the Roman bishops. These tactics consisted in the use of totalitarian techniques of censorship and terrorism against the freedom of communication and discussion essential to the continuance of democracy. Catholic Action, as manipulated by the episcopate, not merely refused to enter with good faith into public discussion of policy with the intention of discovering new truth, but took effective measures to silence discussion and prevent general knowledge of unwelcome truths. This is the unforgivable sin for liberal democracy. One may be a Tory and a liberal democrat, or a Socialist and a liberal democrat. But one cannot be a liberal democrat and seek to restrict the liberty to form judgments and to support them by public speech, press, radio, or organization. " There is no threat to political democracy in a shift of emphasis from private to public regulation, or from state to Federal control, or from the legislative to the executive branches of government. The real threats are the forces that corrupt or abridge free discussion." [5]

The activities of the American Roman bishops in the case of Franco illustrated on an impressive scale the Catholic contempt for democratic discussion. The censorship by boycott, which terrorizes virtually every American newspaper, book publisher and distributor, magazine publisher, movie producer and theater owner, newsstand owner and librarian, is far more widespread and more morally corrupting than is generally realized. It withdraws a sixth of the American people from participation in democratic policy-making by making it a sin for them to listen to the other side on any social or political issue where the prelates have taken a line. In addition it succeeds in preventing millions of non-Catholic Americans from learning what those prelates would prefer to have them ignorant of. Catholics had a right to abstain from reading this or that periodical, or from seeing this or that movie. But with these democratic rights the hierarchy was not content. It was elaborating totalitarian techniques for controlling all means of public communication and for foreclosing the possibility of democratic discussion.

The effect of this censorship on both art and scholarship was equally deleterious, and indeed it displayed a sour Irish prudery that made the most blue-nosed New England Puritans a touch ribald in retrospect. But it was in the handling of political issues, of both foreign and domestic policy, where democracy as such was wounded.

This is the context, moreover, in which the bitter controversy over Roman Catholic education is to be understood. Americans had more than a suspicion that Roman Catholic parochial schools maintained a nondemocratic political tradition in their teaching of history and the social sciences as well as preventing by segregation that development of personal community relations in which democratic discussion would later flourish. The educational policy and methods followed in these schools were not subject to scrutiny or discussion by the community, but were settled by the representatives of an alien absolute ruler without any sympathy for democracy. Academic freedom did not exist within the system. The teaching nuns indoctrinated their students with principles contrary to the democratic constitutional provisions for religious liberty and the separation of Church and State, and in the whole range of concrete political and social issues on which the hierarchy had taken a line these schools censored out all other views. The American people generally were still willing to exempt these schools from taxation and to account them satisfactory equivalents for public schools in meeting compulsory education laws, with only perfunctory inspection of their performance. But the American people displayed an increasing resistance to the bishops' effort to subsidize these schools out of tax funds. And considerable resentment was felt at the effect of these confessional schools in weakening the public schools in many communities.

There is, to be sure, no easy and simple solution to the problem of the relation of Church to State in the school system of a democracy. The American public school system was not really born until the middle third of the nineteenth century. The problem of how the constitutional separation of Church and State should be applied therein has not yet been resolved. The system first attempted and then rejected may yet prove to be the best compromise. Horace Mann endeavored to have the schools present the least common framework of Judaeo-Christian ethics and natural theology, which the several Churches might then supplement with their more specific doctrines. What could be more compatible with the whole system of separation of the spheres of nature and grace which was the key to Puritan Protestant society? This pattern was destroyed, however, by the intransigence of Protestant Fundamentalists, and even more of Roman Catholics, who largely occasioned that " secularization " of the public schools to which they now point in horror. The secularized public school of the late nineteenth century could be accepted, with some reluctance, by American Protestants when schooling involved only a few years of elementary work. But when public education grows to a near monopoly of the studying time and energy of children until late in their teens, no Christian group can accept it with equanimity if it is really " secular." This argument inclined a growing minority of Protestants in this generation to look with more sympathy on the Catholic system of confessional schools. An aggressive minority of dogmatic secularists among public school men, moreover, gave some color to the Catholic attacks on the public school.

The large majority of American Protestants, however, were not persuaded that the public schools were irredeemably secularized. They doubted if American democracy, fed from so many cultures, could long survive without the personal relations and common memories of the public school and its free discussion. The Roman Catholic policy led to a radical pluralism incompatible with democracy. A congeries of segregated religious and cultural colonies could achieve a common policy only by barter and treaty, and the whole democratic system would grind to a halt in the style of the Weimar Republic. To be sure, neither Roman Catholics nor anyone else could be forced to enter freely into the democratic process. But at least the democratic community should abstain from subsidizing the Catholics in their withdrawal from it. The controversy grew steadily more heated during and after the Second World War, and the authoritative interventions of the Supreme Court in the Everson and McCollum cases did little to clarify the fundamental issues.

From another aspect the parochial school system was simply a conspicuous manifestation of the general Catholic policy in America of living in a self-imposed cultural ghetto. The clergy were unwilling to expose their dignity to the danger of being sometimes disagreed with in public discussion. They preferred to constrict American Catholics into colonies, chiefly in the large cities of the Northeast, in which they could enjoy a theocratic clerical rule and from which they could make demands and sorties on the larger State and culture. The impact of Catholicism on American democracy was perhaps most tangible in the municipalities run by bishops and Catholic dictators: Hague's Jersey City, Curley's Boston, Kelly's Chicago. Municipal corruption was not peculiar to the Catholic Irish in America, although they had more than their share of it. What was peculiar was the systematic substitution of clericalism for democracy on most of the range of issues on which we observed a clash in our analysis of the Syllabus. There would be something to say about the Roman Catholic views of property, the judiciary, marriage and sex legislation, social welfare and charitable agencies, as well as the issues we have already described. And in general, to turn the matter about, Roman Catholics have been conspicuously absent from the periodic attempts to reform political corruption in America. The mentality trained by the Roman Church, even when not aggressively clerical, is not that of lay initiative for righteousness, of the responsibilities of the " consciences of private men " in politics.

Just here lay the crux of the clerical dilemma, indeed, the dilemma of Catholic Action in general. The bishops could control the modern world only behind and through the laity, but the more the laity were pushed into public combat and discussion with non-Catholics, the more of them decided on inspection that they preferred liberal democracy to clericalism. The attempt to hold and occupy democratic America by the shock troops of Catholic Action resembled in this respect the attempt of the Russians to occupy Western Europe. As was often said in Germany, Stalin made two mistakes in this project: he let Europe see the Red Army and he let the Red Army see Europe. The very effort to conquer a liberal democratic society for clericalism exposed the clerical forces to vistas of possibilities of Christian freedom and resulted in tremendous leakages.

3. FOREIGN POLICY

The area in which the Roman hierarchy, in contrast to Protestantism, most conspicuously injured liberal democracy, was foreign policy. Here more than anywhere else the alien character of the Roman Catholic community in America was evident. Unlike all other large American Churches, which draw their political and international perspectives from the liberal democratic tradition, the American Catholic hierarchy officially and boldly campaigned between wars in the interests of Fascism and against liberal democracy, following the cue of Pius XI. It was to the American and democratic interest in Europe and Latin America to strengthen wherever possible the moderately reformist parties as against the Communists and revolutionary nationalists at the two extremes. To support the reactionary extreme, as did Pius, was to strengthen the Communists also by reaction, and to increase the likelihood of forcing social issues to civil war. But in all this tendency the American hierarchy, which has probably less independence as against Italian officialdom than any other major episcopate of the Roman Catholic world, put all its considerable resources of propaganda and intrigue to manipulate the diplomatic agencies of the American people contrary to all their tradition and natural sympathies.

It may seem strange at first sight that a minority group should be able to exert such influence on foreign policy contrary to the natural bent of American tradition. But America was unprepared psychologically and technically for the responsibilities of statecraft suddenly thrown upon it in the twentieth century. American Senators were still in the habit of booming out the changes on Washington's warnings about "no entangling alliances," and Wilson's League propaganda proved unable to reverse wholly the isolationist tradition. There was no substantial and consistent tradition of liberal democratic foreign policy in the State Department, to say nothing of the Congress. Between wars American foreign policy was bumbling and inconsistent. In such a situation a closely knit and disciplined group of Romanist technicians in foreign affairs could make themselves felt out of all proportion to their number. The Jesuits established an excellent school of international relations at Georgetown, and usually had on hand well-trained personnel when vacancies in the State Department needed to be filled, especially on the less conspicuous lower levels. No one would have seen grounds for questioning the presence of an undue number of Episcopalians in key positions in foreign affairs. Why were Catholics different? The fact that Catholics are under discipline to obey Italian prelates on pain of eternal damnation as well as various lesser discomforts has never been digested by the American people. The fact that Roman Catholics are bound in certain official positions, such as judges, police officials, diplomatic agents, to serve the Roman curia even contrary to the instructions of the community whose officers they are was believed only with reluctance. It would seem " bigotry " to suggest that Roman Catholic officials should be by their mere religion disqualified from holding certain offices, or at least from performing specific responsibilities of those offices. Under these circumstances a common policy enforced from the Vatican by a merely proportionate number of Catholics in the State Department would have had a disproportionate influence as against other Christians responsible only to God and the nation. And in fact in both Britain and the United States a disproportionate number of Catholics were trained for and secured positions in diplomacy and foreign service. A survey of the American representatives in crucial diplomatic posts in the years after World War II (Moscow, Paris, Berlin, Athens, Korea) reveals not merely a disproportionate number but a near monopoly of Roman Catholics.

Evidence as to the operations of the Roman agents in Government service is not generally accessible. Some indication of the general outline of the policy they were serving, however, can be discerned from the propaganda activities of the hierarchy among the population at large. The crises in which this activity was most apparent were the establishment of the Italian dictatorship; the proposal of American military action against Mexico; the Italian assault on Ethiopia, and the consequent question of " sanctions "; relations between the United States and Latin America in the '30's; and the " personal " embassy at the Vatican. In most if not all of these issues the considerable weight of American Catholicism was thrown against the interests of liberal democracy, and sometimes successfully.

We may note parenthetically the propaganda of outright Fascist organizations. In both Britain and America the small Fascist movements drew disproportionate strength from Roman Catholics. Sir Oswald Moseley's following in Britain drew heavily on Catholics, some estimates running to 80 per cent of the key men.[6] In America the most notorious and dangerous Fascist and anti-Semite was Father Coughlin. By permission of the bishop of Detroit, who defended Coughlin as "the voice of God,"[7] the latter became the chief disseminator of the notorious forgeries, the *Protocols of Zion*. In 1938 he was reproducing the Nazi Streicher's anti-Semitic propaganda wholesale and became the idol of the *Bund*. At the first mass meeting of American Nazis in Madison Square in 1939, the Detroit priest drew the greatest applause. Millions of American Catholics detested the work of this priest, and the brutal street beatings of Jews carried out by his "Christian" Front in various cities. But no such restraining hand was exercised by the hierarchy as in the case of several priests and laymen who dared to criticize Franco. In both Britain and America, as we shall see, the prevailing line of the Catholic press created a favorable atmosphere for the propaganda of the Moseleys and the Coughlins.

The most highly developed avowedly Fascist movement in the English-speaking world was in French Canada (if that is to be included in the English-speaking world), and it was in close league with Roman clericalism. For generations the Roman clergy in Quebec had been the chief focus of cultural and political nationalism and isolationism. They were similar to Latin-American and Spanish clergy also in preferring that their people remain poor and ignorant so that they could be better controlled. They opposed education and economic development, controlled labor, and savagely fought international labor unions such as the C.I.O. Civil liberties were treated in practice as suggested by the Syllabus of Pius IX. Public officials like Mayor Houde and Premier Duplessis, at the prodding of Cardinal Villeneuve, encouraged the suppression of free speech, press, and assembly. The military units of outright Fascists such as Adrien Arcand and Bouchard were subject to no such Government control as were the American and British efforts to organize private armies. The Canadian hierarchy frankly confessed to sympathies for a corporative state, like that of Mussolini or Salazar, in contrast to liberal democracy with its parties, discussion, and freedom. As the cardinal said of liberal democracy: "Paganism has many offers. Among them are freedom of speech, freedom to insult our traditions, our beliefs, and our religion."[8]

Let us consider briefly the chief international issues in which the sympathies of the Roman Church were made evident. With regard to Fascism, while Mussolini's thugs were beating up the last outspoken Catholic defenders of liberal democracy in Italy, the American hierarchy was unctuous in his praise. To go down the line of command, the cue was given by the archbishops and cardinals. Cardinal O'Connell, of Boston, observed a "marvelous transformation" in Italy in 1924. "I see perfect order, cleanliness, work, industrial development." Two years later he described the dictator as "a genius in the field of government, given to Italy by God to help the nation continue her rapid ascent toward the most glorious destiny." [9] In 1934, Mussolini was still "the miracle man." Meanwhile, Cardinal Mundelein, of Chicago, had saluted Mussolini in 1925 as "a great big man — the man of the times," and sported a Fascist decoration. The incumbent of what is known in New York politics as "the power house," Cardinal Hayes, accepted four or five such awards from Mussolini in return for similar services rendered. Cardinal Dougherty, archbishop of Philadelphia, was enthusiastically applauded by the Fascist League of North America for his speech in praise of the regime in 1926. The bishop of Cleveland exalted the "man of destiny" in 1929 at a celebration of the birthday of Fascism. This was the line that was passed down from rank to rank of the clergy in sermons and poured out through the N.C.W.C. press bureau into the three hundred or so diocesan papers and such sheets as Father Parsons' *America* and thence into the unprepared ears of would-be liberal democrats.

The chronic Church-State controversy in Mexico, meanwhile, led twice in our period to hysterical Catholic attempts to precipitate American armed intervention. In 1926 newly elected President Calles proposed to enforce the punitive ecclesiastical provisions of the constitution of 1917 which had been disregarded in the interval. The constitution had been originally adopted out of resentment against the Church's resistance to social, agrarian, and educational reform. And the degree to which this nominally Catholic people felt that the Church deserved punishment was illustrated by the failure of the hierarchy's attempt to organize an interdict and economic boycott in protest against Government persecution. The American hierarchy now set the Knights of Columbus, their chief political stalking-horse, to demanding American military action. Cardinals Hayes and Mundelein condemned the Mexican Government without even a suggestion of the scandalous history of the Mexican Church. The Coolidge Government refused to be bullied, however, and Pius XI called off the American Romanist campaign as likely to be self-defeating.

The same process was repeated at the end of 1934. A joint pastoral disclaimed any desire for armed intervention, but summoned the United

States to all pressure short of war. At once the mobilization of opinion recently drilled by the Legion of Decency went into action. Èvery Catholic paper and every pulpit reveled in atrocity stories. A Knights of Columbus deputation to Secretary Hull demanded the recall of Ambassador Josephus Daniels, who had dared to approve Calles' campaign for an expanded State school system, in a country where the Church had left 85 per cent of the people illiterate. They wanted a threat of diplomatic rupture. The Mexican consulate was being picketed and Mexican goods boycotted by Catholics. Senator Borah agreed to demand an investigation, and many bishops were violent in their language against President Roosevelt as he evaded active intervention. Catholics were aggrieved at the mild support they received from Protestants on this great crusade for liberty of religion, forgetting the grim stream of news reports that Mexico had so long furnished of clerically inspired lynchings of Protestant ministers and laity, and forgetting the current atrocities of the Mexican clerical *Cristeros.* As with Spain the next year, neither truth nor justice could be appealed to from the interests of the infallible institution. And worldly matters like the Good Neighbor policy would of course weigh still less in the balance.

The next occasions when the Roman line was patently opposed to democratic policy concerned the Fascist attacks on Ethiopia and Spain. In contrast to the Mexican situation, Anglo-American prelates now did their best to prevent any sort of intervention or sanctions and to allow the dictators a free hand to buccaneer. We have already noticed the attitude of the Italian clergy and the pope in condoning or justifying the Abyssinian outrage. The American and British hierarchies, in general, poured out the same disgusting apologies through their well-greased propaganda machinery. Some British Catholics attempted to evade the party line and to explain away the papal complicity. Archbishop Hinsley, of Westminster, pleaded for understanding of the situation of Pius XI, " a helpless old man." But *The Catholic Times* rejoiced " that in the hour of need the pope has not joined the Nordic chorus of hypocrisy." *The Catholic Herald* argued that " granted Fascism, a Fascist empire may have been a necessity " and justified dropping poison gas by air " in retaliation for uncivilized methods of warfare." [10] To be sure, this predominant pro-Fascist tendency of the British Catholic press was not wholly representative of British Catholic opinion. Mr. Binchy urges to the contrary, that at least 75 per cent of British Catholics supported the Labor Party. We have had occasion before, however, to notice the relative effectiveness of majority opinion and hierarchical opinion in the Roman communion.

Spain provided the most notorious instance of Roman pressure on

Anglo-American policy in the interests of dictatorship. Here again the Catholic masses were democratic in sympathy, but the pro-Fascist hierarchy was able to lash them into a virtually monolithic front. The first great clerical Fascist victory was the capture of the means of communication, which are the first condition of democratic discussion. The diocesan papers, closely tied to N.C.W.C. news and policy, bombarded the Catholic population of the country with an insistent pro-Fascist propaganda. Even more striking, however, was the success of the Catholic intimidation and corruption of the public press. Early in 1936 this American press was overwhelmingly in favor of the legitimate republican government of Spain. By the end of the year, with scattered exceptions, that press had been bullied into what was in effect a pro-Fascist slanting of all news, by the pressure of the Roman hierarchy. The A.P. doctored its reports and permitted member papers, such as the Hearst press, to violate its regulations and further color its dispatches, as by inserting " Reds " and " Communistic " in description of the Madrid government.[11] *The New York Times* refused to print its own correspondent's report of Mussolini's troops in action in Spain.[12] In the same way the evidence that Franco was a Fascist and boasted of it was played down or suppressed because of fear of Catholic reprisals. " On small papers throughout the United States the Catholic pressure forced columnists out of their jobs." As Heywood Broun had said: " There is not a single New York editor who does not live in mortal terror of the power of this group. It is not a case of numbers but of organization." [13]

Organization, indeed, and hitting below the belt. In every parish of the United States and Canada, agencies were established to watch the press and to coerce it. Coercion was preferred to any attempt to persuade. Instead of arguing, the Church hits through the business office. Cardinal Dougherty, for example, turned the Philadelphia archdiocese on the *Record* for identifying the cause of the Spanish Republic with democracy. Boycott of the newspaper was urged in Catholic pulpits throughout the city as well as by the diocesan paper. Pamphlets were distributed at Masses, with the suggestion that recipients show them to the advertising managers of department and other stores that advertised in the *Record*. The New York and Baltimore prelates similarly bullied great newspapers into warping their news by threats of advertising boycotts. The Legion of Decency achieved similar results in the movies. The same technique was applied in the case of the magazines. A systematic campaign of letters and post cards to advertisers in magazines was used to suppress free expression. These are the devices by which a small minority of a minority sect was able to control the news of a great war in a neutral press and simultaneously to poison the springs of democratic discussion in America and contribute to the establishment of a totalitarian state in Spain. They have been employed elsewhere in the English-speaking world, as in Australia and Britain, with similar if less sweeping success.

Occasionally one would hear of a publisher, movie producer, or department store owner who challenged the insolence of the bishop, and in such cases he often won a complete victory. There was the case of the famous department store owner who refused to take the local bishop's order to withdraw his advertising from an offending newspaper. When the bishop then announced that he would impose a boycott on the store also, the owner merely asked to be notified in advance of the time of the boycott. The bishop's agent asked why. The businessman replied that at that time all Roman Catholic employees of the store would receive their final checks, with a letter explaining the reasons for their dismissal. At this the episode ended. It serves to illustrate the point that as yet these Roman tactics of coercion could succeed only in the half-light of surreptitious conferences and backstairs threats. Once brought into the full daylight of publicity in a democratic country, they could be fought. Teachers often fought them successfully, but newspapermen unfortunately had less pride and sense of responsibility and were more vulnerable to economic pressure.

The pressure continued and in 1938 was transferred to the sphere of clerically instructed voting. Early in 1938 some sixty Congressmen sent a cable of greeting to the Spanish Congress of Montserrat: " We realize the significance of your heroic and determined fight to save the democratic institutions of your young republic from its enemies both within and without Spain." [14] At once the Catholic machine leaped into action and the signers were warned that unless they recanted the Catholic bloc would have its revenge at the polls next fall. The N.C.W.C. kept the tally as one by one these spokesmen for democracy came to heel. A few had the stomach to stand up and face the intrigue of the prelates in their communities. Among them were courageous democratic Catholics. Priests instructed the laity to vote against them. " It is questionable whether there were a round dozen priests who refrained from using their pulpits for pro-Franco purposes." [15] Hundreds of thousands of Catholics were instructed from the altar during Mass to send letters and telegrams to the Government urging retention of the embargo on arms for the Spanish Republic.

More direct action was called for in May when *The New York Times* reported that repeal of the embargo which paralyzed the legally constituted government of Spain was assured in Congress and that the State Department approved. " High church dignitaries came to Washington and talked cold politics." [16] The majority of American Catholics were Democrats and supporters of Mr. Roosevelt. The majority of American Catholics also, to be sure, were indifferent or hostile to Franco, as was the case in Britain. But what is a Catholic's conscience against the bishop's party line? The President capitulated. As a political reporter put it, " Mr. Roosevelt, who has braved concentrated wealth, has not braved the risk of losing the votes around Boston, New York, Chicago, Detroit, Baltimore." At the behest of the American prelates, President Roosevelt and the Congress agreed to starve the Spanish Republic of the war materials necessary to defend itself against the Axis powers.

At the same time the weight of the American State Department was being used to further the Fascist-clerical drive in Latin America against democracy. The strength of the Latin-American Roman Church had always rested with the ignorant women and the conservative landed group who used it as a weapon of social control. The hierarchy consequently was little interested in social justice and had the reputation of being opposed to aid to the Indians. Latin America had heard little or nothing of *Rerum novarum,* but a great deal of the Syllabus. The majority of the people, whether or not they considered themselves Catholic, were indifferent or hostile to the antidemocratic hierarchy and its friends. Against all the efforts of the hierarchy, freedom of religion had been incorporated in twenty constitutions, and eleven of them had separated Church and State. Most Latin Americans were proud of this legally established liberty. They would have liked to look for liberal democratic support from the great republic beyond the Rio Grande. They had often been puzzled as to why the United States had so often supported Latin-American dictatorship. In the past the reasons had usually been financial. Now a strange new turn was to be seen, the State Department of the Protestant and democratic United States nursing a Roman Catholic-Fascist alliance in Latin America.

At the time of the Spanish War the papal secretary of state Pacelli toured Latin America. Within a few months openly Fascist movements appeared in various places on Franco's and Mussolini's models. Mexican "Sinarquism" was the strongest. The Spanish diplomatic service, meanwhile, was used as a network for espionage and propaganda for Hitler, Mussolini, and Franco. Cardinal Goma of Spain blessed this campaign against Protestant America, Pan-Americanism, the Good Neighbor Policy, the Lima Congress, in the name of the revival of the former Spanish empire, " *Hispanidad.*" The press in several countries, Peru, Chile, Argentina, was dominated largely by Nazi and Fascist advertisers. And everywhere the most consistently anti-United States and pro-Fascist section of society was the Roman clergy. It must be remembered that a notable proportion of Latin-American clergy were Spanish- or Italian-trained (700 of the 1,600 priests in Bolivia, e.g., were foreign-born). In Peru the papal nuncio was giving lectures on Fascism while supporters of the Spanish Republic were actually jailed.[17] After all, if the pope saluted Franco as " the savior of Christianity," why not put at Axis disposal the machinery of Latin-American Romanism?

And yet the only important North American supporters of Franco, besides the *Bund,* the Italian-American Fascists, and the Coughlinites, namely, the United States Roman hierarchy, were able to get the State Department to play Franco's game. The State Department developed a policy of using only Roman Catholics in consular service or as cultural attachés. Its propaganda played up Roman Catholicism in the United States to the point of gross distortion. Latin Americans brought to the United States for cultural exchange were selected as good Catholics, which often meant good Fascists, and on their return they used the connections for the Fascist cause. Other Latin Americans brought to the states by the Government expressed surprise and even resentment at the manner in which they were solicitously confined to American Catholic circles.[18] And when the American State Department began to discriminate on religious grounds against Protestantism in issuing passports, many Latin Americans were affronted. " Among us freedom of religion is established by our constitutions, and it offends us to think that an inquisitorial office has been established in some passport department which decides to whom we are to extend our hospitality." [19] After all, Latin Americans knew that the United States was predominantly Protestant. The common people wondered why the United States aided in destroying the Spanish Republic, why it was so concerned to cultivate and aid the one Latin-American group that has always been against freedom and democracy. A revealing incident occurred in 1942, when the Roman hierarchy of Peru, the most reactionary and priest-ridden state in the continent, tried to bar a Protestant youth conference. The Argentine, Uruguayan, Mexican, Bolivian, and Chilean ambassadors were glad to try to help in the name of religious liberty. But the Peruvian youth committee knew better than even to ask the ambassadors from constitutional United States for support! [20]

In 1942 the United States hierarchy launched a campaign against Protestant missionaries in Latin America as the " greatest obstacle to the Good Neighbor policy." The press, radio, and magazines carried this theme all over the states, with the crudest insults to Latin-American Protestants. The bishops were worried, of course, because Latin-American Protestantism had increased 400 per cent since 1914.

That particular canard, however, was blown sky-high when George Howard set out to canvass Latin-American opinion. It soon became evident that the whole theory had been concocted in N.C.W.C. offices. Howard had toured six countries and interviewed hundreds of people in all walks of life before he found anyone — save three Roman bishops — who agreed with the United States hierarchy.[21] The overwhelming response was approval of Protestant missions, and Howard presented an unanswerable accumulation of affidavits to that effect. (The entire cabinet of Chile, for example, with three ex-presidents, considered these missions a genuine contribution to friendly relations. President Ferraz, of the Brazilian Court of Appeals, and Dr. Sagarna, of the Argentine Supreme Court, testified similarly.) But this was only a single case of overreaching; the American hierarchy had been working more quietly and successfully for years in the State Department. Anyone who knew any history would be aware that the cause of liberal democracy in Catholic countries was always carried by the laymen who had the boldness to face down the hierarchy, and that through the hierarchy itself nothing was to be had. But the American State Department was solicitous to work through clerical " channels."

This persistently antidemocratic clerical pressure on American foreign policy reached its culmination at the end of the 1930's with the establishment of Roosevelt's " personal " diplomatic representative at the Vatican. Negotiations had reached the point of overt action at the time of the Spanish war when the papal secretary Pacelli and Archbishop Spellman conferred with Mr. Roosevelt. Secretary of State Pacelli had been the chief administrator of the Vatican's pro-Fascist policies in the Abyssinian war and in the Spanish war, as well as the negotiator of the deal with Hitler by which the Center Party was disbanded in Germany. He was profoundly concerned to cut the last lifeline of Spanish democracy. Roosevelt, on the other hand, wished to cultivate the Roman Church as the most considerable religious support of progressive social policy in the United States. Internationally he might hope to exert some influence through the Roman Church, perhaps in Italian affairs.

In the year in which the German invasion of Poland finally precipitated the Second World War, President Roosevelt broke the continuous diplomatic tradition of the United States by establishing diplomatic relations with the sovereign by divine right of international Roman Catholicism. Nearly a century before the United States had accredited some ten ministers to the papal states for a twenty-year period in the pontificate of Pius IX, but their instructions had related them only to the political and commercial activities of the state of central Italy, and not to the Holy See as the government of all Catholics. There had been an American consulate for such commercial purposes in the papal states from 1797. When this mission was elevated to a chargé d'affaires in 1848, his instructions read in part as follows: " Most, if not all, of the Governments that have diplomatic representatives at Rome are connected with the pope as the head of the Catholic Church. In this respect the Government of the United States occupies an entirely different position. . . . Your efforts, therefore, will be devoted exclusively to the cultivation of the most friendly civil relations with the papal government, and to the extension of the commerce between the two countries." [22] The commercial advantages hoped for never materialized, and, in 1867, Congress allowed the mission to lapse. Three years later the state to which the American ministers had been accredited disappeared from the map of Italy.

When Roosevelt embarked on his constitutional experiment, accordingly, he was attaching an American emissary to the Holy See in that capacity which the nineteenth century American Government specifically and scrupulously declined to recognize: " the pope as the head of the Catholic Church," as political sovereign over American and other Catholics. Herein lies the constitutional difficulty for States whose fundamental law denies political status to any ecclesiastical body. Diplomatic recognition of the papacy implies a division of jurisdiction over American citizens between the law of the United States and the Codex Juris Canonici. It is not comparable to the recognition of any foreign State. Formally it would be comparable to the diplomatic recognition of the Comintern. At the moment the most considerable segment of the papal subjects in terms of size of episcopate, political subserviency, and financial power, is the American Catholic bloc. To recognize the pope as a sovereign over Catholics is to recognize the pope as a sovereign in America. In Catholic or totalitarian countries this division of jurisdiction is usually stated (if not resolved) by a " concordat." In Protestant countries where there is an established Church, as in England or Hohenzollern Germany, diplomatic recognition of the papacy has also been constitutionally feasible. It is very hard to see, on the other hand, how either a concordat or diplomatic recognition of the political curia is compatible with the American constitutional separation of Church and State. The Vatican, of course, has never concealed its desire to change the American Constitution in this regard to a regime of Roman privilege and official intolerance. The American laity and even prelates, however, continued through the '30's to dissimulate on this matter. In public such heretical manifestoes as Al Smith's *Credo of an American Catholic* were allowed to pass without conspicuous rebuke, while in its school system the hierarchy was laboring to bring the laity to the official line by means of such texts as Ryan and Boland's *Catholic Principles of Politics*. The textbook on public ecclesiastical law used at the Pontifical University in Rome, where the elite of the American clergy are trained, makes the duty of Catholics in the United States very clear: " Catholics must make all possible efforts to bring about the rejection of this religious indifference of the State and the instauration, as soon as possible, of the wished-for union and concord of State and Church. . . . Whether tolerance of non-Catholic religions is promised under oath by a statutory law or not, it can never be admitted." [23] The first, and still very cautious, public attack on the principle made by the American episcopate came in its letter of November, 1948. [24]

By his under-the-table Vatican embassy, President Roosevelt unquestionably abetted the Roman Catholic hierarchy in its attempt to undermine the American democratic principle of separation of Church and State. In itself the action was not so significant as the implications that could be drawn from it. The assessment of what the President gained from this bargain would take us beyond the limits of this discussion. There is some reason to think, however, that as with the French renewal of diplomatic relations with the Vatican in the 1920's, the results were disappointing.

In the interval between wars we have thus seen how the weight of American Catholicism was consistently and often effectively thrown on the side of antidemocratic foreign policy on orders from Italy. In contrast, then, to a record superior to that of Protestantism in industrial issues, the Roman Church showed itself a dangerously antidemocratic force in foreign affairs. It was becoming increasingly apparent that adherence to the Roman Church was an adequate *political* ground for questioning the suitability of candidates for offices related to American foreign policy. There is every indication that this Romanist intrigue extended its operations during and after the Second World War, but this history is too recent for us to attempt to narrate it.

EPILOGUE

✤ ✤ ✤

THE RELATIONSHIP of modern democracy to the several Christian traditions has remained more constant than is generally appreciated. Liberal democracy has consistently been allied with that Protestant tradition which we have called "Puritan," but which includes Scandinavian Lutheranism and the Swiss and Dutch Reformed as well as the main concentration in the English-speaking world. Here liberal democracy was born, and to these frontiers it has been almost beaten back in the totalitarian revolutions of the twentieth century. The illiberal, egalitarian democracy of the European Continent, on the other hand, first appeared in a Roman Catholic setting, and its later Marxist form has had its successes in Lutheran Germany and Orthodox Catholic Russia as well as in Roman Catholic societies. In all these last three Christian communions, however, the Churches themselves have steadily opposed this democracy, and by their opposition unquestionably contributed to its dogmatic materialism and ruthless radicalism. Liberal democracy was positively molded and informed by Puritan Protestantism; egalitarian and illiberal democracy crystallized out of the conflict with illiberal ecclesiasticism. Three hundred years of Western civilization down to the middle of the twentieth century have witnessed only minor and temporary deviations from this prevailing pattern of correlations.

Such consistency, together with the expressed views of many of the leading historical figures on the relation of Christianity to liberal democracy, argues that religion was indeed a major causal factor in this history. The social effects of technological advance, the rise of new urban mercantile, professional, and industrial classes, older patterns of social stratification or fluidity have also been very important. We have indeed suggested that such social and economic factors contributed significantly to the patterns of expansion, if not to the actual formation, of Puritan Protestantism as the Christian nurse of democracy. With all these qualifications, however, we are still ready to subscribe to the conclusion of Ernst Troeltsch on the political and social influence of Puritan Protestantism. " It has become one of the basic causes of immense changes in modern society," he wrote. " This spirit has been brought into Catholic and Lutheran countries only from outside. It would never have been created by the new economic, political, and technical conditions of the modern world." [1]

The type of influence we have sought to locate is, in the first degree, not directly doctrinal, either in terms of theology or of political ethics. It is, rather, the influence of certain habits, of attitudes, of types of community relationships formed by the faith and discipline of the particular religious community. These habits have their theological justifications and their political tendencies, but are more popularly influential and persistent than either. They are the folkways of the religious community itself, which may or may not be articulated theologically, and which are translated to the civil state more or less consciously, as things taken for granted. It is in reference to the early history of democracy, when this transference from the religious to the civil community was first effected, that we analyzed most carefully the divergent patterns of the contrasted religious traditions.

The contribution of Puritan Protestantism to modern democracy, as we have noted, may be seen in four successive stages of development. The first significant advances in this direction were made by classical Calvinism and " right-wing " theocratic Puritanism, especially in Switzerland, Holland, Scotland, England, and New England in the sixteenth and early seventeenth centuries. Ultimate authority in the Calvinist's Church lay with the risen Christ; in the State, with the moral law. In neither case was there a specific seat of institutional sovereignty that might claim to embody wholly this ultimate authority. No clergyman, or group of clergy, could claim to be infallible spokesmen for the risen Christ, just as no monarch could safely be honored as strictly " sovereign." In the Church, the executive must always be subject to correction by the will of Christ, for which a partial criterion was at hand in the Scriptures. In the State, the executive must always be under the law, which might have partial statement in a constitution. Estates-general and parliaments, particularly, were strengthened as means of limiting the power of the executive. In both Church and State, the duty of holding the executive to his proper standards was distributed over a group of officers, as a safeguard against the error and sin to which every ruler, political or ecclesiastical, is subject. The principle of appeal from positive law to moral principle, even to the point of resistance, revolution, and tyrannicide, was thus made practically effective as in no other religious tradition.

These liberal aspects of the Calvinist political ethic were held in check by a strongly felt conservatism with regard to the religious character and necessity of political authority. The office of a magistrate was considered to be a high calling from God, and a habit of sober tenacious responsibility was inculcated in Calvinist rulers at all levels of government. Magistrates, as good Christians, were subject to the guidance and discipline of the Church. But as their ultimate obedience was to God, and not to the clergy, the responsibility for decision lay with them. This dualism of the civil and ecclesiastical arms avoided the absolutist centralization of priestly theocracy on the one side, and, on the other, the subservience of religion to political interest in State-Churchism. Political rights and duties were confined to an elite, and conformity to Biblical principles was enforced in Church and State, for nothing like modern democracy was a live possibility within the class structure and educational conditions of the age. But both the extent of participation in government and the principles on which it was rested were a long step toward democracy beyond the government by divine right universal in Roman Catholic, Anglican, and Lutheran societies, or beyond the secular theories of political sovereignty.

The second stage in the political development of Puritan Protestantism is best analyzed in England and its American colonies from the Puritan through the American Revolutions. In this period left-wing Puritans challenged and eventually displaced theocratic Puritanism; State-Church Calvinism passed into Free Church Calvinism. The final stabilization of the English Revolution domesticated left-wing Puritanism as tolerated " Dissent," and the specific bearers of liberal democracy in this period were the " three old denominations " of English nonconformity — Congregationalists, Baptists, and Presbyterians. The conversion of the first and last from right- to left-wing Puritanism, to be sure, took place by degrees and at different times in England and its colonies. Many Anglican laymen also supported nonconformist Whig politics, as is most conspicuous in the make-up of the American colonial conventions.

The left-wing Puritans retained the general temper of Calvinist political ethics, the sense of duty to mold the whole common life in accordance with God's will, the refusal to concede absolute powers to any human authority, the appeal to the higher law, belief in the divine ordination of political rule, and the responsibility of the magistrate to God for the actualization of these principles. But within this common tradition, left-wing Puritanism introduced three new elements in particular which effected a transformation of the intolerant theocratic aristocracy of classical Calvinism into modern liberal democracy.

The most fundamental principle of liberal democracy, first of all, the determination of policy by free discussion, is the secular reflection of the left-wing Puritan procedure of determining the counsel of the Holy Spirit in the Church. It was the Quakers who developed the practice farthest, with the use of silence in meetings and the requirement of unanimity for decisions. But in greater or less degree all the Puritan denominations were influenced, and even the most Biblicistic and legalistic increasingly recognized the importance of the testimony of the Holy Spirit as a necessary correlative to the objective expression of God's word in the Scriptures. The democratic process formally consists of just such a determination in free discussion of the bearing in specific instances of accepted ethical principles and a common loyalty.

The democratic principle of consent, of government responsible to the people, is similarly the secular reflection of the left-wing Puritan practice of " gathering " a church and founding it upon a " church covenant." It was the political thinkers of Puritan background, such as Locke, who adapted to the State this conception of voluntarism and the " social contract." Every single individual became a church member only by deliberately undertaking personal responsibilities for testimony and discipline, and the Church was constituted by a social contract of such individuals under God's law. In the State, similarly, the vocational responsibility which Catholicism confined to the monarch and which Calvinism distributed among all the magistrates was now extended to every private citizen. The State was now conceived as formed by the social contract of all its members, and they were each severally responsible before God for the moral character of its policy.

The release into secular politics of these Church practices, and of allied conceptions of the liberty and fraternity of Christian men, was made possible by the third left-wing modification of classical Calvinism. First of all by the " Levelers " the demand was expressed that the State should be ecclesiastically neutralized and that the Church should be free of political interference. This demand implied a repudiation of the right-wing theocratic attempt to govern the whole community by the Bible and the Church. It was not, however, an abandonment of the State to the powers of evil, as with earlier Anabaptists. The Christian man was still expected to exercise his Christian vocation in politics in the Calvinist tradition, but while doing so he was to guide himself simply by the moral law as evident to all men of good will, rather than appealing to special revelation or ecclesiastical authority. The ethical energies released by Christian redemption were thus available to the community at large, but not under the Christian label. And devotion to the moral law was continually strengthened and clarified by the politically unrecognized nurture of the citizen by the standard of Jesus Christ. These are the presuppositions of the peculiar type of separation of Church and State in America, which produced a political society more devoted to the rule of the natural law than any State with an established Church.

Such a State might include as citizens members of a variety of religious traditions so long as they respected the moral law accessible to all, and so long as they did not seek to impose on the civil community further directives from their specific revelations. So far as the State was concerned, the Calvinist theocratic urge was retained, but henceforth it was to be a theocracy not defined in terms of specific Christian revelation, but a theocracy of " common grace," or general revelation — a theistic or deistic theocracy, if you will. In purely civil matters, consequently, as well as on the issue of separation of Church and State, deistic rationalists like Jefferson might find their strongest supporters among orthodox evangelical Puritans, Baptists, perhaps, or Presbyterians. And from the end of the eighteenth century this principle of separation has meant that Puritan Protestantism, as a whole, has founded its political, social, and economic ethic on natural law, the " higher law," rather than directly on the Bible. Only so could modern democratic society have come to be.

The third stage in the political development of Puritan Protestantism built upon the classical Calvinist and the left-wing Puritan heritage. It was the work of Anglo-American " Evangelicalism," which arose in the middle of the eighteenth century, dominated the nineteenth, and, in the United States at least, was still the prevailing type of religion up to the First World War. Evangelicalism changed the character of a major section of Anglicanism, of the " three old denominations " as a whole, and added to them a new denomination, Methodism. Evangelicalism represented the revival of the central conceptions of sin and salvation of the Reformation in a radically individualized form and in association with a thoroughgoing acceptance of the left-wing Puritan transfer of political and economic ethics from the sphere of the Church and revelation to that of the ecclesiastically neutral community under natural law. This was the form of religion that was the silent partner of the American democratic faith of the nineteenth century, the reservoir of its moral energies. This was the religion that had most to do with freeing the slaves, with the widening of the franchise, with popular education, with the limitation of commercialized alcoholism; that conducted the " moral courts of the American frontier "; and that, in a vast missionary expansion, founded in Asia, Africa, and South America " younger Churches " which would be the chief hope of liberal democracy for the future of these lands.

At the end of the nineteenth century this Evangelicalism split into two distinct wings. They shared a devotion to the liberal democratic State. The one held to the old individualistic utilitarian ethic, suspicious of government and laissez faire in business. The other was ready to use the State for social and moral goals, even to regulation of industry and trade where it seemed necessary to maintain the conditions of a democratic society. British democratic socialism and the American New Deal represented the tendency of this new type of Evangelicalism. In both varieties of Evangelicalism the social and political position rested on general social theory independent of Christian convictions, and the traditional separation of the spheres of reason and revelation was maintained. And, at least at the beginning and in the large, the two wings agreed on theological issues. Increasingly, however, the representatives of the social gospel tendency came to share a liberal theology, in which the Evangelical heritage was displaced by an intense faith in progress and by moralism.

Out of the dissolution of this liberal social gospel Evangelicalism there crystallized in the generation between the World Wars the fourth stage in the democratic ethic of Puritan Protestantism. While it is too near to us for an evaluation of its achievements, or even for an assured characterization of its structure, some things can be said. There was a much sharper sense of the distinctively Christian basis of social ethics than in any type of Evangelicalism. While it was generally recognized that some kind of confessionally neutral moral law was necessary to maintain modern democracy, nevertheless the disintegration of moral conviction in the general society made evident the fact that belief in moral law was not likely to be sustained without more specific faith in revelation. And while the problem of defining a discipline for Christians distinct from the code of the larger community in social and political questions was only talked about, nevertheless the sense of distinctive community and destiny, the awareness of the *Church,* was much heightened. Some aspects of the seventeenth century debates of right- and left-wing Puritans were reopened in new guises. And for practical achievements, one might at least say that the Christian and liberal democratic interpretation of the Second World War by some of the Protestant theologians was as clear and as deep as any of the rival attempts to read the meaning of the crisis. Many democrats who had disdained the Church viewed it with new respect if they did not themselves believe.

While Calvinism and Puritanism were developing these related patterns of life and government within the civil and within the religious community, and while Scandinavian and American Lutheranism, at least, tended in the same direction, Roman Catholicism had a very different history. In Church organization, as in worship and theology, modern Roman Catholicism in many ways became an anti-Evangelical "Protestantism." Elements of the common heritage that the Reformation had recovered from obscurity were now systematically suppressed. Features that the Reformers had protested against were moved from the background to the forefront. With regard to the nature of the Church, for example, in reaction to the Reformation recovery of the organic sense of the community indwelt by the Holy Spirit, a communion of those touched by God and ministering to each other of what they had received, the new Romanism defined the Church primarily in terms of jurisdiction and ecclesiastical authority. To belong to the Church was less to belong to the organic community of Christ than to be one of many individuals submitted to one ecclesiastical sovereign.

The papal Church constituted in this way the archetype of sovereignty by divine right to modern Europe. It represented an elective but absolute monarchy. The Church's monarch, to be sure, was theoretically subject to Christ, but there were no means to realize this subordination in case of need. Just so the Catholic king was theoretically bound to natural law, but there were no agencies to enforce this claim of the law upon him. In Church and State the practical result was that the executive was above the law and defined the law. The very possibility of limited government, a precondition of liberal democracy, was thus precluded. Within the Church as within the State, in Roman Catholic countries, the members of the community were not trained to initiative or called to responsible participation in the determination of policy. The governed did not delegate powers to their rulers, nor have the right to withdraw them, nor were their opinions or consent solicited by either Church or State. They were, rather, trained to accept decisions and policies on external authority without looking too closely into their intrinsic moral character. Dissent was treated as disobedience and sin in the penitential discipline of the Church, which inculcated habits of unquestioning submission. Discussion was simply forbidden on the important issues of policy. The democratic principle of discussion was diametrically opposed by the system of Index and Inquisition. The whole community was knit together, not as with the Protestants, by the mutual ministry of all to all, but by common submission to the one central and superimposed autocratic rule.

As regards the relations of Church and State, finally, there were always seeds of liberty in the potential conflicts of kings and popes. According to ultramontane theory, the Roman see had the right to overrule civil authorities and, if necessary, to depose kings. The Roman claim was always for clerical supremacy in the State. In practice, however, the popes of the seventeenth and eighteenth centuries could not often make this claim good. Most Catholic monarchs refused to recognize such papal supremacy in temporal matters. These struggles over jurisdiction rarely affected the ordinary citizen and layman in any case, since it was to the interests of both rivals to keep him in the habit of unquestioning obedience to authority.

Up to the end of the eighteenth century the simple contrast between the two classical sociological types of Western Christianity stood forth almost as baldly as in this schematic presentation. Roman Catholicism maintained as much of medieval feudalism as could be reconciled with absolute monarchy. Puritan Protestantism in Britain, the new United States of America, Holland, and Switzerland was constitutionalist and republican or democratic in tendency. Here had appeared the various "bills of rights," the written constitutions, the systems of political parties and parliaments and elections, all based on faith in the supremacy of law and the determination of policy by discussion.

With the French Revolution there appeared a new phenomenon, democracy of sorts in the Roman Catholic cultural sphere. But while this democracy was consciously modeled on British and American institutions, it never shared their basic motivation, the desire to preserve an institutional sphere for the inalienable political responsibilities of the Christian citizen. Jacobin democracy was really closer to the Roman Catholic monarchism it sought to displace than it was to liberal democracy. This is also true of the Continental democracy derived from it and finally of the Communism of the twentieth century, which is still recognizably of the school of Rousseau. There is more kinship between twentieth century Communism and the clerical Fascism which is the heir of Catholic monarchism than there is between either of them and liberal democracy.

The analysis of the political influence of Roman Catholicism in the nineteenth and twentieth centuries must be pursued along two divergent paths. Puritan Protestantism throughout this period maintained its positive affiliation with liberal democracy without producing any considerable opposition. Roman Catholic political absolutism, however, served by its positive support to maintain monarchism and absolutism throughout this period. By the reaction which it called forth at the same time, Roman Catholic political absolutism contributed to the development of anticlerical and illiberal democracy, of Marxist Communism, of anarchism. These are all phenomena peculiar to the Roman Catholic world and to that segment of Lutheranism which similarly held to autocratic patterns in Church life and in politics.

The history of the Roman Catholic alliance with political absolutism in the last century and a half can be summarized in terms of the suppression of five successive efforts to achieve a synthesis of Catholicism and democracy. The first effort, of course, was the French Revolution, in the first stages of which a majority of the lower clergy favored constitutional reform. The Roman Court, however, condemned the *Declaration of the Rights of Man* as regards civil and religious liberty, popular sovereignty, responsible government. Those French Catholics, like Grégoire, who believed in democracy as well as Catholicism were forced into the schismatic " Constitutional Church," which was finally liquidated by Napoleon a decade later. And when the Bourbons succeeded Napoleon, they showed themselves less reactionary than the pope, who protested the constitution of 1814 as too liberal.

Forty years after the outbreak of the great French Revolution, another rising took place in France against Restoration clericalism and divine-right monarchy. This was the Revolution of 1830, at the time of the American Jacksonian revolution and the first reform of the oligarchic British Parliament. This French Revolution of 1830 produced the constitutional monarchy of Louis Philippe, which endured for eighteen years. Even more notable was its expression in the Low Countries, where Catholic Belgium won its independence from the Calvinist Dutch king and promulgated the most liberal constitution on the Continent of Europe. The great body of the French hierarchy and the papacy had opposed the Revolution of 1830 as they had the Revolution of the 1790's, but there had again been a corporal's guard who had sought to reconcile Catholicism and liberalism. Led by Lamennais, they achieved their triumph in Belgium while defeated in France. At the same time O'Connell in Ireland won Catholic emancipation by the threat of civil war on the basis of a clerically organized popular movement. The ideas of Catholic liberalism, however, were once again and even more explicitly and unqualifiedly condemned by the Church in *Mirari vos* and *Singulari nos*. Lamennais was excommunicated.

The first time any considerable fraction of the Roman hierarchy ever flirted with democracy was just one hundred years ago, in the Revolution of 1848 and its aftermath. The Revolution had been prepared in Catholic circles by propaganda and the organization of the Catholic electorate in the preceding ten or fifteen years, especially in France, Germany, Holland. The effect of the Revolution was to extend the Belgian pattern of a partial alliance of Catholicism with liberalism to the western Continental countries where Catholicism was a minority and needed protection against the State. Thus the new semiliberal constitutions of Holland and Prussia gave Catholicism new rights and won Catholic support. In the dominantly Catholic cultures of Italy and France, however, the initial Catholic sympathy for the revolution turned rapidly to counterrevolution. Catholics were the chief support for the dictatorship of Napoleon III in France, by which the second French Republic was stamped out, and in Italy Pius IX and Antonelli did everything in their power to repress the liberal democratic movement. French and Italian Catholic liberals were again disgraced. The manifesto of this antiliberal and antidemocratic Roman reaction was published in 1864 in the Syllabus of Errors, which has remained authoritative for all Catholics ever since.

The fourth wave of Catholic democracy occurred in the 1890's under the encouragement of Pope Leo XIII, and was brutally purged away in the dozen years before the First World War by his successor, Pius X. Here again it was primarily a matter of dominantly Catholic countries, France, Italy, Belgium. Leo was concerned to break the ruinous identification of French Catholicism with monarchism and disloyalty to the Republic, and to cultivate the new laboring classes before they should fall completely into the hands of the Marxists. His successor, schooled in divine-right monarchy and social reaction, had no answers to social and political unrest save military repression and paternalistic charity. He broke up the Catholic democratic movements and once again authoritatively forbade to Catholics the principles of liberal democracy in *Pieni l'animo* and especially in his letter condemning the *Sillon* in 1910.

For the generation between the First World War and the Second, it is perhaps inaccurate to speak of a fifth wave of Catholic democracy. There was something of such a movement in the 1930's, particularly in France and Belgium, as represented by the Jocists and such intellectuals as Sturzo and Maritain. But, on the whole, the picture is one of antidemocratic aggression, of official Catholic encouragement and support of Fascist totalitarianism. In Italy, Germany, Austria, Spain, as well as elsewhere, the Roman hierarchy deliberately chose between democracy and Fascism, and materially aided the latter, both to overthrow legally established governments by violence, and, in more than one case, to break international order by naked aggression. By such violence and injustice, moreover, the Vatican everywhere strengthened the case and the cause of world Communism, thus weakening the position of liberal democracy against both its chief rivals.

The Catholic alliance with Fascist counterrevolution in this last generation pointed up again the purely external and opportunistic basis on which Roman Catholicism had come to terms here and there with democracy. There was no intrinsic kinship between Roman Catholicism and liberal democracy. Unlike Protestantism, the Roman Church had never fought for democracy when democracy was weak. The Roman Church had accommodated itself to democracy when democracy, supported by other systems of thought, had proved itself a power to be reckoned with. And then it had never given wholehearted support to liberal democracy, but only to those democratic liberties by which the Roman Church itself could profit. From Lamennais on down, the Catholic democrats had been clericals at heart, and were simply urging that the priests could control modern society by manipulating the press, the ballot, and the political machinery of democracy. And where a monarchist restoration or a military dictatorship became a possibility, the Roman Church generally turned with relief to such types of governments as more familiar to its traditions and better suited to its methods. Clerical Fascism is the normal and safest type of modern government from the Roman viewpoint. Apart from ideological conflicts, indeed, Communist dictatorship is also more congenial to Roman Catholicism than is liberal democracy.

In the dominantly Protestant English-speaking world, meanwhile, the homeland of liberal democracy, the Roman Church had cautiously increased its discipline. At the beginning of the nineteenth century, American and British Roman Catholics had been released from civil disabilities, in part on the strength of their protestations that they did not accept those political claims of the pope that were later to be officially promulgated by the Syllabus and the Vatican Council. From the 1830's, the Catholic section in England, Scotland, America, and Australia increased by leaps and bounds, not by conversion, but by mass immigration from poor Catholic countries. Up to the time of the First World War, the Roman Church exerted little appreciable political influence, being preoccupied with the problem of organizing the heterogeneous immigration. In the last generation, however, the Roman Church has felt itself sufficiently rooted, oriented, and secure in these democratic societies to begin to exert political pressure in accordance with its own traditions. These traditions, as we have seen, are not merely undemocratic, but antidemocratic. As a result there is considerable tension between the " teaching Church," the hierarchy, and the laity, largely molded by the surrounding democratic culture. Internal discipline, however, has been steadily strengthened. The authority of the priest over the laity, the co-ordination of the episcopate, and the direct control of Rome over the whole has steadily increased in America in the last four generations. There is ever less hope of liberal democracy in the governing bodies of the Church. The influence of the general democratic culture has also doubtless increased as the Catholic laity have come out of their ghetto and mixed actively in the State and society.

The result of this tension has been a tightening of discipline and of anti-democratic policy within the Church, and an unremitting stream of rebels out of the Church.

The antidemocratic influence of the Roman see and bishops showed itself in the democratic world chiefly in the attempt to interfere with the freedom of communication and the determination of policy by discussion. In addition their pressure on foreign affairs was against international law and for Mussolini, the Abyssinian invasion, the Axis capture of Spain, and the general support of clerical Fascism everywhere. Not everything the Roman episcopate stood for, however, was *ipso facto* antidemocratic. In both education and in law the Roman Church insisted vigorously on the reference to ultimate norms where Protestants were often less vociferous. And in social and economic policy the Roman Church, because of its sociological location as the Church of the urban worker, played a more active role in the support of trade-unionism and in winning political recognition for this disadvantaged class than did Protestantism as a whole. These contributions, however important, were only accidentally democratic, and were used by the hierarchy as steppingstones for its further undemocratic program.

The Puritan Protestantism of the English-speaking world displayed a certain embarrassment and indecision in this between-wars generation before the aggressiveness of totalitarianism abroad, both Fascist and Communist, and the new allied clericalism within. The social and political ethic that it had nourished for over a century no longer seemed adequate. The faith in progress, in the automatic harmony of economic and political interests, in education and enlightened self-interest — all these first principles of the liberal utilitarian ethic were called into question by the events of history. And the Churches, which had forgotten on what basis and under what conditions they had accepted this ethic, were perplexed. Even the mighty system of voluntary societies for the welfare of workers — mutual insurance societies, co-operatives, trade-unions, and the like — which Puritan Protestantism had helped to build up, seemed no longer adequate in the increasing concentration and bureaucratization of business. The paternalist and undemocratic Churches, Lutheran, High Anglican, and Roman Catholic, seemed more relevant to the situation, with their greater readiness to use State intervention in such matters. As men were increasingly consolidated into great political and economic masses, the highly decentralized Church structure of Puritan Protestantism seemed ever less able to address itself to the problems that were presented on a regional or national basis. Only the large and centralized Churches such as the Roman Catholic seemed to be in a position to apply themselves effectively to the kind of social and political issues that were now dominant. Even psychologically, the depersonalization and *Vermassung* of modern life seemed to require more in the way of unifying symbolism and central authority in a religious community than Puritan Protestantism appeared to possess.

The problem of Puritan Protestantism as a religious tradition in the mid-twentieth century is thus closely analogous to the problem of liberal democracy in the State. Is it possible for the traditions that have exalted personal responsibility and freedom, voluntary initiative, and the method of discussion, to achieve, nevertheless, enough of self-discipline, organization, and unity to meet the problems of an increasingly bureaucratized, industrialized, militarized society? Can Puritan Protestantism in its ecumenical efforts transcend congregational and denominational autonomy and still maintain a vital practice of congregational self-government — and a real priesthood of all — within a more inclusive and powerful framework? Can the liberal State accept the social and economic controls which seem indispensable and still remain liberal in fact? As at their origin, three hundred years before, the destinies of Puritan Protestantism and of liberal democracy are indissolubly joined. Holding precious the same heritage, they face the same perils, and, beneath all the perplexities, with the same faith.

From the viewpoint of Western culture, or the world as a whole, there were three religious and political blocs to be distinguished. The Roman Catholic world was, save in so far as it had adopted protective coloration in the English-speaking countries, politically authoritarian and dogmatically antiliberal. Marxist countries shared the same formal pattern. Each bloc attempted to define the issues so as to carry with them the Puritan democrats. It was " Democracy against Fascism," or it was " Christian civilization against atheist Communism." It was extremely important both politically and religiously that in this tension Puritan Protestantism retain a very distinct sense of its unique tradition and refuse to be hoodwinked by either of these slogans. Whatever temporary alliances might be expedient, Puritan Protestantism was responsible to God alone and could yield its conscience to no infallible interpreters — neither to a party nor to a hierarchy.

SUGGESTED READINGS

✣ ✣ ✣

THE BIBLIOGRAPHY of this topic is enormous, although its quality is very uneven and many aspects still need careful study. Most of the works here listed will guide the reader to primary sources and secondary discussions.

Perhaps the best definition of democracy is found in the works of Lord Lindsay of Balliol. His *Modern Democratic State* (London: Oxford University Press, 1943) has few, if any, rivals. The historical chapters exhibit clearly the relation of early democracy to Puritanism, a relation illuminated again in his *Essentials of Democracy* (University of Pennsylvania Press, 1929). For the careful discrimination of the political ethics of the various Churches, on the other hand, there is nothing to compare with Ernst Troeltsch, *The Social Teaching of the Christian Churches* (The Macmillan Company, 1931). Troeltsch is difficult reading, but careful study of the table of contents will enable one to pick out the crucial passages in this connection.

The standard histories of political thought should of course be consulted, such as G. H. Sabine, *History of Political Theory* (Henry Holt and Company, Inc., 1937); W. A. Dunning, *A History of Political Theories from Luther to Montesquieu* (The Macmillan Company, 1905); and, again, *From Rousseau to Spencer* (1920). The Roman Catholic writers are more extensively discussed in P. Janet, *Histoire de la science politique, tome* 2, F. Alcan, Editeur (Paris: Ancienne librairie Germer Baillière et Cie, 3d ed., 1887). There are also the eight volumes of essays on various figures edited by F. J. C. Hearnshaw from 1930, the titles of which usually run: "The Social and Political Ideas of Some Great Thinkers of Such and Such a Period." On nineteenth century Roman Catholic thought there is R. H. Soltau, *French Political Thought in the 19th Century* (London: E. Benn, 1931), and C. T. Muret, *French Royalist Doctrines Since the Revolution* (Columbia University Press, 1933).

The later chapters of Father Figgis' *From Gerson to Grotius* (Cambridge: At the University Press, 1931) are valuable for the Reformation and Counter Reformation. H. D. Foster's *Collected Papers* (Hanover, New Hampshire: privately printed, 1929) contain three or four essays on the political influence of Calvinism. F. S. Scott Pearson's books on Thomas Cartwright; Harold

Laski's edition of the *Vindiciae contra tyrannos* (London: George Bell & Sons, Ltd., 1924); Winthrop Hudson's *John Ponet* (The University of Chicago Press, 1942) illustrate significant contributions to that tradition supplied with excellent editorial introductions.

Among the many books on English Puritanism and democracy, one might mention T. C. Pease, *The Leveller Movement* (American Historical Association, 1916), and Woodhouse' brilliant introduction to *Puritanism and Liberty* (London: J. M. Dent & Sons, Ltd., 1938). G. P. Gooch's *The History of English Democratic Ideas in the 17th Century* (Cambridge: At the University Press, 1898), while ancient, is still worth reading. While less precise in its historical definitions, Ralph Barton Perry's rather diffuse account of American Puritanism, *Puritanism and Democracy* (Vanguard Press, 1944), is exhaustive in its ethical analysis and especially rich in bibliographical indications. Charles Borgeaud's *The Rise of Democracy in Old and New England* is another older work that is still useful.

Ruggiero's *History of European Liberalism* (London: Oxford University Press, H. Milford, 1927) is a notable exception to a general dearth of literature on that subject. Walter Nigg, *Geschichte des religiösen Liberalismus* (Zurich: M. Niehans, 1937), approaches the subject from theology. Ruffini's *Religious Liberty* (G. P. Putnam's Sons, 1912) is particularly instructive in its contrast of the motives and results of toleration and of liberal democracy. Arthur Rosenberg's *Democracy and Socialism* (London: George Bell & Sons, Ltd., 1939) sets forth the relations from a Marxian viewpoint and is not least illuminating in its bizarre misconception of American democracy. A sketch of socialism in Christian history is found in *The Christian Origins of Social Revolt,* by W. D. Morris (London: George Allen & Unwin, Ltd., 1949).

For the attitude of the Roman Church since the French Revolution there is a very useful collection of documents by Michon, *Les documents pontificaux sur la démocratie moderne* (Paris: Rieder, 1928). Weill's *Histoire du catholicisme libéral en France* (Paris: F. Alcan, 1909) is perhaps the best history of that ill-starred movement.

The social and political encyclicals of Leo XIII are available in English in Wynne, S. J., *Great Encyclical Letters of Leo XIII* (Benziger Brothers, 1903), and in Husslein, S. J., *Social Wellsprings* (Bruce, 1940–1942), Vol. I. (Volume II is devoted to the comparable deliverances of Pius XII.) For Pius X, one must seek out his encyclicals, such as that on the *Sillon* or those dealing with the separation of Church and State in France, in the files of some such periodical as the *American Catholic Quarterly Review*. B. B. Carter has translated two volumes of Eduardo Soderini's account of the reign of Leo XIII. The first of them, *The Pontificate of Leo XIII* (London: Burns, Oates, and Washbourne, 1934), deals with his social and political policy. Nitti's *Catholic Socialism* (The Macmillan Company, 1895) is a useful accumulation of materials up to 1891. Williams' *Catholic Social Thought* (Ronald Press, 1950) came to hand too late to be used for this study.

With regard to Dissent, see A. Lincoln, *Some Political and Social Ideas of English Dissent, 1763–1800* (Cambridge: At the University Press, 1938); also

E. D. Bebb, *Nonconformity and Social and Economic Life, 1660–1800* (London: Epworth Press, 1935). The social and political history of Methodism has been much canvassed. We may mention M. L. Edwards' trilogy, *John Wesley and the 18th Century* (London: George Allen & Unwin, Ltd., 1933); *After Wesley* (London: Epworth Press, 1935); *Methodism and England* (London: Epworth Press, 1943), as well as Wellman J. Warner, *Wesleyan Movement in the Industrial Revolution* (London: Longmans, Green & Co., Inc., 1930); R. T. Wearmouth, *Methodism and the Working-Class Movements of England, 1800–1850* (London: Epworth Press, 1937); also *Methodism and the Common People of the 18th Century* (London: Epworth Press, 1945); E. R. Taylor's *Methodism and Politics, 1791–1851* (Cambridge: At the University Press, 1935). The well-known writings of J. L. and Barbara Hammond should be compared with these for a hostile evaluation of Methodism's influence.

On the Evangelical Awakening as a whole, see Halévy, *History of the English People in 1815* (London: Penguin Books, Ltd., 1937), and the twelfth lecture of Dicey's *Lectures on the Relation Between Law and Public Opinion in England During the Nineteenth Century* (The Macmillan Company, 1905). F. J. Klingberg deals with the *Antislavery Movement in England* (Yale University Press, 1926). H. V. Faulkner's *Chartism and the Churche 1 Study in Democracy* (Columbia University Press, 1916) is a particularly revealing cross section of the Churches. A schematic generalized comparison of the same sort was made by T. C. Hall, *The Social Meaning of Modern Religious Movements in England* (Charles Scribner's Sons, 1900). Of all the literature about the " Christian socialism " of Maurice and Ludlow, we may be content here with Canon C. E. Raven's *Christian Socialism, 1848–1854* (London: The Macmillan Company, 1920).

The Church of England has been relatively well supplied with historians of its recent political and social ethics. D. O Wagner's *The Church of England and Social Reform Since 1854* (Columbia University Press, 1930) is full of useful information. Maurice Reckitt has published three books of interest here: *Maurice to Temple* (London: Faber and Faber, 1948); *Faith and Society* (Longmans, Green & Co., Inc., 1932) (the historical chapters also include one on the United States); and (with Hudson) *The Church and the World* (London: George Allen & Unwin, Ltd., 1938). G. C. Binyon's *The Christian Socialist Movement in England* (The Macmillan Company, 1931) includes a little on the Free Churches apart from Methodism in the latter half of the nineteenth century, but in general that subject seems to have been little studied. H. F. Lovell Cocks's expanded lecture, *The Nonconformist Conscience* (London: Independent Press, 1940), and D. T. Jenkins' *Church Meeting and Democracy* (London: Independent Press, 1944) are suggestive.

The literature on the social ethic of the American Churches is not so extensive as that of the British, nor so sophisticated either in theology or political and social thought. One might mention Alice Baldwin's *The New England Clergy and the American Revolution* (Duke University Press, 1928) and Humphrey's *Nationalism and Religion in America, 1774–1789* (Chipman

Law Publishing Co., 1924), for the period of the Revolution. For the humanitarian movement in general, there is Alice F. Tyler's *Freedom's Ferment, Phases of American History to 1860* (University of Minnesota Press, 1944), which is comprehensive but something of a jumble, and on the most important single issue, G. H. Barnes's *The Anti-slavery Impulse, 1830–1844* (D. Appleton-Century Company, Inc., 1933). Tocqueville's *Democracy in America*, newly edited by Bradley (Knopf, 1945), must be consulted. For the period between the Civil War and World War I, three accounts of the many available may be noticed: C. Howard Hopkins' *Rise of the Social Gospel* (Yale University Press, 1940); Abell's *Urban Impact on American Protestantism, 1865–1900* (Harvard University Press, 1943); and May's *Protestant Churches and Industrial America* (Harper & Brothers, 1949). Abell's article on " The Reception of Leo XIII's Labor Encyclical in America, 1891–1914," *Review of Politics* (Vol. 7, 1945, pp. 464–495), helps to fill the lack of an account of American Roman Catholic political and social ethics in the period. Visser 't Hooft's *The Background of the Social Gospel in America* (Haarlem: H. D. T. Willink & Zoon, 1928) is much more acute and penetrating than any of the American works cited, but is based on inadequate factual information. Ralph Gabriel's *Course of American Democratic Thought* (Ronald Press, 1940) is perhaps the most indispensable single volume. Anson Phelps Stokes's monumental compilation, *Church and State in America* (Harper & Brothers, 1950), provides profuse source materials.

The predominant tendency of German Lutheranism to antidemocratic absolutist attitudes is set forth at length in the historical sections (pp. 92–371) of Georg Wünsch, *Evangelische Ethik des Politischen* (Tübingen: J. C. B. Mohr [Paul Siebeck], 1936). The Nazi sympathies of the author may even incline him to put the contrast with Puritan Protestantism somewhat too sharply.

The most substantial study of Roman politics since the First World War is D. A. Binchy's *Church and State in Fascist Italy* (London: Oxford University Press, 1941). Most of the literature on the period, as one might expect, is more journalistic in character. Gerald Brenan's *The Spanish Labyrinth* (The Macmillan Company, 1943) has valuable chapters on the role of the Church. Gedye's *Betrayal in Central Europe* (Harper & Brothers, 1939) deals with Austria and Czechoslovakia and Charles Gulick offers a thorough account of *Austria from Habsburg to Hitler* (University of California Press, 1948). For Germany, there might be mentioned Duncan-Jones's *The Struggle for Religious Freedom in Germany* (London: V. Gollancz, Ltd., 1938), and Micklem's *National Socialism and the Roman Catholic Church* (London: Oxford University Press, 1939). Avro Manhattan's *Vatican and World Politics* (Gaer Associates, 1949) is irritatingly casual about its documentation, but worth-while if used with care.

There is no wholly satisfactory work on the political influence of the Roman Church in Britain and America between wars. For the former, there are a few indications in C. J. Cadoux, *Roman Catholicism and Freedom* (London: Independent Press, Ltd., 1936). Three books might be mentioned for the United States: E. Boyd Barrett's *Rome Stoops to Conquer* (Julian Messner, Inc., 1935); George Seldes' *The Catholic Crisis* (Julian Messner, Inc., 1945); and Paul Blanshard's *American Freedom and Catholic Power* (The Beacon Press, Inc., 1949). The first is a witty, somewhat belletristic presentation by a former Jesuit, the last more factual and less well-balanced, written from a naïvely dogmatic secular viewpoint. Seldes is a crusading journalist of liberal-socialist sympathies. Some publisher should make more generally accessible the lectures of G. La Piana, "A Totalitarian Church in a Democratic State. The American Experiment," now available only in the *Shane Quarterly*, April, 1949.

The hopeless contradictions and incoherences of the democratic Catholic position can be exhibited from such a work as Maritain's *The Rights of Man and Natural Law* (Charles Scribner's Sons, 1943), sometimes from consecutive pages. Rommen's *State in Catholic Thought* (Herder, 1945), though repetitive, is much better than the well-known American text by Ryan and Boland, *Catholic Principles of Politics* (The Macmillan Company, 1940). Fascist sympathies are evident in the writings of the most distinguished English Catholics: C. Dawson's *Religion and the Modern State* (London: Sheed & Ward, Inc., 1938), De la Bedoyère's *Christian Crisis* (Benziger Bros., 1940), and Hilaire Belloc's journalistic pieces.

Of various constructive efforts to restate the Christian tradition of liberal democracy in the mid-twentieth century, four writers might be singled out of many. Reinhold Niebuhr sets forth the Reformed doctrine of man in its political bearings with his usual vigor in *The Children of Light and the Children of Darkness* (Charles Scribner's Sons, 1944). Eduard Heimann's *Freedom and Order* (Charles Scribner's Sons, 1947) has not received the attention it merits. The Swiss Reformed theologian Emil Brunner similarly discusses political ethics in *Justice and the Social Order* (Harper & Brothers, 1945) and *Christianity and Civilization* (Charles Scribner's Sons, 1945). Archbishop Temple's little Penguin Book, *Christianity and the Social Order* (1942) had an extraordinary reception in Great Britain.

NOTES

✣ ✣ ✣

AUTHOR'S PREFACE

1 Ernst Troeltsch, *The Social Teaching of the Christian Churches*, Vol. II, pp. 688–691, 807–820.

CHAPTER I

1 H. J. Laski (ed.), *Vindiciae contra tyrannos*, p. 1.
2 H. D. Foster, *Collected Papers*, p. 148.
3 J. N. Figgis, *From Gerson to Grotius*, pp. 120 f., 118.
4 Hans Baron, "Roots of Calvinist Republicanism," *Church History*, March, 1939, p. 34.
5 John T. McNeill, "Natural Law in the Teaching of the Reformers," *Journal of Religion*, July, 1946, p. 171.
6 Figgis, *op. cit.*, p. 118.
7 *Ibid.*, p. 167.
8 John T. McNeill, *Unitive Protestantism*, p. 118. Abingdon Press, 1930.
9 *Ibid.*, p. 113.
10 *Ibid.*, pp. 89, 93 f., 115.
11 P. T. Forsyth, *Faith, Freedom and the Future*, p. 41. Hodder & Stoughton, Ltd., 1912.
12 John T. McNeill, "The Democratic Element in Calvin's Thought," *Church History*, September, 1949, p. 160.
13 *Ibid.*, p. 165.
14 Figgis, *op. cit.*, pp. 155 ff., 167.
15 *Religion and the Rise of Capitalism*, end of Chapter IV. John Murray, 1926.
16 Christopher Dawson, "Religious Origins of European Disunity," *Dublin Review*, October, 1940, pp. 151 f., 153 f.
17 A. D. Lindsay, *The Churches and Democracy*, p. 24. The Epworth Press, London, 1934.
18 Woodhouse, *Puritanism and Liberty*, p. 53.

19 Dicey, *Introduction to the Study of the Law of the Constitution*, pp. 197, 198, 3d ed., 1889, The Macmillan Company, cited by Perry, *Puritanism and Democracy*, pp. 287 f.
20 Woodhouse, *op. cit.*, Introduction, for a thorough analysis.
21 Bogue and Bennett, *History of Dissenters*, Vol. IV, p. 152. London, 1808–1812.
22 Cited, A. Lincoln, *Some Political and Social Ideas of English Dissent, 1763–1800*, p. 17.
23 D. Schaff, "The Jefferson-Bellarmine Legend," *Papers of the American Society of Church History*, Series 2, Vol. 8. G. P. Putnam's Sons, 1928.
24 Perry, *op. cit.*, p. 358.
25 *Ibid.*, pp. 188 f.
26 Bryce, *The American Commonwealth*, Part I, Chapter XXVI, 3d ed., 1893. The Macmillan Company.
27 Cited, Lincoln, *op. cit.*, p. 39, n. 4.
28 *Ibid.*, p. 3.

CHAPTER II

1 R. H. Soltau, *French Political Thought in the 19th Century*, p. xxix.
2 A. Sorel, *L'Europe et la révolution*, Vol. I, p. 101. E. Plon, Nourrit et Cie, 1885.
3 Soltau, *op. cit.*, p. xxii.
4 *Ibid.*, p. xxix.
5 Michon, *Les Documents pontificaux sur la démocratie moderne*, pp. 32 f.
6 *Ibid.*, p. 37.
7 *Ibid.*, pp. 38 f.; cf. pp. 52 f.
8 *Ibid.*, pp. 40 f.
9 *Ibid.*, p. 54.
10 *Ibid.*, p. 45.
11 *Ibid.*, pp. 59 f.

12 *Ibid.*, p. 63.
13 See p. 21.
14 Ruggiero, *History of European Liberalism*, p. 163.
15 Lecanuet, *Montalembert*, Vol. II, p. 3. J. de Gigord, Paris, 1912–1920.
16 Lamennais, *Affaires de Rome*, p. 349. Garnier Frères, Paris [n.d.].
17 Michon, *op. cit.*, p. 75.
18 Lamennais, *op. cit.*, p. 418.
19 *Ibid.*, pp. 150 f.

CHAPTER III

1 E. R. Taylor, *Methodism and Politics, 1791–1851*, pp. 10 f.
2 Cited, *ibid.*, p. 1.
3 *Minutes of Conference, 1766*, I, p. 61.
4 Cited, Taylor, *op. cit.*, p. 44.
5 Cited, *ibid.*, p. 46.
6 Cited, *ibid.*, p. 79.
7 Cited, *ibid.*
8 Webb, *Story of the Durham Miners*, pp. 22 f.; cited, R. T. Wearmouth, *Methodism and the Working-Class Movements of England, 1800–1850*, p. 227.
9 *Ibid.*, p. 216.
10 M. L. Edwards, *John Wesley and the 18th Century*, p. 184.
11 Cited, M. L. Edwards, *After Wesley*, p. 156.
12 Taylor, *op. cit.*, p. 206.
13 Cited, Bready, *England: Before and After Wesley*, p. 84. Hodder & Stoughton, Ltd., 1938.
14 Edwards, *John Wesley and the 18th Century*, p. 119.
15 Eayrs, *Letters*, p. 489. Hodder & Stoughton, Ltd., 1915.
16 W. S. Hudson, "Puritanism and the Spirit of Capitalism," *Church History*, March, 1949.
17 Quoted, H. R. Niebuhr, *Social Sources of Denominationalism*, pp. 70 f. Henry Holt and Company, Inc., 1929.
18 Halévy, *History of the English People in 1815*, p. 9.
19 Dicey, *Law and Opinion in England*, p. 402; cited, Edwards, *John Wesley and the 18th Century*, p. 188.
20 Halévy, *op. cit.*, p. 215.
21 Cf. Ruth Kenyon, "Social Aspect of the Catholic Revival," in *Northern Catholicism*, eds. N. P. Williams and C. Harris, S. P. C. K., London, 1933; and W. G. Peck, *The Social Implications

of the Oxford Movement*, Charles Scribner's Sons, 1933.
22 Cited, Reckitt, *Maurice to Temple*, p. 52.
23 *Life of Maurice*, Vol. II, p. 137.
24 R. H. Gabriel, *Course of American Democratic Thought*, p. 38.
25 Troeltsch, *op. cit.*, Vol. II, p. 675.
26 *Ibid.*, pp. 652, 812.
27 Morley, *Life of Gladstone*, Vol. I, p. 563; cited, *ibid.*, p. 938.

CHAPTER IV

1 Ernst Troeltsch, *The Ideas of Natural Law and Humanity*, in O. Gierke, *Natural Law and the Theory of Society, 1500 to 1800*, Vol. I, pp. 201, 202. Cambridge: At the University Press, 1934.
2 Lecanuet, *Montalembert*, Vol. III, p. 38.
3 Cited, C. S. Phillips, *Church in France, 1848–1908*, p. 49. The Macmillan Company, 1936.
4 Veit, *Kirchengeschichte*, IV, 2, S. 255.
5 Quoted, G. Weill, *Histoire du catholicisme libéral en France, 1828–1908*, pp. 99 f. F. Alcan, Paris, 1909.
6 Cf. Montalembert, *L'Eglise libre dans l'état libre*. C.˙Douniol, Didier et Cie, 1863.
7 Phillips, *op. cit.*, p. 95.
8 Lecanuet, *op. cit.*, Vol. III, pp. 373 f.
9 Nielsen, *History of the Papacy in the Nineteenth Century*, Vol. II, p. 344. E. P. Dutton & Co., Inc., 1906.
10 Debidour, *Histoire des rapports de l'église et de l'état*, p. 721. F. Alcan, Paris, 1898. For the text of the Syllabus, cf. Schaff, *Creeds of Christendom*, Harper & Brothers, 1877, or Gladstone and Schaff, *The Vatican Decrees*, Harper & Brothers, 1875.
11 Baunard, *Pie*, Vol. II, p. 215. Cited, Nielsen, *op. cit.*, p. 263.
12 Michon, *op. cit.*, p. 110.
13 Nielsen, *op. cit.*, p. 269.
14 Volume XIV, pp. 368 f.
15 Liguori, *Praxis confessarii*, Capit. primum, §II, circa medici officium, 8; Koch-Preuss, *Handbook of Moral Theology*, Vol. II, p. 164. B. Herder Book Company, 1919–1925; McHugh and Callan, *Moral Theology*, Vol. II, p. 703. Joseph F. Wagner, Inc., 1929–1930.
16 Liguori, *op. cit.*, 9; Koch-Preuss, *op. cit.*, p. 165.
17 Acton, "The Vatican Council," in *Es-

says on Freedom and Power, pp. 302 f.,
326. The Beacon Press, Inc., 1948.
[18] Figgis and Laurence, eds., *Lord Acton's Correspondence*, p. 121. Longmans, Green & Co., Inc., 1917.
[19] *Ibid.*, p. 122.
[20] *Ibid.*
[21] *Ibid.*, pp. 41–43.
[22] Gladstone, "Vaticanism," in *Rome and the Newest Fashions in Religion*, pp. 14, 16, 17. John Murray, 1875.

CHAPTER V

[1] Kantorowicz, *Der Geist der englischen Politik*, p. 15. E. Rowohlt, Berlin, 1929.
[2] E.g., Gustaf Aulén, *Church, Law, and Society*. Charles Scribner's Sons, 1948.
[3] A. D. Lindsay, *The Modern Democratic State*, p. 184.
[4] R. Gabriel, *Spiritual Origins of American Culture*, Hazen Pamphlet, Series I, No. 14.
[5] R. Gabriel, *Course of American Democratic Thought*, p. 100.
[6] Pound, *Spirit of the Common Law*, p. 42. Marshall Jones Company, 1921.
[7] Pound, *Encyclopedia of Social Sciences*, Vol. IV., p. 55. The Macmillan Company, 1931.
[8] R. C. K. Ensor, *England: 1870–1914*, pp. 137 f. Oxford: At the Clarendon Press, 1936.
[9] A. Bryant, *English Saga (1840–1940)*, p. 135. William Collins Sons & Company, Ltd., with Eyre & Spottiswoode, London, 1940.
[10] A. M. Schlesinger, "Critical Epoch in American Religion," in *Massachusetts Historical Society Proceedings*, LXIV, October, 1930, pp. 523–548.
[11] A. I. Abell, *Urban Impact on American Protestantism, 1865–1900*, p. 164.
[12] D. O. Wagner, *The Church of England and Social Reform Since 1854*, p. 186.
[13] C. H. Hopkins, *Rise of the Social Gospel*, p. 156.
[14] Quoted, Abell, *op. cit.*, p. 136.
[15] Quoted, E. A. Payne, *The Free Church Tradition in the Life of England*, p. 102. Student Christian Movement Press, London, 1944.
[16] *The Nonconformist Conscience*, p. 56.
[17] Quoted, Wagner, *op. cit.*, p. 175.
[18] Quoted, R. V. Holt, *The Unitarian Contribution to Social Progress in Eng-*

land, p. 231. George Allen & Unwin, Ltd., 1938.
[19] "The Reception of Leo XIII's Labor Encyclical in America, 1891–1914," in *Review of Politics*, Vol. 7, 1945, p. 468.
[20] Purcell, *Life of Cardinal Manning*, Vol. II, p. 714. The Macmillan Company, 1898.
[21] *Ibid.*, p. 781.
[22] *Ibid.*, p. 715.
[23] Quoted, Hofstadter, *Social Darwinism*, p. 173. University of Pennsylvania Press, 1944.
[24] Wagner, *op. cit.*, p. 240.
[25] *Ibid.*, p. 326.
[26] Reckitt, *Maurice to Temple*, p. 146.
[27] Reckitt, *Faith and Society*, p. 201.
[28] Reckitt, *Maurice to Temple*, p. 151.
[29] Reckitt, *Faith and Society*, p. 215.
[30] "The Church and the Workingman," in *Catholic World*, September, 1909, p. 781.
[31] Reckitt, *Maurice to Temple*, p. 156.
[32] Kantorowicz, *op. cit.*, pp. 74 ff.
[33] *Ibid.*, p. 167.

CHAPTER VI

[1] Michon, *op. cit.*, p. 109.
[2] Soderini, *Il Pontificato di Leone XIII*, Vol. I, p. 250. A. Mondadori, Milan, 1932.
[3] Purcell, *op. cit.*, pp. 572–580.
[4] Soderini, *The Pontificate of Leo XIII*, pp. 156, trans. B. B. Carter.
[5] Husslein, S. J., *Social Wellsprings*, Vol. I, pp. 50 f.
[6] Soderini, *op. cit.*, p. 150.
[7] Rommen, *State in Catholic Thought*, pp. 469 f., 459 f.
[8] Ryan and Boland, *Catholic Principles of Politics*, p. 84.
[9] Husslein, *op. cit.*, p. 83.
[10] *Ibid.*, p. 138.
[11] *Ibid.*, p. 89.
[12] Phillips, *op. cit.*, p. 201.
[13] Ryan and Boland, *op. cit.*, p. 705.
[14] Husslein, *op. cit.*, p. 159.
[15] *Ibid.*
[16] *Ibid.*, p. 160.
[17] *Ibid.*, p. 19.
[18] *Ibid.*, pp. 56 f.
[19] *Ibid.*, p. 102.
[20] Rommen, *op. cit.*, p. 475.
[21] Husslein, *op. cit.*, p. 16.
[22] *Ibid.*, p. 68.
[23] *Ibid.*, p. 84.

[24] *Ibid.*, pp. 81 f.
[25] *Ibid.*, p. 130.
[26] *Ibid.*, p. 138.
[27] Soderini, *op. cit.*, p. 175.
[28] J. J. Wynne, S. J., *The Great Encyclical Letters of Leo XIII*, pp. 323, 324.
[29] L. Bergstraesser, *Politischer Katholizismus*, Vol. II, pp. 146–148. Drei Masken Verlag, München, 1923.
[30] Will, *Life of Cardinal Gibbons*, p. 336. E. P. Dutton & Co., Inc., 1922.
[31] Laveleye, "Le Parti clérical en Belgique," in *The Fortnightly Review*, November 1, 1872, pp. 516, 512.
[32] Husslein, *op. cit.*, p. 156.
[33] Laveleye, *op. cit.*, p. 514.
[34] W. H. Dawson, *Bismarck and State Socialism*, p. 24. S. Sonnenschein, 1891.
[35] Soderini, *op. cit.*, p. 181.
[36] H. Somerville, *Studies in the Catholic Social Movement*, p. 87. Burns, Oates & Washbourne, Ltd., 1933.
[37] Husslein, *op. cit.*, p. 186.
[38] *Ibid.*, p. 189.
[39] *Ibid.*, p. 168.
[40] *Ibid.*, p. 197.
[41] *Ibid.*, pp. 195 f.
[42] Lecanuet, *La Vie de l'église sous Léon XIII*, p. 629. F. Alcan, Paris, 1930.
[43] *Ibid.*, p. 627.
[44] G. J. Weill, *Histoire du mouvement social en France*, p. 399. F. Alcan, Paris, 1904.
[45] M. Turmann, *Le Développement du catholicisme social*, p. 191. F. Alcan, Paris, 1909.
[46] Wynne, *op. cit.*, p. 483.
[47] Soderini, *op. cit.*, p. 208.
[48] Wynne, *op. cit.*, p. 493.
[49] R. Bazin, *Pius X*, pp. 104, 162 ff. Sands & Company, Ltd., London, 1928.
[50] Cited by A. Lugan, "*L'Action française and Catholicism,*" *Catholic World*, Vol. 125 (1927), pp. 145–154, 353–359, 506–514, and Vol. 128 (1928), pp. 72–81.
[51] Lecanuet, *op. cit.*, p. 685.
[52] Cited, *American Catholic Quarterly Review*, Vol. 35 (1910), p. 699.
[53] *Ibid.*, p. 701.
[54] *Ibid.*, p. 710.
[55] *Mémoires*, Vol. III, p. 194. E. Nourry, Paris, 1930–1931.
[56] E. Barbier, *Histoire du catholicisme libéral et social*, Vol. V, Chapter 12, Impr. Y. Cadoret, Bordeaux, 1924.

[57] Luzzi, "Roman Catholic Church in Italy," *Hibbert Journal*, Vol. 9, pp. 310 f., 1910–1911.
[58] A. L. Lilley, "Modernism," in Hastings' *Encyclopedia of Religion and Ethics*. Charles Scribner's Sons, 1916.

CHAPTER VII

[1] Mendizabal, *Martyrdom of Spain*, p. 18. Charles Scribner's Sons, 1938.
[2] D. A. Binchy, *Church and State in Fascist Italy*, p. 113. Oxford University Press, 1941.
[3] *Ibid.*, pp. 85 f.
[4] *Ibid.*, p. 138.
[5] *Ibid.*, p. 383.
[6] *Ibid.*, p. 377.
[7] *Ibid.*, pp. 744 f.
[8] H. Belloc, *Essays of a Catholic*, p. 242. Cited, Blanshard, *American Freedom and Catholic Power*, p. 245.
[9] Husslein, *op. cit.*, Vol. II, p. 244.
[10] *Ibid.*, p. 248.
[11] *Christendom*, Winter, 1937.
[12] Binchy, *op. cit.*, p. 678.
[13] *Ibid.*, p. 640.
[14] W. Teeling, *Pope Pius XI and World Affairs*, p. 138. Frederick A. Stokes Company, Inc., 1937.
[15] *Ibid.*, p. 272.
[16] Binchy, *op. cit.*, p. 648.
[17] *Ibid.*, p. 651.
[18] B. Menne, *The Case of Dr. Bruening*, p. 21. Hutchinson & Company, Ltd., London, 1942.
[19] *Ibid.*, p. 28.
[20] *Ibid.*, p. 48.
[21] De la Bedoyère, *Christian Crisis*, p. 100.
[22] Husslein, *op. cit.*, Vol. II, p. 213.
[23] Quoted, Seldes, *The Catholic Crisis*, p. 271.
[24] *Ibid.*, p. 275.
[25] Brenan, *The Spanish Labyrinth*, p. 41, n. 3.
[26] *Ibid.*, pp. 52 ff.
[27] Cited, Seldes, *op. cit.*, p. 284.
[28] *Ibid.*, p. 281.
[29] Mendizabal, *op. cit.*, p. 126.
[30] Cited, A. Manhattan, *Vatican in World Politics*, p. 88.
[31] Brenan, *op. cit.*, pp. 49 f.
[32] Manhattan, *op. cit.*, p. 104.
[33] Seldes, *op. cit.*, p. 267.
[34] Manhattan, *op. cit.*, p. 314.
[35] *Catholic Herald*, July 12, 1940.

36 Dawson, *Religion and the Modern State*, pp. 134–136.
37 Coudenhove-Kalergi, *Crusade for Pan-Europe*, p. 173. G. P. Putnam's Sons, 1943.

CHAPTER VIII

1 *Malvern, 1941,* p. 10, Longmans, Green & Co., Inc., 1941.
2 *Ibid.,* p. 121.
3 *Official Report, World Conference on Church, Community, and State, Oxford, 1937,* p. 230, ed., J. H. Oldham. Willett, Clark & Company.
4 Dawson, *op. cit.,* p. 106.
5 Quoted, Hutchison, *We Are Not Divided,* p. 195. Round Table Press, Inc., 1941.
6 *Ibid.,* pp. 109 ff.
7 *Ibid.,* p. 134.
8 Tippy, *Annals of the American Academy of Political Science,* 1922, p. 125.
9 Hutchison, *op. cit.,* p. 111.
10 Jerome Davis, *Business and the Church.* The Century Company, 1926.
11 Hutchison, *op. cit.,* p. 119.
12 *Ibid.,* p. 113.
13 Reckitt, *Faith and Society,* p. 122.
14 Hutchison, *op. cit.,* p. 121.
15 *Ibid.,* p. 120.
16 W. A. Visser 't Hooft, *The Background of the Social Gospel in America,* p. 65.
17 Reckitt, *Maurice to Temple,* p. 160.
18 Reckitt, *Faith and Society,* p. 114.
19 Reckitt and Hudson, *The Church and the World,* pp. 172 f.
20 Reckitt, *Faith and Society,* p. 131.
21 F. E. Johnson, *The Social Gospel Re-examined,* p. 4. Harper & Brothers, 1940.
22 *Ibid.,* p. 130.
23 *Ibid.,* p. 9.
24 Gabriel, *Course of American Democratic Thought,* p. 417.
25 *Malvern, 1941,* p. 220.
26 *Ibid.,* pp. 14 f.
27 *Official Report,* p. 13.
28 Hutchison, *op. cit.,* p. 253.
29 *Official Report,* p. 79.
30 *Ibid.,* p. 155.
31 *Malvern, 1941,* p. 50.
32 Iremonger, *William Temple,* p. 434. Oxford University Press, 1948.
33 *Malvern, 1941,* p. 197.

34 *Information Service,* Federal Council Bulletin, May 15, 1948; Liston Pope, "Religion and the Class Structure," in *Annals of the American Academy of Political Science,* March, 1948; Wesley and Beverly Allinsmith, "Religious Affiliations and Politico-economic Attitude, A Study of Eight Major U.S. Religious Groups," in *Public Opinion Quarterly,* Fall, 1948, pp. 377–389.

CHAPTER IX

1 O'Hea, S. J., in M. Spencer, *Social Discipline,* p. 74. Longmans, Green & Co., Inc., 1926.
2 Reckitt and Hudson, *op. cit.,* p. 186.
3 Husslein, *op. cit.,* Vol. II, p. 232.
4 H. Fey, *Can Catholicism Win America?,* p. 18. Reprinted from *The Christian Century,* November 29, 1944 to January 17, 1945.
5 Perry, *op. cit.,* pp. 542 f.
6 C. J. Cadoux, *Religious Liberty,* p. 63. Cf. Binchy, *op. cit.,* p. 719.
7 *Time,* September 14, 1936.
8 Seldes, *op. cit.,* pp. 296 f.
9 Cited by G. Salvemini, "Seeking for Truth," *Free World,* September, 1943, pp. 237 f.
10 Cadoux, *op. cit.,* p. 194.
11 Seldes, *op. cit.,* pp. 188 f.
12 *Ibid.,* p. 199.
13 *Ibid.,* p. 186.
14 *Ibid.,* p. 141.
15 *Ibid.,* p. 147.
16 Max Lerner, *Nation,* May 28, 1938.
17 Carleton Beals, quoted, Seldes, *op. cit.,* pp. 322 f.
18 G. P. Howard, *Religious Liberty in Latin America?,* p. 4. The Westminster Press, 1944.
19 *Ibid.,* p. 7.
20 *Ibid.,* p. 20.
21 *Ibid.,* p. 57.
22 L. F. Stock, *United States Ministers to the Papal States,* p. 3. Catholic University Press, Washington, D.C., 1943.
23 Cited, La Piana, *Shane Quarterly,* April, 1949, pp. 92 f.
24 *Ibid.,* Lecture IV.

EPILOGUE

1 Troeltsch, *op. cit.,* Vol. II, p. 818.

INDEX

INDEX

✢ ✢ ✢